Early Medieval Winchester

Early Medieval Winchester

Communities, Authority and Power in an
Urban Space, *c.* 800–*c.* 1200

edited by

Ryan Lavelle, Simon Roffey
and Katherine Weikert

OXBOW | books
Oxford & Philadelphia

Published in the United Kingdom in 2021 by
OXBOW BOOKS
The Old Music Hall, 106–108 Cowley Road, Oxford, OX4 1JE

and in the United States by
OXBOW BOOKS
1950 Lawrence Road, Havertown, PA 19083

Hardback edition: ISBN 978-1-78925-623-9
Digital Edition: ISBN 978-1-78925-624-6

A CIP record for this book is available from the British Library

Library of Congress Control Number: 2021943928

Printed in Malta by Melita Press

Typeset in India by Lapiz Digital Services, Chennai.

For a complete list of Oxbow titles, please contact:

UNITED KINGDOM
Oxbow Books
Telephone (01865) 241249
Email: oxbow@oxbowbooks.com
www.oxbowbooks.com

UNITED STATES OF AMERICA
Oxbow Books
Telephone (610) 853-9131, Fax (610) 853-9146
Email: queries@casemateacademic.com
www.casemateacademic.com/oxbow

Oxbow Books is part of the Casemate Group

Front cover: Winchester Cathedral from St Giles's Hill © Copyright Peter Trimming and licensed for reuse under Creative Commons Licence CC BY-SA 2.0.

Contents

vi   *Contents*

Editors' Preface

The papers in this volume have developed from those delivered at a conference, 'Winchester: An Early Medieval Royal City', held at the University of Winchester in July 2017. The focus of the publication has changed slightly in the process of editing this volume, with an appreciation for the recognition of the importance of communities in the approach to the city, but the sense of the royal city that drove through that conference was invaluable in providing the energy for this volume.

The conference was held with the support and encouragement of Hampshire Cultural Trust, and with the help of the organisational brilliance of Gemma Holsgrove; this volume has been published with the backing of one of the University's research centres, the Wessex Centre for History and Archaeology. We are grateful to all of them for their support, as without them this volume could not have been published.

A global pandemic probably isn't anyone's first choice of backdrop for contributing to or editing a collection of essays. We would like to express our gratitude to colleagues in our institution and in our fields of study, including the anonymous referees who have helped us in the editing of this volume, and of course to the contributors to this volume. The contributors' willingness to respond to editorial queries, often at very short notice, their patience and good humour with the occasional bump in the road have been an enormous help to us with the publication of this volume. We are also grateful to our editors Felicity Goldsack and Jessica Hawxwell and their colleagues at Oxbow, for their help and forbearance in bringing this volume to publication.

While this book cannot be the final word on an important period in the history and archaeology – or indeed the literary culture – of medieval Winchester, we hope that the collection of important work in this volume can stand as a testament to much of the great scholarship undertaken on and in Winchester and moreover, to the way in which the scholarship on the city is developing in the twenty-first century.

Ryan Lavelle
Simon Roffey
Katherine Weikert

Winchester, June 2021

List of Contributors

Karl Christian Alvestad is Associate Professor in the Department of Culture, Religion and Social Studies, University of South-Eastern Norway.

Mark Atherton is Senior College Lecturer at Regent's Park College, University of Oxford and Stipendiary Lecturer at Mansfield College, University of Oxford.

Martin Biddle is Emeritus Professor of Archaeology at the University of Oxford, Emeritus Fellow of Hertford College, Oxford and Director of the Winchester Research Unit.

Toni Griffiths is a visiting fellow at the Parkes Institute, University of Southampton.

Alexander James Langlands is Senior Lecturer in Medieval History at Swansea University.

Eric Lacey is Senior Lecturer in English at the University of Winchester.

Ryan Lavelle is Professor of Early Medieval History at the University of Winchester.

David McDermott is an honorary research fellow at the University of Winchester.

Simon Roffey is Reader in Medieval Archaeology at the University of Winchester.

Sharon M. Rowley is Professor of English at Christopher Newport University.

Alexander R. Rumble is a retired reader in Palaeography at the University of Manchester.

Katherine Weikert is Senior Lecturer in Early Medieval European History at the University of Winchester.

Barbara Yorke is Emeritus Professor of Early Medieval History at the University of Winchester and Honorary Professor at the Institute of Archaeology, University College London.

List of Illustrations

List of Tables

Chapter 1

Communities, Authority and Power in Winchester, *c.* 800–*c.* 1200

Katherine Weikert, Ryan Lavelle and Simon Roffey

Winchester, though now a quiet and rather small city, contains hidden depths in its past as a place of settlement for over two thousand years. Its place at the heart of the interests of an early medieval ruling family who dominated Wessex and England gives it part of that lustre, but its timeline stretches long before the years on which this volume focuses.[1] As the location of two Iron Age settlements, one of which morphed into the Roman city, the ancient and medieval layers provide a palimpsest of urban landscapes which remains to this day. Its size and population throughout the early and into the central Middle Ages distinctly reflect the development of an urban centre and growth of its population during the period covered by this volume, at the height of its power and influence. By the seventh century, as a central place within the West Saxon kingdom, the city contained its own bishop and bishopric, established in the building known as the Old Minster, which began the start of centuries of Wintonian episcopal power matching that of its royal and political significance. The period of the tenth and eleventh centuries, bridging into the twelfth, saw Winchester shift from the focus of the West Saxon royal family to the then-nascent English kingdom, propelling the city, its culture, community and peoples into a central city in the affairs of the kingdom.

With this centrality, and the centuries of evidence available, writing medieval Winchester as a city of power and community can, and does, take many angles. There is sometimes-sporadic written evidence such as chronicles, particularly the *Anglo-Saxon Chronicle*, which originated as an Alfredian, Wessex-centric view of the past.[2] The rich monastic traditions of hagiography, especially with Winchester's internationally-

---

[1] Although Anglocentric scholars often tend to draw on 1066 for a division between the 'early Middle Ages' and the increasingly common 'central Middle Ages' for historical periodisation, 'early medieval' has been used as the label of historical convenience for this volume, which has the added benefit of drawing some continuities across the period of the Norman Conquest. The term 'central Middle Ages', referring here broadly to a period of the eleventh and twelfth centuries, is occasionally employed in this chapter. For comments on periodisation here, see Lavelle 2015.

[2] For a useful review of the evidence and scholarship, see Jorgensen 2010, 11–14.

revered St Swithun, give great insight into the thriving medieval religious, civic and intellectual city.[3] Charters from the period tell of the network of royal, ecclesiastical and aristocratic interests associated with the city, with the records of estates held in the city's hinterland and sometimes within the urban space itself revealing competing interests and rivalries, particularly between the Old and New Minsters.[4] There were also other records: Domesday Book was kept in the royal castle in the form of the Exchequer manuscript, sometimes known as 'Great Domesday'; as Sally Harvey has noted, its contemporary title as the 'Book of Winchester' is intrinsically linked with the governmental functions of the city in the eleventh century and in that manner the creation and very survival of such a valuable 'Book of the Treasury' (another medieval name) should be seen as evidence of Winchester's early medieval importance.[5]

The Hampshire folios of Domesday Book do not provide a separate record of the city itself as a shire town in the manner of many other eleventh-century English towns, including neighbouring Southampton.[6] The Domesday record does provide us with indications of the wealth of city institutions in its entries of landholdings of the bishopric and the New Minster, as well as the Nunnaminster, known by the later eleventh century as St Mary's Abbey.[7] Domesday entries also reveal the many royal and aristocratic estates with attached properties in the city, perhaps functioning as *pieds-à-terre*, the estates' owners retaining a stake in the urban economy and urban politics.[8] However, the city has its own surveys in the manuscript known as Winton Domesday. The Winton Domesday manuscript, written at the orders of Bishop Henry of Blois in the middle of the twelfth century, records one earlier survey and one from Henry's own time. The first of these surveys records information from the reigns of Henry I and, like Great Domesday, of Edward the Confessor, regarding royal properties, mainly on the High Street; the second is concerned with a greater number of properties in the mid-twelfth century city and provides evidence on details of the lives and the wealth of the inhabitants of areas of the city.[9]

Perhaps even more importantly, the material remains of medieval Winchester play the dual role of not only interpreting the city, but in the development of archaeological techniques and methodologies themselves. Major excavations in the 1960s and early

---

[3] See Lapidge 2003 and Karl Alvestad's contribution to this volume, pp. 257–74.
[4] For property in the city, see Rumble 2001.
[5] Harvey 2014, 1–31. See also Biddle 1987, 314, who discusses the link between the castle, treasury, and the *Liber de Thesauro*, recorded in the early twelfth century.
[6] Munby 1982, S1–3. However, for useful comments on the fact that summaries of data for towns are not the Domesday norm, and that the information on Winchester was to hand, see Roffe 2007, 118–19.
[7] Knowles 1966, 702–3, provides totals of the gross (annual) income of religious houses in Domesday; according to his calculations, which are admittedly open to debate, depending on how one calculates Domesday income, the Old Minster received £600 (making it sixth of the 46 pre-Conquest houses in the kingdom, with Glastonbury's £827 as first), the New Minster £390 and the Nunnaminster £65 (placing it 32nd).
[8] Darby 1977, 310, and fig. 105, discussing Winchester in a wider discussion of urban-rural properties (309–13). For a review of the status of urban properties in the hands of social elites, see Fleming 1993.
[9] Biddle 1976, 32–141.

1970s investigated nearly 12,000 square metres of urban settlement within the walls, making Winchester not only one of the most extensively excavated medieval towns in England, but also a training ground for an entire generation of British archaeologists.[10] Many of the finds from these extensive excavations were diagnostically 'Anglo-Saxon,' roughly 700–1100, pointing to the impact this period had on the development of the city – including the secular and sacred politics and communities which the city hosted. Winchester, for all its small-town feel in the present, was a hub of not only local and regional power and networks, but one that extended throughout the West Saxon and English kingdoms and indeed western Europe, home of many communities and a part of important transnational exchanges of ideas and culture.

There is, as Martin Biddle's contribution to this volume makes clear, a significant element of antiquity to the city as a place already settled before the Middle Ages, and the topography of the earlier history affected the medieval city. The Iron Age enclosures on the edges of the city at St Catherine's Hill (an impressive double-ringed hill fort) to its south-east and at Oram's Arbour to its north-west gave first shape to the growing city (see Fig. 1.1 and Chapter 2, Fig. 2.1). Aspects of Oram's Arbour were retained by the first-century Roman establishment of a walled city with the status of *civitas*, a planned and organised local government centre. For example, a road and site roughly along modern Jewry Street, at the bottom of Oram's Arbour, were settled before Roman occupation, and were folded into the Roman town as both a major street and the main road north out of the walled city.[11] Roman Winchester, *Venta Belgarum*, named after the Iron Age Belgae, became one of the larger towns in *Britannia*.[12] Even if very little of the Roman wall is actually visible *in situ* today, the shape of Roman Winchester can still be roughly seen in the modern city topography – Eastgate, Southgate and North Walls streets marking each boundary.[13] After the withdrawal of Roman imperial control in the fifth century, the archaeological evidence of Winchester suggests that while there was minimal continuous urban occupation, particularly when compared with the continuity of Roman cities in continental Europe, the city continued to have a significance as a regional centre.[14] The Roman walls ultimately provided an area for a comparatively large medieval city (58.2 ha).[15]

With the growth and intensification of royal power in Britain in the seventh century, especially with newly established monastic and episcopal networks emerging through

---

[10] See Martin Biddle's contribution to this volume, pp. 19–39.
[11] Ford and Teague 2011.
[12] For the significance of the Belgae in the Roman identity of Winchester, see King 2020.
[13] For a comprehensive survey of the walls, see Ottaway *et al.* 2019.
[14] On towns in the post-Roman world generally, see Wickham 2005, 591–2, discussing the differences north of the Alps from the Mediterranean region at 674–92. Biddle 1973, 232–4 discusses the affinities of late Roman era (and 'early Anglo-Saxon') grave goods with northern France, the Low Countries and Rhineland. Stuckert 2017, 219–37, discusses the evidence for early Anglo-Saxon population continuity and change.
[15] Biddle 1973, 229.

connections to continental Europe and particularly Gaul,[16] interest grew in the symbolic power of direct connection with Rome and the Romanised world. Winchester, with its Roman ruins and *spolia*, would provide a locus of political and ecclesiastical power for the fledgling kingdom with its powerful bishop and probably a royal palace.[17] By the mid-seventh century, Winchester had its first cathedral at the Old Minster and its first bishop, Wine – albeit a figure whose incumbency was short-lived and who fell out with the then-king, according to Bede.[18] This episcopal seat had been transferred to Winchester from the earlier foundation at Dorchester-on-Thames as the West Saxon dynasty's interests shifted from the Thames Valley in the face of Mercian pressure (and probably also related to the West Saxons' interests in territory to the south of Winchester); the body of the West Saxons' first bishop, Birinus, was also transferred from Dorchester by the end of the seventh century.[19] Excavations directed by Martin Biddle have revealed that the Old Minster's active community encouraged an almost continuous programme of building, rebuilding and expansion through to the tenth century (see Biddle's contribution to this volume, Chapter 2). To this establishment were added the royal foundations of Nunnaminster, by King Alfred's widow Ealhswith (d. 902), probably after Alfred's death in 899, on the site of her own estate in Winchester, and New Minster, by Alfred's son Edward.[20] The connection between royal and ecclesiastical rule, almost always important in the Middle Ages, reached new heights via the connection between the house of Wessex, the kings of England and the bishops of Winchester.

Winchester's regional significance in the (eventually dominant) West Saxon kingdom provided a major link in its importance in the central Middle Ages. The intersecting factors of a significant and diverse urban population, a major palace complex, an important episcopal centre and a Roman past combined to their fullest fruition as an expression of power. This is somewhat removed from the popular portrait of a sub-Roman palatial complex in the *Last Kingdom* books of Bernard Cornwell, recently adapted for television, which might give an impression of a permanent royal sanctuary in the city. Winchester's 'capital' authority was a mixture of the influence of ecclesiastical communities coupled with economic wealth for a peripatetic royal governance over a diverse population with (then as now) some extraordinarily wealthy residents.

Contrary to popular belief, though, Winchester has never been a 'capital' of England or even of Wessex. But it certainly was a city of great importance, perhaps even a central city, which was both symbolic and practical in its use and need by dint of the royal and episcopal investment in its worth. Eugen Ewig argued for the link between '*residence et capitale*' in the Roman Empire's successor polities, noting the significance of the idea of the permanence of a central place and the importance of a palatial

---

[16] For the significance of Gaulish/Frankish connections, underplayed in Bede's account but important in terms of the West Saxon church, see generally Campbell 1986, 53–67.
[17] Cf. Yorke 1982.
[18] Bede, *HE* III.7.
[19] *Ibid*. On the shift to Winchester, see Yorke 1995, 58–9.
[20] Rumble 2001, 231.

residence within an urban space, even if it became increasingly difficult to achieve in practice, and for the early Carolingian ruling family, there was a notable absence of urban centres used as the locations for palaces. This may simply have been an issue of policy and even expediency for rulers who needed to remain on the move.[21] Most early medieval societies operated without a permanent, central location as a 'capital' and early medieval England was no different. Many of the 'principal' cities of power in the early Middle Ages operated similarly: the establishment of Baghdad by the Abbasid Caliphate in 762 as a 'disembedded capital', but also the centre of intellectual culture and trade; the importance of Córdoba (and its associated palace city, Madinat al-Zahra) to the Umayyad rulers of Al-Andalus in the tenth century; the undeniable significance of Constantinople, Jerusalem and Rome to multiple empires and religions.[22] On a smaller scale, Winchester fits this model alongside cities such as Aachen, where the royal chapel was structurally integral with the Carolingian palace, in one – but not the only – of the imperial cities, or Nidaros (now Trondheim), seat of Norway's first metropolitan see which was – not coincidentally – built in the 1070s on the gravesite of the saintly warrior King Olav II. In these places, as in Winchester, location and proximity played a key part in the landscape of power in the cities. Aachen's chapel and palace occupied the same physical structure, the palatine complex constructing the identity of secular and sacred power.[23] At Nidaros, King Sverre Sigurdsson built his castle in early 1180s on the hill above the town and cathedral.[24] Sverre was in conflict with the church throughout his reign,[25] and the location of his stronghold would not have been a coincidence. The castle and cathedral were physically separated by about two miles, but the sightlines between indicate tension in the relationships: the king's castle towered over both the archbishop's cathedral and palace.[26] Even if the evidence for Winchester does not suggest tensions as pronounced as those of Nidaros, the topographical relationships between royal residences and important cathedrals in an urban landscape are echoed in Winchester: the early medieval palace was located to the immediate west of the Old and New Minsters, and William's Norman palace expanded this to the north, encroaching onto the medieval High Street.[27] The royal nunnery of St Mary's sat just to the immediate north-east of the male houses (at least until New Minster moved to the northern suburb of Hyde in 1110), and most of the south-east of the city was a quarter of royal, ecclesiastical and monastic importance.[28]

   The role of Alfred the Great as the West Saxon founding father of Winchester is now more debatable than it once was, particularly given that the mid-ninth-century

---

[21] Ewig 1963, esp. 53–8. Roach 2011 investigates the political significance royal itineraries in an English context.
[22] See Liu 2011; van Bavel *et al.* 2014; Joffe 1998; Clarke 2011.
[23] For the relationship between urban and palatial space, see Rollason 2016, esp. 171–201.
[24] Sverresborg Trøndelag Folkemuseum, n.d.
[25] Bagge 2014, 81.
[26] Kulturminnesøk, n.d.
[27] *RRAN I*, 37; Biddle and Keene 2017, 38.
[28] For a recent study of the significance of this, see Foxhall Forbes 2011.

incumbency of Bishop Swithun was a time at which a bridge was built over the River Itchen. This, Martin Biddle suggests, indicates that the medieval east gate, in a different position from the Roman east gate and an essential part of the new street layout of the city from the ninth century, was already open before Alfred's reign.[29] The remodelling and recalibration of the Roman street plan in Winchester may not have been repeated with quite such verve in other southern English cities but the relationship between the lengths of the city walls and the resources allocated to the city seems to have provided a model for the development of an urban policy in southern England, in the form of the measurements used in the Burghal Hidage (which, though surviving as an early tenth-century manuscript, probably signifies the late ninth-century policies of Alfred the Great).[30] The only act in Winchester for which there is direct evidence of the presence of a living King Alfred in the city, however, is his order of the execution of two Viking ships' crews caught on the Sussex coast, recorded in the *Anglo-Saxon Chronicle* for 896. This act may, however, be telling of Winchester's regional and even national significance in in a city which has considerable evidence, in the form of execution burials, of the operation of justice (or at least displays of justice).[31] However, Winchester's urban and royal influence for the wider English kingdom is perhaps rooted in the later tenth century and during the reign of Cnut the Great (1016/17–35), who is connected to the city both through his gifts to the New Minster as well as the promulgation of his lawcode in Winchester in 1020 or 1021.[32] This relationship moves smoothly into the mid-eleventh century, when the city saw the coronations of Edward the Confessor in 1043, and the 'confirmation' coronation of William I in 1070.[33]

The intertwining of royal and religious power can be seen in Winchester as the location for some of the most dynamic relationships between kings and religious men throughout the early Middle Ages. Alfred relied heavily on Grimbald of St Bertin for his cultural programme of literary and educational endeavours, having convinced Archbishop Fulco of Rheims to send him to aid in Alfred's reform of culture and education in southern England. Grimbald did not receive the bishopric that Fulco saw him worthy of, but Grimbald appears to have been important in Winchester. His installation in his own *monasteriolum* in Winchester and his association with the

---

[29] Biddle and Keene 2017, 26–7. For the evidence for the relationship between Alfred and Winchester (and especially the limits of direct evidence), see Yorke 1999, 5–7.

[30] Yorke 1995, 115–21. See Lavelle 2021, 86–9 for a review of recent work on the relationship between the Burghal Hidage and Alfred; Keene and Biddle 2017, 26–7 discuss the archaeological evidence for the possible early medieval investigation of the lengths of the wall – an intriguing suggestion which shed light on the notion of Winchester as a city providing a 'blueprint' for other early medieval burhs.

[31] See the short discussion of this in Ryan Lavelle's contribution to this volume, p. 137.

[32] On Cnut and Winchester, see Yorke forthcoming (although Yorke does hold some reservations about the relationship between the king and the city). British Library Stowe MS 944 fol. 6r; British Library Cotton Nero MS A I fols 3r-41r.

[33] For Edward: Licence 2020, 85–9; for William I: Bates 2016, 336; Gathagan 2004 places the 1068 coronation of Matilda of Flanders in Winchester; however, her coronation at Whitsun (OV II, 214–15; John of Worcester III, 6–7) would have taken place at Westminster as William wore his crown at Westminster on Whitsun (see below).

later foundation of New Minster are indicative of the esteem in which Grimbald was held.[34] Relationships between kings and church were perhaps at an apex in the tenth century reforms, enacted by the partnership of King Edgar and Æthelwold, bishop of Winchester, with influence from the important reformed monasteries at Fleury, Cluny and St Peter's, Ghent.[35] The city itself saw some of the earliest changes of this horizon, with the (possibly violent) expulsion of secular clerks from Winchester in 964 under Æthelwold's demand and support from Edgar's men.

The bright, if short-lived, flame of tenth-century monastic reform began changes that were accelerated in the post-Conquest era. Throughout this period, there was a confidence and affinity between the kings of England and the bishops of Winchester.[36] Even if bishops were not always close allies, as with the much-maligned Stigand (who held his Winchester see in plurality with the archbishopric of Canterbury until 1070), their roles as intermediaries were invaluable.[37] Wakelin, the first Norman bishop of Winchester, was a royal chaplain to William, and began the process of building the Norman cathedral still visible today in the north and south transepts. William Giffard, bishop for most of the earlier twelfth century, served as something akin to a chancellor to both William Rufus and Henry II; Henry of Blois, bishop from 1129, was the brother of King Stephen (and first cousin of the Empress Matilda).[38] The bishopric of Winchester grew into one of the most powerful in the kingdom. Until the Dissolution of the Monasteries after the 1534 Act of Supremacy, Winchester was the wealthiest bishopric in the kingdom, and to this day, the bishop of Winchester is still third in precedence behind the archbishops of Canterbury and York, alongside the bishops of London and Durham.[39] As political power grew in Winchester, so did that of the bishop.

Religious life, with its connections not just through England but through the continent, shaped the city. Although less discussed than other cities such as Canterbury or Durham, Winchester, with its access to wealth and its influential patrons, saw a flourishing of arts and intellectual culture during this period. We might only be able to imagine the sound of an organ reputed to have been established by Bishop Æthelwold in the Old Minster and enlarged by his successor, Ælfheah, in the last years of the tenth century; Wulfstan the Cantor claimed it could be heard all over the city. But the description does give some flavour to the innovative nature of the other musical developments that accompanied the tenth-century reformation, which can be seen and, with a little help, heard from the interpretation of words and notation on surviving manuscripts.[40] Manuscripts of music, in fact, were one of the strengths

---

[34] Pfaff 2004; Keynes and Lapidge 1983, 185–6; Keynes 1996, 16.

[35] See generally Yorke 1988.

[36] However, on Æthelstan, see this chapter, p. 11.

[37] On Stigand's importance in Winchester, see Harvey 2014, 29.

[38] Franklin 2004; for Henry of Blois see generally Kynan-Wilson and Munns 2021.

[39] House of Lords Precedence Act 1539, 31 Hen 8, §3.

[40] Berry 1988, with discussion of the 'Winchester organ' at 157–60. A rendering of 'Alleluia, Dies sanctificatus' from the tenth-century *Winchester Troper*, performed by the Schola Gregoriana of

of the lost Winchester library (see below). The influence of Carolingian artistry can be seen in the detailed illuminations of the tenth- and eleventh-century Winchester Style manuscript illustrations, and the apex of the artistry of the monastic scriptoria is seen in the mid-twelfth century Winchester Bible, produced under the patronage of Bishop Henry of Blois with artists drawn both locally but also specifically called in from Sicily.[41]

The work of Steven F. Vincent and, more recently, the late and sorely missed Claire Donovan have demonstrated important libraries at the monastic institutions of Winchester. From what can be reconstructed of the libraries, history and hagiography were particular strengths, and they also contained manuscripts about music, theology, classics and works in or about the Greek language.[42] Not coincidentally, the Winchester monasteries also had a strong medical tradition with libraries including works on science and medicine.[43] One the of the earliest medical treatises, Bald's *Leechbook*, compiled in the ninth century, is solely known to us from a tenth-century copy, likely made in Winchester by the same scribe responsible for the Cathedral library's copy of the Old English version of Bede's *Historia Ecclesiastica* and a number of entries in the *Anglo-Saxon Chronicle*.[44] Although it is difficult to draw a direct line of causation, with such a legacy it is perhaps unsurprising that early Norman Winchester became home to one of the earliest hospital foundations at St Mary Magdalen, to the east on a down above the city.[45] This intellectual culture also fostered writing from Winchester authors, between the composition of the *Regularis Concordia* at the start of the tenth-century reforms, to Lantfred and Wulfstan the Cantor locally producing hagiography, and Winchester-trained Ælfric of Eynsham creating both hagiography as well as a famous and popular *Grammar*. Though the Winchester Cathedral library was largely dispersed in the Dissolution of the Monasteries, manuscript production in the monastic precincts speak to the religious and intellectual culture of the city and their intersections.

The connections and interactions between Winchester's citizens and influential monastic communities was certainly limited, particularly after enclosing the monastic and ecclesiastical precinct in the south-west of the city. These limitations were no doubt exacerbated by Benedictine reforms dictating limited contact between monks and lay people. But its large number of parish churches – fifty-seven by the end of the twelfth century – indicates smaller religious communities in a city whose population may have been as many as 12,000 by *c.* 1110.[46] Without accounting for

---

Cambridge and directed by Mary Berry, is available at: https://www.youtube.com/watch?v=i-OuElxgC1o.

[41] Donovan 2021.

[42] Donovan 2021; Vincent 1981.

[43] Vincent 1981.

[44] British Library Royal MS 12 D XVII (see cataloguing information at http://searcharchives.bl.uk/primo_library/libweb/action/dlDisplay.do?docId=IAMS040-002106754&fn=permalink&vid=IAMS_VU2); British Library Cotton MS Otho B XI; Cambridge, Corpus Christi College MS 173. See Sharon Rowley's chapter in this volume, pp. 81–102.

[45] Roffey 2012.

[46] Martin Biddle and Derek Keene in Biddle 1976, 440–1, estimate 6,500 from the properties in Winchester

non-Christian citizens, parish sizes or population density, this indicates an average parish of around 210 people (allowing, of course, for a very considerable amount of variation). These smaller communities would have encouraged spirituality and created the patterns of life where the secular intersected with the spiritual – from saints' days to regular church attendance – and created friendship and kinship groups in smaller neighbourhoods in what was a large medieval city.[47]

The Christian communities, though, were not the only ones in medieval Winchester. The city was home to a sizeable Jewish community, established before 1148 and witnessed by multiple means though, for the twelfth century, primarily through documentary sources.[48] Richard of Devizes of the cathedral priory of St Swithun's chronicled some of the atrocities and accusations against the Jews throughout England in the late twelfth century (including an accusation of ritual murder in Winchester following the coronation of Richard I).[49] More prosaically, Winchester was home to one of the *archae*, the record-keeping locations of Jewish financiers (literally, arcs or chests). Like all communities, the Jewish population of Winchester probably contained a small number of very wealthy magnates, but the percentage of the community which had income sufficient enough to pay the 1159 *donum* to Henry II ranked Winchester as the fourth-wealthiest Jewish community in England after London, Norwich and Lincoln, tied with Cambridge.[50] In 1177, the establishment of a cemetery for the Jewish population was another important mark of acknowledgement of the community's presence and importance in the city, as previously Jewish people throughout England were only allowed burial in London.[51]

The Winchester Jews settled largely in the north-west of the city along what is now called Jewry Street (known in the twelfth century as *Scowrtenestret* [shoemaker's street]).[52] Although the exact location of the synagogue, the spiritual heart of the community, is unknown, it too was along Jewry Street. With their particular relationship to the crown, the Jewish community also had a physical and proximal relationship with Winchester's royal castle on the south-west of the city inside the walls, close to the Westgate. Although out of the era of this book, when Simon de Montfort the Younger went on his rampage in 1265 on his march towards his father at Evesham, he killed all the Wintonian Jews save those who had taken refuge at

---

in *c.* 1110, extrapolating the estimate to upwards of 8,000. The estimate is revised (Biddle 1987, 329–30) to about 12,000.

[47] Sadly, the death in 2019 of a talented Winchester University research student, Susan Nightingale, prevented the completion of her PhD thesis on southern English urban communities, in which Winchester parish affiliations were due to provide a significant strand of discussion. We remain grateful to her for influencing our thoughts on these issues.

[48] Hillaby and Hillaby 2013, 2. See the chapter in this volume by Toni Griffiths, pp. 225–39.

[49] Stevenson 1838, 5–6.

[50] Hillaby 2001, 64; see also Mell 2017, 187, 174, 215.

[51] Riley 1853, 457–8.

[52] This, coincidentally, is also the rough location of the Iron Age road leading out of the city to the north, referenced above (Fig. 1.1)

the castle.[53] Outside the terrible acts, though, medieval Winchester held a thriving Jewish community numbering a few hundred at most, some occupied with finance but others in the wool trade, and most in trades unknown to us, like many medieval people. Much like their non-Jewish neighbours, wealth was concentrated with a few families, but the majority were not particularly wealthy, a matter which is borne out by the skeletal evidence from the partially excavated Jewish cemetery in the city's western suburbs.[54]

Wealth, however, was a significant factor in Winchester's medieval history. Although the majority of its medieval population would not have been wealthy, the city itself held great amounts of wealth. This stems partly from its early medieval mints: between the late ninth and twelfth centuries, Winchester was one of the four great royal mints of England. The major Winchester mint reflects the royal power into the city, but adds the wealth that mints created not only in coinage but in wealth of the system itself. With a major minting industry came commensurate influence and opportunities to the medieval city. The Winton Domesday, for example, provides the names and often the location of residences for a number of Winchester moneyers, perhaps dozens if all possible identifications are correct. Their homes tend to be clustered to the immediate west of the cathedral, close to the palace, in streets that held higher rent values compared to the rest of the city.[55] There is further evidence of the relative wealth of the city of Winchester in comparison to other eleventh-century towns (particularly London, whose prosperity is obvious from the early medieval evidence). The comparable evidence of the number of moneyers and the value of taxable property in the city of Winchester, not to mention the presence of high-status goods and the evidence of the investment in luxury manuscripts in the city, are worthy of note.

The relationship between the cities of Winchester and London is particularly prominent throughout this period, just as the relative affluence of the city of Winchester today is reliant on a short link between Winchester and London: the two cities were (and still are) within one another's orbit, even if it now (and probably then) matters less to those in London than to those in Winchester. Eleventh- and twelfth-century rulers moved rapidly and frequently between Winchester and London, and the bishop of Winchester's property in Southwark is a recognition of the historical significance of the bishop's diocesan authority right up to the Thames in Surrey. If there was a discernible moment that tipped of the scales from one city to the other, it may have started to take place by the early eleventh century. Martin Biddle's observation on the production of coin 'as an index of commercial activity' indicates that during the middle of the tenth century London surpassed Winchester in terms of wealth and population to the point that, with Norwich, Lincoln and York, Winchester was firmly in the second tier of urban centres after the Norman Conquest

---

[53] Hillaby and Hillaby 2013, 391.
[54] Ottaway and Qualmann 2018, 224–41.
[55] Biddle 1976, 396–422. For the evidence of coins themselves over a longer period, see Biddle 2012, 6–23.

(although London alone occupied the first tier).[56] Furthermore, Edward the Confessor's investment in the extra-mural palace and abbey at Westminster in the mid-eleventh century provided English kings with a church of ceremonial importance to match the wealth of London. Winchester was fortunate that the burials of its kings were not translated to Westminster in the manner that West Saxon and pre-Conquest English rulers sometimes moved their ancestors (see Barbara Yorke's chapter in this volume pp. 59–80), a matter which may help explain the continuing significance of the city into the later eleventh century.

The royal bones in the minsters notwithstanding, perhaps were it not for Cnut's interest in the city of Winchester – or at least antagonism toward London – Winchester's post-Conquest significance may have been less pronounced. The importance of Winchester for West Saxon kings of England was not a *fait accompli*, either. In the tenth century, the bishop's support for Æthelstan's brother, the short-lived Ælfweard, who succeeded his father Edward in Wessex in 924 for a matter of days, may have led to a souring of relations between crown and what Sarah Foot calls the 'Winchester establishment',[57] while Æthelred's focus on the control of London in the early eleventh century may have stemmed from a pragmatic need to retain control of its wealth, as well as the strategic importance of a city that was situated to control lands beyond Wessex.[58]

The symbolic nature of power in the city was continuously recognised through the Conquest period, though. William I, according to the *Anglo-Saxon Chronicle*, wore his crown at Easter in Winchester every year that he was in England for the festival (Pentecost was spent at Westminster and the Christmas festival in Gloucester).[59] The grandeur of a crown-wearing occasion helped to remind all involved of the seriousness of the duty in secular and Christian terms: the crown was the greatest symbol of the position, the responsibility it carried, and the authority which came with it. William's son William Rufus continued this tradition in his reign, with Easter crown-wearings in Winchester.[60] The location of the royal treasury at Winchester through the mid-twelfth century was also a crucial component to its continuing significance after the eleventh century. For these kings, the practical importance of the possession of the royal treasury in Winchester provided a pairing with the importance of acclamation in London. Indeed, it was a pattern for conquerors or, say, unexpected heirs such as William, William Rufus and Stephen to make certain to control both London and

---

[56] Biddle 1987, 330; Yoshitake 2015; Green 2017, 198–220, highlights the growth of London's political significance in tandem with its economic growth from the later tenth century. Though there is no direct comparison between the two cities, Winchester warrants three pages (187–9). For the relative significance of the evidence of the Winchester mint's production between Edgar and the Norman Conquest (6.6% of all then-known coins (44,000), placing Winchester fourth after London, York and Lincoln), see Biddle 2012, 5.

[57] Foot 2011, 39–41 (quotation at 39).

[58] Naismith 2018, 180–1.

[59] ASC E for 1087. Biddle 1985; Bates 2020, 522–4.

[60] Barlow 1983, 211.

Winchester in quick succession to secure their rule.[61] But a royal treasury, like saintly bones, are portable. In the mid-twelfth century, the treasury was finally moved to London, and the royal palace was dismantled by 1148.[62] Perhaps the final show of Winchester's strategic importance came with the Treaty of Winchester in 1153, which settled the nearly twenty-year 'Anarchy' between Stephen and Matilda with the agreement that Matilda's son Henry would succeed Stephen. Negotiated by Henry, bishop of Winchester (and Stephen's brother), this crucial treaty signalled both the importance of the city but also was a final act of significance in the period. Perhaps a sign of the times was that the treaty was duly confirmed by charter in Westminster later in the same year.[63]

Through this later period, though, as London waxed and Winchester waned, Anglo-Norman and Angevin rulers were still drawn to Winchester not only for its symbolic importance but also because of its proximity to the coast ports of southern England that allowed access to Normandy. Going to a place like Winchester instilled rulers with a certain gravitas en route to or from Rouen or Caen, particularly when coupled with the opportunities to express rulership through hunting in the royal New Forest, less than a day's journey away.[64] Perhaps in the wake of London's eclipsing of Winchester, it was this convenience that maintained much of Winchester's standing in the south of England.[65] But a principal city, even of the second tier, cannot rely on a main role as a stopover destination, however exclusive. The significant loss of Normandy in 1204 was also likely a significant blow to Winchester, given that members of the royal family no longer needed to travel to the duchy quite so frequently as they had done for more than a century. Winchester would continue to have royal links into the thirteenth century and beyond – Henry III magnificently rebuilt the twelfth-century castle; Mary I married Phillip of Spain in the cathedral; Charles II intended to create a pleasure palace to the west of the city fit to rival Versailles – but from at least the end of the twelfth century, Winchester's star had diminished.

***

---

[61] For William II, Barlow 1983, 54–63, provides an assessment of the circumstances of an eleventh-century coup. On the treasury, see Yoshitake 2015. Barlow notes that William Rufus' possession of the treasury in Winchester second to his coronation would denote the right order of things, that he was not 'in company with those who seized the throne in irregular circumstances', 1983, 55.

[62] For discussion of the latter, see Biddle 1976, 292–302. For the treasury, Yoshitake 2015.

[63] White 1990, 11; Holt 1994, 295–6.

[64] This (not coincidentally) led to opportunities for accidental death. Both Richard of Normandy (d. *c.* 1070), William the Conqueror's son, and William Rufus (d. 1100) perished in hunting accidents in the New Forest. William Rufus was certainly buried in Winchester Cathedral, and it is likely that Richard was as well; see Barlow 1983, 429; Bates 2016, 330; BBC News 16 May 2019.

[65] On the significance of Wessex and William I's 'Cross-Channel Empire', see Bates 2020, 530–3. Bates also discusses the significance of hunting in the local infrastructure at 522–7. Rollason 2016, 150–64, provides a valuable indication of the projection of power (rather than simply leisure pursuit) associated with hunting.

This volume explores many of these interrelated issues of royal, ecclesiastical and community expressions of power, placing early and central medieval Winchester in regional, national and transnational context as a city at the nexus of might and influence. In many ways those expressions and influences of power intersected with one another. As a political city, as an ecclesiastical city, as a city of communities, Winchester's early medieval foundations and exchanges formed the city into a locus of power. Thus, this volume seeks to examine these aspects that made Winchester into a city at the heart of the kingdom in the early and central Middle Ages. As well as that, far from being an insular-focussed city, this volume also highlights some of Winchester's continental connections in the period.

That the city was symbolically, physically and emotionally important for secular and royal power is in no doubt. Reaching back into the days of Alfred, the Old Minster and, later, the cathedral became intended memorial sites for the West Saxon, the Anglo-Scandinavian and the Anglo-Norman royal families. Some of these connections, both through royal burial and the association of powerful nobility with the city, are explored in this volume with Barbara Yorke discussing royal burial, and David McDermott's investigation of the close connections between Winchester and members of the ruling family, whose associations with the city advanced their claims to power. The importance of the city as a physical location for acts and symbols of authority is examined in two chapters by Ryan Lavelle and Alexander Langlands. Winchester as an important place in the time of contested successions is highlighted by Katherine Weikert, who examines the actions of Queen Matilda and Empress Matilda during the rout of Winchester in 1141.

There are, though, significant links between the royal and ecclesiastical power of the city, and this manifests in many ways. Sharon Rowley's dynamic chapter demonstrates how political, religious and intellectual cultures combined into a single tenth- and eleventh-century Winchester-created treatise to represent the close relationships between king, bishops and people. The intellectual and cultural weight of Winchester is further seen in the monastic, ecclesiastical and intellectual city – the home of Wulfstan the Cantor, Bishop Æthelwold and Bishop Henry of Blois. Alexander Rumble's chapter, for example, examines the attempts made by Henry of Blois to raise Winchester to a metropolitan see, a move that would have levelled Winchester with the archbishoprics of Canterbury and York. Moving the lens past the city, Karl Christian Alvestad explores how Winchester's 'local' St Swithun was hardly that, by examining the evidence and reasons for the transmission of St Swithun into medieval Norway.

But finally, the city is more than royal and episcopal power. The city is also stories and people: stories of the residents, the visitors and their impact here and elsewhere. This includes within the modern city, where the creation of an archaeological community linked by a decades-long excavations programme explored the city and created significant knowledge of Winchester's medieval past, discussed in this volume by Martin Biddle. The vibrant archaeological investigations in Winchester also

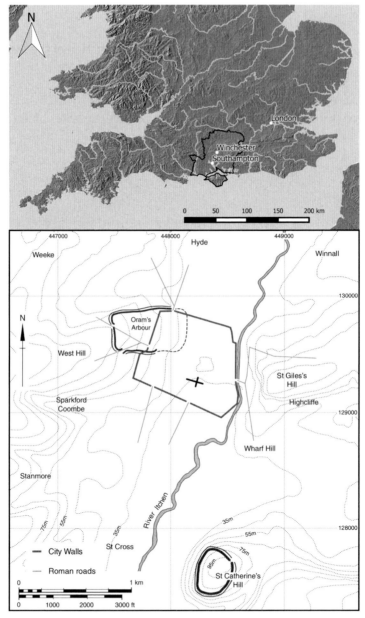

Fig. 1.1: Top: Winchester in its southern English geographical setting, showing the pre-1974 county boundaries of Hampshire. Topographical map data from Copernicus Land Monitoring Service of the European Environment Agency: European Union Digital Elevation Model (EU-DEM), available at: https://land.copernicus.eu; rivers and boundary data from Ordnance Survey. © Crown copyright and database right, 2018; Bottom: Winchester in its geographical and topographical setting, showing the location of Winchester and Iron Age settlements of Oram's Arbour and St Catherine's Hill. Bottom map after Ottaway 2017, 5, fig. 1.1, used with grateful acknowledgements to the author, Winchester City and Historic England. © Crown copyright 2017 OS 1000019531.

present the opportunity for Simon Roffey's creative exploration of a twelfth-century Winchester pilgrim, which tells a transnational story of a pious man who ended his life, and was buried, in Winchester. Toni Griffiths' examination of the medieval Jewish people in Winchester, and their modern memorialisation and presence in the city, gives witness to a materially lost community and the efforts to restore them through heritage initiations. Mark Atherton, in treating Lantfred as a Frankish 'outsider' investigating the miracles of Swithun, explores how the monk was able to write about features of the citizens of Winchester in the process. Equally focused on Lantfred's life of St Swithun, Eric Lacey presents a wholly different story, which had been related to the Frankish writer. It may be too much to hope Lacey has revealed the city's earliest-known folktale, but in his detailed analysis of the supernatural revealed in a familiar topographical setting, it isn't unreasonable and certainly, as Lacey notes, puts a different perspective on the better-known musings on Winchester's famous water meadows.[66]

Ultimately, this volume seeks to explore Winchester's many early and central medieval facets for what they were: part of intertwined networks of power and meaning, each related to and encouraging the other. From the religious to the secular to the everyday; from Lantfred's *The Translation and Miracles of St Swithun* to a single burial on a hill overlooking the city, from flourishing religious minorities to rebellious earls and empresses, the medieval city of Winchester tells us of many pasts and gives us the means to explore them, illuminating a powerful city at its absolute height.

Abbreviations

ASC	Anglo-Saxon Chronicle. Plummer, C. (ed.) 1889. *Two of the Saxon Chronicles Parallel (787–1001 A.D.): with Supplementary Extracts from the Others: A Revised Text.* Oxford: Clarendon Press.
Bede, *HE*	Colgrave, B. and Mynors, R. A. B. (ed. and trans.) 1969. *Bede's Ecclesiastical History of the English People,* Oxford: Clarendon Press.
ODNB	*Oxford Dictionary of National Biography,* 2004 (online edition), https://www.oxforddnb.com/.
OV	Chibnall, M. (ed. and trans.) 1968–80. Orderic Vitalis, *The Ecclesiastical History of Orderic Vitalis,* 6 vols. Oxford: Oxford University Press.
RRAN I	Davis, H. W. C. (ed.) 1913. *Regesta Regum Anglo-Normannorum 1066–1154, Volume I.* Oxford: Clarendon Press.

Bibliography

Manuscripts
Cambridge, Corpus Christi College MS 173.
London, British Library Cotton MS Nero A I.
London, British Library Cotton MS Otho B XI.

---

[66] For a collection of Winchester literature, which understandably does not include Lantfred's 'Furies', see Locke 1913.

London, British Library Royal MS 12 D XVII.
London, British Library Stowe MS 944.

Primary Sources

Darlington, R. R., McGurk, P. and Bray, J. (eds) 1995. *The Chronicle of John of Worcester: Volume II: The Annals from 450 to 1066*. Oxford: Oxford University Press.

House of Lords Precedence Act. 1539. 31 Henry VIII. Available at: https://www.legislation.gov.uk/aep/Hen8/31/10. (Accessed 27 May 2021).

Keynes, S. D. and Lapidge, M. (eds) 1983. *Alfred the Great: Asser's Life of King Alfred and Other Contemporary Sources*. Harmondsworth: Penguin.

Lapidge, M. (ed.) 2003. *The Cult of St Swithun*, Winchester Studies, 4.ii. Oxford: Clarendon Press.

Munby, J. (ed.) 1982. *Domesday Book: Hampshire*. Chichester: Phillimore.

Riley, H. T. (ed.) 1853. *The Annals of Roger de Hoveden*. London: H. G. Bohn.

Schola Gregoriana of Cambridge, dir. Mary Berry. 2020. 'Alleluia, Dies sanctificatus.' https://www.youtube.com/watch?v=i-OuElxgC1o. (Accessed 16 July 2021).

Stevenson, J. (ed.) 1838. *Chronicon Ricardi Divisiensis de rebus gestis Ricardi primi regis Angliae*. London: English Historical Society.

Secondary Sources

Bagge, S. 2014. *Cross and Scepter: The Rise of the Scandinavian Kingdoms from the Vikings to the Reformation*. Princeton: Princeton University Press.

Barlow, F. 1983. *William Rufus*. London: Methuen.

Bates, D. 2016. *William the Conqueror*. New Haven and London: Yale University Press.

Bates, D. 2020. William the Conqueror and Wessex, in A. Langlands and R. Lavelle (eds), *The Land of the English Kin: Studies in Wessex and Anglo-Saxon England in Honour of Professor Barbara Yorke*, 517–37. Leiden: Brill.

BBC News. 16 May 2019. 'Queen's bones' found in Winchester Cathedral royal chests. Available at: https://www.bbc.co.uk/news/uk-england-hampshire-48281733 (Accessed 19 June 2021).

Berry, M. 1988. What the Saxon Monks Sang: Music in Winchester in the Late Tenth Century, in B. Yorke (ed.), *Bishop Æthelwold: His Career and Influence*, 149–60. Woodbridge: Boydell Press.

Biddle, M. 1973. Winchester: The Development of an Early Capital, in H. Jankuhn, W. Schlesinger and H. Steuer (eds), *Vor- und Frühformen der europäischen Stadt im Mittelalter. Bericht über ein Symposium in Reinhausen bei Göttingen in der Zeit vom 18. bis 24. April 1972*, vol. 1, 229–61. Göttingen: Vandenhoeck & Ruprecht.

Biddle, M. (ed.) 1976. *Winchester in the Early Middle Ages: an edition and discussion of the Winton Domesday*, Winchester Studies, 1. Oxford: Clarendon Press.

Biddle, M. 1985. Seasonal Festivals and Residence: Winchester, Westminster and Gloucester in the Tenth to the Twelfth Centuries, *Anglo-Norman Studies*, 8, 51–72.

Biddle, M. 1987. Early Norman Winchester, in J. C. Holt (ed.), *Domesday Studies: Papers Read at the Novocentenary Conference of the Royal Historical Society and the Institute of British Geographers, Winchester, 1986*, 311–31. Woodbridge: Boydell Press.

Biddle, M. (ed.) 2012. *The Winchester Mint and Coins and Related Finds from the Excavations of 1961–71*, Winchester Studies, 8. Oxford: Clarendon Press.

Biddle, M. and Keene, D. 2017. *The British Historic Towns Atlas Vol. VI: Winchester*. Oxford: The Historic Towns Trust and Winchester Excavations Committee.

Campbell, J. 1986. *Essays in Anglo-Saxon History*. London: Hambledon Press.

Clarke, N. 2011. Medieval Arabic Accounts of the Conquest of Cordoba: Creating a Narrative for a Provincial Capital, *Bulletin of the School of Oriental and African Studies, University of London*, 74:1, 41–57.

Darby, H. C. 1977. *Domesday England*. Cambridge: Cambridge University Press.

Donovan, C. 2021. Bishop Henry's Bible, in W. Kynan-Wilson and J. Munns (eds), *Henry of Blois: New Interpretations*, 145–84. Woodbridge: Boydell Press.

Ewig, E. 1963. Résidence et capitale pendant le haut Moyen Age, *Revue Historique*, 230, 25–72.

Fleming, R. 1993. Rural Elites and Urban Communities in Late-Saxon England, *Past and Present*, 141, 3–37.

Foot, S. 2011. *Æthelstan. The First King of England*. New Haven and London: Yale University Press.

Ford, B. M. and Teague, S. 2011. *Winchester, a City in the Making: Archaeological Excavations Between 2002-2007 on the Sites of Northgate House, Staple Gardens and the Former Winchester Library, Jewry Street*. Oxford: Oxford Archaeology Monograph.

Foxhall Forbes, H. 2011. Squabbling Siblings: Gender and Monastic Life in Late Anglo-Saxon Winchester, *Gender and History*, 23, 653–84.

Franklin, M. J. 2004. William Giffard (d. 1129), ODNB. Available at https://doi.org/10.1093/ref:odnb/10655. (Accessed 10 June 2021).

Gathagan, L. 2004. The Trappings of Power: The Coronation of Matilda of Flanders, *Haskins Society Journal*, 13, 21–39.

Green, J. 2017. *Forging the Kingdom: Power in English Society, 973-1189*. Cambridge: Cambridge University Press.

Harvey, S. 2014. *Domesday: Book of Judgement*. Oxford: Oxford University Press.

Hillaby, J. 2001. Testimony from the Margin: The Gloucester Jewry and its Neighbours, c. 1159–1290, *Jewish Historical Studies*, 37, 41–112.

Hillaby, J. and Hillaby, C. 2013. *The Palgrave Dictionary of Medieval Anglo-Jewish History*. London: Palgrave Macmillan.

Holt, J. C. 1994. 1153: The Treaty of Winchester, in E. King (ed.), *The Anarchy of King Stephen's Reign*, 294–317. Oxford: Oxford University Press.

Joffe, A. H. 1998. Disembedded Capitals in Western Asian Perspective, *Comparative Studies in Society and History*, 40:3, 549–80.

Jorgensen, A. 2010. Introduction: Reading the Anglo-Saxon Chronicle, in A. Jorgensen (ed.), *Reading the Anglo-Saxon Chronicle: Language, Literature, History*, 1–28. Turnhout: Brepols.

Keynes, S. (ed.) 1996. *The Liber Vitae of the New Minster and Hyde Abbey, Winchester*. Copenhagen: Rosenkilde & Bagger.

King, A. 2020. Venta Belgarum: What is in the Name for Roman Winchester? in A. J. Langlands and R. Lavelle (eds.), *The Land of the English Kin: Studies in Wessex and Anglo-Saxon England in Honour of Professor Barbara Yorke*, 13–25. Leiden: Brill.

Knowles, D. 1966. *The Monastic Order in England: A History of its Development from the Times of St Dunstan to the Fourth Lateran Council 943-1216*. Cambridge: Cambridge University Press.

Kulturminnesøk. n.d. Sverresborg, Forsvarsanlegg. Available at: https://www.kulturminnesok.no/. (Accessed 9 June 2021).

Kynan-Wilson, W. and Munns, J. (eds.) 2021. *Henry of Blois: New Interpretations*. Woodbridge: Boydell Press.

Lavelle, R. 2015. Sous la lumière d'Alfred le Grand ou dans l'obscurité des Vikings? Quelques problèmes et possibilités dans la périodisation de l'histoire anglaise 'pre-Conquest', in J.-F. Dunyach and A. Mairey (eds.), *Les âges de Britannia : Repenser l'histoire des mondes britanniques (Moyen Âge-XXIe siècle)*, 33–54. Rennes: Presses Universitaires de Rennes.

Lavelle, R. 2021. The 'Dark Matter' Evidence for Alfredian Military Reforms in their Ninth-Century Context, in E. Bennett, G. M. Berndt, S. Esders and L. Sarti (eds), *Early Medieval Militarisation*, 80–95. Manchester: Manchester University Press.

Licence, T. 2020. *Edward the Confessor: Last of the Royal Blood*. New Haven and London: Yale University Press.

Liu, X. 2011. A Silk Road Legacy: The Spread of Buddhism and Islam, *Journal of World History*, 22:1, 55–81.

Locke, A. A. 1913. *In Praise of Winchester: An Anthology in Prose and Verse.* London: Constable and Co.

Mell, J. L. 2017. *The Myth of the Jewish Moneylender, Vol. 1.* New York: Palgrave Macmillan.

Naismith, R. 2018. *Citadel of the Saxons: The Rise of Early London.* London: I. B. Tauris.

Ottaway, P. and Qualmann, K. E. 2018. *The Anglo-Saxon, Medieval and Later Suburbs: Excavations 1971–86.* Winchester: Winchester Museums Service.

Ottaway, P., Qualmann, K., Scobie, G. and Zant, J. 2019. *Winchester's Roman and Medieval Defences: A Report on Excavations 1974–86 and a Gazetteer.* Winchester: Hampshire Cultural Trust.

Pfaff, R. W. 2004. Grimbald [St Grimbald] (d. 901?), ODNB, https://doi.org/10.1093/ref:odnb/11634. (Accessed 9 June 2021).

Roach, L. 2011. Hosting the King: Hospitality and the Royal *Iter* in Tenth-century England, *Journal of Medieval History*, 37, 34–46.

Roffe, D. 2007. *Decoding Domesday.* Woodbridge: Boydell Press.

Roffey, S. 2012. Medieval Leper Hospitals in England: An Archaeological Perspective from St Mary Magdalen, Winchester, *Medieval Archaeology*, 56, 170–80.

Rollason, D. 2016. *The Power of Place: Rulers and their Palaces, Landscapes, Cities, and Holy Places.* Princeton and Oxford: Princeton University Press.

Rumble, A. R. 2001. Edward the Elder and the Churches of Winchester and Wessex, in N. J. Higham and D. H. Hill (eds), *Edward the Elder 899–924*, 230–47. London: Routledge.

Stuckert, C. M. (ed.) 2017. *The People of Early Winchester.* Winchester Studies 9.i. Oxford: Oxford University Press.

Sverresborg Trøndelag Folkemuseum. n.d. The Castle – Sion. Available at: https://sverresborg.no/en/the-castle-zion. (Accessed 9 June 2021).

Van Bavel, B., Campoplano, M. and Dijkman, J. 2014. Factor Markets in Early Islamic Iraq, c. 600–1100 AD, *Journal of the Economic and Social History of the Orient*, 57:2, 262–89.

Vincent, S. F. 1981. The Monastic Libraries of the Diocese of Winchester during the Late Anglo-Saxon and Norman Periods, unpublished MA thesis, Western Michigan University.

White, G. J. 1990. The End of Stephen's Reign, *History*, 75:243, 3–22.

Wickham, C. 2005. *Framing the Early Middle Ages: Europe and the Mediterranean 400–800.* Oxford: Oxford University Press.

Yorke, B. 1982. The Foundation of the Old Minster and the Status of Winchester in the Seventh and Eighth Centuries, *Proceedings of the Hampshire Field Club and Archaeological Society*, 38, 75–83.

Yorke, B. (ed.) 1988. *Bishop Æthelwold: His Career and Influence.* Woodbridge: Boydell Press.

Yorke, B. 1995. *Wessex in the Early Middle Ages.* London: Leicester University Press.

Yorke, B. forthcoming. Cnut and Winchester, in R. North, E. Goeres, and A. Finlay (eds), *Anglo-Danish Empire: A Companion to the Reign of Cnut the Great.* Kalamazoo: Medieval Institute Publications.

Yoshitake, K. 2015. The Place of Government in Transition: Winchester, Westminster and London in the Mid-Twelfth Century, in P. Dalton and D. E. Luscombe (eds), *Rulership and Rebellion in the Anglo-Norman World, c. 1066–c.1216: Essays in Honour of Professor Edmund King*, 61–76. Aldershot: Ashgate.

Chapter 2

Capital Considerations: Winchester and the Birth of Urban Archaeology

Martin Biddle

Outlining the programme of archaeological excavations in Winchester between 1961 and 1971, this chapter explores the social context for the development of archaeology and the establishment of archaeological units for the investigation of towns. The chapter draws on some of the key factors in the development of archaeological practice and the impact this had on the study of medieval towns both in the UK and internationally.

'Time and Chance' were the words used by Dame Joan Evans (1893–1977), the first benefactor of our work in Winchester, to describe the discovery of Knossos by her much older brother, Sir John Evans (1851–1941).[1] They are equally applicable to the start of excavations in Winchester in 1961.

The catalyst was the decision of Messrs. Trust Houses Ltd. to build the Wessex Hotel in the centre of Winchester. In 1957 and 1961, in two pioneering papers, Roger Quirk, CB, had set out the written and topographical evidence for the location of the sites of the Anglo-Saxon royal churches of the Old and New Minsters to the north of the present cathedral, ending both papers with a plea for excavation.[2] The proposed new hotel was to be built on what he then believed was the site of the New Minster church founded by King Alfred. Quirk, himself a Wykehamist and an under-secretary in Lord Hailsham's Ministry of Science and Technology, moved at once to secure the support of Robin McCall, Town Clerk of Winchester and of the then Ministry of Works, for an archaeological excavation of the site of the proposed new hotel, then an open space used as the Cathedral Park. The present writer, just down from Cambridge, who had excavated King Henry VIII's Nonsuch Palace two years before, was asked to direct the excavation.

The site of the car park had been used as a cemetery since the end of the Middle Ages down to the 1860s but was otherwise undisturbed, providing an intact sequence of archaeological deposits from the beginning of the Roman period down to the early

---

[1] Evans 1943.

[2] Quirk 1957, 28–68, esp. 67–8 and fig. 1; 1961, 16–54, esp. 37 and fig. 6.

twelfth century, after which the area had apparently lain open as part of the outer close of the cathedral. The Roman remains included a north–south street which had been relaid many times to a total thickness of over two metres, flanked to the west by the east range of the forum of the Roman town of *Venta Belgarum* and to the east by a Roman house with a long structural history. The site appears afterwards to have lain open until the tenth century when a cemetery associated with an 'oval' chapel (*i.e.* with an apse to both west and east) came into use. This was followed by a major building complex now thought to be the residence of the abbot of New Minster from the later eleventh century down to the move of New Minster to Hyde in 1110.

These Roman and medieval buildings were represented by a depth of over three metres of undisturbed archaeological stratigraphy. Their investigation in 1961 on a scale previously unmatched by any excavation in Winchester gave rise to a wholly new appreciation of the wealth of the city's buried past.[3] There was, however, at that time no legal protection of any kind for the buried remains of the urban past, or indeed for any remains of the past except for the relatively few scheduled ancient monuments. Things are different today, but at that time it was clear that special arrangements would have to be made to place the future of archaeology in Winchester on a formal basis. The then mayor, Mrs Dilys Neate, JP, made this a feature of her mayoralty and under her guidance the Winchester Excavations Committee was formed by decision of a public meeting attended by an audience of hundreds in the Great Hall of Guildhall on 27 February 1962.

The report on the 1961 excavation included the setting up of this committee.[4] The second interim report on the work carried out in 1962 and 1963 laid out what was to become in effect the first of a series of manifestos for the future of its work in Winchester.[5] The aim was as follows:

> to undertake excavations, both in advance of building projects and on sites not so threatened, aimed at studying the development of Winchester as a town from its earliest origins to the establishment of the modern city. The centre of interest is the city itself, not any one period of its past, nor any one part of its remains. But we can hope that this approach will in particular throw light upon the end of the Roman city and on the establishment and development of the Saxon town, problems as vital to our understanding of urban development in this country, as they are difficult to solve.

It was stressed that it was:

> essential to this approach that the study and interpretation of the documentary evidence should go hand in hand with archaeological research, for the existence of documentary materials greatly enhances the possibilities of interpretation inherent in the archaeological results and vice-versa.

---

[3] *I Interim.* This became the first of a series of ten interim reports published in the *Archaeological Journal*, 119 in 1962 and in the *Antiquaries Journal*, 44–50, 52, 55, from 1964 to 1975.

[4] *I Interim*, 150.

[5] *II Interim*, 188.

By the third interim report at the end of the fourth season in 1964, the objectives had been further clarified.[6]

> Important research programmes into various scientific problems, biological, botanical and physical have begun and throughout emphasis has been, and will continue to be, laid on the use of all the available evidence, documentary, archaeological, scientific, to study the development of Winchester as an urban environment and of the inhabitants in inter-relation with that environment over a period of two thousand years.

During these first four seasons from 1961 to 1964 the project evolved in stages from a rescue operation to the beginnings of a major planned excavation programme which was to last a decade. Trench I on Cathedral Green in 1962 took barely a month but located what was shown in 1964 to be the site of the seventh-century high altar of Old Minster. In 1963 the line of that first trench was extended north. It confirmed the site of the Anglo-Saxon Old Minster and identified the nave of the late ninth or early tenth-century New Minster immediately to its north, a vivid demonstration of the accuracy of the written evidence that the two churches lay so close together a man could scarcely walk between them.[7] This was the beginning of an investigation on the Cathedral Green that was to continue until 1970.

The 1963 excavation was considerably larger than the two previous seasons, involving work at the castle and at Wolvesey Palace as well as on the Cathedral Green and on Lower Brook Street where work would eventually result in the examination of twelve houses and the churches of St Mary and St Pancras.[8] These sites were all to continue: the pattern set in the years 1962 and 1963 was to last for the next eight years until 1971.

An event in the 1963 season came to influence all that was to follow. On the afternoon of 29 July, Margaret Wood, the doyenne of the study of medieval timber-framed buildings in England, brought her friend Professor Urban T. Holmes Jr. of the University of North Carolina at Chapel Hill and his wife Peggy to see the excavation of medieval houses on the west side of Lower Brook Street, the medieval Tanner Street. Professor Holmes, who had just republished his *Daily Living in the Twelfth Century*,[9] the century which was the centre of his intellectual life, looked down on the massive surviving stump of one of the major timber uprights of what we called House IV. He could scarcely contain his feelings: here were the actual remains of one of the houses he had been studying from the documents but had not imagined he would ever see. By April 1964 I was at Chapel Hill, speaking on the excavations at Winchester and recruiting volunteers for the dig. That summer we were joined by students from the University of North Carolina at Chapel Hill and from Duke University nearby in an association formulated by Professor Holmes that was to last with notable financial

---

[6] *III Interim*, 261.
[7] Quirk 1957, 65, para. 7.
[8] See below, p. 30.
[9] Holmes 1962.

support each year for seven seasons, including in 1967 a major grant from the United States National Endowment for the Humanities. It was at this stage that the work at Winchester changed from a purely local project to a major international undertaking.[10]

The 1965 season lasted for eleven weeks with increased participation and funding, notably from the two American universities and from the Old Dominion Foundation in New York, as well as from the Ministry of Public Building and Works, the Hampshire County and Winchester City councils, the British Museum, the British Academy and the Society of Antiquaries. This was a pattern of support which was to last into the next decade. The number of people taking part each year rose to about five hundred with the participation of volunteers from many countries, including the United Kingdom and Commonwealth, the United States, most European countries and Saudi Arabia. Nineteen sites were investigated in total over an eleven-year period at a cost of £149,811.[11] The collaboration with the University of North Carolina at Chapel Hill and Duke University proved vital in the procurement of volunteers and funds (providing 18.5 per cent of the total cost of the excavations).[12] Excavators such as Shepherd Fere and John Wacher in the late 1950s began to move away from the earlier model of using paid labourers for heavy digging, instead utilising volunteers.[13] This was taken even further in the excavations at Winchester. Approximately 3,000 volunteers from as many as thirty-five countries took part in the excavations over the years 1964–71. Through the support of the Winchester City Council and Hampshire County Council, the Winchester Excavations Committee was able to make use of disused buildings around the city of Winchester to house the volunteers. These ranged from the army base of Bushfield Camp, to local schools, pubs and the Bendicks chocolate factory. In addition to half-board accommodation, volunteers staying two weeks or more were provided with a daily lunch allowance of 4 shillings. Site-supervisors at Winchester were initially appointed on the recommendations of others, but a policy of promoting internally from among the volunteers was soon established.[14] Whilst Winchester was quite different from other excavations taking place across the UK and Europe at the same time, the influence of the variety of cultures upon the excavation method and procedure is clear. Most notable perhaps was the impact of the Danish archaeologist, Birthe Kjølbye, who would transform Winchester's methods of excavation and recording.[15] In 1966 the work of the Winchester Excavations Committee received one of the Duke of Edinburgh's first Awards for International Co-operation.

The association with the United States was the happy result of chance personal contact. The association with Poland was by contrast deliberately sought. It was becoming clear as early as 1964 that the archaeology of individual medieval towns was a significant focus of research in Poland where, as Professor Witold Hensel was later to write, 'the scarcity of written sources concerning the Slav towns in the

---

[10] Professor Holmes died on 12 May 1972.
[11] Biddle 1983, 98.
[12] *Ibid.*, 98, n. 2.
[13] Collis 2011, 80.
[14] *Ibid.*
[15] See below, p. 24.

period before the thirteenth century made a wider discussion of their beginnings impossible'.[16] With the help of Hugo Blake of the Association for Cultural Exchange contact was established in December that year with Professor Aleksander Gieysztor of the University of Warsaw and through him with Dr Krzystof Dambrowski of the university's Institute for the History of Material Culture who was leading urban excavations in the ancient Polish city of Kalisz. As a result of these contacts students from Poland and what was then Czechoslovakia took part in the 1966 season led by Dr Andrej Kempisty from the University of Warsaw who joined as a site-supervisor. This resulted in an invitation to visit Poland after that season to see the work in urban archaeology being carried out in some of the major Polish cities of medieval origin. During September, Birthe Kjølbye of the University of Aarhus, the site-supervisor of the excavation of Old Minster north of Winchester Cathedral, and I visited Warsaw and a series of Polish towns, including Gdańsk, Kraków, Opole, Łódź, Poznań and Wrocław, among other places, and saw how the archaeological work in each was in the hands of a dedicated individual urban team.

The lesson for Winchester was obvious. In addition to the annual summer excavation seasons, however large, something more permanent was necessary to see the programme of excavations brought to a conclusion and the results written up in the context of a thorough understanding of the extensive documentary evidence available for the history of Winchester from the tenth century onwards. Steps towards the creation of a 'Winchester Research Unit' began at once on our return from Poland. Support had to be gathered and funds secured. The Unit came into being on 1 October 1968 with a permanent office in Parchment Street. Our initial hopes were set out in the concluding paragraph of the seventh interim report, on the 1968 season:

> This work will probably require five years and is being undertaken by the Winchester Research Unit, which has a staff of eight under the writer's direction. The Unit was established in October 1968 by generous grants from the Calouste Gulbenkian Foundation, the Hampshire County Council, the City of Winchester and the Ministry of Public Building and Works. The unit will prepare for publication a series of perhaps twelve monographs, which will be published by the Clarendon Press and will cover all aspects of the city's physical evolution, changing character and economic development, as revealed by the excavations and documentary research of 1961–70.[17]

These hopes were to prove optimistic. The annual excavations, originally planned to come to an end with a ninth season in 1970, were extended for a final season in 1971, ten years after excavation began in 1961.[18] The work of the Winchester Research Unit in analysing the excavation records and finds, which by 1976 had over forty members, laid down the groundwork for all the Winchester Studies volumes to follow.[19] The

---

[16] Hensel 1969, 51–60.

[17] *VII Interim*, 326.

[18] There were in fact eleven seasons in all, but the brief work in 1962 was amalgamated with that of the first full-scale season in 1963 to form the second interim report, *II Interim*.

[19] See Appendix.

Research Unit continues its work today in 2021 (although with a much smaller team), sixty years since work started on the Cathedral Car Park in 1961.

This paved the way for the establishment of professional archaeological 'units' across the country, notably the York Archaeological Unit founded in 1972, the Urban Research Unit of the City of London which began work in 1973 and the Canterbury Archaeological Unit founded in 1975, all of which continue to this day and, of special notice, the *Laboratoire Archéologie et Territoires* founded at the University of Tours by Henri Galinié in 1992, inspired by his work on the Winchester excavations from 1969 to 1971. Many of the techniques developed in Winchester during the excavations became standard archaeological practice throughout Britain with many remaining in practice today. Notable innovations included the introduction of metric measurements in 1965, the development of standardised sheets of plastic drawing film, the development of open-area excavation and methods for dealing with sites with complex stratigraphy and the excavation of 'robbed' structures.[20] A number of these innovations were the direct result of the arrival in 1964 of Birthe Kjølbye, whose Danish experience helped transform the practices in Winchester.

The Nature of Winchester

Winchester is more than just a city of ancient, indeed Roman, origin. Even then its precursors in the valley stretched back into the prehistoric past. Still visibly dominant today a mile to the south of the present city, the Iron Age hillfort of St Catherine's Hill (Fig. 2.1) on the east bank dominated a great east–west route across southern England and from at least as early as the third century BC controlled its crossing of the Itchen river. Matched on the west bank from perhaps the first century BC was a vast enclosure (under the west half of the walled city and the western suburb of the present city) surrounded by a ditch and presumably a bank, known today only from excavation. This too controlled the crossing of the river on the same long-distance west–east route along the chalk hills of what we today call Wessex.

The Roman walled town of *Venta Belgarum* inherited the control of this ancient crossing and as its name implies was the focus of the tribal area inhabited by the 'Belgic' people. It was one of the largest of the so-called 'cantonal capitals' of the peoples of Roman Britain and survived as such into the troubled decades at the end of the fourth and beginning of the fifth century AD.

What happened then is still a matter of great uncertainty. The evidence suggests that already by the sixth century and possibly the fifth, some leading element of the incoming Saxons had become established not only in the area around Winchester, where there is a grouping of pagan Anglo-Saxon cemeteries, but already within the

---

[20] See below, p. 27. For a detailed discussion on the techniques developed during the Winchester excavations including the introduction of the metric recording system and the procedures developed for the recording and interpretation of buildings from robber-trenches, see Biddle and Kjølbye-Biddle 1969. For a more detailed discussion of the organisational model for Winchester, its methods of excavation and its impact on archaeological practices in Britain, see Collis 2011.

*Fig. 2.1: Aerial view looking east across the Iron Age hillfort of St Catherine's Hill, Winchester.
© Winchester Excavations Committee.*

walls, possibly in or around one of the major Roman buildings in the central part
of the former Roman town (Fig. 2.2). The evidence is slight: an important amethyst
pendent, some decorated metalwork, a triangular bone comb, some vessel glass, a few
pieces of pottery, a coin and two spearheads, but sufficient to indicate a significant
early Saxon presence inside the walls.[21]

These fragments of evidence explain the foundation within the walls of the former
Roman town in or about 648 of a church dedicated to St Peter and St Paul, later known
as Old Minster. Cenwalh, the recently converted king of Anglo-Saxon Wessex, was the
founder, presumably to serve an existing royal residence and as the see of the first
of its line of now ninety-seven bishops.

The Four Principal Excavations in Winchester, 1963–71

By 1963 four sites had become the focus of investigation and on these, work was
to continue for the next eight or nine years. Other sites were undertaken as need
arose, principally in advance of development, but the excavation of the Old Minster

---

[21] See WS 11, 20–5. A report on the detailed analysis and interpretation of the evidence of Roman
Winchester and its finds is forthcoming, see Appendix, WS 3.i.

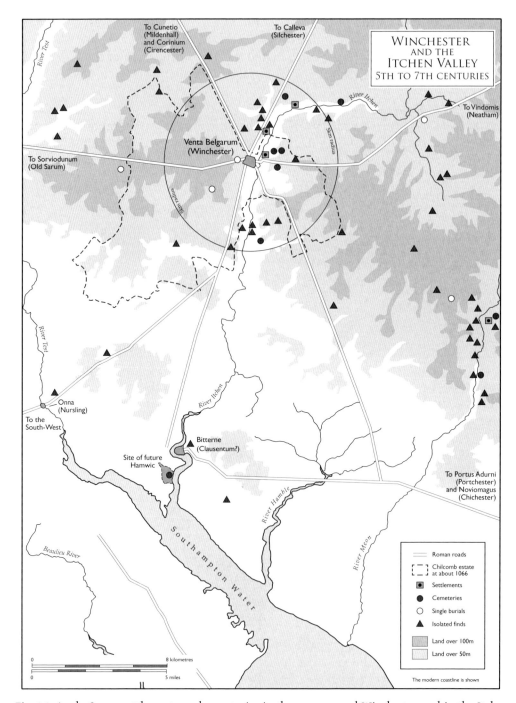

Fig. 2.2: Anglo-Saxon settlements and cemeteries in the area around Winchester and in the Itchen Valley, from the fifth to seventh centuries AD. Map by Giles Darkes. WS 11, fig. 14, after Biddle and Kjølbye-Biddle 2007. © Winchester Excavations Committee and The Historic Towns Trust.

immediately north of the present cathedral, at the castle on the west side of the city, at Wolvesey Palace in the south-east corner of the walled area and along the west side of Lower Brook Street represented the bulk of the work of the Winchester Excavations Committee over the remaining eight years.

Cathedral Green 1962–9

The excavation of the site of Old Minster, the Anglo-Saxon cathedral of Winchester, located in 1962–3, was especially difficult and different from the other sites. This was because its walls had been almost wholly removed when the minster was demolished in 1093–4 leaving behind only the lines of the trenches from which the materials of its walls had been robbed-out, 'the robber-trenches', and the massive foundations on which those walls had been built during the long development of the church from around 650 until its final extension and reconstruction in the late tenth century (Fig. 2.3). The church had grown over the centuries to a total length of over 72 m (some 235 feet) and was excavated through several seasons in sections: centre, east end and west front, with a return to the central area in 1969, with the result that only part of the surviving remains could ever be seen at one time. Most dramatic perhaps was the area immediately west of the original seventh-century church where huge lateral apses were erected in the later tenth-century on foundations of rammed chalk to north and south of the westward extension of the original nave (Fig. 2.4). The overall development of Old Minster over some five centuries is best seen in a diagram of its growth over time (Fig. 2.5). [22]

Castle Yard, 1967–71

Immediately after the Battle of Hastings in October 1066 the Norman army moved north-west to take control of Winchester, the principal

Fig. 2.3: The plan of the cathedral of Old Minster in its final form marked out in modern brick in the grass alongside the present nave of Winchester Cathedral, looking west, reconstructed from the 'robbed' foundations. The plan of the first church of the mid-seventh century is laid out in red brick. © John Crook.

[22] For an overview of the excavation and interpretation of the Anglo-Saxon Minsters, see Biddle 2017. The final report is in preparation, see Appendix, WS 4.i.

Fig. 2.4: *The chalk foundations of the north apse of Swithun's martyrium at Old Minster c. 975, looking north.* © *Winchester Excavations Committee.*

town of the late Anglo-Saxon kingdom. The royal palace and treasury in the heart of the walled town, immediately north-west of the cathedral church, appear to have fallen to the Normans without resistance. Almost at once they began to build a fortified enclosure in a salient on the west wall of the Roman town, on the highest ground in the town within the walls, immediately south of the Roman and Anglo-Saxon west gate. This was the beginning of the castle, in which the royal treasure was to be kept for several centuries until it was moved to Westminster in the 1180s. The excavation of the north end of the castle, to the north of the thirteenth-century Castle Hall, took place for the Hampshire County Council at intervals in the sixties and early seventies during construction of the new Law Courts (Fig. 2.6). This made it possible to establish the long sequence of change in this part of the castle from the Roman period to the thirteenth century (Fig. 2.7).

Wolvesey Palace, 1963–71

At the opposite corner of the city a bishop of Winchester, probably Æthelwold (963–84), began the development in the south-east angle of the Roman walls of a residence which was to serve the bishops of Winchester down to the present day. Built on an open cultivated field, 'Wulf's island', now Wolvesey, a slightly higher area

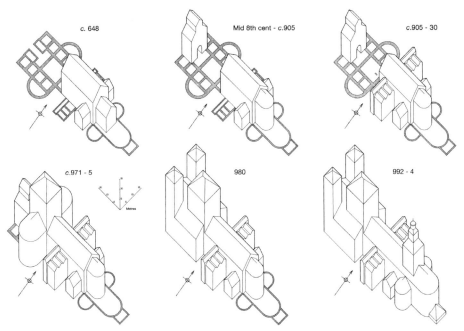

Fig. 2.5: The development of Old Minster from c. 648 to its final form in 992–4: c. 648, the original cross-plan church; mid-eighth century–c. 905, a gatehouse was added to the west, followed by the addition of an apse to the original east end; c. 905–30, a western façade was added and six chapels were built behind the façade; c. 971–5, St Swithun's body was moved from outside the west door, where he had been buried in 863, into the church in 971 and a vast building with two apses was constructed around the site of the saint's original grave; 980, the foundations of this building failed and it was rebuilt as a huge square tower dedicated in 980; 992–4, the east end was rebuilt with an eastern and two lateral apses, focused on the high altar where St Swithun's body now lay. © Winchester Excavations Committee.

in the low-lying valley floor, this was to become the first of three successive palaces. It lies today under an orchard and has never been investigated. The second, begun after the conquest by the second Norman bishop William Giffard (1100–29), lasted for seven centuries as the residence of the bishops of Winchester and became one of the greatest of all houses in medieval England. The third was built to one side of the medieval palace and on a vast scale by Sir Thomas Fitch for Bishop Morley in 1684. It is in the one surviving wing of this third palace that the present bishop lives today. The vast surviving ruin of the second palace is now a scheduled monument in the care of English Heritage whose predecessor in 1962 asked the Winchester Excavations Committee to undertake its investigation and to elucidate its development over seven centuries (Figs 2.8 and 2.9).[23]

---

[23] See Biddle 2021.

Martin Biddle

Fig. 2.6: Castle Yard 1969: looking north-west across the foundation of an early twelfth-century square tower at the north end of the castle. © Winchester Excavations Committee.

Lower Brook Street, 1965–71

The fourth of these major sites was completely different: an area in the heart of the medieval city, along the west side of the former Tanner Street, now Lower Brook Street, one of the north–south streets of the Anglo-Saxon planned town laid out in the later ninth century (Fig. 2.10).[24] Here, from 1965 onwards for seven annual summer seasons, it was possible to excavate in detail the sites of four medieval town houses throughout their history. Two lay to either side of their parish church, St Mary in Tanner Street (Figs 2.11 and 2.12). Another church, St Pancras, lay behind in the middle of the block between Tanner Street and Wongar Street (now Middle Brook Street). These small houses were the opposite of the great buildings under investigation elsewhere in the city, private properties (albeit rented from greater landlords), the homes over some five centuries of ordinary inhabitants of the city, from the tenth or eleventh century until abandoned with the fall in population from the 1500s onwards. All began as wooden structures, and some remained that way although they were often rebuilt. Some went through many changes, being rebuilt on stone foundations. The archaeological evidence was limited to the below-ground evidence and none of these houses survived the later fifteenth century, but the history of the inhabitants

---

[24] See Biddle 2020 and WS 11, 26–35.

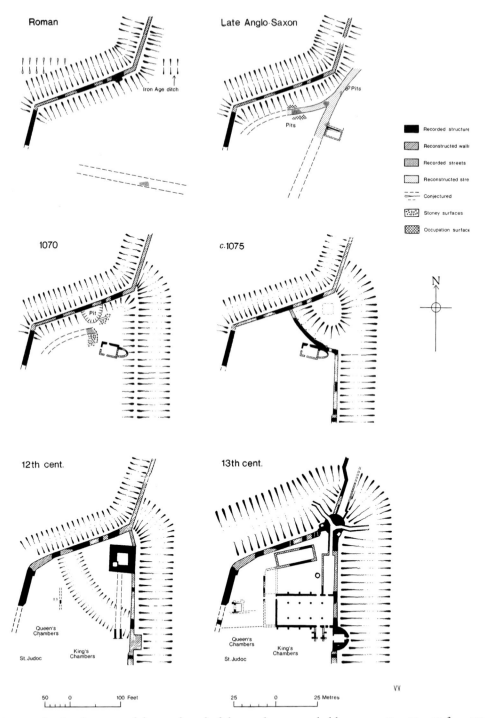

Fig. 2.7: The development of the north end of the castle as revealed by excavation. Fig. 29 from WS 6.i. © Winchester Excavations Committee.

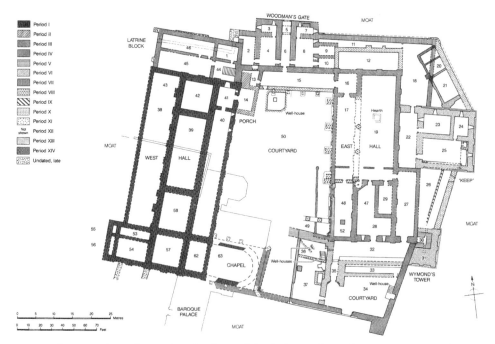

Fig. 2.8: Wolvesey Palace: the medieval palace of the bishops of Winchester, as excavated 1963–71.
© Winchester Excavations Committee.

of each could be traced from the thirteenth or fourteenth century onwards from the surviving documents, linking the bare bones, as it were, to the living inhabitants.[25]

The liturgical arrangement of their churches in Tanner Street (Lower Brook Street today) and behind could also be followed in detail in so far it is survived in the ground,[26] something impossible to do in medieval churches surviving in use today (Fig. 2.11). Only one person was buried in the tiny church of St Mary on Tanner Street, and that in the later north aisle, with the result that the complex evidence of the medieval floors in the body of the church had survived undisturbed by the digging of graves. This meant that details such as the introduction and movement of the font, or the division between the body of the church and the area of the altar could be followed in ways not otherwise possible (Fig. 2.12).

Publications

The ongoing work of excavation from 1961 to 1971 was reported annually in a series of ten 'Interim Reports'. These were published (except for the first year) in the

---

[25] See WS 2, ii, 758–61, 763–4, figs 81–3, 87–8.
[26] *Ibid.*, 741–4, 761–3, figs 85, 89.

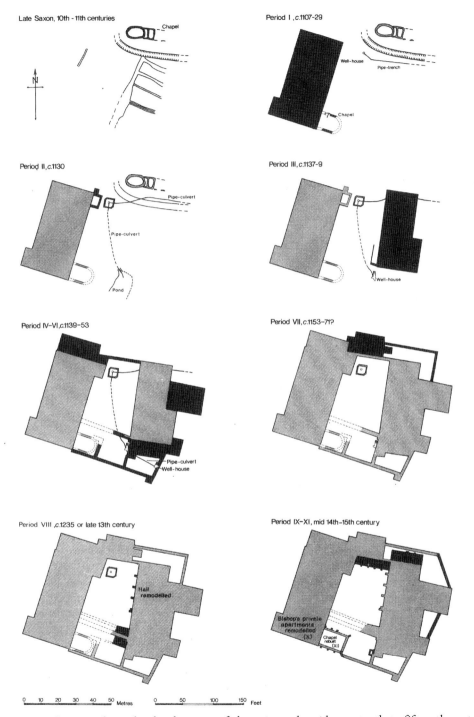

Fig. 2.9: Wolvesey Palace: the development of the episcopal residence, tenth to fifteenth century.
© *Winchester Excavations Committee.*

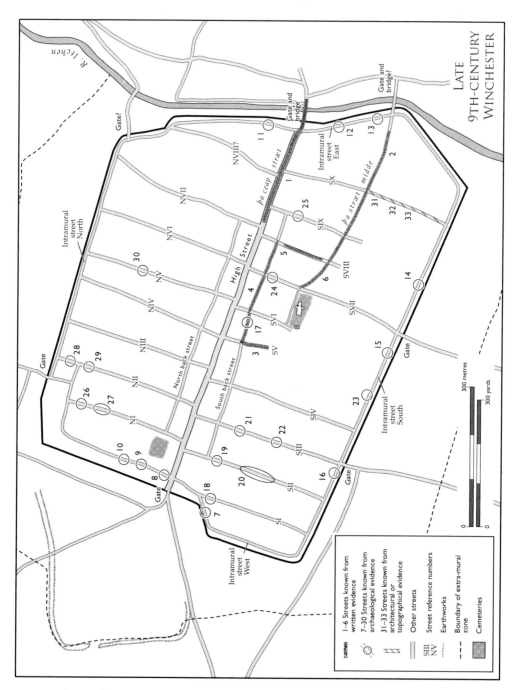

Fig. 2.10: The Anglo-Saxon street plan of the mid-ninth century. Tanner Street is shown as street NVII. From WS 11, fig. 16. Drawn by Giles Darkes. © Winchester Excavations Committee and The Historic Towns Trust.

Fig. 2.11: Lower Brook Street 1970: the walls of the church of St Mary in the later eleventh century, flanked to north and south by the sites of medieval houses, looking north-west. © Winchester Excavations Committee.

Antiquaries Journal.[27] In 1968 it was decided that full reports on the excavations and the associated documentary research would be published in a series of 'Winchester Studies', nine volumes of which have now been published in ten parts, with four more volumes nearing submission to the press (Appendix). The scale and variety of the archaeological excavations in Winchester have enabled us to reconstruct not only the royal and ecclesiastical quarter of the city but also to study the city as a whole through two thousand years. The reports that form the *Winchester Studies* series attempt to provide a comprehensive study of Winchester from the Iron Age, through *Venta Belgarum*, the fifth largest city of Roman Britain, the planning of the city by Alfred the Great in the late ninth century, the Norman city with a new cathedral and castles, the decline of the later Middle Ages, to the emergence of modern Winchester in the eighteenth and nineteenth centuries.[28]

Objects Found on the Excavations

Now on Display

Selected artefacts from the excavations in Winchester can be seen in the Winchester City Museum, in the Castle Hall, in the associated display by the Hampshire County

---

[27] See above, nn. 3 and 13.

[28] For a bibliography by Anthony King which includes all the occasional publications on the Winchester excavations by either or both Martin Biddle and Birthe Kjølbye-Biddle up to 2009, see Henig and Ramsay 2010. For an insider's view from one who was part of the team from 1961 onwards for many years, see Collis 2011, with excellent images.

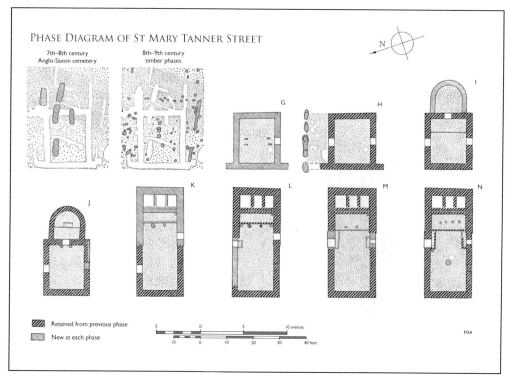

Fig. 2.12: Lower Brook Street: the development of the site and church of St Mary in Tanner Street: the seventh- to eighth-century Anglo-Saxon cemetery, the eighth- and ninth-century timber phases, the stone house (Phases G and H), the tenth- to late twelfth-century (Phases I–N) of the church. Drawing by Fred Aldsworth. First published in X Interim, fig. 15. © Winchester Excavations Committee.

Council next to the Castle Hall and in the exhibition 'Kings and Scribes' in the Triforium Gallery of Winchester Cathedral.

The Excavation Archive
The excavation archive of the Winchester Excavations Committee and Research Unit, both records and finds, are cared for by the Hampshire Cultural Trust in their stores at the Bar End Industrial Estate, Winchester.

Abbreviations

I Interim	Biddle, M. and Quirk, R. N. 1962. Excavations near Winchester Cathedral, 1961, *Archaeological Journal*, 109, 150–94.
II Interim	Biddle, M. 1964. Excavations at Winchester, 1962–63. Second interim report, *Antiquaries Journal*, 44, 188–219.

III Interim	Biddle, M. 1965. Excavations at Winchester, 1964. Third interim report, *Antiquaries Journal*, 45, 230–61.
VII Interim	Biddle, M. 1969. Excavations at Winchester, 1968. Seventh interim report, *Antiquaries Journal*, 49, 295–329.
X Interim	Biddle, M. 1975. Excavations at Winchester, 1971. Tenth and final interim report, *Antiquaries Journal 55, 96–126; 295–337.*
WS 2	Keene, D. J. 1985. *Survey of Medieval Winchester*, Winchester Studies 2 in two parts. Oxford: Clarendon Press.
WS 11	Biddle, M. and Keene, D.J. (eds) 2017. *Winchester*, The British Historic Town Atlas vol. 6, Winchester Studies 11. Oxford: Oxbow Books.

Bibliography

Biddle, M. 1983. The Study of Winchester: Archaeology and History in a British Town, 1961–83, Albert Reckitt Archaeology Trust Lecture, *Proceedings of the British Academy, 69, 93–135.*

Biddle, M. 2017. *The Search for Winchester's Anglo-Saxon Minsters.* Oxford: Archaeopress.

Biddle, M. 2020. Winchester: A City of Two Planned Towns, in A. Langlands and R. Lavelle (eds), *The Land of the English Kin: Studies in Wessex and Anglo-Saxon England in Honour of Professor Barbara Yorke,* Brill Series Early Middle Ages 26. Leiden: Brill.

Biddle, M. 2021. Wolvesey: Henry of Blois's *domus quasi palatium* in Winchester, in W. Kynan-Wilson and J. Munns (eds), *Henry of Blois: New Interpretations,* 119–44. Woodbridge: Boydell Press.

Biddle, M. and Kjølbye-Biddle, B. 1969. Metres, Areas and Robbing, *World Archaeology,* 1.ii, 208–19.

Biddle, M. and Kjølbye-Biddle, B. 2007. Winchester: from *Venta* to *Wintancæstir*, in L. Gilmour (ed.), *Pagans and Christians – from Antiquity to the Middle Ages: Papers in Honour of Martin Henig, presented on the Occasion of his 65th Birthday,* BAR International Series 1610, 189–214. Oxford: British Archaeological Reports.

Collis, J. 2011. The Urban Revolution: Martin Biddle's Excavations in Winchester, 1961–1971, in J. Schofield (ed.), *Great Excavations: Shaping the Archaeological Profession,* 74–86. Oxford: Oxbow Books.

Evans, J. 1943. *Time and Chance: The Story of Arthur Evans and his Forebears.* London: Longmans.

Henig, M. and Ramsay, N. (eds) 2010. *Intersections: The Archaeology and History of Christianity in England, 400–1200: Papers in Honour of Martin Biddle and Birthe Kjølbye-Biddle.* Oxford: British Archaeological Reports.

Hensel, W. 1969. The Origins of Western and Eastern Slav Towns, *World Archaeology,* 1.i, 51–60.

Holmes Jr., U. T. 1962. *Daily Living in the Twelfth Century.* Madison: University of Wisconsin Press.

Quirk, R. N. 1957. Winchester Cathedral in the Tenth Century, *Archaeological Journal,* 114, 28–68.

Quirk, R. N. 1961. Winchester New Minster and its Tenth-century Tower, *Journal of the British Archaeological Association,* 3rd ser. 24, 16–54.

Appendix

Winchester Studies

11 studies in 17 volumes (1976–2021 and ongoing)
9 volumes published up to April 2021 in black, 2 volumes forthcoming and 6 volumes in preparation.

WS 1   Biddle, M. (ed.) 1976. *Winchester in the Early Middle Ages: an edition and discussion of the Winton Domesday*, Winchester Studies, 1. Oxford: Clarendon Press.

WS 2   Keene, D. J. 1985. *Survey of Medieval Winchester*, Winchester Studies 2 in two parts. Oxford: Clarendon Press.

Pre-Roman and Roman Winchester

WS 3.i   Morris, F. M. and Biddle, M. forthcoming. *Venta Belgarum: Prehistoric, Roman, and Post-Roman Winchester.*

WS 3.ii   Clarke, G. 1979. *The Roman Cemetery at Lankhills.* Oxford: Clarendon Press.

The Anglo-Saxon Minsters of Winchester

WS 4.i   Kjølbye-Biddle, B. and Biddle, M. in preparation. *The Anglo-Saxon Minsters of Winchester.*

WS 4.ii   Lapidge, M. 2003. *The Cult of St Swithun.* Oxford: Clarendon Press.

WS 4.iii   Rumble, A. 2002. *Property and Piety in Early Medieval Winchester: Documents Relating to the Topography of the Anglo-Saxon and Norman City and its Minsters*, Winchester Studies 4.iii. Oxford: Clarendon Press.

Residences and Other Town Sites in Medieval Winchester

WS 5   Biddle, M., Kjølbye-Biddle, B. and Ottaway, P. in preparation. *The Brooks and other Town Sites of Medieval Winchester.*

WS 6.i   Biddle, M. and Clayre, B. in preparation. *Winchester Castle: Fortress, Palace, Garrison, and County Seat.*

WS 6.ii   Biddle, M. in preparation. *Wolvesey Palace.*

Artefacts from Medieval Winchester

WS 7.i   Barclay, K. in preparation. *Ceramics of Medieval Winchester.*

WS 7.ii   Biddle, M. (ed.) 1990. *Object and Economy in Medieval Winchester*, 2 vols. Oxford: Clarendon Press.

WS 8   Biddle, M. (ed.) 2012. *The Winchester Mint and Coins and Related Finds from the Excavations of 1961-71*, Winchester Studies, 8. Oxford: Clarendon Press.

Human, Animal and Plant Biology

WS 9.i   Stuckert, C. M. (ed.) 2017. *The People of Early Winchester*. Oxford: Clarendon Press.

WS 9.ii   Maltby, M. (ed.) in preparation. *The Animals of Early Winchester*.

WS 10   Biddle, M., Renfrew, J. and Ottaway, P. (eds) forthcoming. *Environment, Agriculture, and Gardens in Early Winchester*.

The Origin and Development of Winchester

WS 11   Biddle, M. and Keene, D.J. (eds) 2017. *Winchester*, The British Historic Town Atlas vol. 6, Winchester Studies 11. Oxford: Oxbow Books.

Chapter 3

The King's Stone: Peace, Power and the Highway in Early Medieval Winchester

Alexander James Langlands

Bringing together scattered historical references to an ancient cross known as the 'King's stone' this chapter establishes the location of a lost landmark to the north of Winchester. Whilst the form and style of the monument eludes us, comparing its situational context to other such examples can do much to further our understanding of how royal power was being articulated in the early medieval landscape of Wessex and western Mercia. Considered alongside the evidence for major routeways and emerging citadels, an archaeology of movement can be reconstructed within which the notion of 'peace', an imagined Roman past, the rise of popular pilgrimages and sacred urban space are explored. The 'King's stone' is part of an increasing body of evidence that supports the case for a sophisticated road network being in place in Wessex as early as the ninth century.

The evidence for standing stone crosses from Anglo-Saxon England has long garnered the attentions of antiquarians and archaeologists and the *Corpus of Anglo-Saxon Stone Sculpture* serves as testimony to an enduring scholarship within which, for the most part, art historical analysis and considerations of form and style have taken precedence.[1] This is a circumstance that has largely been determined by the fact that so many crosses – or, rather, fragments of crosses – no longer survive in their original locations. As such, for a significant number of surviving examples, we are therefore robbed of the opportunity to interrogate situational contexts. Quite the opposite set of circumstances presents itself to us in the case of the King's stone. Whilst we may have a location, we have no physical object for analysis.

Clearly, provenance can prove an important element in our understanding of early medieval standing stone crosses and it is in their locational settings that studies of such monuments from across the British Isles and beyond have been greatly advanced

---

[1] Regional corpora can be found at *The Corpus of Anglo-Saxon Stone Sculpture*. Available at: http://www.ascorpus.ac.uk/ and see volumes IV for South-East England and VII for South-West England.

in recent times.[2] Beyond passive memorialisation, the requirement to proactively commemorate looms large in the ambitions of many crosses, and particularly those that bare a close association with cemetery settings.[3] Collections of stones scattered across more expansive areas have also been shown to represent key elements in the construction of sacred landscapes, where pre-existing mythical and 'natural' landscape features were purposefully drawn into a conceptual framework aligned to the veneration of saints with local, regional and international appeal.[4] These functions extend to individual standing stones identified in landscape contexts, where it is clear that there is much more of value that we can take from the relationship they enjoyed with surrounding topographical features such as other existing monuments, major routeways and arenas of intervisibility.[5]

In tighter topographical settings, clusters of stone monuments allow for the examination of inter-relationships with other such edifices and archaeological evidence. On Inishmurray, Co. Sligo, for example, crosses are proposed to have served as station points during penitential processions around the wider monastic complex.[6] Here the potent combination of landscape and material culture is employed in the propagation of the belief in the power of saints in an arrangement where the procession – the movement between stones – is a key element. The same kind of movement, one with salvation as its end goal, has been proposed for the so-called 'Street of the Dead' on Iona, furnished as it is with at least seven monumental free-standing crosses.[7] More widely across Medieval Britain it is clear that standing crosses played an important role in the articulation of pilgrim routes.[8]

In these latter examples, procession – *movement* – the journey from one place to another, both physical and conceptual, and the role that such monuments played in informing that movement stands as a key element in the grammar of their architectural location. This paper presents the evidence for a now lost early medieval standing stone cross that once occupied a site some three miles north of the city of Winchester. Whilst the exact location of the monument eludes us, its broader landscape setting – one that was almost certainly determined by the layout of major routes in the area – provides us with an opportunity to explore not just aspects of commemoration, remembrance and a constructed identity with both a past and future, but also to examine the materiality of an emerging style of power propagated by the royal elite of Wessex in the ninth and early tenth centuries.

---

[2] Williams *et al.* 2015.
[3] Williams 2006; Devlin 2011.
[4] Stopford 1994; Edwards 2001; Gondek 2007; Gondek and Noble 2010; Hall 2012.
[5] Orton 2006; Murrieta-Flores and Williams 2017; Everson and Stocker 2017; Kirton 2015.
[6] Ó Carragáin 2009.
[7] Campbell and Maldonado 2020, 20–5.
[8] Locker 2015 passim.

The Documentary Sources for the King's Stone

The boundary marks from a number of Anglo-Saxon charters describing grants of land made to the immediate north of Winchester can be located with a degree of certainty, enabling aspects of the tenth-century landscape to be reconstructed cartographically.[9] In particular, the line of the Roman road from *Venta Belgarum* (Winchester) to *Leuchomagnus* (near Andover), and various monuments along its course, are recorded in some detail. The *fulan flode* recorded as a boundary mark in the grant of *Eastune* (Easton) to Brihthelm, Bishop, by King Edgar (AD 961) equates broadly with present-day Fulflood, and from here the boundary passes along the *stret* (Roman road) to the *heafod stoccan* (head stakes), the latter of which also appears in the boundary clause for a grant of land at *Worðige* (now Headbourne Worthy) and is to be associated with present-day Harestock (Fig. 3.1).[10] The term *heafod stoccan* has been archaeologically and historically associated with the judicial practice, prevalent in Anglo-Saxon England, of displaying the heads of executed individuals on stakes.[11] Excavations conducted at Old Dairy Cottage, on the line of the Roman road, recovered fifteen graves containing the remains of at least seventeen individuals. Each individual appeared to have been decapitated with the head placed towards the foot of the grave.[12] Radiocarbon dating of two burials suggests a date range between the late eighth and the early eleventh century, and the long-term function of this place of execution is indicated by the 'Gallows Field' recorded in the 1840s Tithe Award.[13]

With these boundary marks reliably positioned, a number of the following landmarks recorded in the *Worðige* charter can be conjecturally assigned locations:

> *of heafod stocca . and lang stræt to lusan þorne . of lusan þorne to deopan delle . up to kinges stane . from kincges stane . up to holan stane . of holan stane . up to fyrd geate . of fyrd geate . to wic herpaðe . and lang wic herpæðes . æft to kynges stane .*

> From the head stakes, along the street to the lousy thorn. From the lousy thorn to the deep dell [quarry/pit] up to the King's stone. From the King's stone up to the hollow [or holey] stone. From the hollow stone, up to the host-army gate. From the host-army gate, to the *wic* raiding-army path. Along the *wic* raiding-army path back to the King's stone.[14]

Whilst the 'lousy' thorn and the deep dell are today beyond recovery, that the King's stone is a monument returned to in the perambulation does much to aid in the fixing of certain landmarks around a triangle of land known by the nineteenth century as

---

[9] Langlands 2019, 80–7; Brooks 2000; Grundy 1921; Grundy 1924; Grundy 1926; Grundy 1927; Klingelhöfer 1990.

[10] S 695, BCS 1076, KCD 1230; S 309, BCS 473, KCD 1055. Although S 309 is dated to AD 854 but widely considered to be a fraudulent charter, there appears no reason to doubt that the boundary clause is of at least early eleventh-century date, Keynes 1994.

[11] Reynolds 2009, 31, 119, 243; Cubitt 2009, 1027 n. 26, n. 27.

[12] Nenk *et al.* 1991.

[13] Reynolds 2009, 119.

[14] S 309, BCS 473, KCD 1055.

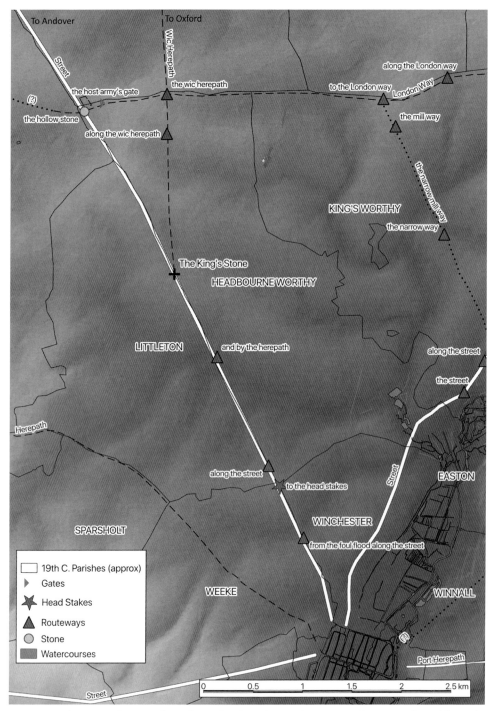

Fig. 3.1: Winchester and its northern hinterland in the tenth century, showing selected boundary marks from Anglo-Saxon charters.

'Worthy Down'. In this endeavour some support comes from the lines of nineteenth-century parish boundaries, long recognised as a valid source for the extents of early medieval landholding, especially where they follow the lines of ancient trackways.[15] So, both the western and northern parish boundaries of Headbourne Worthy parish seem likely to represent the bounds of the tenth-century estate. There is a deviation from the modern bounds returning south as the line of the *wic herpaðe* is used in the tenth century. Elsewhere, the evidence for this road representing an important trade route between Oxford and Winchester (and *Hamwic*/Southampton beyond) from at least the ninth century has been considered in detail.[16] It is mentioned explicitly as the *wic herpaðe* in boundary clauses where it passed through land at *Clere* (High Clere) some 30 km to the N of Winchester.[17] As such, therefore, the evidence points to the King's stone being positioned at the junction where the *wic herpaðe* converges on the Roman road. The hollow stone might very well be located at the north-west corner of the estate, given that stones, as well as posts, trees and other 'point' features often mark sharp turns in boundary orientations. The *fyrd geate* presumably sits somewhere on the major route that the parish boundary follows on an east–west axis. This route, latterly known as the Lunway,[18] is recorded in the *eastune* charter as the *lunden weg* (London Way), appears in a charter for Crawley as the *lunden hærpaðe*, survives in the place-name Lunway's Cross, and has been projected as far west as Ilchester.[19] An *ealden fyrd gat* (old *fyrd* gate) appears in a boundary clause that records a boundary running *andlang Worði saetna mearc* (along the boundary of the people of Worthy) and it seems likely that this is one and the same as the gate referred to in the bounds of Headbourne Worthy.[20] If ever there was a place in southern Anglo-Saxon England where the *fyrd* – the 'host' army – might usefully intercept the *here* – the 'raiding' army – then the crossroads of the London Way with the Oxford to Winchester *herepath* is it.

This location for the King's stone is further supported by a reference in Lantfred's *Translatio et miracula S. Swithuni*, written after AD 971. The document records a series of miracles performed posthumously at the tomb of St Swithun and included in the various stories are aspects of the journeys which pilgrims made to seek cures for a range of ills.[21] The narrative's purpose, as much as anything else, is to elaborate on the power of the English saint as a force for righteousness and the restoration of health and as such is not without its problems.[22] But there is little reason to suspect some of the more mundane details of travel made by people coming locally from the province of 'Ham' (Hants), Collingbourne (Wilts.) and the Isle of Wight or, further afield, from

---

[15] Bonney 1979; Reed 1984; Rackham 1986, 79.
[16] Langlands 2020.
[17] S 680, BCS 1051, KCD 1225.
[18] Hawkes 1925, 325–6.
[19] S 695, BCS 1076, KCD 1230; S 381, BCS 629, KCD 1096; Grundy 1918, 153–4; Hill 1981, 116, fig. 199, although the rationale for extending the road this far is uncertain.
[20] S 374; Grundy 1927, 308–10; Forsberg 1950, vol. 9, 202–3; Miller 2001, 40–5.
[21] Lapidge 2003, 217–331.
[22] See papers by Mark Atherton and Eric Lacey in this volume, pp. 169–89 and 191–214.

Bedfordshire, London, Rochester, *Hunum* (? Hunts.), 'far away areas to the west' and 'various regions of England'. In one particular account we are told of a blind man and his young guide coming to rest at 'a large, tall, shining stone cross…, put up to the glory of Christ', 'nearly three miles distance' from Winchester.[23] Lantfred's work is given a literary overhaul at the hands of Wulfstan the Cantor, in a hexametric poetical version of events completed in the final decade of the tenth century and it is in this latter work that the author takes the opportunity to provide some further details. The large shining stone cross is referred to in this slightly later account as '*uexillum quoniam de rupe uetusto erectum sublime crucis*' [a replica in ancient stone of the sublime cross] '*quem lingua 'Petram' uocat Anglia 'Regis*'' [which the English tongue calls the King's stone].[24]

Drawing together the details from both accounts, the following can be concluded: that the form of the monument is a cross (*crux/crucis*, *staurus*), that it is constructed in 'ancient' stone and is 'shining' or 'bright', that it is 'nearly' (*pene*) three miles out from the city and that in the English tongue it is known as the 'King's stone'. The final piece of supporting evidence is spatial: the junction of the *wic herpaðe* with the Roman road into Winchester, the proposed location for the King's stone, is marked by a milestone indicating three miles distance from the city.[25]

Renovatio, Romanitas and the King's Peace on the Highway

Because the King's stone no longer survives, we can only speculate upon its artistic merits. The reader will need to judge for themselves on the evidence presented here how safe an inference it is to place the monument exactly where it is located in Figure 3.1. The significance of the stone's name and it lying 3 miles from the city is alone of some importance, but even if we can only situate it imprecisely within a broader area, our options for extended commentary on its relationship to its immediate surroundings are limited. On whether the cross occupies a site with longer-term numinous associations, we can't be certain as there is no obvious evidence for prehistoric monuments in the immediate vicinity, nor the kind of natural hillock that might have invited articulation; ritual, commemorative, or otherwise.[26] The setting is characterised by shallow, sweeping and expansive undulations of open farm land today and, if the evidence of charter boundary clauses is to be believed, much of this landscape would have been open chalk downland in the tenth century. On a recent visit in mid-February, it felt like a bleak and featureless landscape, accompanied only by the roar of passing trunk road traffic. It is the roads themselves, their convergence as they approach the city, and their crossing of the major east–west London Way, that appears to be the defining context for the position of the King's stone.

[23] '*Erat autem ubi repausabant ingens crux lapidea, tria passuum milia pene distans a prefata urbe*' and '*Staurus hic est saxea fulgens grandis altissima, ad laudem Christi posita*', Lapidge 2003, 317–19.

[24] *Ibid.*, 528–9.

[25] See the 25 inch to the mile OS series, Hampshire and Isle of Wight, Sheet XL.4, revised 1894, published 1896.

[26] Semple 2010, 21–4.

Crossroad locations have long been identified as key landscape features required to play their role in the widespread conversion of the rural people, either through sanctification or demonisation.[27] The hanging of 'nefarious ligatures' and the worship of spirits is inveighed against in numerous Church Fathers' texts,[28] whilst the manumission of slaves suggests more positive Christian associations.[29] Such crossroads may have been of great antiquity at the point at which they attracted this interest; the intersections between an age-old prehistoric network and the Roman roads that served an entirely different set of aspirations was no doubt marked. But if the case for a relatively extensive phase of early medieval road building is to be believed,[30] new crossroads and junctions would have arisen as a result. As Andrew Fleming has argued in the case for purposefully maintained long-distance roads in early medieval Wales, sequences of crossroads and junctions may in themselves have served as key nodal points in the conceptualisation of these highways and in this sense, the junction at the King's stone is worthy of remark.[31] Whilst there is no reason why the line of the *wic herpaðe* should not have its origins in either the prehistoric or Roman period, the name alone, and the rise of Oxford as an economically important centre by (at least) the early ninth century,[32] suggests a route of national significance for middle and later Anglo-Saxon commercial exchange and peer-polity relations. The fact that it appears to spur from the Roman road also indicates that it post-dates this stretch of *strete* which in other boundary clauses is referred to as a *herepath*,[33] and therefore is likely to be in active service to traffic heading north-north-west towards Cirencester, Gloucester and Worcester beyond.

The King's stone was therefore positioned at an important and potentially quite lively junction. Contingents of tradespeople, pilgrims and dignitaries – the great and the good – from two of the three Mercian burhs to appear in Version B of the Alfredian Burghal Hidage,[34] would have converged on the King's stone before making their way along the final three miles of their journey on a paved ancient street to the gates of Winchester, the heart of the West Saxon kingdom. The King's stone was a new monument, serving a new junction on an ancient imperial road in an emerging landscape of royal power, and a location therefore ripe for monumental inscription.

A very similar set of circumstances have been observed in the case for a now lost standing stone in the northern hinterland of Anglo-Saxon Worcester. Michael Hare has drawn attention to a narrative passage written into a charter purporting to date to the eighth century but clearly forged in the eleventh century in order to provide some form of written evidence for land St Peter's Worcester effectively

---

[27] Flint 1994, 89, 205–7.
[28] See *e.g.* Barlow 1969, 79; McNeill and Gamer 1990, 334, 331; Meaney 1984.
[29] Pelteret 1995, 143–5; Radford 1975, 6–7.
[30] Langlands 2019, 164–96.
[31] Fleming 2010, 13.
[32] Blair 1994, 52–4, 87–92, 146–9.
[33] S 376, BCS 620/1, KCD 342; Grundy 1921, 164–73; Grundy 1927, 340; Biddle 1976, 256–7.
[34] Hill 1969.

controlled.[35] Concerning the fate of two decorated stone crosses of early medieval date, the passage includes two short parts: the first refers to a stone cross, skilfully built above the benefactors' – Wiferd and Alta – graves, destroyed (*destructam*) and incorporated into the fabric of an enlarged presbytery constructed in Edward the Confessor's reign. The second concerns a 'White Stone' placed at a distance of one mile from the first, outside the city to the north, and likewise destroyed in the time of King William the Elder. It is the White Stone that concerns us here and the original location of this monument appears to be preserved in the name of Whitston Priory, a thirteenth-century nunnery which stood almost exactly one mile to the north of the cathedral.[36] As with Winchester's King's stone, two pieces of corroborating historical evidence allow for a relatively tight location to be proposed for the White Stone, but further similarities can be observed in their respective topographic settings. Like the King's stone, the White Stone appears to stand close to the junction of two important routes into the city, that of the Droitwich and Kidderminster roads as they converge, before the crossing of the Barbourne Brook (Fig. 3.2).

Both stones provide a useful *terminus ante quem* for the junctions that they furnish, in the sense that to make investment in such a grandiose statement worthwhile their construction must, theoretically, be responding to a road using audience. The study of early medieval route networks is notoriously hindered by the absence of direct evidence for their presence and as a consequence, early medieval scholarship has found itself assumptively reliant on the network of Roman roads with which to furnish its maps. Recent scholarship has invited us to place movement more prominently within our examination of the archaeological record and if monumental stones are key signatures in an archaeology of movement, then joining up the dots, so to speak, may very well lead us to a network of specifically early medieval routes.[37]

The King's stone is almost certainly evidence of a monument type playing its part in the substantial physical infrastructures of pilgrimages that archaeological investigations have found elsewhere and for Anglo-Saxon England in the later ninth century, there is a demonstrable rise in the popularity of pilgrimages amongst a greater section of society.[38] An increase in pilgrims created a greater need for roadside dedication and this function is explicitly being fulfilled by the King's stone when we are told of how the blind man who has taken rest there goes on to pray at the monument, is relieved of his blindness and is able, once the glaucoma has receded from his eyes, to gaze upon the city. Upon arriving at his destination, he informs the monks of the place at which he received the miracle cure.[39] However, such monuments

---

[35] I am grateful to Michael Hare for pointing out the clear similarities between the King's stone and a similar monument recorded to the north of Worcester, Hare 2014, 26. I also owe Michael a debt of gratitude for kindly reading a draft of this text and making a number of useful observations from which the final text has benefited enormously.

[36] *Ibid.*, 28, 31, fig. 5.1.

[37] Aldred 2020; Langlands 2019, 137–63.

[38] Graham-Campbell 1994; Stopford 1994; Rollason 1989, 187.

[39] Lapidge 2003, 317–18.

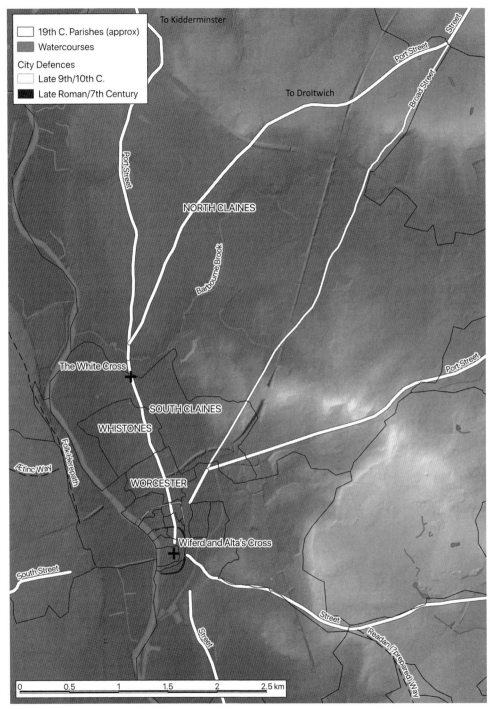

Fig. 3.2: Late Saxon Worcester and its northern hinterland, showing the location of the White Stone and Wiferd and Alta's Stone (after Hare 2014 and Hooke 1980).

may also be conveying subliminal messages, operating below the threshold of popular consciousness but within the measurably specific ideological context of Christian kingship. There is much, therefore, that the King's stone could have achieved in the construction of sacred space, drawing on an imagined imperial tradition sustained through the imposition of law and order.

The king's role in the stone may have come about because of royal patronage and a large part of St Peter, Old Minster's endowment was made generously, if intermittently, at the hands of the West Saxon kings in the seventh and eighth centuries. It was with dynastic developments in the ninth century however that a permanent and potent link was made between the Old Minster and the royal family of Wessex, where moral authority was a clear trade-off for such munificent patronage.[40] Yet, a political agenda may also be in evidence in a stone clearly intended to serve as a component part in a monumental repertoire that sought to evoke *Romanitas*.[41] This elite strategy is seen as equivalent to the contemporary literary narratives of power and conversion, and was being used to bring a renewed Christian authority in line with the surviving physical edifices of *imperium*.[42]

That we are told that the King's stone is fashioned from 'ancient' stone is of interest. But so too is the distance it is said to lie from the city. Again, parallels can be drawn with the Worcester White Stone which is both constructed in very similar work (*opere consimili*) to the stone commemorating Wiferd and Alta's donation, but is also said to stand one mile from it. In both this case and that of the King's stone, mile intervals are being marked on major routes, and together they beg the question whether the recreation of the Roman *miles* system of measurement is also part of the project of imperial *renovatio*. Are these early medieval stones located where they are because in the ninth century there were still enough Roman milestones remaining *in situ* to influence the setting of later stone monuments? We are reminded of William of Malmesbury's account of the death and funeral cortège of Aldhelm, where *biscepstanes* were erected along the course of the Roman Fosse Way at the overnight resting points of the saint's body on its journey back to Malmesbury.[43] We also see from the charter boundary evidence for land between the Wylye and Avon in south Wiltshire the presence of 'stone columns' at regular intervals along an 'old herepath', and elsewhere Roman milestones appear reused as important commemorative monuments.[44] As Sarah Semple has pointed out, the 'ancient' was valuable to the church as much as it was to kings and more specifically, in terms of stone sculpture itself, the deliberate appropriation of Roman sites is clearly a reflection of a desire on the part of both institutions to establish a new 'Rome of Christ'.[45]

---

[40] Yorke 1982.
[41] Blair 2005, 189–90.
[42] Semple 2013, 133.
[43] Preest 2002, 261.
[44] Langlands 2019, 147–8; Nash-Williams 1950, no. 258.
[45] Semple 2013, 135; Hawkes 2003, 82.

This project of the ninth-century West Saxon kings manifests itself most famously in the gridded street layout of Winchester, said to demonstrate 'symbolic intent' and clear allusions to the secular organisation of Rome.[46] In this context, the King's stone plays its part in what has been termed 'memory work' – a mediation of 'a history and mythology' with a material world.[47] The active construction of a perceived Roman past may very well have been the objective, but it also served as a reminder of the role played by secular power in ensuring the present day enactment of Christian ideas around the freedom and protection afforded to the wayfarer, the trader, the pilgrim, and other road users of Christian kind. Of course, many people, going about their daily business in the landscape of ninth-century central Wessex, may very well have been largely oblivious to these elite aspirations for the re-investiture of Roman *imperium*, in much the same way that they may have been unversed in the attendant political philosophy that is clearly in evidence in our surviving documentary sources from the royal court.[48] For them the stone's *materiality* may have been a signifier of other important parameters to contemporary life. Its association with the made road (again, in stone), would have served as a timely reminder of the king's presence, and the command over the highway that royal power enjoyed. A range of textual evidence suggests that this control, first explicitly evident in the legal treatise of laws known as the *Leges Henrici Primi*, has its origins in the Anglo-Saxon period.[49] Of particular relevance is the stipulation in a prefatory note that all *herestrete* pertain wholly to the king, and all *qualstowa* (literally 'killing places'), pertain totally to the king and are in his soke.[50] This arrangement is borne out by archaeological and topographical evidence from across Anglo-Saxon England but more locally by Hampshire execution cemeteries at Meon Hill and Stockbridge Down, both of which lie directly on the main highway from Winchester to Old Sarum.[51] In this context then, the King's stone takes its place alongside the 'head-stakes' and execution cemetery further along the Roman road in what appears very much like a 'carrot and stick' approach to ensuring law-abiding use of the highway. Royal protection and its deep Christian links announce themselves as one passes the King's stone, whilst God's judgement awaits the evil doer is the clear message conveyed by the grisly (but probably quite reassuring) sight of the heads of felons displayed on stakes.

Whilst it seems likely that the promotion of the *frið* in later Anglo-Saxon legislation has much to do with mercantile activity and the lucrative growth of an economy based on an increasingly stable cash nexus, it has also been apparent for some time that it reflects the notions of a public peace and a form of protection that was extended to all people in the kingdom.[52] The connection between peace and the highway might

---

[46] Biddle 2020; Keene 2017.
[47] Williams *et al.* 2015, 8–9.
[48] Pratt 2007.
[49] Cooper 2000; Cooper 2002; Cooper 2016.
[50] Downer 1972, ch. 10.2.
[51] Langlands 2019, 170; Reynolds 2009, 117.
[52] Stubbs 1903, 198–202.

be inferred from a chapter in one of Æthelred's law codes where a link between the peace, coinage, fort and bridge work is made.[53] But one intriguing miscellaneous legal memorandum from the *Textus Roffensis* does much to draw together these notions of peace, godly protection, justice, the king *and* the 3 mile mark from the city. Known as *Pax*, a single line of legislation surviving in the *Textus Roffensis* and likely linked with Æthelred II's later law codes,[54] it sets out exactly, to a grain of barley corn, how far the king's peace extends from the city gate. It reads:

> Ðus feor sceal beon þæs cinges grið, fram his burhgeate þær he is sittende, on feower healfe his. Ð>æt< is iii mila 7 iii furlang, 7 iii æcera bræde, 7 ix fota, 7 ix scæftamunda, 7 ix berecorna.

> Thus far shall be the king's peace, from his city gate [or 'gatehouse'] where he is seated, on its four sides. That is 3 miles, and 3 furlongs, and 3 acres, and 9 feet, and 9 spans, and 9 barley corns.[55]

Sacred Space, Busy Roads and the Rise of Towns

Michael Lapidge suggested that the King's stone of Wulfstan's account may have been a boundary marker on the limits of the ancient *territorium* of the Roman city.[56] In this sense, the location doesn't quite fit with the territorial boundaries proposed for this area in the eighth century and beyond.[57] But we might entertain that a different kind of boundary is being traversed at this location. Whilst we can't say which way the King's stone was facing, there is definitely a sense, because of its position at the junction of converging major routes, of its marking an arrival, an 'entering' into a special place, especially if a deep-rooted association between standing stones and 'entry points' is informing its architectural grammar.[58] Although their use primarily as boundary markers has been called in to question,[59] where such monuments are purposefully designed to furnish routes radiating out of church centres, the result *is* a kind of boundary, and in this case into a sacred and *peaceful* space. In a study of early medieval standing crosses in the ecclesiastical parish of Dewsbury (West Riding of Yorkshire), cross bases were identified on roads radiating out of the centre in a manner in which they appear to define the 'heart' of the ecclesiastical estate.[60] The same scenario might be proposed for case-studies in Cornwall, and Martin Carver's study of the Tarbut stones demonstrates clear evidence for the marking out of a 'holy' landscape.[61] A pair of roadside early medieval stones dating to at least the eleventh

[53] V Atr. 26.1, Attenborough 1922, 243.
[54] Naismith 2019.
[55] Monk 2017.
[56] Biddle 1976, 256–7; Lapidge 2003, 529, n. 715.
[57] Brookes 2020, esp. fig 13.2; after Eagles 2015.
[58] Andrén 1993.
[59] Blair 2005, 478–80.
[60] Coatsworth 2015, 136.
[61] Thomas 1967, 86–100; Preston-Jones and Langdon 1997; Carver 2017.

century may be achieving the same message in South-West England. Whilst on a macro-geographical level the Copplestone Cross is situated at a major crossing axis of north-east/south-west and south-east/north-west roads in central Devon, in its immediate location it sits at the convergence of roads from Bude and Barnstaple *en route* to Crediton, the site of the tenth-century episcopal see.[62] Its highly decorated granite cross-shaft, with evidence of Scandinavian influences, provides a tentative link with the now lost *Chenutdestana* (Cnut's Stone), the 1086 name for Knowstone, Devon, a stone marking the main route from Barnstaple to Tiverton.[63] What begins to emerge from this evidence is the very real prospect of an increasing level of sanctification being imposed, in material form, on much wider landscapes, and the drawing of liminal and remote parts of the kingdom into a sphere of Christian holiness.

On a practical and methodological level, the dating of both the King's stone and the White Stone provide us with useful evidence for *movement*, in this case, the development of route networks in the hinterlands of two key regional Anglo-Saxon urban sites. For both stones to operate successfully, there must already have been pre-existing audiences of a volume sufficient to warrant the investment in this form of monumental architecture. Both monuments were clearly crosses, perhaps decorated, but were referred to in the vernacular tongue as 'stones' and this has implications for how we read other 'stones' both in the placename and charter boundary clause evidence – especially when they are associated with major junctions in areas where glacial erratics are absent.[64] This volume of traffic, in turn, suggests that a relatively sophisticated network of routeways is already in operation throughout these areas. For Winchester and its links to the north, the term *wic herpaðe* (Fig. 3.1), used to describe the road to Oxford, is perhaps a reference to the trade coming ultimately from *Hamwic*. Although recorded as late as the tenth century, the name may very well have derived from an eighth century context, and suggests a purposely maintained route for trade and exchange.[65]

Like Winchester, Worcester clearly lay at the centre of a network of routes leading in from all directions, making their way across a relatively prosperous and well-developed agricultural countryside.[66] It is also clear that the 'Port Street' from Droitwich superseded the line of the Roman road as the main approach road to Worcester from the north-east'.[67] The White Stone, and the need to mark this junction, suggests that this supersession is earlier than the ninth century. Evidence suggests that when the dues owed on the profits of the Droitwich salt industry are being divided up in the late ninth, it is already flourishing with the transhipment

---

[62] S 795, BCS 1303, although with a boundary clause dating to the mid-eleventh century; Langlands 2019, 88–90, figs 24, 25; Reynolds and Langlands 2011.

[63] Cramp 2006, 82–3; Mawer and Stenton 1932, 340.

[64] Hare 2010, 140; 2012, 181–2, appendix 3.

[65] Langlands 2020.

[66] Hooke 1980, 40.

[67] *Ibid.*, 45.

point at Worcester on the River Severn being key to this success.[68] The consensus on Worcester's urban development sees the street system as one laid out in the tenth century.[69] Yet, a body of work has recently made the case for urban planning and the setting out of 'burghal' topography in the late ninth century and in Worcester's case this is seen as an episode contemporary with the order by Æthelred and Æthelflæd (884 x 901) to build the *burh* for the protection of all the people.[70] Wagons are explicitly mentioned in a reservation of dues here and cause us again to think about the level of infrastructural improvement to road surfaces that is required to make carting viable. Elsewhere the evidence for substantial river crossings and bridges in early medieval England, Ireland and Wales suggests something important, in a civic and infrastructural sense, is happening as early as the eighth century.[71]

The point here is that whilst the archaeological evidence for urban growth across Anglo-Saxon England may be confined to the tenth century, with slow urban growth in the first half of the century followed by a phase of rapid expansion in to the eleventh, the route network upon which it is predicated must be a precursor.[72] We may have to wait until the tenth century to see the blossoming of a sophisticated landscape of urbanism, and debate what elements of it were already in place by the ninth, but the evidence from important roadside monumental architecture relating to Winchester and Worcester suggests that the ambitions for it can be projected back into the early ninth century.

Abbreviations

BCS   Birch, W. de Gray. 1885–99. *Cartularium Saxonicum*, 3 vols. London: Whiting & Company.

KCD   Kemble, J. M. 1839–48. *Codex Diplomaticus Aevi Saxonici*, 6 vols. London: Sumptibus Societatis.

S   Sawyer, P. H. 1968. *Anglo-Saxon Charters: an Annotated List and Bibliography*, Royal Hist. Soc. Guides and Handbooks, 8, London: Royal Historical Society. Also available at: *The Electronic Sawyer: Online Catalogue of Anglo-Saxon Charters* https://esawyer.lib.cam.ac.uk/.

Bibliography

Primary Sources
Attenborough, F. L. 1922. *The Laws of the Earliest English Kings*. Cambridge: Cambridge University Press.
Barlow C. W. (trans.) 1969. *Iberian Fathers: Martin of Braga, Paschasius of Dumium and Leander of Seville*. Washington: Catholic University of America Press.

---

[68] Maddicott 2005.

[69] Baker *et al.* 1992; figure 5 of this paper provides the most useful overview of the sequence; Baker and Holt 1996; Holt 2010.

[70] S 223, BCS 579, KCD 1075; Haslam, 2012; Haslam 2014; Kelly 1992, 17.

[71] Harrison 2004; Langlands 2019, 164–73; O'Sullivan and Boland 2000; Fleming 2010, 13–14.

[72] Hodges 1989, 156; Hinton 2000, 230–5.

Biddle, M. (ed.) 1976. *Winchester in the Early Middle Ages: an edition and discussion of the Winton Domesday*, Winchester Studies, 1. Oxford: Clarendon Press.

Downer, L. J. 1972. *Leges Henrici Primi*. Oxford: Oxford University Press.

Lapidge, M. 2003. *The Cult of St Swithun*, Winchester Studies, Vol. 4. Oxford: Oxford University Press.

McNeill, J. T. and Gamer, H. M. 1990. *Medieval Handbooks of Penance: A Translation of the Principal 'Libri Poenitentiales' and Selections from Related Documents*. New York: Columbia University Press.

Miller, S. 2001. *Charters of The New Minster, Winchester*, British Academy, Anglo-Saxon Charters Series, vol. 9. Oxford: Oxford University Press.

Monk, C. 2017. *The Anonymous Fragment of Law Known as Pax ('Peace'): Textus Roffensis, f. 38r; Translated from Old English and Edited*. Rochester: Rochester Cathedral Research Guild.

Ordnance Survey 1896. 25 inch to the mile OS series map, Hampshire and Isle of Wight, Sheet XL.4 (revised 1894).

Preest, D. (trans.) 2002. *William of Malmesbury: The Deeds of the Bishops of England (Gesta Pontificum Anglorum)*. Woodbridge: Boydell Press.

Secondary Sources

Aldred, O. 2020. *The Archaeology of Movement*. London: Routledge.

Andrén, A. 1993. Doors to Other Worlds: Scandinavian Death Rituals in Gotlandic Perspectives, *Journal of European Archaeology Archive*, 1:1, 33–56.

Baker, N., Dalwood, H., Holt, R., Mundy, C. and Taylor, G. 1992. From Roman to Medieval Worcester: Development and Planning in the Anglo-Saxon City, *Antiquity*, 66:250, 65–74.

Baker, N. J. and Holt, R. 1996. The City of Worcester in the Tenth Century, in N. P. Brooks and C. Cubitt (eds), *St Oswald of Worcester: Life and Influence*, 129–46. Leicester: Leicester University Press.

Biddle. M. 2020. Winchester: A City of Two Planned Towns, in A. J. Langlands and R. Lavelle (eds), *The Land of the English Kin: Studies in Wessex and Anglo-Saxon England in Honour of Professor Barbara Yorke*, 26–49. Leiden: Brill.

Blair, J. 1994. *Anglo-Saxon Oxfordshire*. Stroud: Alan Sutton.

Blair, J. 2005. *The Church in Anglo-Saxon Society*. Oxford: Oxford University Press.

Bonney, D. J. 1979. Early Boundaries and Estates in Southern England, in P. H. Sawyer (ed.), *English Medieval Settlement*, 41–51. London: Edward Arnold.

Brookes, S. 2020. On the Territorial Organisation of Early Medieval Hampshire, in A. J. Langlands and R. Lavelle (eds), *The Land of the English Kin: Studies in Wessex and Anglo-Saxon England in Honour of Professor Barbara Yorke*, 276–93. Leiden: Brill.

Brooks, N. P. 2000. The Micheldever Forgery, in N. Brooks (ed.), *Anglo-Saxon Myths: State and Church 400-1066*, 239–74. London: Hambledon Press.

Campbell, E. and Maldonado, A. 2020. A New Jerusalem 'At the Ends of the Earth': Interpreting Charles Thomas's Excavations at Iona Abbey 1956–63, *Antiquaries Journal*, 100, 1–53.

Carver, M. O. H. 2017. Sculpture in Action: Contexts for Stone Carving on the Tarbat Peninsula, Easter Ross, in S. M. Foster (ed.), *Able Minds and Practiced Hands: Scotland's Early Medieval Sculpture in the 21st Century*, 13–36. Leeds: Maney.

Coatsworth, E. 2015. Landmarks of Faith: Crosses and Other Free-Standing Stones, in G. R. Owen-Crocker and M. Clegg Hyer (eds), *The Material Culture of the Built Environment in the Anglo-Saxon World*, 117–36. Liverpool: Liverpool University Press.

Cooper, A. 2000. The King's Four Highways: Legal Fiction Meets Fictional Law, *Journal of Medieval History*, 26, 351–70.

Cooper, A. 2002. The Rise and Fall of the Anglo-Saxon Law of the Highway, *Haskins Society Journal*, 12, 39–69.

Cooper, A. 2016. Once a Highway, Always a Highway: Roads and English Law, c. 1150–1300, in V. Allen and R. Evans (eds), *Roadworks: Medieval Britain, Medieval Roads*, 50–73. Manchester: Manchester University Press.

Cramp, R. 2006. *Corpus of Anglo-Saxon Stone Sculpture: Volume VII: South-West England*. Oxford: Oxford University Press.

Cubitt, C. 2009. 'As the Lawbook Teaches': Reeves, Lawbooks and Urban Life in the Anonymous Old English Legend of the Seven Sleepers, *English Historical Review*, 124:510, 1021–49.

Devlin, Z. 2011. Putting Memory in its Place: Sculpture, Cemetery Topography and Commemoration, in M. F. Reed (ed.), *New Voices on Early Medieval Sculpture in Britain and Ireland*, 32–41. Oxford: British Archaeological Reports.

Eagles, B. N. 2015. Small Shires and Regiones in Hampshire and the Formation of the Shires of Eastern Wessex, *Anglo-Saxon Studies in Archaeology and History*, 19, 122–50.

Edwards, N. 2001. Monuments in a Landscape: The Early Medieval Sculpture of St David's, in H. Hamerow and A. MacGregor (eds), *Image and Power in the Archaeology of Early Medieval Britain*, 53–77. Oxford: Oxbow Books.

Everson, P. and Stocker, D. 2017. 'The Cros in the Markitte Stede'. The Louth Cross, Its Monastery and Its Town, *Medieval Archaeology*, 61:2, 330–71.

Fleming, A. 2010. Horses, Elites … and Long-Distance Roads, *Landscapes*, 11:2, 1–20.

Flint, V. I. J. 1994. *The Rise of Magic in Early Medieval Europe*. Oxford: Clarendon Press.

Forsberg, R. 1950. *A Contribution to a Dictionary of Old English Place-Names*. Uppsala: Nomina Germanica, IX.

Gondek, M. 2007. Early Historic Sculpture and Landscape: A Case Study of Cladh a'Bhile, Ellary, Mid-Argyll, *Proceedings of the Society of Antiquaries of Scotland*, 136, 237–58.

Gondek, M. and Noble, G. 2010. Together As One: The Landscape of the Symbol Stones at Rhynie, Aberdeenshire, in S. T. Driscoll, J. Geddes and M. A. Hall (eds), *Pictish Progress*, 281–305. Leiden: Brill.

Graham-Campbell, J. 1994. *The Archaeology of Pilgrimage*, World Archaeology, 26, 1:2. London: Taylor and Francis.

Grundy, G. B. 1918. The Ancient Highways and Tracks of Wiltshire, Berkshire and Hampshire, and the Saxon Battlefields of Wiltshire, *Archaeological Journal*, 75, 69–194.

Grundy, G. B. 1921. The Saxon Land Charters of Hampshire with Notes on Place and Field Names, *Archaeological Journal*, 28, 55–173.

Grundy, G. B. 1924. The Saxon Land Charters of Hampshire with Notes on Place and Field Names, *Archaeological Journal*, 31, 31–126.

Grundy, G. B. 1926. The Saxon Land Charters of Hampshire with Notes on Place and Field Names, *Archaeological Journal*, 33, 91–253.

Grundy, G. B. 1927. The Saxon Land Charters of Hampshire with Notes on Place and Field Names, *Archaeological Journal*, 34, 160–340.

Hall, M. 2012. Three Stones, One Landscape, Many Stories. Cultural Biography and the Early Medieval Sculptures of Inchyra and St Madoes, Carse of Gowrie, Perthshire, Scotland, in S. H. Dudley, A. J. Barnes, J. Binnie, J. Petroc and J. Walklate (eds), *Narrating Objects, Collecting Stories: Essays in Honour of Professor Susan M. Pearce*, 85–102. London: Routledge.

Hare, M. J. 2010. A possible Commemorative Stone for Æthelmund, Father of Æthelric, in M. Henig and N. Ramsay (eds), *Intersections: The Archaeology and History of Christianity in England, 400–1200. Papers in Honour of Martin Biddle and Birthe Kjølbye-Biddle*, 135–48, BAR British Series 505. Oxford: Archaeopress.

Hare, M. J. 2012. Deerhurst's Earliest Patrons: Æthelmund and Æthelric, *Transactions of the Bristol & Gloucestershire Archaeological Society*, 130, 151–82.

Hare, M. J. 2014. Hemming's Crosses, in G. R. Owen-Crocker and S. D. Thompson (eds), *Towns and Topography: Essays in Memory of David Hill*, 26–36. Oxford: Oxbow Books.

Harrison, D. 2004. *The Bridges of Medieval England: Transport and Society 400–1800*. Oxford: Clarendon Press.

Haslam, J. 2012. *Urban-rural Connections in Domesday Book and Late Anglo-Saxon Royal Administration*, BAR British Series 571. Oxford: Archaeopress.

Haslam, J. 2014. Planning in Late-Saxon Worcester, *Anglo-Saxon Studies in Archaeology and History*, 19, 153–72.

Hawkes, C. H. C. 1925. Old Roads in Central Hants, *Proceedings of the Hampshire Field Club and Archaeological Society*, 9, 324–33.

Hawkes, J. 2003. Iuxta Morem Romanorum: Stone and Sculpture in Anglo-Saxon England, in C. E. Karkov and G. Brown (eds), *Anglo-Saxon Styles*, 69–100. New York: State University Press.

Hill, D. 1969. The Burghal Hidage: The Establishment of a Text, *Medieval Archaeology*, 31:1, 84–92.

Hill, D. 1981. *An Atlas of Anglo-Saxon England*. Oxford: Blackwell.

Hinton, D. A. 2000. The Large Towns 600–1300, in D. M. Palliser (ed.), *The Cambridge Urban History of Britain, Volume 1: 600-1540*, 217–43. Cambridge: Cambridge University Press.

Hodges, R. 1989. *The Anglo-Saxon Achievement*. London: Duckworth.

Holt, R. 2010. The Urban Transformation in England, 900–1100, *Anglo-Norman Studies*, 32, 57–78.

Hooke, D. 1980. The Hinterland and Routeways of Late Saxon Worcester: The Charter Evidence, in M. O. H. Carver (ed.), *Medieval Worcester: An Archaeological Framework*, 38–49. Worcester: Transactions of the Worcestershire Archaeological Society.

Keene, D. 2017. Early Medieval Winchester: Symbolic Landscapes, in H. B. Clarke and A. Simms (eds), *Lords and Towns in Medieval Europe: The European Historic Towns Atlas Project*, 419–44. London: Routledge.

Kelly, S. E. 1992. Trading Privileges from the Eighth Century, *Early Medieval Europe*, 1, 3–28.

Keynes, S. 1994. The West Saxon Charters of King Æthelwulf and His Sons, *English Historical Review*, 109, 1109–49.

Kirton, J. 2015. Locating the Cleulow Cross: Materiality, Place and Landscape, in H. Williams, J. Kirton and M. Gondek (eds), *Early Medieval Stone Monuments: Materiality, Biography, Landscape*, 35–61. Woodbridge: Boydell Press.

Klingelhöfer, E. 1990. Anglo-Saxon Manors of the Upper Itchen Valley: Their Origin and Evolution, *Proceedings of the Hampshire Field Club and Archaeological Society*, 46, 31–9.

Langlands, A. J. 2019. *Ancient Ways of Wessex: Travel and Communication in an Early Medieval Landscape*. Oxford: Windgather Press.

Langlands, A. J. 2020. Ceapmenn and Portmenn: Trade, Exchange and the Landscape of Early Medieval Wessex, in A. J. Langlands and R. Lavelle (eds), *The Land of the English Kin: Studies in Wessex and Anglo-Saxon England in Honour of Professor Barbara Yorke*, 294–311. Leiden: Brill.

Locker, M. 2015. *Landscapes of Pilgrimage in Medieval Britain*. Oxford: Archaeopress.

Maddicott, J. R. 2005. London and Droitwich, c. 650–750: Trade, Industry and the Rise of Mercia, *Anglo-Saxon England*, 34, 7–58.

Mawer, A. and Stenton, F. M. 1932. *The Place-Names of Devon, Part 2*. Cambridge: Cambridge University Press.

Meaney, A. L. 1984. Ælfric and Idolatry, *Journal of Religious History*, 13, 119–35.

Murrieta-Flores, P. and Williams, H. 2017. Placing the Pillar of Eliseg: Movement, Visibility and Memory in the Early Medieval Landscape, *Medieval Archaeology*, 61:1, 69–103.

Naismith, R. 2019. The Laws of London? IV Æthelred in Context, *The London Journal*, 44:1, 1–16.

Nash-Williams, V. E. 1950. *The Early Christian Monuments of Wales*. Cardiff: University of Wales Press.

Nenk, B., Margeson, S. and Hurley, M. 1991. Medieval Britain and Ireland in 1990, *Medieval Archaeology*, 35, 157–8.

Ó Carragáin, T. 2009. The Saint and the Sacred Centre: The Early Medieval Pilgrimage Landscape of Inishmurray, in N. Edwards (ed.), *The Archaeology of the Early Medieval Celtic Churches*, 207–26, Society for Medieval Archaeology Monograph, 24. Leeds: Maney.

Orton, F. 2006. At the Bewcastle Monument, in Place, in C. A. Lees and G. R. Overing (eds), *A Place to Believe in: Locating Medieval Landscapes*, 29–66. University Park: Pennsylvania State University Press.

O'Sullivan, A. and Boland, D. 2000. *The Clonmacnoise Bridge: An Early Medieval River Crossing in County Offaly*, Archaeology Ireland Heritage Guide No. 11. Bray: Wordwell.

Pelteret, D. 1995. *Slavery in Early Medieval England from the Reign of Alfred until the Twelfth Century*. Woodbridge: Boydell and Brewer.

Pratt, D. 2007. *The Political Thought of King Alfred the Great*. Cambridge: Cambridge University Press.

Preston-Jones, A. and Langdon, A. 1997. St. Buryan Crosses, *Cornish Archaeology*, 36, 107–28.

Rackham, O. 1986. *The History of the Countryside*. London: J. M. Dent and Sons.

Radford, C. A. R. 1975. The Pre-Conquest Church and the Old Minsters of Devon, *Devon Historian*, 2, 2–11.

Reed, M. 1984. Anglo-Saxon Charter Boundaries, in M. Reed (ed.), *Discovering Past Landscapes*, 261–306. London: Croom Helm.

Reynolds, A. J. 2009. *Anglo-Saxon Deviant Burial Customs*. Oxford: Oxford University Press.

Reynolds, A. J. and Langlands, A. J. 2011. Travel as Communication: A Consideration of Overland Journeys in Anglo-Saxon England, *World Archaeology*, 43, 410–27.

Rollason, D. 1989. *Saints and Relics in Anglo-Saxon England*. Oxford: Blackwell.

Semple, S. J. 2010. In the Open Air, in M. O. H. Carver, A. Sanmark and S. J. Semple (eds), *Signals of Belief in Early England*, 21–48. Oxford: Oxbow Books.

Semple, S. J. 2013. *Perceptions of the Prehistoric in Anglo-Saxon England*. Oxford: Oxford University Press.

Stopford, J. 1994. Some Approaches to the Archaeology of Christian Pilgrimage, *World Archaeology*, 26, 1:2, 57–72.

Stubbs, W. 1903. *The Constitutional History of England*. Oxford: Clarendon Press.

Thomas, C. 1967. *Antiquities of Cambourne*. St. Austell: H. E. Warne.

Tweddle, D., Biddle, M. and Kjølbye-Biddle, B. 1995. *A Corpus of Anglo-Saxon Stone Sculpture*, Volume IV: South-East England. Oxford: Oxford University Press.

Williams, H. 2006. *Death and Memory in Early Medieval Britain*. Cambridge: Cambridge University Press.

Williams, H., Kirton, J. and Gondek, M. (eds) 2015. *Early Medieval Stone Monuments: Materiality, Biography, Landscape*. Woodbridge: Boydell Press.

Yorke, B. A. E. 1982. The Foundation of the Old Minster and the Status of Winchester in the Seventh and Eighth Centuries, *Proceedings of the Hampshire Field Club and Archaeological Society*, 38, 75–83.

Chapter 4

Royal Burial in Winchester: Context and Significance

Barbara Yorke

A project to examine the bones of kings and bishops contained in Winchester Cathedral's mortuary chests has required a new consideration of which early medieval kings were buried in Winchester and in what circumstances. The number of seventh- and eighth-century West Saxon kings buried at Old Minster has to remain uncertain, but was probably fewer than some post-Conquest historians believed. Winchester became a favoured place of royal burial under Æthelwulf, Alfred and Edward the Elder, including the foundation of New Minster as a place of burial for Edward and his immediate family, and again for Anglo-Danish and early Norman kings in the eleventh century. But less than half the royal burials between 858–1066 took place in Winchester, and understanding the circumstances of royal burial in the city requires consideration of the alternative choices that were made. Disputed successions in the context of regional factionalism and affiliations can help explain the range of places chosen for royal burial, and why the time was not yet right in later Anglo-Saxon England for the emergence of an exclusive site of royal burial.

One of the most apparent manifestations of Anglo-Saxon royal interest in Winchester is that up until the twelfth century it had the largest number of recorded burials of rulers of Wessex and England. It was probably first used as a burial place of kings in the seventh century and was intermittently used for royal burials in every century thereafter, up to that of the last recorded king to be buried in Winchester, William II 'Rufus' who was killed in the New Forest in 1100. Two major churches were used for royal burials, the Old and New Minsters that stood in close proximity to each other in the south-eastern quarter of the city.[1] The Old Minster was the cathedral church founded in the seventh century and considerably redeveloped in the later tenth century, while the New Minster was founded in 901 by King Edward the Elder (899–924), at least in part to serve as a place of burial for himself and his immediate

---

[1] Biddle 2018.

family. The aim of this paper is firstly to identify which kings are known to have been buried in Winchester (establishing a definitive list is not an entirely straightforward matter), and secondly, to seek to understand why some rulers chose Winchester as their burial place for it was never exclusively the choice for burial of either kings of Wessex or kings of all England. The question of 'why Winchester?' therefore also needs one to consider 'why *not* Winchester?'.

Kings Buried in Winchester: New Minster

Identifying which members of the royal house were buried in New Minster is relatively straightforward as it was only used for royal burials for a restricted period between *c.* 901 and 957, and the burials are recorded in an early medieval history of the foundation incorporated into the house's own *Liber Vitae* from the time of Abbot Ælfwine (1031–57).[2] King Edward the Elder (899–924) seems to have made foundation of the new house a priority soon after his accession 'for the sake of the souls' of himself and his father, King Alfred (871–99).[3] Although King Alfred had been buried in Old Minster after his death on 22 October 899, Edward appears to have had his body removed to New Minster at the earliest possibility.[4] Work was sufficiently advanced to enable Edward's mother Ealhswith to be buried in New Minster after she died in December 902.[5] Subsequently Edward's younger brother Æthelweard was buried in the church on his death in either 920 or 922.[6] Edward himself was interred there in 924 (d. 17 July) as was his son Ælfweard who ruled for just a few weeks after him (d. 2 August).[7] The last known member of the royal house to be buried in New Minster was Edward's grandson King Eadwig (955–7).[8] In the time of Abbot Geoffrey (1106–25) the foundation moved from its site in the cathedral close to a new site in the northern suburb of Hyde.[9] It is presumed that the bodies of members of the Anglo-Saxon royal house were transferred to the new church, but only those of Alfred, Ealhswith and Edward are specifically referred to in later records. The recent recalibrated radiocarbon date of 892x985 for a hip bone (partial right os coxa) found with burials redeposited after the dissolution of Hyde Abbey has aroused considerable interest as the possible remains of either Alfred or Edward.[10]

New Minster would seem to have been founded with a primary purpose of serving as a mausoleum for King Edward the Elder and his immediate family.[11] Why Edward should have felt the need to build a new church rather than, say, extending the

---

[2] Birch 1892; Keynes 1995.
[3] Miller 2001, xxvi, nos. 2, 4 and 5.
[4] Birch 1892, 5; Miller 2001, xxv–vii.
[5] *ASC* CD 903; Keynes, 1995, 3.
[6] Miller 2001, xxvi–vii.
[7] *ASC* CD 924; Birch 1892, 6.
[8] Birch 1892, 7.
[9] Miller 2001, xxi; Qualmann *et al.* 2021.
[10] Tucker 2014 and in Qualmann *et al.* 2021, 235–300.
[11] Miller 2001, no. 4, 26–30 refers to prayers to be said daily at New Minster for the souls of Alfred, Edward and their ancestors.

neighbouring cathedral church in which his father and other family members were already buried is a topic that will be considered later in the paper, together with the issue of why, when all subsequent rulers of the Anglo-Saxon royal house were descended from Edward the Elder, only his grandson Eadwig was buried in New Minster. For the moment discussion will turn to the rather more complex topic of identifying which kings were buried in the Old Minster.

Kings Buried in Winchester: Old Minster

The most striking resource for studying the royal burials in Old Minster are the remains of early medieval kings that, together with those of Queen Emma and several Anglo-Saxon bishops of Winchester, are contained in the mortuary chests that stand on top of the presbytery screens in Winchester cathedral. Recent renovations at the east end of the cathedral required the temporary removal of the chests and so provided an opportunity to check on the conservation status of the chests and their bones. All required attention, and the opportunity was also taken to institute a thorough scientific examination of the bones by Kate Robson-Brown of the University of Bristol and Heidi Dawson-Hobbis (now of the University of Winchester) with the aim of reassembling and identifying the individual skeletons, in so far as that was possible. Analysis is still ongoing at the time of writing but is sufficiently advanced for some initial results to be displayed in the refurbished triforium museum in Winchester Cathedral (opened May 2019), including copies of the surviving female bones (most likely those of Queen Emma) and the skull of a juvenile male (possibly Richard, the son of William I).[12] Initial radiocarbon dating has confirmed that the bones are indeed early medieval in date.

Work has been hampered because of the poor state of the bones. In 1642 Civil War troops emptied out the contents of the mortuary chests and destroyed five, or possibly six of the chests. The bones were retrieved in 1661, and placed in the four, surviving, early sixteenth-century mortuary chests and two newly made copies. A plaque on one of the new chests recorded the destruction and retrieval.[13] Inevitably the bones were hopelessly jumbled when they were thrown out of the chests, and most of the 20 skeletons reconstructed by Kate Robson-Brown and Heidi Dawson-Hobbis are incomplete. A starting point for identifying the kings originally buried in Old Minster is therefore the inscriptions on the surviving chests. These produce the names of Cynegils (611–42), Cynewulf (757–96), Ecgbert (802–39), Æthelwulf (839–58), Eadred (946–55), Edmund (probably Ironside 1016), Cnut (1016–36) and William II Rufus (1087–1100) (as well as that of Queen Emma). The tomb of Harthacnut (1040–2)

---

[12] Richard, son of William I was born *c.* 1055 and died 1069×74: Barlow 1983, 13. A second unrecorded juvenile discovered in the mortuary chests and with similar dating was possibly a second, Richard, grandson of William I and son of William's eldest son Robert who also died in a hunting accident in the New Forest in 1100, the same year as his uncle William Rufus, Barlow 1983, 419; Aird 2008, 96–7, 193–4.

[13] Biddle 1993, 275–8; Crook 1994, 167–8.

is recorded as lying beneath the north screen of the presbytery on a sixteenth-century plaque.[14] Late twelfth-century inscriptions in a similar position beneath the south side of the presbytery screen refer to the tombs there of Edmund, Earl Beorn, the nephew of Cnut killed in 1049, and Richard, son of William I who died in a hunting accident in the New Forest sometime between 1069 and 1075.[15] The evidence for these tombs has enabled Martin Biddle and Birthe Kjølbye-Biddle to reconstruct the likely original arrangement of Anglo-Danish and Norman burials in the Norman presbytery. The area was remodelled in the fourteenth and fifteenth centuries and some of the burials, including those of Cnut and Emma, were displaced to forerunners of the mortuary chests on top of the screens.[16] Although it had been assumed that the tombs incorporated into the bases of the presbytery screens still contained their skeletons, the presence of a juvenile who may be Prince Richard in the mortuary chest collections, and the record of Edmund as being both in one of the tombs and in one of the mortuary chests, has raised the possibility that all the royal burials from the presbytery tombs were moved to the mortuary chests at an unknown date.

The members of the royal house whose remains are recorded on the mortuary chests and on the presbytery screen inscriptions are compared in Table 4.1 with records of the burials for these rulers found in Anglo-Saxon and later medieval written sources. Burial in Old Minster is recorded in manuscripts of the *Anglo-Saxon Chronicle* for Cynewulf, Æthelwulf, Eadred, Cnut and William Rufus (the last in the newly completed Norman cathedral). The burial of Harthacnut in Old Minster is recorded in the D version of the *Anglo-Saxon Chronicle* and on his tomb, which apparently survives on the north side of the north screen of the presbytery (and this apparent surviving burial has been assumed to be why he is not one of the kings named as included in the mortuary chests).[17] Recent investigations by John Crook have suggested that this tomb no longer contains a body; it is possible that his remains were placed in one of the mortuary chests at some unrecorded point.[18] The *Anglo-Saxon Chronicle* records Edmund Ironside as being buried at Glastonbury,[19] but the twelfth-century inscription in the south presbytery screen which reads 'Here lies King Edmund, son of King Æthelred' is strong evidence to support a hypothesis that his body, or part of it, may have been transferred to Winchester. Martin Biddle and Birthe Kjølbye-Biddle suggest this may have been done as part of the creation of a burial place for the family of Cnut at the east end of the Old Minster.[20] One version of the *Anglo-Saxon Chronicle* records that Edmund and Cnut had sworn ties of brotherhood when they met at Deerhurst

---

[14] Biddle and Kjølbye-Biddle 2016, 238–41.
[15] Chibnall 1972, 114–5 (V, 2); Van Houts 1995, 217; *GRA*, 502–5.; see also n. 12.
[16] Biddle and Kjølbye-Biddle 2016.
[17] *Ibid.*, 222–3.
[18] Crook forthcoming.
[19] *ASC* CDE 1016.
[20] Biddle and Kjølbye-Biddle 2016, 224–6.

Table 4.1: Kings named on surviving mortuary chests.

Kings named on mortuary chests	Other references to burial in Winchester
Cynegils d. 641/2	
Cynewulf d. 786	*ASC 757*
Ecgbert d. 839	*Winchester Annals*
Æthelwulf d. 858	*Annals of St Neot*; *ASC 855*
Eadred d. 955	*ASC 955 D*
Edmund Ironside d. 1016	Twelfth-century inscription on south screen presbytery, Winchester cathedral
Cnut d. 1035	*ASC 1035*
Emma/Ælfgifu d. 1052	*ASC 1051 C*
William II Rufus d. 1100	*ASC 1100 E*

in 1016,[21] and these claims are elaborated by John of Worcester.[22] The inclusion of Edmund in what was to become the mausoleum of Cnut's family would have been a demonstration of such claims and their implications for Cnut's rightful inheritance of the throne. Cnut's visit to the grave of his 'brother' Edmund at Glastonbury in 1032 with Archbishop Æthelnoth of Canterbury recorded by William of Malmesbury could well have been when the translation was arranged.[23]

Rather surprisingly the burial place of King Ecgbert, the grandfather of King Alfred, is not recorded in any source from the Anglo-Saxon period. The twelfth-century *Winchester Annals* of Richard of Devizes which does include reference to Ecgbert's burial in Winchester is a far from ideal source that has been characterised as belonging to the Geoffrey of Monmouth school of historical writing, with legendary material mixed with genuine historical evidence with the aim of glorifying the past of the city.[24] For instance, Richard also has Ecgbert crowned king of all Britain in Winchester after his victory at *Ellendun*.[25] Nevertheless, the claim that Ecgbert was buried in the Old Minster is a distinct possibility; no other place of burial is known for him and his son Æthelwulf was buried there. Æthelwulf's son and successor Æthelbald leased land at Farnham (Surrey) from Bishop Swithun in 858 with the promise that it would return after his death 'for the love of God, and for the remedy of my soul and of [the souls] of my *parentes*, that is, my grandfather Ecgberht and my father Æthelwulf' which could possibly be an indication that both were buried at Winchester and so under the care of Swithun.[26]

[21] *ASC D* 1016; Townend 2017.
[22] Darlington and McGurk 1995, 492–7; Lawson 1993, 138–9.
[23] *GRA*, 330–1; McDermott 2020, 349–51.
[24] Gillingham 2015.
[25] Luard 1865, 7–8.
[26] S 1274.

The chests claim to contain the body of King Cynegils (611–42), the first West Saxon king to be converted to Christianity. No place of burial is recorded for him in any early source. Bede records that the body of Birinus, the first bishop of the West Saxons who had baptised Cynegils, was moved by Bishop Haedde (676–705) from Dorchester-on-Thames, the site of the first West Saxon see where he had been buried, to Winchester.[27] Birinus subsequently became a significant saint of Old Minster, but neither Winchester nor Dorchester-on-Thames seem to have recorded any traditions relating to him and even the date of his death is unknown.[28] It could be supposed that Cynegils had also been buried at Dorchester and that his body was moved with that of Birinus to Winchester, but there is no evidence beyond the mortuary chest for the claim. There might be a greater expectation that his son Cenwalh (642–72) would have been buried in the Old Minster for it was in his reign that Old Minster had been founded.[29] The fifteenth-century Winchester chroniclers believed that he was buried in the western crypt (possibly beneath the high altar platform) and this would be an appropriate tribute to the founder of the original Saxon cathedral.[30] There may, however, have been some confusion between Cynegils and Cenwalh in medieval Winchester because a hybrid 'Cynewalh' appears in some of the later charters that claim grants of royal privileges from the seventh century.[31]

The *Winchester Annals* claimed that Æscwine (674–6) and Centwine (676–85) for whom no burial places are otherwise known were buried in Winchester. These two plus Æthelheard (726–40) are also recorded as buried in the cathedral in the fifteenth-century Winchester *Liber Historialis* (probably written by Thomas Rudborne), who cites lost *acta* of the Winchester bishops Henry Giffard and Henry of Blois.[32] There is no corroboration from pre-Conquest sources, but we do know that Centwine retired to a religious house that he had founded and so is perhaps more likely to have been buried there than in Winchester.[33] In the medieval cathedral there was the potential for confusion between rulers who were patrons and those who were actually buried within it. The early fourteenth-century screen in the cathedral was decorated with statuettes that an inscription declared were 'the bodies of saints [who] lie here buried in peace'.[34] In fact, as the surviving *tituli* show, the names are those of various kings of Wessex and England and bishops of Winchester. They include the names of many of those named on the mortuary chests, but also others such as Edward the Elder, Æthelstan, Æthelred Unræd and Edward the Confessor known to have been buried elsewhere.

---

[27] Bede, *HE*, 232–3.
[28] Love 1996, xlix–l, 1–48.
[29] *ASC* 642.
[30] Crook forthcoming.
[31] S 229; Rumble 2002, no. V, 106.
[32] Crook forthcoming.
[33] Lapidge and Rosier 1985, 47–8.
[34] Crook 1994, 183–7.

Excavations on the site of Old Minster by Martin Biddle and Birthe Kjølbye-Biddle provide additional information about its royal burials.[35] Two graves were excavated in the seventh-century nave. Grave 68 contained the fittings from an elaborate iron-bound coffin that had been broken apart when the body within it had apparently been removed. But the adjoining grave 67 retained its body, a young man, of perhaps 25–35 years,[36] buried with remains of a gold-fringed cloth and headdress and garter-tags of niello in Trewhiddle style.[37] The garter-tags imply a ninth-century date for this burial; the headdress could suggest royal status as does the prestigious location in the nave. The strongest putative candidate in the likely timeframe is King Æthelwulf's eldest son Æthelstan. When Æthelwulf succeeded Ecgbert as king of the West Saxons in 839, he made Æthelstan king of the recently acquired areas of the south-east, that is the provinces of Kent, the East Saxons, South Saxons and Surrey.[38] Æthelstan predeceased his father and so never became king of the main West Saxon kingdom, but is given the title of 'king' in the *Anglo-Saxon Chronicle* and in Kentish charters of his father which he attested.[39] Æthelstan's last recorded activity was a naval victory over a Viking fleet at Sandwich in 851.[40] The burial places of Æthelwulf's four other sons who ruled Wessex are recorded in the common text of the *Anglo-Saxon Chronicle* – Æthelbald (d. 860) and Æthelbert (d. 865) at Sherborne and Æthelred (d. 871) at Wimborne. Alfred (d. 899) was buried initially in Old Minster but moved (as discussed above) soon after to New Minster. Æthelstan is the only known ninth-century West Saxon ruler of the right sort of age from the West Saxon royal house whose place of burial is not otherwise recorded. So, while there can be no certainty over identity, grave 67 may be the oldest royal burial excavated *in situ* in a church in recent times, not just in Winchester, but in England as a whole.

Grave 68, which abuts 67 and was emptied out, could possibly have been that of Æthelwulf himself, but King Eadred (d. 955) is another possibility. The fill of the grave contained a penny of King Edmund (939–46) who was Eadred's brother and so could be interpreted as a possible grave-offering.[41] The removal of the occupant of grave 68, but not that of grave 67, provides possible corroboration for only certain burials being exhumed as part of the process which would eventually lead to reinterment in the mortuary chests, and would seem to imply that the names of the occupants of the graves were clearly recorded in some way.[42] No traces of possible earlier royal burials were found within Old Minster though burial outside the church may have begun soon after its foundation.[43] This is not conclusive evidence that kings of the

---

[35] Biddle 1965, 256–8; Biddle and Kjølbye-Biddle forthcoming.
[36] Dawson-Hobbis pers. comm.
[37] Wilson 1965; Crowfoot 1990, 468–72.
[38] *ASC* 839; Keynes 1993, 120–8.
[39] *ASC* 851; Keynes 1993, 124–6.
[40] *ASC* 851.
[41] Biddle and Kjølbye-Biddle forthcoming.
[42] For methods of identification of royal burials in Canterbury see below nn. 57 and 58.
[43] Kjølbye-Biddle 1992, 222–4.

seventh and eighth centuries were not buried within the church, as only part of the original Old Minster was excavated. The southern portion of the church, which may well have contained a porticus to match that located on the north side, could not be excavated because of its proximity to the modern cathedral. The royal burials at Canterbury were made in the southern porticus of Christchurch.[44] It is also possible that coffins could have stood on the stone floor of the east end without showing any discernible trace in excavations.

It is not certain what happened to the existing royal burials when Bishop Æthelwold began his replanning of the west end of the cathedral between 971 and 974. The promotion of the cult of St Swithun was an integral part of the rebuilding and an area outside the seventh-century Old Minster, where St Swithun had been buried originally, was enclosed and developed. Clustered around the now empty grave of Swithun, over which his main reliquary was placed, were a series of stone coffins. Did these contain the remains of some former kings (and/or bishops)? Four stone coffins were excavated, two with bodies *in situ* and two reused for later burials, and there was a robbed-out emplacement for a fifth coffin.[45] More coffins could have stood to the south which was not excavated because of its proximity to the cathedral. At some point in the early Norman period, probably after work had begun on the new cathedral in 1079–80, the area was turned into 'a memorial court' by laying down a covering of pink plaster between the coffins.[46] When the Old Minster was finally demolished in 1079–80, the court would have stood in the open air. It was possibly the 'unsuitable place' from which Henry of Blois had the remains of Saxon kings and bishops removed in 1148 and placed in lead sarcophagi – forerunners of the mortuary chests – inside the cathedral.[47] The most recent consideration suggests it is more likely that the remains of many of the Saxon kings and bishops had first been deposited in the cathedral crypt, and one account suggests that the bones of the individuals in this group had already been jumbled together.[48] The remains of Cnut and other family members had probably been removed directly to the east end of the cathedral from Old Minster. Martin Biddle and Birthe Kjølbye-Biddle have suggested the probable arrangement of their burials in the Norman presbytery which was constructed 1079–93, and suggested that this may have mirrored arrangements at the east end of the Old Minster from which they were transferred directly to the presbytery soon after its completion.[49]

The Choice of Royal Burial Places

The dead, it is said, do not bury themselves, but it would appear that many rulers had established long before their deaths where they wished to be buried and marked

---

[44] Bede, *HE*, 150–1; Welch 2007, 238–9.
[45] Crook 1994, 173–6.
[46] Biddle 1968, 278.
[47] Biddle and Kjølbye-Biddle 2016, 217–9.
[48] Crook 2011, 174–5; Crook forthcoming.
[49] Biddle and Kjølbye-Biddle 2016, 219–28.

their choices by conspicuous patronage in life, though some royal burials appear
to have been more *ad hoc*. Some royal bodies were moved some distance to ensure
burial in Winchester. Edward the Elder died in Farndon (Cheshire),[50] Eadred in Frome
(Somerset)[51] and Cnut in Shaftesbury (Dorset).[52] Other rulers – or those in charge of their
burials – seem to have been equally determined that they were to be buried elsewhere.
Whatever kings may have desired in their lifetimes, in death they were dependent on
family members or the clergy of particular foundations for what actually occurred. For
instance, though there are indications – particularly in the suggested transfer of the
body of Edmund Ironside – that Cnut had plans for a family mausoleum in Old Minster,[53]
it was his widow Queen Emma and Bishop Ælfsige II (a former royal chaplain) who
can be presumed to have overseen its development and the burial of Cnut and other
family members (Harthacnut and Earl Beorn, the nephew of Cnut). There are therefore
many different facets to be considered when seeking to understand why Winchester
was chosen, or not chosen, as a place of royal burial, and these could vary over time.

Before the ninth century bishoprics were not especially favoured as places of
Anglo-Saxon royal burial, either in Wessex or elsewhere (with the caveat that the
burial places of many Anglo-Saxon kings are not known). The only one of the Anglo-
Saxon kingdoms where there were regular royal burials in a cathedral see was Kent
where nearly all its major kings of the seventh and eighth centuries were buried
in Canterbury. However, they were not buried in the cathedral, but outside the city
walls in accordance with Roman custom which presumably influenced members of
the Gregorian mission.[54] Æthelbert (d. 616 or 618) and his Frankish wife Bertha were
buried in the south porticus, dedicated to St Martin, of the church of SS Peter and
Paul, founded by Augustine as his monastic church.[55] Æthelbert's son Eadbald (616×40)
subsequently founded a new church of St Mary,[56] in alignment with SS Peter and Paul's
east end, and in eleventh century Canterbury it was believed that all subsequent kings
of Kent were buried there.[57] Coffin-plates of this date identifying the original burials
survive.[58] Episcopal sites appear to have been only used occasionally for royal burial in
other Anglo-Saxon kingdoms, and in each instance for one recorded burial only. King
Saebbi of the East Saxons (d. 692×4) was buried in St Paul's, London,[59] King Ceolred of
Mercia at Lichfield[60] and the head of King Edwin of Deira in York.[61]

---

[50] *ASC* 924 BCD.
[51] *ASC* 955 A.
[52] *ASC* 1035.
[53] Biddle and Kjølbye-Biddle 2016.
[54] Welch 2007; Kelly 1997, 34–7.
[55] Bede, *HE*, 150–1.
[56] *Ibid.*, 156–7.
[57] Welch 2007, 238–9.
[58] Shaw 2018, 193–204 suggests that inscriptions from foundation stones and epitaphs from tombs were
    a major source of Bede's information on the Kentish royals and ecclesiastics buried in Canterbury.
[59] Bede, *HE*, 362–9.
[60] *ASC* 716.
[61] Bede, *HE*, 204–5.

In the seventh to ninth centuries, it seems to have been the norm for a wide range of sites to be used for royal burials with different branches of royal houses often having their own favoured minsters.[62] When the *Anglo-Saxon Chronicle* records, after an unsuccessful attack by the atheling Cyneheard on King Cynewulf in 786, that '[Cynewulf's] body is buried at Winchester and the atheling's at Axminster',[63] it may indicate the different ecclesiastical affiliations of these rival royal lines. In eighth and ninth century Mercia there was a vogue for burial in nunneries that had been founded by members of the royal house and which were run by royal women who could then be responsible for organising appropriate care and commemoration of their dead kinsmen.[64] Æthelbald (716–57) was buried at Repton,[65] Offa (757–96) at Bedeford (probably Bedford),[66] Coenwulf (796–821), probably, at Winchcombe,[67] and Wiglaf (827–40) at Repton.[68] The sites of only a few such nunneries that are known to have existed in Wessex are specifically named. Beorhtric (786–802), the son-in-law of Offa, was buried at Wareham, which was certainly a nunnery when Asser was writing at the end of the ninth century,[69] and Alfred's brother Æthelred (865–71) at Wimborne which had been founded by members of their family in the eighth century.[70] The only one of the tenth-century West Saxon kings to be buried in a nunnery was the murdered King Edward the Martyr (975–8) at Shaftesbury.[71] The circumstances of Edward's death and burial were highly unusual and politically sensitive. Shaftesbury, founded by King Alfred for his second daughter, had continuous close ties with the royal house and so could safely be entrusted with developing the cult of Edward.

Therefore, an issue that needs to be explained is why Winchester became such a key place for royal burial in the ninth century and after. In many ways it could be seen as a logical choice and, of course, had already been used for some royal burials. King Ecgbert greatly boosted the fortunes of Wessex when in 825 he had turned tables on the previously all-powerful Mercians and moved the former kingdoms of the south-east – Kent, Sussex, the East Saxons and Surrey – from Mercian to West Saxon control. Wessex was doubled in size and Winchester, a former Roman town and the premier bishopric, was conveniently placed as its central point.[72] At one level the use of Winchester for royal burial can be seen as a facet of the town's refurbishment in the

---

[62] Yorke 2013.

[63] *ASC* 757.

[64] Yorke 2003, 112–18; burial in royal nunneries can be found in several other kingdoms as well.

[65] *ASC* 757; Biddle and Kjølbye-Biddle 1985.

[66] Cubitt 1995, 225–6.

[67] Bassett 1985.

[68] Rollason 1981 and 1983, 5–9.

[69] Asser, ch. 49, 36–7 (trans. Keynes and Lapidge 1983, 82; see their notes at 245).

[70] *ASC* 718 and 871; the nunnery is said to have been founded by Cuthburh and Cwenburh sisters of King Ine and of Ingeld from whom the Ecgbertings claimed to be descended.

[71] Rollason 1983; Ridyard 1988, 154–75; Keen 1999. The late Anglo-Saxon nunneries were also used for the burial of other members of the royal house, including princes *e.g.* Edmund the son of King Edgar and Ælfthryth who was buried in Romsey in 972 (*ASC* G); Yorke 2003, 112–18.

[72] Yorke 1984.

ninth century. This has traditionally been associated with King Alfred as part of his wider campaign of burh-building during the Viking wars.[73] More recent reassessments suggest revival may have begun around the middle of the ninth century, during the episcopacy of Swithun (852–63) and in the reign of Alfred's father and elder brothers.[74] Swithun himself is credited with building the east gate over the river Itchen in 859 in a Latin poem of late eleventh-century date that was once inscribed upon the bridge itself.[75] The implication may be that the gate was needed because of increased traffic into the town. The West Saxon mint may have been transferred by this date from Hamwic to Winchester.[76] The coins are without a mint-signature so certainty is not possible, but it can be suggested that major raids on Hamwic in the 840s may have made a transfer of some functions and population to the more defensible site of Winchester an attractive option.[77] Recent excavations in the north-west quarter have also advanced the idea that parts of the town were being redeveloped around the middle of the ninth century.[78] A major Viking attack on Winchester during the reign of King Æthelbert (860–5) when great booty was taken seems to suggest that it rather than Hamwic was the place in southern Hampshire worth attacking by that date.[79]

But Winchester was far from being the only site chosen for royal burial between the ninth and eleventh centuries as Table 4.2 and Figure 4.1 show.[80] Of the nineteen kings who ruled between Æthelwulf and Edward the Confessor, eight were buried in Winchester (nine if one counts the probable transfer of remains of Edmund Ironside from Glastonbury). This is considerably more than at the next contenders, Glastonbury and London-Westminster, with three burials each, and Sherborne, the other major see of original Wessex, where two of Alfred's brothers were buried, but it is the case that over half the kings buried between 858–1066 were buried somewhere besides Winchester (actual numbers are complicated by transfer of the some bodies). There were potentially various factors at work when it came to the choice of a site for royal burial, and their interplay was not always the same. Who decided where a king was to be buried could be one variable. Edward the Elder was clearly committed at the start of his reign to establishing New Minster as a place of burial for himself and his

---

[73] Biddle and Hill 1971.

[74] Ford and Teague 2011; Biddle 2018, 6–9. However, Alfred's elder brothers were not buried in Winchester, and this can be connected with tensions between the areas east and west of Selwood that formed the bishoprics of Winchester and Sherborne respectively. This rivalry is considered further below, see also Yorke 1984.

[75] Lapidge 2003, 781–2.

[76] Dolley 1970; Naismith 2012, 128–33.

[77] Morton 1992, 70–7.

[78] Ford and Teague 2011.

[79] *ASC* 860; Asser chs 17–18.

[80] It is an obvious point, but all these sites of royal burial are either in Wessex or London-Westminster. Although eventually kings of all England, when it came to choosing burial places or placing female relatives in nunneries the kings of the later Anglo-Saxon period stuck to their West Saxon roots. This can be seen as one of the indications that there were limits to the unification of England within this period, Molyneaux 2015.

Table 4.2: Burial places of Anglo-Saxon Kings 858–1066 (OM: Old Minster; NM: New Minster).

King	Burial place
Æthelwulf d. 858	Steyning then Winchester OM
Æthelbald d. 860	Sherborne
Æthelbert d. 865	Sherborne
Æthelred d. 871	Wimborne
Alfred d. 899	Winchester OM, then NM
Edward d. 924	Winchester NM
Ælfweard d. 924	Winchester NM
Æthelstan d. 939	Malmesbury
Edmund d. 946	Glastonbury
Eadred d. 955	Winchester OM
Eadwig d. 959	Winchester NM
Edgar d. 978	Glastonbury
Edward d. 978	Wareham, then Shaftesbury
Æthelred d. 1016	St Paul's, London
Edmund Ironside d. 1016	Glastonbury, then Winchester OM?
Cnut d. 1035	Winchester OM
Harald Harefoot d. 1040	Westminster, then St Clements, London
Harthacnut d. 1042	Winchester OM
Edward d. 1066	Westminster

family. His son Æthelstan made an equally decisive choice of Malmesbury where not only he was buried, but also his two cousins who died at the battle of Brunanburh.[81] Generous patronage of these foundations underscored their choices.[82]

In some other instances the identification of who made the choice of burial-place can be uncertain. According to the *Annals of St Neots* Æthelwulf was buried in Steyning (Sussex),[83] but the *Anglo-Saxon Chronicle* record of his death refers to him as buried in Winchester.[84] Presumably his body was transferred from Steyning to Winchester, but we do not know when, which of his sons organised it or whether it was what Æthelwulf had himself intended.[85] Unlike Edward the Elder and Æthelstan, not all kings necessarily

[81] *GRA*, 220–1; Foot 2011, 186–8.
[82] Miller 2001, lv–vi, nos. 2–8; Kelly 2005, 103, nos. 25–8 (though these charters are problematic); Foot 2011, 186–8.
[83] Dumville and Lapidge 1985, 51; Gardiner 1993. For further explanation of how Æthelwulf came to be buried in Steyning in the context of the rebellion against him by his son Æthelbald see below.
[84] *ASC* 855.
[85] Though see above for S 1274, a lease from Bishop Swithun to King Æthelbald, which could imply that both the bodies of Ecgbert and Æthelwulf were under the bishop's care in Winchester, and so that it

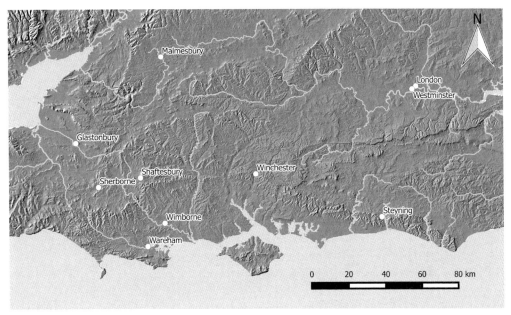

Fig. 4.1: Burial places of Anglo-Saxon kings, 858–1066. Topographical map data from Copernicus Land Monitoring Service of the European Environment Agency: European Union Digital Elevation Model (EU-DEM), <https://land.copernicus.eu>; rivers and boundary data from Ordnance Survey (© Crown copyright and database right, 2018).

committed themselves from an early stage in their reign to a particular place of burial. In his will King Eadred (946–55) left gifts and money to the place where he wished to be buried but does not identify it.[86] The will then refers to three estates granted to Old Minster (where Eadred was subsequently buried), but with no indication that it was his own choice of burial-place. The grants of land in the will never seem to have reached the intended recipients and it is thought likely that Eadred's nephew and successor Eadwig revoked the will. Perhaps it was also Eadwig, in conjunction with Bishop Ælfsige I of Winchester (951–59) who was a significant figure at his court, who decided that Eadred was to be buried in Old Minster.[87] The burial of Æthelred Unræd in St Paul's, London is likely to have been dictated by the circumstances of his death in London while defending his kingdom against Cnut.[88] His eldest son Æthelstan who died shortly before him makes clear in his will his intention to be buried in Old Minster, Winchester,[89] and that may have been Æthelred's intention as well before he was overtaken by events.

---

was shortly after his death in 858, but within the reign of Æthelbald, that Æthelwulf was moved to Winchester (*i.e.* between 858 and 860).

[86] Miller 2001, no. 17, 76–81.
[87] Marafioti 2014, 68–71.
[88] Keynes 2012; Marafioti 2014, 84–96.
[89] Whitelock 1930, no. 20, 56–63, 167–74.

Kings it would appear could move bodies of their predecessors if they so desired, just as they could translate the remains of saints; in both cases the aims can be seen as broadly political.[90] An extreme example was when Harthacnut had the body of his predecessor Harald Harefoot dug up from Westminster and thrown into a fen.[91] The probable transfer of all or part of the body of Edmund Ironside from Glastonbury to Old Minster by Cnut was more benign, but was also self-serving in the way it was used to suggest that Cnut and his heirs were the natural successors of the West Saxon kings.[92] The Normans in their turn stressed their links with Cnut's family by transferring their burials from the Old Minster to the cathedral presbytery and through associated burials of some members of their own family.[93] Reburial of the remains of Edward the Martyr, who had been buried without due respect after his murder, was a necessary requisite for the reconciliation of rival factions and acceptance of the rule of his brother Æthelred.[94] Possession and allocation of the body of a dead king could in certain circumstances be an overt political statement. After King Alfred died in 899 his nephew Æthelwold made a bid for the throne and one of the places he seized was Wimborne where his father King Æthelred was buried.[95] Æthelwold was forced to flee, but while he still remained at large and a threat, the successful King Edward founded New Minster which could be seen as a counter demonstration that a new line had been founded claiming descent from Alfred not Æthelred. The rivalry of Æthelwold and Edward shows, as Nicola Marafioti in particular has argued, how royal burial and succession politics could be linked,[96] though unlike Westminster Abbey later, neither Winchester (with the exception of the coronation of Edward the Confessor), nor any other favoured site for tenth- or eleventh-century royal burials, became a place of royal inauguration as well as of royal burial.[97]

Burial and Regional and Factional Politics

Many of the places where kings were buried can be seen as regional centres of active political factions, and Winchester can certainly, at times, be interpreted in this way. An example which has received much discussion is the support in Winchester for Edward the Elder's sons by his second wife Ælfflaed. When Edward died in 924 Æthelstan, his eldest son from his first marriage, was declared king in Mercia, but Wessex supported Ælfweard, Edward's elder son by Ælfflaed. In the event, Ælfweard died a few weeks after

---

[90] Rollason 1986; Marafioti 2015, 205–9 for a possible instance of sanctuary claimed at the tomb of King Alfred.

[91] *ASC* CD 1040; Darlington and McGurk 1995, 528–31; Marafioti 2014, 125–60; the body was subsequently reburied in a Danish cemetery in London, possibly St Clement Danes.

[92] Biddle and Kjølbye-Biddle 2016, 224–6.

[93] Bates 2020, 529–30.

[94] Ridyard 1988, 154–71; Keen 1999; Marafioti 2014, 161–91.

[95] Lavelle 2009; Marafioti 2015, 209–12.

[96] Marafioti 2014.

[97] Palliser 2004.

his father but Æthelstan was not fully accepted as king of Wessex until the following year.[98] There are suggestions of a plot against Æthelstan being planned in Winchester and Ælfweard's brother Edwin seems to have lived under the protection of Winchester clergy. In this instance we can probably assume that Æthelstan's opponents included the bishop and clergy of Winchester and the family of Ælfflæd whose father had been ealdorman of Wiltshire, the most significant ealdormanry in the Winchester diocese. Small wonder that Æthelstan preferred to choose a different location for his own burial at Malmesbury in a region with which his own maternal family may have been connected.[99]

Regional divisions and regional leaders, including the bishops, can also be seen as playing key roles in the ninth-century politics that may lie behind varying use of Winchester and Sherborne as royal burial places. The division between the two dioceses, east and west of Selwood, was an ancient one that was still significant in ninth-century Wessex.[100] Asser had heard that when the return of King Æthelwulf was opposed by his son Æthelbald, who had been ruling the country in his absence, it was the bishop of Sherborne and the ealdorman of Somerset, the two major powers west of Selwood, who were behind it.[101] Æthelwulf was forced to accept a demotion and rule only in the recently acquired south-eastern areas (which presumably explains why he was buried originally in Steyning). Possibly the favour shown to Winchester and its bishop Swithun had fed resentment in the Sherborne diocese.[102] The choice of Sherborne for the burials of Æthelbald and his brother Æthelbert, and possibly that of Wimborne for the burial of Æthelred, while other members of the family were buried in Winchester, can be seen as a reflection of this political rivalry within the two dioceses.

A third distinctive region – though not a bishopric – was composed of the northern parts of Wiltshire and Somerset, home to two additional religious houses that were used for royal burial in the tenth century, Malmesbury and Glastonbury. This was an area that had long been disputed between Wessex and Mercia and these houses had been able to draw on patrons from both kingdoms.[103] It had been under Mercian control in the reign of Offa (757–96), perhaps administered as part of the ealdormanry of the Hwicce, as in 802 the ealdorman of the Hwicce faced the ealdorman of Wiltshire in battle at Kempsford (on the Wiltshire/Gloucestershire border) for control of the region.[104] Both ealdormen were killed, but the Wilsaetan were victorious, paving the way for the area's incorporation into Wessex as part of the shires of Wiltshire and Somerset.[105] The victory was also presumably associated with the succession of King Alfred's grandfather Ecgbert and the death of Offa's son-in-law Beorhtric in the same year.

---

[98] Yorke 1984; Foot 2011, 37–43; Marafioti 2014, 54–65.
[99] For this see further discussion and references below.
[100] Yorke 1995, 22–4; *ASC* 893.
[101] Asser, ch. 12, 9–10; Keynes and Lapidge 1983, 70.
[102] Yorke 1984.
[103] Yorke 1995, 61–4; Kelly 2012, 26–37.
[104] *ASC* 802; Hare 2012.
[105] Draper 2006, 56–74.

It would appear likely that the family of King Æthelstan's mother Ecgwynn, the first wife of King Edward the Elder, came from this region and was related to the family of Dunstan, abbot of Glastonbury and, eventually, archbishop of Canterbury.[106] The information can be inferred from B's *Life of St Dunstan* which refers to a widow Æthelflaed, who lived at Glastonbury and was niece (*neptis*) of King Athelstan and related to Dunstan.[107] To fit the timescale Æthelflaed must have been the daughter of Æthelstan's full sister (and even then the chronology is tight and Æthelflaed would have been a young widow). The only way Æthelflaed could be niece (or possibly some other relation) of Æthelstan and related to Dunstan was if Æthelstan's mother was related to Dunstan's family as Dunstan is not said to have been related to any other members of the royal house. The marriage of Edward and Ecgwynn took place towards the end of his father's reign,[108] and could be seen as linked to his policy of bringing the western Mercian province of the Hwicce (the diocese of Worcester) into closer alignment with Wessex.[109] The leading families of both regions are likely to have developed links when northern Wessex was ruled from Mercia (for instance, Dunstan is also said to have been related to Bishop Cynesige of Lichfield).[110] It is part of the background that explains why the succession of Æthelstan was supported in Mercia, while Wessex (and more specifically, the Winchester diocese) supported the sons of Edward's second marriage to the daughter of an ealdorman of Wiltshire.[111] It is also part of the background that explains why Malmesbury and Glastonbury became places of royal burial in the tenth century.

Æthelstan was buried in Malmesbury, a foundation of the royal saint Aldhelm who had been the first bishop of Sherborne,[112] and apparently the subject of some devotion from Æthelwulf and Alfred, as well as Æthelstan himself.[113] It was thus a place with impeccable West Saxon credentials, but one that had sometimes been controlled by Mercian kings and so an appropriate choice for the burial of Æthelstan – a member of the West Saxon royal house, but with strong Mercian connections that seem to have been crucial for his succession as king.[114] Æthelstan's half-brother and successor Edmund was buried in Glastonbury after his unexpected death at Pucklechurch (Gloucestershire) in 946.[115] Was it Edmund's intention to have been buried at Glastonbury? He was a generous patron of Glastonbury and had appointed Dunstan as abbot,[116] but he was also a donor of land to New Minster, Winchester, and, according to its *Liber Vitae* had commissioned new work

---

[106] Yorke 1988, 67–70.
[107] *Lives*, 32–41.
[108] Yorke 2001; Foot 2011, 28–34.
[109] Keynes 1998; Yorke 2019.
[110] *Lives*, 68–9.
[111] Yorke 1988; Foot 2011, 37–40.
[112] Barker and Brooks 2010.
[113] Kelly 2005, 13–22.
[114] Foot 2011, 34–9; Marafioti 2014, 56–64.
[115] Halloran 2015.
[116] Kelly 2012, 56–61, nos. 27–37.

on its church before his untimely death.[117] These works have been identified with a major extension to the east end found in Martin Biddle's excavations which could have been an appropriate place for further royal burials.[118] The earliest *Vita* of Dunstan does not claim it was Edmund's intention to have been buried at Glastonbury, but rather implies that the decision was the initiative of Dunstan who was present at Pucklechurch when Edmund was killed.[119] Whatever the circumstances, Edmund's burial at Glastonbury paved the way for the burial there of his son King Edgar and ultimately for Edgar's grandson Edmund Ironside.[120] Like the oscillation between Sherborne and Winchester in the ninth century, royal burial fluctuated between Winchester and Glastonbury in the tenth century. It seems to have reflected the rivalry between two prominent ecclesiastics, Dunstan and Bishop Æthelwold of Winchester and the different factions of which they were prominent members which may have had origins in regional rivalries with deeper roots.[121] Æthelwold's impressively rebuilt Old Minster, in which the bodies of earlier West Saxon kings as well as St Swithun were honoured and displayed, had to wait until plans were put in train for a mausoleum for the family of Cnut and Emma before receiving further royal burials.[122] It seems reasonable to suggest that Bishop Æthelwold and his immediate successors had not anticipated that there would have been such a hiatus.

Conclusion

Seen in an early medieval European context Winchester can be interpreted as unusually prominent as a place of royal burial between the ninth and eleventh centuries. In Francia and Ottonian Germany the complex and divided political arrangements mitigated against any one place achieving such dominance, though locations might be reused especially if there were political reasons for emphasising connections with particular individuals.[123] Many of the places selected – such as St Denis, Aachen, Rheims and Metz – had significant Roman backgrounds and associations with key events or saints. The selection of Winchester in the ninth century by the Ecgbertings can be seen as part of this broader European trend. For incoming Danish and Norman dynasties the need to demonstrate continuity with the West Saxon dynasty must have been a significant factor in continuing use of Winchester as a site of royal burial. The pull of particular places was offset by the desire of individual rulers to ensure that their

---

[117] Birch 1892, 6–7.

[118] Biddle and Kjølbye-Biddle forthcoming; Biddle pers. comm.

[119] *Lives*, 60–1; 92–5; Marafioti 2014, 65–77; Halloran 2015.

[120] McDermott 2020, 349–51.

[121] There is not room to discuss how these tensions may have operated in favour of Glastonbury becoming the place of Edgar's burial rather than Winchester but suffice it to say that when the kingdom was divided between Eadwig and his brother Edgar, Dunstan who had been exiled from Eadwig's court was received at Edgar's. Although as a boy Edgar had been at Abingdon with Æthelwold that did not mean that there was a rapport between them, perhaps rather the contrary. See further discussions in Yorke 1988 and Scragg 2008.

[122] Biddle 1975 and 2018.

[123] Nelson 2000; Rollason 2016, 344–86.

souls were expertly looked after in churches that they had founded or of which they were major patrons,[124] and this factor helps account for the wide choice of places by the later Carolingian and Ottonians, such as Lorsch, Regensberg, Magdeburg and Bamberg. Edward the Elder's foundation of New Minster both continued his family's established links with Winchester and emphasised the new dynasty in which descendants of King Alfred ousted claims of heirs of other family members. Sherborne, Malmesbury and Glastonbury may have had the appeal of new places of patronage, but their selection, like that of their European counterparts, can also be linked with regional politics and affiliations. These factors help explain why Winchester failed to achieve the dominance that Westminster did for the Plantagenets in a period when the rules of succession had become more rigid and government more centralised.[125] Royal government never became fixed in one location in Anglo-Saxon England, and in the ninth and tenth centuries kings needed to balance the interests of regionally based elites within Wessex, especially its bishops and ealdormanic families, in order to rule successfully. It is this final factor that helps explain why Winchester, although the prime site of royal burial in later Anglo-Saxon England, failed to achieve complete dominance and was not selected by all its rulers as their last resting-place.

Acknowledgements

I would like to thank fellow members of the Winchester Cathedral Mortuary Chest project, especially Martin Biddle, John Crook, Kate Robson-Brown and Heidi Dawson-Hobbis for discussing evidence and sharing unpublished material with me. Ryan Lavelle and an anonymous reviewer made many helpful suggestions, and Ryan kindly produced the map for me.

Abbreviations

ASC   *Anglo-Saxon Chronicle*. Plummer, C. (ed.) 1889. *Two of the Saxon Chronicles Parallel (787–1001 A.D.): with Supplementary Extracts from the Others: A Revised Text*. Oxford: Clarendon Press.

Asser   Stevenson, W. H. (ed.) 1904. *Asser's Life of King Alfred, together with the Annals of St Neots erroneously ascribed to Asser*. Oxford: Clarendon Press.

Bede, *HE*   Colgrave, B. and Mynors, R. A. B. (ed. and trans.) 1969. *Bede's Ecclesiastical History of the English People*. Oxford: Clarendon Press.

GRA   Mynors, R. A. B., Thomson, R. M. and Winterbottom, M. (ed. and trans.) 1998, *William of Malmesbury, Gesta Regum Anglorum, the History of the English Kings*, Volume I. Oxford: Clarendon Press.

---

[124] The financial advantages that bishops and abbots might derive from a royal burial in one of their ecclesiastical foundations should not be overlooked when considering how royal burials came about (*e.g.* Dunstan's intervention for Glastonbury discussed above).

[125] Palliser 2004.

Lives   Winterbottom, M. and Lapidge, M. (ed. and trans.) 2012. *The Early Lives of St Dunstan*. Oxford: Clarendon Press.
S   Sawyer, P. H. 1968. *Anglo-Saxon Charters. An Annotated List and Bibliography.* Guides and Handbooks 8. London: Royal Historical Society.

Bibliography

Primary Sources
Birch, W. de G (ed.) 1892. *Liber Vitae: Register and Martyrology of New Minster and Hyde Abbey Winchester.* Winchester: Warren and Son.
Chibnall, M. (ed. and trans.) 1972. *The Ecclesiastical History of Orderic Vitalis*, Volume III (Books V and VI). Oxford: Clarendon Press.
Darlington, R. R. and McGurk, P. (ed. and trans.) 1995. *The Chronicle of John of Worcester. Volume II.* Oxford: Clarendon Press.
Dumville, D. N. and Lapidge, M. (eds) 1985. *The Anglo-Saxon Chronicle. A Collaborative Edition: 17, The Annals of St Neots with Vita Prima Sancti Neoti.* Cambridge: D. S. Brewer.
Kelly, S. (ed.) 2005. *Charters of Malmesbury Abbey*, Anglo-Saxon Charters 11. London: British Academy, Oxford University Press.
Kelly, S. (ed.) 2012. *Charters of Glastonbury Abbey*, Anglo-Saxon Charters 15. London: British Academy, Oxford University Press.
Keynes, S. and Lapidge, M. (trans.) 1983. *Alfred the Great. Asser's Life of King Alfred and Other Contemporary Sources.* Harmondsworth: Penguin Books.
Lapidge, M. 2003. *The Cult of St Swithun*, Winchester Studies 4ii. Oxford: Clarendon Press.
Lapidge, M. and Rosier, J. L. (trans.) 1985. *Aldhelm: The Poetic Works.* Cambridge: D. S. Brewer.
Love, R. C. (ed. and trans.) 1996. *Three Eleventh-Century Anglo-Latin Saints' Lives: Vita S. Birini, Vita et Miracula S. Kenelmi and Vita S. Rumwoldi.* Oxford: Clarendon Press.
Luard, H. R. (ed.) 1865. *Annales Monasterii de Wintonia.* London: RS.
Miller, S. (ed.) 2001. *Charters of New Minster, Winchester*, Anglo-Saxon Charters 9. London: British Academy, Oxford University Press.
Van Houts, E. (ed. and trans.) 1995. *Gesta Normannorum Ducum of William of Jumièges, Orderic Vitalis, and Robert of Torigni*, 2 vols. Oxford: Clarendon Press.
Whitelock, D. (ed. and trans.) 1930. *Anglo-Saxon Wills.* Cambridge: Cambridge University Press.

Secondary Sources
Aird, W. M. 2008. *Robert Curthose, Duke of Normandy c. 1050-1134.* Woodbridge: Boydell Press.
Barker, K. and Brooks, N. 2010. *Aldhelm and Sherborne: Essays to Celebrate the Founding of the Bishopric.* Oxford: Oxbow Books.
Barlow, F. 1983. *William Rufus.* London: Methuen.
Bates, D. 2020. William the Conqueror and Wessex, in A. Langlands and R. Lavelle (eds), *The Land of the English Kin: Studies in Wessex and England in Honour of Professor Barbara Yorke*, 517–37. Leiden and Boston: Brill.
Bassett, S. 1985. A Probable Royal Mausoleum at Winchcombe, Gloucestershire, *Antiquaries Journal*, 65, 82–100.
Biddle. M. 1965. Excavations in Winchester, Third Interim Report, *Antiquaries Journal*, 45, 230–64.
Biddle, M. 1968. Excavations in Winchester, Sixth Interim Report, *Antiquaries Journal*, 48, 250–84.
Biddle, M. 1975. *Felix Urbs Winthonia*: Winchester in the Age of Monastic Reform, in D. Parsons (ed.), *Tenth-Century Studies. Essays in Commemoration of the Millennium of the Council of Winchester and Regularis Concordia*, 123–40. Chichester: Phillimore.

Biddle, M. 1993. Early Renaissance at Winchester, in J. Crook (ed.), *Winchester Cathedral. Nine Hundred Years 1093-1993*, 257–304. Chichester: Phillimore.

Biddle, M. 2018. *The Search for Winchester's Anglo-Saxon Minsters*. Oxford: Archaeopress and the Winchester Excavations Committee.

Biddle, M. and Hill, D. 1971. Anglo-Saxon Planned Towns, *Antiquaries Journal*, 51, 70–85.

Biddle, M. and Kjølbye-Biddle, B. 1985. The Repton Stone, *Anglo-Saxon England*, 14, 233–92.

Biddle, M. and Kjølbye-Biddle, B. 2016. Danish royal burials in Winchester: Cnut and his Family, in R. Lavelle and S. Roffey (eds), *Danes in Wessex: The Scandinavian Impact on Southern England, c.800 – c.1100*, 212–49. Oxford: Oxbow Books.

Biddle, M. and Kjølbye-Biddle, B. forthcoming. *The Anglo-Saxon Minsters of Winchester*, Winchester Studies 4.i. Oxford: Archaeopress.

Crook, J. 1994. 'A Worthy Antiquity': The Movement of King Cnut's Bones in Winchester Cathedral, in A. Rumble (ed.), *The Reign of Cnut. King of England, Denmark and Norway*, 165–92. London: Leicester University Press.

Crook, J. 2011. *English Medieval Shrines*. Woodbridge: Boydell Press.

Crook, J. forthcoming. The Royal and Episcopal burials in Winchester Cathedral, *Antiquaries Journal*, 102.

Crowfoot, E. 1990. Textiles, in M. Biddle (ed.), *Object and Economy in Medieval Winchester*, Winchester Studies 7.ii, 467–88. Oxford: Clarendon Press.

Cubitt, C. 1995. *Anglo-Saxon Church Councils c. 650-c.850*. London: Leicester University Press.

Dolley, R. H. M. 1970. The location of the pre-Ælfredian mints of Wessex, *Proceedings of the Hampshire Field Club and Archaeological Society*, 27, 57–61.

Draper, S. 2006. *Landscape, Settlement and Society in Roman and Early Medieval Wiltshire*, BAR British Series 419. Oxford: BAR Publishing.

Foot, S. 2011. *Æthelstan. The First King of England*. New Haven and London: Yale University Press.

Ford, B. and Teague, S. 2011. *Winchester - A City in the Making. Archaeological Excavations between 2002 and 2007 on the sites of Northgate House, Staple Gardens and the former Winchester Library, Jewry Street*, Monograph 12. Oxford: Oxford Archaeology.

Gardiner, M. 1993. The Excavation of a Late Anglo-Saxon Settlement at Market Field, Steyning, 1988–9, *Sussex Archaeological Collections*, 131, 21–67.

Gillingham, J. 2015. Richard of Devizes and 'A Rising Tide of Nonsense'. How Cerdic met King Arthur, in M. Brett and D. A. Woodman (eds), *The Long Twelfth-Century View of the Anglo-Saxon Past*, 141–56. Aldershot: Ashgate.

Halloran, K. 2015. A Murder at Pucklechurch: The Death of King Edmund, 26 May 946, *Midland History*, 40, 120–9.

Hare, M. 2012. Deerhurst's earliest patrons; Æthelmund and Æthelric, *Transactions of the Bristol and Gloucestershire Archaeological Society*, 130, 151–82.

Keen, L. (ed.) 1999. *Studies in the Early History of Shaftesbury Abbey*. Dorchester: Dorset County Council.

Kelly, S. 1997. The Anglo-Saxon Abbey, in R. Gem (ed.), *English Heritage Book of St Augustine's Abbey Canterbury*, 33–49. London: Batsford.

Keynes, S. 1993. The Control of Kent in the Ninth Century, *Early Medieval Europe*, 2, 111–32.

Keynes, S. (ed.) 1995. *The Liber Vitae of the New Minster and Hyde Abbey, Winchester*. Copenhagen: Rosenkilde and Bagger.

Keynes, S. 1998. King Alfred and the Mercians, in M. A. S. Blackburn and D. N. Dumville (eds), *Kings, Currency and Alliances: History and Coinage of Southern England in the Ninth Century*, 1–46. Woodbridge: Boydell Press.

Keynes, S. 2012. The Burial of King Æthelred the Unready at St Paul's, in D. Roffe (ed.), *The English and Their Legacy 900-1200. Essays in Honour of Ann Williams*, 129–48. Woodbridge: Boydell Press.

Kjølbye-Biddle, B. 1992. Dispersal or concentration: the disposal of the Winchester dead over 2000 years, in S. Bassett (ed.), *Death in Towns: Urban Responses to the Dying and the Dead, 100-1600*, 210-47. Leicester: Leicester University Press.

Lavelle, R. 2009. The Politics of Rebellion: the Ætheling Æthelwold and West Saxon Royal Succession, 899–902, in P. Skinner (ed.), *Challenging the Boundaries of Medieval History: The Legacy of Timothy Reuter*, 51–80. Turnhout: Brepols.

Lawson, M. K. 1993. *Cnut: The Danes in England in the Early Eleventh Century*. London and New York: Longman.

Marafioti, N. 2014. *The King's Body: Burial and Succession in Late Anglo-Saxon England*. Toronto: Toronto University Press.

Marafioti, N. 2015. Seeking Alfred's Body: Royal Tomb as Political Object in the Reign of Edward the Elder, *Early Medieval Europe*, 23, 2015, 202–28.

McDermott, D. 2020. Wessex and the Reign of Edmund II Ironside, in A. Langlands and R. Lavelle (eds), *The Lands of the English Kin: Studies in Wessex and England in Honour of Professor Barbara Yorke*, 336–51. Leiden and Boston: Brill.

Morton, A. D. (ed.) 1992. *Excavations at Hamwic: Volume I*, Council for British Archaeology Research Report 84. London: CBA.

Molyneaux, G. 2015. *The Formation of the English Kingdom in the Tenth Century*. Oxford: Oxford University Press.

Nelson, J. 2000. Carolingian Royal Funerals, in F. Theuws and J. Nelson (eds), *Rituals of Power from Late Antiquity to the Early Middle Ages*, 131–84. Leiden: Brill.

Naismith, R. 2012. *Money and Power in Anglo-Saxon England: The Southern English Kingdoms, 757-865*. Cambridge: Cambridge University Press.

Palliser, D. M. 2004. Royal mausolea in the long fourteenth century (1272–1422), in W. M. Ormrod (ed.), *Fourteenth-Century England* 3, 1–15. Woodbridge: Boydell Press.

Qualmann, K., Scobie, G and Zant, J. 2021. *Excavations at Hyde Abbey, Winchester 1972-1999*. Winchester: Hampshire Cultural Trust.

Ridyard, S. 1988. *The Royal Saints of Anglo-Saxon England: A Study of West Saxon and East Anglian Cults*. Cambridge: Cambridge University Press.

Rollason, D. W. 1981. *The Search for St Wigstan, Prince-Martyr of the Kingdom of Mercia*, Vaughan Paper no. 27. Leicester: Department of Adult Education, University of Leicester.

Rollason, D. W. 1983. The Cults of Murdered Royal Saints in Anglo-Saxon England, *Anglo Saxon England*, 11, 1–22.

Rollason, D. W. 1986. Relic-cults as an Instrument of Royal Policy, c.900–c.1050, *Anglo-Saxon England*, 15, 91–103.

Rollason, D. W. 2016. *The Power of Place: Rulers and their Palaces, Landscapes, Cities, and Holy Places*. Princeton and Woodstock: Princeton University Press.

Rumble, A. 2002. *Property and Piety in Early Medieval Winchester: Documents Relating to the Topography of the Anglo-Saxon and Norman City and its Minsters*, Winchester Studies 4.iii. Oxford: Clarendon Press.

Scragg, D. (ed.) 2008. *Edgar, King of the English, 959-75, New Interpretations*. Woodbridge: Boydell Press.

Shaw, R. 2018. *The Gregorian Mission to Kent in Bede's Ecclesiastical History: Methodology and Sources*. London and New York: Routledge

Townend, M. 2017. *The Road to Deerhurst: 1016 in English and Norse Sources*, Deerhurst Lecture 2016. Kings Stanley: Friends of Deerhurst Church.

Tucker, K. 2014. The Unmarked Grave and the Search for Alfred, in E. Albert and K. Tucker, *In Search of Alfred the Great: The King. The Grave. The Legend*, 219–28. Stroud: Amberley.

Welch, M. 2007. Anglo-Saxon Kent, in J. H. Williams (ed.), *The Archaeology of Kent to AD 800*, 187–250. Woodbridge: Boydell Press for Kent County Council.

Wilson, D. 1965. Late Saxon Metalwork from the Old Minster 1964, in M. Biddle, Excavations in Winchester, Third Interim Report, *Antiquaries Journal*, 45, 230–64, 262–4.

Yorke, B. A. E. 1984. The Bishops of Winchester, the Kings of Wessex and the Development of Winchester in the Ninth and Early Tenth Centuries, *Proceedings of the Hampshire Field Club and Archaeological Society*, 40, 61–70.

Yorke, B. A. E. 1988. Æthelwold and the Politics of the Tenth Century, in B. A. E. Yorke (ed.), *Bishop Æthelwold: His Career and Influence*, 65–88. Woodbridge: Boydell Press.

Yorke, B. A. E. 1995. *Wessex in the Early Middle Ages*. London: Leicester University Press.

Yorke, B. A. E. 2001. Edward as Ætheling, in N. Higham and D. Hill (eds), *Edward the Elder 899-924*, 25–39. London and New York: Routledge.

Yorke, B. A. E. 2003. *Nunneries and the Anglo-Saxon Royal Houses*. London: Continuum.

Yorke, B. A. E. 2013. The Burial of Kings in Anglo-Saxon England, in G. R. Owen-Crocker and B. W. Schneider (eds), *Kingship, Legislation and Power in Anglo-Saxon England*, 237–58. Woodbridge: Boydell Press.

Yorke, B. A. E. 2019. *Æthelred, Lord of the Mercians and his Deerhurst Connections*, Deerhurst Lecture 2019. Kings Stanley: Friends of Deerhurst Church.

Chapter 5

Constructing Early Medieval Winchester: Historical Narratives and the Compilation of British Library, Cotton MS Otho B.XI

Sharon M. Rowley

This chapter reconsiders the compilation of British Library MS Cotton Otho B.XI in light of recent developments in codicological theory and from the perspective of Winchester as a place where the manuscript was being copied, added to or otherwise altered. The first phase of copying took place in the middle of the tenth century, when the Otho copy of the Old English version of Bede's Historia Ecclesiastica *was made; the second phase took place at the beginning of the eleventh century, between 1001–12, when additional materials were added to Otho from Cambridge, Corpus Christi College MS 173. These stages correspond to the reigns of Edmund I (939–46), Eadred (946–55), Eadwig (955–9) and Æthelred (978–1016). By looking closely at the contents and differences between the two manuscripts as they changed over time, it is argued that the scribes who expanded Otho did not, as Patrick Wormald suggested, 'wide[n] the scope of the Corpus 173 argument'; rather, the scribes of Otho created an entirely new composite book that provides both a record of and a resource for Christian kingship. In it, the compilers brought together a range of texts that explore the relationship between the king, his bishops and his people; the nation and its boroughs; the part and the whole.*

'Places gather', while manuscripts 'do not stand still but develop'; both can be 'construed as dynamic, lived experience' and studied as 'window[s] onto human activity.'[1] Exploring the idea of Winchester as a place, along with medieval manuscripts as dynamic 'processes',[2] establishes a new perspective from which to examine accounts of Winchester as a royal city in the Old English version of Bede's *Historia Ecclesiastica* (OEHE), the *Anglo-Saxon Chronicle* (ASC) and in the texts associated with them in

---

[1] My opening is a pastiche, combining theories of place with theories about manuscripts by Edward Casey, quoted in Lees and Overing 2006, 5 and 1, and Gumbert 2004, 21.

[2] Johnston and Van Dussen 2015, 4.

British Library, Cotton MS Otho B.XI (hereafter, Otho).[3] More specifically, this essay reconsiders the compilation of Otho in light of recent developments in codicological theory and from the perspective of Winchester as a place where the manuscript was being copied, added to or otherwise altered. The first phase of copying takes place in the middle of the tenth century, when the Otho copy of the OEHE was made; the second phase takes place at the beginning of the eleventh century, between 1001–12, when additional materials were added to Otho from Cambridge, Corpus Christi College MS 173 (hereafter, Corpus; see Appendix).[4] These stages correspond to the reigns of Edmund I (939–46), Eadred (946–55), Eadwig (955–9) and Æthelred (978–1016). By looking closely at the contents and differences between the two manuscripts as they changed over time, I argue that the scribes who expanded Otho did not, as Patrick Wormald suggested, 'wide[n] the scope of the Corpus 173 argument';[5] rather, the scribes of Otho created an entirely new composite book that provides both a record and a resource for Christian kingship. In it, they bring together a range of texts that explore the relationship between the king, his bishops and his people; the nation and its boroughs; the part and the whole. After an introduction to the contents and study of these manuscripts as composite manuscripts, this chapter looks at the ways in which the OEHE in Otho represents Winchester and the house of Wessex in the mid-tenth century, with special focus on the reigns of Edmund I and Eadred. It then reexamines the early eleventh-century additions in the context of Æthelred's rule and recent studies of his 'politics of penance',[6] to argue that Otho was a living book that served practical purposes during the troubled reigns of some of the less well-known kings of Wessex.

Otho and Corpus as Composite Manuscripts

Both Otho and Corpus have been studied in depth.[7] They have also long been studied together; firstly, because the scribe who wrote the annals for *924–55 (except 951) on folios 26r–27v in Corpus also copied most the OEHE in Otho; and secondly, because the ASC, the lists of popes and bishops, and some of the Laws were copied from Corpus into Otho in the early eleventh century.[8] However, scholars disagree as to whether paleographical and codicological findings should be brought to bear on the interpretation of the texts collected in them. According to James Simpson,

---

[3] London, British Library, Cotton MS Otho B.XI (Winchester, s. xmed–s. xi1).
[4] Cambridge, Corpus Christi College MS 173 (Winchester, s. ix/x–xi2). See Parkes 1976 and Rowley 2015.
[5] Wormald 1999, 76.
[6] Cubitt 2012, 179.
[7] Parkes 1976; Bately 1986; Dumville 1992 and 1994; Wormald 1999.
[8] Bately 1986, xxxiv–xxxv and Ker 1940, 81–2 and 1957, 233. This is Scribe 3 in Corpus and Scribe 1 in Otho; cf. Plummer 1889; Parkes 1976; Richards 1986. Dumville agrees for the annals of *924–46, but raises questions about the 955 annal, 1992, 62–3. I agree with Bately's statement: 'I can find no significant differences between this annal and the other entries in this section apart from the annal 951 and would therefore assign it to hand 3', 1986, xxxiv.

'paleographers and codicologists for the most part stick to paleography and codicology. They ... eschew the translation of their findings into literary criticism and cultural history'.[9] David Dumville also warns that 'students of manuscripts are sometimes undesirably free in their attribution of motive to scribes'.[10] This may be one reasons why Wormald qualifies his conclusions about Otho as 'speculative' – though he had some precedent in interpreting compilations.[11]

Despite (or perhaps because of) Dumville's admonition, there has been a tremendous amount of recent scholarship exploring the complexities of miscellaneous and composite medieval manuscripts.[12] Indeed, although Johnston and Van Dussen study later medieval manuscripts, their theories about compilation, homogeneity and miscellaneity are useful when reconsidering the compilation of Otho. They posit three 'theses' in relation to the study of manuscript books: that 'the manuscript is a process as much as it is a product'; that 'because the manuscript as process resulted in its continued and constant evolution, we must focus on a manuscript's entire life cycle, not just its moment of original production'; and that 'the manuscript as a process combined with the manuscript's dynamic life cycle resulted in decentralised forms of authority'.[13] Given that the copy of the *ASC* in Corpus has recently been described as offering 'a single, monolithic vision of English history',[14] the paleographical and codicological evidence demonstrating that this particular copy of the *ASC* has been added to, altered and erased from its earliest stages suggests the importance of considering a manuscript's entire life cycle and heeding the extent to which such interventions create new meanings across shifting contexts.[15]

Composite manuscripts need to be studied on a case-to-case basis. As Barbara Shailor points out, some 'miscellaneous' manuscripts may not be 'as mixed or diverse as they may first appear';[16] others, as Peter Gumbert notes, *can* be 'arbitrarily joined'. Many examples also survive 'where [codicological] units are combined which are not quite independent and yet distinct', though 'it is not certain that medieval ideas on this subject were identical with ours'.[17] For Gumbert, understanding how manuscripts 'grew in stages and/or [were] put together from originally separate pieces ... is vital ... for understanding the text in it, the precise form it takes in this manuscript, and the combination with other texts in which it appears'.[18] Similarly, Arthur Bahr argues that

---

[9] Simpson 2006, 292; quoted in Johnston and Van Dussen 2015, 1.
[10] Dumville 1992, 113.
[11] Parkes 1976; F. Robinson 1980; P. A. Robinson 1980.
[12] Nichols 1990; Bahr 2013; Kwakkel 2013; Ford 2016; Johston and Van Dussen 2015; Friedrich and Schwarke 2016.
[13] Johnston and Van Dussen 2015, 4, 6, 9.
[14] Trilling 2013, 232–3. Trilling concedes that 'the later development of the Chronicle itself begins to undermine the hegemony envisioned by its first West Saxon patrons', 233.
[15] Johnston and Van Dussen 2015, 9. On the complexities of the *ASC* in Corpus, see Keynes and Dumville's 'General Editors' Foreword' to Bately 1986, ix.
[16] Shailor 1996, 167.
[17] Gumbert 2004, 19–20.
[18] *Ibid.*, 18.

'we can productively bring comparable interpretive strategies to bear on the formal characteristics of both physical manuscripts and literary works'.[19] That is that 'the selection and arrangement of texts in manuscripts, like that of words in poetry, can produce ... "metaphorical potentialities," discontinuities and excesses, multiple and shifting meanings'.[20] Bahr contrasts his definition of 'assemblage' and 'compilational reading' with Parkes's definition of *compilatio*, acknowledging that 'Parkes and others' saw 'medieval *compilatio* ...[as] a practical, rather than an aesthetic or literary form of textual engagement; its goal was to streamline difficult texts, making them "*readily ... [and] easily* accessible" – and this in "systematic and convenient form"'.[21] But neither seems to be the case in Otho.

Instead, approaching compilation as a dynamic process of textual engagement by means of which, 'present and past com[e] together to form a constellation',[22] suggests new angles from which to approach the elements in Otho and Corpus considered anomalous by Wormald and Parkes. Parkes, who considered the organising principle of Corpus to be 'dynastic achievement', treated the first 'booklet' of that manuscript as the most coherent.[23] He described the work of the scribes who wrote folios 26–32 (Bately's scribes 3–7) – which include *The Battle of Brunanburh* – as 'scrappy', and suspected that their efforts reflected the death of the earlier 'tradition of historiography' in Winchester.[24] Although he argued that Volume II was probably joined with Volume I in the tenth century in Winchester, when and where Scribe 1 was still able to 'suppl[y the] lacunae', Parkes considered the materials in Volume II to be 'totally unrelated to ... the rest of the manuscript'.[25] I have argued elsewhere that the additions 'assert an early English sense of connection with Christian world history, as well as a teleological and moral sense of time'.[26] Elizabeth Tyler has recently argued that a similar combination of world history and early English 'political discourse' can be seen in the compilation of British Library MS Cotton Tiberius B.i.[27]

Returning to Otho, Wormald echoes Parkes's discomfort with miscellaneity. On the one hand, Wormald argues that 'it is ... possible to make suggestions about the reasons why the collection [in Otho] was made'; on the other hand, he admits that he was 'tempt[ed] to deny' that some of the texts 'belonged to the original collection at all'; these are the 'Seasons for Fasting', the medical recipes and, 'above all *The Burghal Hidage*'.[28] Wormald comes up with a solution, but his hesitation derives from the

---

[19] Bahr 2013, 1.
[20] *Ibid.*, 10.
[21] *Ibid.*, 12.
[22] *Ibid.*, 13.
[23] Parkes 1976, 167, 169.
[24] *Ibid.*, 169; Bately 1986, xxxiv–xxxix.
[25] Parkes 1976, 168–9.
[26] Rowley 2015, 18.
[27] Tyler 2017, 66. I would like to thank my anonymous reader for this reference.
[28] Wormald 1999, 72, 76.

contrast between some of the textual content and his idea that Otho was compiled 'to foster and celebrate the traditions of the English people'.[29]

Although the act of adding the *ASC* and lists of bishops – both of which use Bede's *Historia Ecclesiastica* as a source – to a copy of the OEHE may seem redundant, even Wormald observed the 'sharp contrast between … [the *ASC*'s] emphasis on Wessex and … Bede'.[30] Nevertheless, he read the compilation of Otho as 'widening' the 'argument' of Corpus, which he believed 'was designed to balance the dynastic achievement in battle and in justice'.[31] However, Wormald excluded from his analysis all of Volume II of Corpus, which as Parkes pointed out, substantially altered the character of that compilation in the tenth century; consequently, Corpus as a whole book would have read quite differently when Otho was being copied.[32]

Although their studies remain foundational, there are moments when additions to each of the manuscripts elude the organising principles Parkes and Wormald articulated. Re-examining the compilation of Otho in stages and from the perspective of local or regional interests centering on Winchester suggests that the manuscript was compiled to help rulers in Wessex face the challenges of the mid-tenth and early eleventh centuries. A thorough understanding of this dynamic, however, depends on a clear articulation of the differences between the OEHE and its Latin source, as well as the contexts in which that text was copied in Winchester in the middle of the tenth century.[33]

The OEHE and Otho

The OEHE was translated anonymously sometime in the ninth or early tenth century. It survives in five manuscripts and three excerpts from the late ninth to the late eleventh centuries.[34] Although Bately argued that we cannot place the OEHE in the ninth century, Godden suggested it may be 'a few decades or half-century earlier' than the earliest manuscripts; linguistic evidence as analysed by Fulk confirms this possibility.[35] The OEHE was long believed to have been translated by King Alfred, but the current consensus is that it was not, though some continue to associate it with his programme of education and translation.[36] I have argued elsewhere that the OEHE

---

[29] *Ibid.*, 80.
[30] *Ibid.*, 75.
[31] *Ibid.*, 75.
[32] Parkes 1976, 168, 151–2. Parkes also notes that the Sedulius was catalogued as following the *Chronicle* and preceding the *Laws* by Thomas James in 1600.
[33] Bately 1988, xxxiv–xxxv; Dumville 1992, 126–7.
[34] In addition to Otho, these are: Cambridge, Corpus Christi College 41; Cambridge, University Library Kk.3.18; London, British Library Cotton Domitian A.IX, fol. 11; Oxford, Bodleian Library Tanner 10; and Oxford, Corpus Christi College 279B; see Rowley 2011, 16–25.
[35] Bately 1988, 98; Godden 2009, 121; Fulk 2012, 66–9.
[36] See Rowley 2011, 37–46; see also, Sweet 1876, 197–8; Miller 1890–8; Deutschbein 1901; Whitelock 1962; Waite 2014; Campbell 1951.

was translated independently of Alfred's programme, and that the compilation in Otho suggests that the OEHE alone did not fit his ideological agenda.[37]

At least three translators contributed to the OEHE as we have it. While the bulk of the translation was the work of one main translator, parts of Book III survive in a separate translation in Otho, CCCO 279b and CUL K.k.318. Dorothy Whitelock has also demonstrated that the chapter headings were translated by one (or two) others.[38] Waite has also recently shown that the Preface was the work of yet another translator; he concludes: '[t]he Preface appears to be the pastiche of a writer of the first half of the tenth century (if not the end of the ninth) who had some knowledge of the genuine Alfredian Prefaces, but whose dialect differed from that of Alfred'.[39] Consequently, I believe that the Preface may have been added as a frame for incorporating the OEHE into the Alfredian corpus.[40]

The differences between Bede's *HE* and the OEHE reveal problems with Wormald's interpretation of the OEHE, and thereby the compilation of Otho. The main OEHE translator abridged his source substantially, shortening the descriptions of England and Ireland, cutting most of the Roman and foreign history, and eliminating Bede's account of the Pelagian heresy and Bede's excerpts from Adomnán's descriptions of the holy land. He removed most of Bede's account of the Easter Controversy and almost all of the papal correspondence.[41] Combined, these changes 'suggest that Bede's Old English translators carefully ... revised their source to present a view of early English history that differs from Bede's'. The OEHE steers clear of vocabulary strongly associated with Alfred (such as the use of *Englalond*) to focus on conversion, the development of the Church, key early English saints and the relationship between kings and bishops.[42]

Although Otho does manifest a link between the OEHE and Wessex, because of this extensive revision the OEHE cannot be said to provide a 'blueprint' for Alfred as 'the architect of a kingdom of all the English', as envisioned by Wormald.[43] Indeed, although the OEHE 'is sometimes taken as part of an Alfredian nation-building strategy', George Molyneaux observes that '[w]hen such claims are made, the differences between the *HE* and the [OEHE] are rarely mentioned'.[44] Molyneaux targets the OEHE's omission of 'one of the clearest enunciations of the spiritual unity of the English in the *HE*', where Bede describes Gregory the Great as '*apostolus noster*', asserting that: 'By right we can and should call him our apostle, because,

---

[37] Rowley 2011, 164.

[38] Whitelock 1974, 277–8; Potter 1931; Campbell 1951.

[39] Waite 2015, 85.

[40] On thresholds and frames (Genette's '*seuils*') in translations, see Batchelor 2018.

[41] Rowley 2011, 4.

[42] *Ibid.*, 14 (quotation), 57–70, 131.

[43] Wormald 2004, 20 and 1999, 377. Oxford, Bodleian Library MS Tanner 10 has been associated with Winchester, but Gameson has shown that 'neither its contents, preparation, script, nor its decoration provides positive evidence to support this [localisation]', Gameson 1992a, 129; cf. Gameson 1992b, 176.

[44] Molyneaux 2009, 1304–5.

when he governed the most important see in the whole world ... he made our *gens*, until then enslaved to idols, into a Church of Christ' (*HE*, II.i).[45] This omission from the OEHE is just one example; upon a complete examination it becomes clear that the differences in the translation effectively dismantle Bede's salvation history. If the OEHE 'cannot be assumed to be propaganda', Molyneaux concludes, 'the case for believing the whole collection [in Otho], laxatives and all, had this purpose is greatly weakened'.[46] While the idea that these manuscripts share an interest in 'dynastic achievement' cannot be denied, the miscellany in Otho can be better understood in relation to the challenges of the mid-tenth and early eleventh centuries.

The OEHE and the House of Wessex in the Mid-tenth Century

According to Janet Bately, the script used by the scribe who wrote most of the OEHE in Otho and folios 26r-27v of Corpus is:

> the Square minuscule typical of the 940s and 950s in general and the charters of Eadred and Eadwig in particular. Since the evenness of the script appears to indicate that the annals were entered not year by year but page by page and all at the same time, and since the last annal-number entered by this scribe appears to have been that for *956 ... Ker's dating of mid-tenth century (Wright *ca* 960, Dumville 947x955/6) is unlikely to be mistaken.[47]

This window corresponds to the reigns of Edmund I (939–46), Eadred (946–55) and Eadwig (955–59) in Winchester.[48] These are three kings of Wessex whose troubled reigns have sometimes been elided in studies that focus on English unification. In *Wessex and England* for example, although he also devotes a chapter to Edmund, Dumville emphasises the 'crucial' role of Æthelstan in the 'welding together with Wessex of recently conquered territories'.[49] While Alfred, Æthelstan and (later) Edgar's achievements cannot be denied, Molyneaux cautions that 'the tenth century did not see "English unification", but simply the expansion and consolidation of the territory of a ruling dynasty'.[50] As Janet Thorman reminds us:

> [h]owever strong and stable West-Saxon rule in the tenth century may have been, the *Chronicle* makes it clear that no West-Saxon leader was free of rebellion, invasion, treachery, and the pressures of separate interests pursuing opportunistic strategies. West-Saxon

---

[45] *Ibid.*, 1303.

[46] *Ibid.*, 1306.

[47] Bately 1986, xxxv; cf. Dumville 1992, 126–7.

[48] As always, paleographical dates are somewhat fluid, and a date early in the reign of Edgar cannot be ruled out. See Stenton 1971; Dumville 1992; Molyneaux 2015. Dumville cautions that 'difficulties remain' regarding the Winchester localisation, but Stokes has recently solidified paleographical arguments for Winchester, see Dumville 1992, 63–6; Dumville 1994, 148; Stokes 2014, 43, 80–3, esp. 81.

[49] Dumville 1994, 147; cf. Foot 2011.

[50] Molyneaux 2015, 1.

hegemony was from the start continuously challenged and reasserted in response to contingent events.[51]

Because a cluster of such challenges to West-Saxon hegemony occurs in the mid-tenth century, a look at the reigns of Edmund, Eadred and Eadwig provides rich contexts in which to consider the copying of the OEHE in Otho.

Edmund I, who succeeded Æthelstan in 939, may be better known as the *æþeling* who supported his older brother and king at the *Battle of Brunanburh*.[52] According to Ann Williams, 'Edmund inherited his half-brother's realm, but had to fight hard to retain it; much of his short reign was occupied in struggling against the Viking rulers of Dublin for control of the north-east midlands and the kingdom of York'.[53] The poem 'The Five Boroughs', in the *ASC* (annal for 944) celebrates his recovery of some of this territory.[54] Edmund was also 'concerned with the advancement of religion', but as Dumville puts it, 'not committed … to a single tradition or ideology'.[55] Edmund translated Oda to the archiepiscopacy at Canterbury in 941, sponsored the livings of religious women, and gave Glastonbury to Dunstan, but he expelled Æthelwold (future bishop of Winchester) from court – restoring him only after a 'miraculous escape from death in a hunting accident'.[56] Several good quality books survive from Edmund's reign, including some in English; again according to Dumville, 'original composition of historical and homiletic literature is attested in this period'.[57] Edmund also issued three law codes and his reign seems to have been intellectually lively. Dumville concludes that Edmund 'might … have been remembered as one of the more remarkable kings of Anglo-Saxon England', had he not been killed in a fight in 946.[58]

Edmund's brother Eadred also 'competed with a series of Hiberno-Scandinavian kings for Northumbrian recognition'.[59] Although Eadred was initially accepted as king of Northumbria on his accession in 946, he found himself confronted by Erik Bloodaxe's takeover there almost immediately. Eadred responded by leading an invasion at least as far as Ripon in 948. It was '[d]uring the course of this campaign the minster church at Ripon – which had been founded by St Wilfrid and which housed his remains – was burnt down'.[60] After more changes of leadership and a period of Northumbrian independence from Wessex between 950–4, the Northumbrians expelled Erik, after which Eadred regained control of the region, becoming once again, King of the English.[61]

---

[51] Thorman 1997, 78.
[52] See Beaven 1918; Williams 2004; Foot 2008.
[53] Williams 2004, 766; cf. Molyneaux 2015, 15–34.
[54] Stenton 1971, 356–60, esp. 357.
[55] Dumville 1992, 178.
[56] Williams 2004, 767–8.
[57] Dumville 1992, 182, 178, cf. Williams 2004.
[58] Dumville 1992, 182–4; Williams 2004, 768.
[59] Molyneaux 2015, 32; see also Stenton 1971, 360–3; Yorke 1988, 65–88; Goold 1999, 317–27.
[60] Lapidge 1988, 45.
[61] Stenton 1971, 360–3.

In the meantime, Eadred cultivated good relationships with important bishops and abbots and patronised the Old Minster, Winchester. He appointed Æthelwold to the monastery at Abingdon, and maintained a close relationship with Dunstan, who had already instigated monastic reform at Glastonbury; Dunstan remained one of Eadred's key advisors.[62] The *Vita Dunstani* confirms their close association, stating that Eadred entrusted the 'best' of his charters and treasures to Dunstan.[63] Oda, Archbishop of Canterbury also played a 'major role' in Eadred's 'witan'.[64] The *Vita S. Æthelwoldi* by Wulfstan of Winchester describes Eadred's ill health and some heavy drinking with guests from Northumbria, but it also reports that Eadred was 'a friend and champion of the Old Minster at Winchester, as the ornaments manufactured at his order bear witness: a great gold cross, a gold altar, and the other things that he graciously and generously sent there in honour of the blessed apostles Peter and Paul'.[65] While the D recension of the *ASC* indicated that Eadred 'ordered a great slaughter in Thetford in 952 to avenge the killing of an abbot',[66] William of Malmesbury asserts that 'Eadred devoted his life to God, "endured with patience his frequent bodily pains, prolonged his prayer and made his palace altogether the school of virtue"'.[67]

While this is a brief survey of the reigns of Edmund and Eadred, elements of their reigns can be connected with themes emphasised by the abridgement of the OEHE, including the proper relationship between bishops and kings, the value of patronising churches, ill health as a trial sent by God and the importance of the proper treatment of holy or saintly remains. They fostered the careers of Dunstan and Æthelwold (Eadred moreso with the latter), supported the Old Minster with gifts, and maintained good relations with Archbishop Oda. Whether Oda accompanied Eadred on his Northumbrian raid in 948, possibly participating in the destruction of the minster church at Ripon and translation of Wilfrid's relics (as Eadmer reported), remains unknown. In his prefatory letter to Frithegod's poem in honor of Wilfrid, Oda states that he simply 'reverently received' the remains in Canterbury.[68] Although this *furta sacra* was contested by Ripon, the attention Eadred paid to Wilfrid's remains suggests that he may have been emulating Æthelstan, who venerated the Northumbrian saint Cuthbert. Given these thematic connections, it seems to me plausible that either Edmund or Eadred commissioned the copy of the OEHE in Otho. If it had initially been commissioned by (or for) Edmund, it makes sense that Eadred (or one of his *witan*) continued the work.

Some of the themes outlined above can be found in the chapters of the OEHE dealing with Winchester and Wessex: translations, the founding of churches and the need for good relations between kings and bishops for the maintenance of the realm.

---

[62] Yorke 1988, 74; and Higgitt 1979, 275.

[63] Keynes 1980, 148 and Pratt 2014, 318 n. 111; cf. Winterbottom and Lapidge 2012, 60, 64.

[64] Yorke 1988, 74.

[65] Quoted in Lapidge 1996, 52.

[66] Molyneaux 2011, 87.

[67] Quoted in Goold 1999, 321.

[68] Lapidge 1988, 45, note 3.

The first mention of Winchester in the OEHE relates to the translation to Winchester of the body of Bishop Birinus, who had come from Rome and who first converted the West Saxons. In Book III, chapter 5 of the OEHE: 'Bishop Hædde commanded his body to be taken up and brought to Winchester, and it was buried with honour within the church of the blessed apostles Peter and Paul' (*Hædde biscop heht his lichoman upadon ⁊ lædan to Wintaceastre ⁊ in cirican þara eadiga apostola Petrus and Paulus arwyrðlice geseted is*).[69] Birinus, who pledged to preach 'in the most remote parts of England, where no teaching had ever penetrated before', found plenty of work in Cynegils's Wessex, where he first landed.[70] But Cenwealh, Cynegils's son and heir, 'refused to receive the faith and sacraments of the Heavenly King and shortly after he lost dominion of his earthly kingdom' (*wiðsoc, þæt he geleafan onfenge ⁊ þam geryne þæs heofonlican cyniges; ond sona æfter medmiclum fæce þa meaht forleas þæs eorðlican rices*).[71] Cenwealh converted while in exile and regained his kingdom; after which the OEHE reports how Cenwealh drove two bishops, Agilbert and Wine, out of the kingdom. The OEHE reports that Cenwealh 'frequently suffered severe damage to his dominion at the hands of his enemies' until he remembered what had happened before: 'Then at last he recollected, that his want of faith formerly caused his expulsion, and that on receiving the faith of Christ he recovered his throne' (*ða cwom him æt nehstan to gemynde, þæt hine ær his getreowleasnis of his rice adraf, ond eft, þa he Cristes geleafan onget, þæt he his rice onfeng*).[72] So Cenwealh humbly begged Agilbert to return.

Although this pattern associating the winning of and ability to maintain an earthly kingdom with adherence to Christianity and the respectful treatment of bishops repeats throughout the OEHE, Ecgfrith's expulsion of Bishop Wilfrid in III.17, does not correspond a loss of power. Instead, it leads to the conversion of Caedwalla, king of Wessex 685–7. During his exile, Wilfrid travelled to Rome and worked as a missionary among the South Saxons until he was recalled to his see, at which point, the OEHE reports that 'then they were placed under the bishops of Wessex, who lived at Winchester', expanding Winchester's influence over the region. Caedwalla's case is of special interest here, because he makes a deal with Wilfrid to grant land on the Isle of Wight to 'God's service' if granted victory in war. He was, so he did, giving Bishop Wilfrid three hundred hides 'and the stock beside'.[73] The making of such deals is another motif in the OEHE, for example Oswiu's founding of monasteries in return for victory against Penda. In Book V, the OEHE tells how Caedwalla later abdicated and went to Rome, where he was baptised and buried, emphasising his importance as an exemplary king.[74]

Yorke argues that Caedwalla's successes 'seem to have marked a significant stage in the growth of Wessex, for it is at this point that Bede begins consistently to refer

[69] Miller 1890–8, 168–9.
[70] *Ibid.*, 166–7.
[71] *Ibid.*, 168–9.
[72] *Ibid.*, 170–1.
[73] *Ibid.*, 306–7.
[74] Campbell 2009. On the omission and rearrangement of chapters, see Rowley 2011, 202–3.

to the dynasty as "West Saxons" instead of as "Gewisse"'.[75] So, while Eadred may have burned down the minster church at Ripon accidentally, the opportunity to translate the remains of Wilfrid, who symbolically linked Northumbria and Rome to Wessex and Winchester, was powerfully meaningful. Not only could Eadred atone for burning the church in the first place, but he could also assert a religious bond between the northern and southern regions of his newly reunited kingdom.

While these are just a few examples, the ways in which themes in the OEHE resonate with events in the reigns of Edmund and Eadred, especially the challenges to the northern parts of their earthly domain, the efficacy of supporting bishops and monasteries, and – for Eadred – the linking of Wilfrid to an important early king of Wessex, suggest that the text would have been of special interest. The ways that the OEHE abridges its source allow it to be read as a series of *exempla*, which provide more of a 'mirror' for Christian kings, than a book 'necessary for *all* men to know'.[76] While Eadred's achievements have been eclipsed by those of Alfred, Æthelstan, and Edgar as king and patron, his associations with Dunstan and Æthelwold, along with his support for Abingdon, Glastonbury and the Old Minster prior to the official start of Benedictine reform provide compelling contexts in which to read the copying of the OEHE during his reign. As Parkes, Dumville, Bately and many others have confirmed, the same scribe who copied the OEHE in Otho is also the same one who wrote the medical collection known as Bald's *Leechbook*, British Library, Royal MS 12.D.xvii, which may have been copied for Eadred's health benefit.

That being said, these themes also remain relevant for Eadwig, especially the *exempla* in the OEHE demonstrating the dangers of rejecting bishops.[77] During Eadwig's short reign, attempts to remonstrate his behavior led to Dunstan's exile. Further difficulties created a 'rift ... between Eadwig and some of the most important lay and ecclesiastical nobles of the reigns of his father and uncle'.[78] Eadwig's incestuous marriage to Ælfgifu (renounced in 958) calls to mind not only Sigebert's disobedience to bishop Cedd and murder at the hands of his incestuously married thegn (OEHE III.16), but also Gregory the Great's fifth response to Augustine of Canterbury regarding acceptable degrees of kinship in marriage in the *Libellus Responsionem*, which is included after Book III in the OEHE.[79]

The OEHE closes with warnings of uncertain times in eighth-century Northumbria, dismantles Bede's narrative of salvation history, and focuses on conversion and the relationships between kings and bishops – some of which are rocky – in the sections dealing with Wessex. Because of its abridgement, the lessons in the OEHE arguably

---

[75] Yorke 1995, 59.

[76] Keynes and Lapidge 1983, 126; emphasis added.

[77] On the danger of ignoring episcopal authority in the OEHE, consider: Sigeberht, king of the East Saxons was murdered after (or for) disobeying the orders of Bishop Cedd (III.16) and the Northumbrian king Oswine died soon death after humbling himself before Aidan, who had just berated him for questioning his judgment and valuing a horse above a human (III.14).

[78] Yorke 1988, 74–76.

[79] See Yorke 1988, 76 and Rowley 2011, 128–30; Miller 1890–8, 70–2.

correspond to issues facing the kings of Wessex in the mid-tenth century; these lessons endorse Christian practices and heeding the advice of bishops. As a mirror for princes, the OEHE provided useful and informative *exempla* for Æthelstan's heirs during troubled reigns. The texts added to the OEHE when the Otho manuscript was further confected in the early eleventh century attest to its status as a living book with practical purposes.

The Additions of 1001–13: The *ASC* and *The West Saxon Genealogical Regnal List*

The fact that Otho was burned in the fire at Ashburnham House in 1731 has limited anyone's ability to study that manuscript as a whole book since then. Laurence Nowell made a transcription of most it in 1562, omitting the front matter to the OEHE and augmenting the *Laws* slightly.[80] Humfrey Wanley also described Otho prior to the fire; Roland Torkar has reconstructed its original order and contents.[81] More recently, Greg Waite has discovered that John Smith, in preparation of his 1722 edition of the OEHE, collated Otho against a copy of Abraham Wheloc's 1644 edition of the same. Waite's discovery reveals the state of the front matter of the OEHE in Otho, demonstrating that it contained a Preface and *West Saxon Genealogical Regnal List* (*WSGRL*), as seen in a later copy of the OEHE, Cambridge University Library MS K.k.3.18. This means that in Otho, 'there seem to have been two copies [of the *WSGRL*] (from two different exemplars) made fifty years apart'.[82]

This proves a complicated place to start when considering the additions to Otho made in the early eleventh century. But, sometime between 1001–13 (a date range based on the end of the annals and additions to the episcopal lists) in Winchester,[83] Scribe 2 repaired or supplied the end of the OEHE, then added some of the materials from Corpus; specifically, the second *WSGRL*, the G version of the *ASC*, lists of popes and English bishops, and (probably) the laws of Alfred and Ine. Scribe 3 copied the laws known as *II Æthelstan*, which were positioned before the code of *Alfred-Ine*. (Items 7–11 in the comparative table in the Appendix have been completely lost, so we have no information about the scribes or dating of those sections. Wormald assumed that these texts were more or less contemporaneous with the other added texts.)

As Wormald noted, the addition of these materials took place at 'a time when [England] faced the first of its two great eleventh-century crises'.[84] Because of more recent, detailed studies of this period and Æthelred's reign by Simon Keynes, Catherine Cubitt, Levi Roach and Ryan Lavelle, it is now possible to think about the

---

[80] Now London, British Library Additional 47303; on the laws, see below and Richards 1986, 176.
[81] Torkar 1981, 42–3.
[82] Waite 2015, 32, 54.
[83] Stokes 2014, 88.
[84] Wormald 1999, 76–8; quotation at 80.

combination of texts added to Otho in relation to what Cubitt called Æthelred's 'politics of remorse', and to the range of strategies Æthelred employed during the 990s and early 1000s, as identified by Keynes and Lavelle, from peace-making and penance to local defences.[85]

While the dates of the interventions in Otho leap from *c.* 955 to *c.* 1001, it is worth noting that the monastic reform initiated by Dunstan and partially fostered by Eadred came 'to the fore in the reign of Edgar (959–75)'.[86] This, the Benedictine Reform, articulated and sought to enact what John Higgitt describes as an 'ideal of an alliance of king and monks', based on Continental and Bedan models.[87] Keynes and Cubitt both focus on Æthelred's charter of 993, in which he 'determined to correct for the better what [he had] performed childishly', and the writings of Ælfric and Wulfstan, who were proponents of the reforms of Æthelwold and Dunstan.[88] Keynes reads their influence on Æthelred as forming an alliance of kings and monks like the one described by Higgitt. More specifically, Keynes argues that 'what counts, in relation to the events of 1009, is the organised *combination* of alms-giving, fasting, litanies, and prayer, and its concentration over a specified period in response to a particular emergency'.[89] Keynes also observes that Edgar had 'issued a special code of laws in response to a visitation of the plague'.[90] In addition to providing a rationale for re-copying the genealogy, patterns begin to take shape regarding the copying of historic law codes during ongoing crises.

Bishop Æthelwold's reforming ideal reached directly back to what he saw as the golden age of Bede, so the continued relevance of the OEHE on the part of whoever commissioned the additions to Otho should be clear; in the 990s, we see an expansion of the alliance of kings and bishops, and a development of the combination of acts of supplication. The added lists of popes and bishop also echo parts of the OEHE. Similarly, the two *WSGRLs* perform similar functions, because the OEHE includes several genealogies: from Hengist's to the kings of Kent, the Wuffings, and so on.[91] Here, we can see the ways in which the *ASC* adds to and contrasts with the OEHE, creating both resonances and dissonances. Returning to Bahr's idea of the literary effects of compilation, repetition is one of the most basic. In Otho, we also see an envelope structure, framing the OEHE with the genealogies, placing the OEHE literally and physically within the house of Wessex, thus extending the act of appropriation begun by the addition of an Alfredian-style preface by another translator. Reading the development of Otho as a dynamic process here reveals how the later expansion of this manuscript arguably imitates the conquest of the rest of the island by the West Saxon kings.

---

[85] Keynes 2007, 151–220; Lavelle 2008; Cubitt 2012, 179–192; Roach 2014.
[86] Higgitt 1979, 280.
[87] *Ibid.*
[88] Cubitt, 2012, 182, cf. Roach, 2014, 735–8ff.
[89] Keynes 2007, 184.
[90] *Ibid.*, 184.
[91] Sisam 1990, 146

The additions to Otho not only celebrate the achievements of Alfred, Æthelstan and, in the AG version of the *ASC*, those of Edward the Elder,[92] they also situate Winchester in the world, as well as in relation to biblical history. In some ways, this move is imitative of the combination of Sedulius's biblical poem with the *ASC* in Corpus,[93] but the different combination of text offers a new perspective on Winchester and Wessex. In these additions, Winchester is not, as it is in the OEHE, the first stop en route to the wildest and remotest parts of England; rather, it is the most frequently mentioned city. Winchester is named seventeen times, as opposed to ten mentions each for Canterbury and Rochester.[94] While Winchester is not the first English city mentioned in the text, it is one of the first not named as place of battle; rather, in 643, 'Cenwealh had built the church in Winchester' (*Cenwealh het atimbran þa ciricean on Wintanceastre*).[95] While a small handful of baptisms, consecrations and episcopal seats are mentioned earlier, this is the first church. So Cenwealh's command to build the first English church in Winchester is striking, not exactly true, but rhetorically powerful. Given that the first several cities mentioned in the Chronicle are Bethlehem, Antioch, Rome and Jerusalem, the fact that the first naming of Winchester corresponds to the first building of *þa ciricean* on royal command can be read as a claim to precedence – one that differs dramatically from the OEHE. The expansive, poetic commemoration of successful West Saxon kings in the *ASC*, specifically concerning Edward and Edmund, develops this claim to precedence, providing as much of a model for Æthelred as the *exempla* from the OEHE may have for Eadred or Eadwig.

The annals about Edward add important descriptions of the king travelling around his domain and fortifying key places, including Maldon. Lavelle's suggestions, first that the nature of the Viking raids in the 980–90s were such that Æthelred would not have been expected to ride out before the scale of the attacks changed in 1001, and second that Æthelred may have waited until the line of succession was secure before he did so, make good sense. It may also be possible to read the Edward annals as copied in Otho after 1001 as praise for his riding out to battle, like his great ancestors, or as a nudge to do more of the same.[96] However, the copy of the *ASC* in Otho ends (with its exemplar) in 1001, so it does not include the large-scale attacks starting in 1006. But, as both Keynes and Cubitt observe, Æthelred's 'politics of penance' began in 993, after Byrhtnoth's defeat at Maldon and the sack of Bamburgh (in Northumbria).[97] According to Keynes, 'a chronicler writing at Winchester early in the first decade of the eleventh century provides a contemporary account of the events of 1001', which included the betrayal of Æthelred by Pallig, brother-in-law to Svein.[98] Changing times

---

[92] Dumville 1992, 126n. 326: 'This group of six annals is found only in MSS AG'. For the G version, see Lutz 1981.

[93] See Rowley 2015, 18.

[94] Bately 1986, 119–124.

[95] Bately 1986, 29

[96] Lavelle 2008, 116, 102.

[97] Keynes 2007, 154ff; Cubitt 2012, 179.

[98] Keynes 2007, 157–8.

require kings to have a thorough grasp of history and military strategies, along with a sense of the roles and duties of individuals and groups.

The Laws, the Lists, the Recipes, the Burghal Hidage and Some Concluding Remarks

The lists of popes and English bishops follow the end of the *ASC* in Otho and precede the Laws, so the order in Otho differs from that of Corpus. The lists in Otho are also continued to 1012, according to Wanley, in a hand other than that of Scribe 2 or 3.[99] These lists could be mnemonic or encyclopedic, but in their current position they reinforce the importance of the church and the ongoing relationships between kings and bishops found in the *ASC* and OEHE. The laws, in turn, continue to connect Winchester to the world: combined with Alfred's biblical preface to the Laws, they focus on immediate and often secular problems.

Mary Richards points out that 'the joint codes of Alfred and Ine' in Corpus 'epitomize two of the most striking features of the OE laws. First, the more recent code takes priority ... [and s]econdly, an earlier code supplements the later code in an integral way'.[100] These features hold true in Otho, which inserts the code known as *II Æthelstan* (which is not in Corpus) before the *Alfred-Ine* code. Just as Alfred's laws add to and clarify Ine's, the laws of Æthelstan in Otho 'attempt', as Richards puts it, 'to bring internal peace to the land'; they also address 'problems concerning ...exchange and purchase' and 'refe[r] to the laws of Alfred and Ine (*sio domboc*) for lists of fines applying to these crimes'.[101] Richards suggests that the inclusion of the laws and 'The Seasons for Fasting' in Otho gives the collection 'a specific practical function ... to communicate certain legal matters to the laity' via the church.[102] Problematically, however, two of the law codes Richards discusses were not in Otho, which changes their focus slightly.

Part of the difficulty here arises from the problem that Nowell transcribed several law codes, and layered additional commentary onto his transcription of the laws in Otho. He added materials from another (lost) manuscript to the end of his transcript of Otho; these are the passages from *V Æthelstan*, the *Judex*, and (possibly) the end of *II Æthelstan*. According to Torkar, Otho contained the *Alfred-Ine* laws, a short section of 'penalties for adultery' not in Corpus, and *II Æthelstan*, which includes regulations for minting coins in addition to the laws concerning exchange and purchases, as well proper witnessing and oaths and the proper locations for markets and exchanges.[103] Consequently, the laws in Otho had a secular and financial emphasis. They address the proper witnessing and taxation

---

[99] See Wormald 1999, 72.
[100] Richards 1986, 173.
[101] *Ibid.*, 174.
[102] *Ibid.*, 176.
[103] See Torkar 1981, 42–3 and Dammery 1990. These are Ker's items 5b and c. Ker 1957, 232.

of all exchanges and purchases, and regulate money-making, so that all monies were issued by the proper authority, whether king, bishop or abbot. This would be as useful and important in the early 1000s as it was in 924, given the large sums of money Æthelred was paying out in *heregild*.[104] The regional and city-based rules for moneyers, along with provisions for the regular repair of *burhs* in *II Æthelstan*, also resonate with the itemisation of regional defenses found in the Burghal Hidage, which follows the Laws in Otho.[105]

Significantly, the copy of the Burghal Hidage in Otho contains a paragraph missing from the other branch of transmission of the hidage, and which lays out the computation for exactly how many hides and men are required for 'the maintenance and defense of the wall'.[106] Given, as Lavelle points out, further treacheries and the weakening of the bonds between the different regions of England under the stress of the early eleventh-century attacks,[107] the inclusion of the Burghal Hidage in Otho can be read in conjunction with the emphasis on Winchester found in its *ASC*, as clear directions for the defense of Wessex and Winchester, the heart of Æthelred's England. Advice found in the Burghal Hidage can be read as working in tandem with the *exempla* from the OEHE, and the regulation by the Laws and the 'Seasons for Fasting' for combined spiritual health and preservation of earthly dominion.

In fact, the 'Seasons for Fasting' correspond closely to 'politics of penance' described by Cubitt and Keynes. Cubitt sees an important shift happening by the time Wulfstan preached his famous *Sermo lupi ad anglos* in 1014, by which the people assume some of 'responsibility for the loss of God's favour', instead of the king bearing the full brunt himself.[108] While 1014 is later than Otho, several texts in the manuscript, especially the 'Seasons', the Hidage and the Laws, do consider the proper roles and actions of individuals in certain conditions and places, such as on the wall, during exchanges and in their fasts or almsgiving. The 'Seasons' depict the *leod* (the people) as they participate in *leodscipe*, and are educated by their *leodfruma* (prince or leader), as playing a key role beginning, rather repetitively, in the first two stanzas of the poem. The poem does go on to articulate a strong sense of English tradition based, like Bede's, on the teachings of Gregory the Great. But as it does so, 'Seasons' also emphasises the importance of individual people, similar to the way that the Burghal Hidage emphasises the importance of individual places, and how they should be manned. With few exceptions, we almost never hear about people who are not kings, queens, saints or bishops in the OEHE. In contrast, although kings dominate parts

---

[104] Lavelle 2008, 24.

[105] As Torkar and Dammery point out, some of the differences have led to questions as to whether the Laws were copied from Corpus or from a very closely related manuscript. Dumville indicates that he questioned the connection based on crucial textual differences, but that Wormald convinced him that the differences stemmed from Otho being corrected against another manuscript when it was copied in the early eleventh century. Dammery 1990, 126–35; Dumville 1992, 57n. 13; Torkar 1981, 129–35.

[106] See Hill and Rumble 1996; Keynes and Lapidge 1983, 193–4.

[107] Lavelle 2008, 114–15.

[108] Cubitt 2012, 190–1.

of the *ASC*, the importance of individuals and local places permeate the subsequent texts copied into Otho, not only in terms how to regulate or defend them, but also in terms of their spiritual and physical wellbeing.

Although 'Seasons' is incomplete, and although there are signs of missing pages in Nowell's transcript suggesting that the medicinal recipes may have been copied at another time or place, the recipes resonate with the medical advice offered by John of Beverly in Book V of the OEHE. It is also true that the recipes arguably bring the microcosm-macrocosm, or part-to-whole, dynamic I have been teasing out across the compilation to its logical conclusion. The medical recipes can be interpreted as combining practical and spiritual guidelines that should operate, efficaciously, on the human body in the way that royal gifts to monasteries or fasting and prayers might combine with four fighting men per pole on the wall to defend the city in the Burghal Hidage.[109]

As a composite manuscript, Otho is quite different from Corpus. Just as the differences between the OEHE and its source challenge readers familiar with those differences to reconsider how the OEHE re-presented history and what it meant to audiences in mid-tenth-century Winchester, Otho re-presents the *ASC*, the regnal and episcopal lists, and the *Laws* from Corpus, placing them in different historical, textual and codicological contexts. Framed by the OEHE, the Burghal Hidage, the 'Seasons for Fasting' and medical texts by scribes working in the first decade of the eleventh century, these texts tell new and different parts of the history of Winchester and Wessex, connecting them to the world and the biblical history omitted from the OEHE. These differences, along with those between the OEHE and the *ASC*, resonate as they invite reflection about how the past can be used as well as commemorated.

While Otho shares an interest in dynastic achievement and history, it can also be read as an evolving process, the form and content of which reflects the changing concerns and needs of user-producers in Winchester during the reigns of Edmund, Eadred and Eadwig, and later during that of Æthelred; it speaks to both the continuities and the challenges of their reigns. These are kings whose places in history have been somewhat eclipsed by Alfred, Æthelstan and Edgar, but a closer look at the compilation of Otho provides a glimpse of the interests and ideas captured by the combination of texts brought together and transmitted by its scribes. The fact that Cnut took over and ruled from Winchester, continuing some of the practices employed by the Anglo-Saxon kings of Wessex, suggests that the symbolic significance of Winchester, produced in and by the texts of BL Cotton Otho B.XI, played no small role in the continuing life cycle of Winchester as an early medieval royal city.

---

[109] Keynes and Lapidge 1983, 194.

Appendix: Comparative Table of Manuscript Contents[110]

CCCC 173	BL Cotton Otho B.XI + membra disiecta
1.1 fols. 1v–32r *Anglo-Saxon Chronicle* (A)	1. fols. 1–38 + B.x fols. 55, 58, 62 The Old English Bede
*1.2. fols. 32rv *Acta Lanfranci*	2. Add. 34652, fol. 2: West-Saxon Genealogy to Alfred
2. fols. 33r–52v Laws of Alfred and Ine (w/chapter headings)	3. fols. 39–47 Fragments of the *Anglo-Saxon Chronicle* (G) (seven out of probably thirty-four leaves)
3. fols. 53r–56v Lists of popes and English Bishops	4. Lost lists of popes and English bishops (described by Wanley, copied by Nowell at the start of Add. 43703)
*4.1 fols. 57r–58v Sedulius, Letter 1 to Macedonius	**5. fols. 48, 51 Laws (originally four leaves): Add. 43703 fols. 233r–236r/15 or 20, II Æthelstan's 'Grately' code.
*4.2. fols. 59r–79v Sedulius, *Carmen paschale*	6. fols. 49, 50, 52, 53 Laws, Alfred-Ine (three out of probably nineteen leaves). Ker: 'Closely related to no. 39'.)
*4.3. fols. 79v–80r Sedulius, Hymn *A solis ortus cardine*	**7. Add. 43703 f. 255r/12–19 Legal section, "⁊ ymb æbricas"
*4.4. fols. 80–81r Sedulius, Letter II to Macedonius	**8. Add. 43703 fol. 255rv Burghal Hidage
*4.5. fols. 81r–81v Verses of Damsus on St Paul	**9. Add. 43703 fols. 255v–256 Note on hides and defense
*4.6. fols. 81v–82 v Sedulius, *Elegia*	**10. Add. 43703 fols. 257–260 "Seasons for Fasting" (incomplete when Nowell copied)
*4.7. fols. 82v–83v Augustine, *De ciuitate Dei*, xviii.23 (excerpts) with three versions of Sibylline prophecies	**11. Add. 43703 fols. 261–4 Medicinal recipes (probably also incomplete when Nowell copied)

* = Not in BL Cotton Otho; Vol. I = items 1–3; Vol. II = item 4–4.7
** = Not in CCCC 173

Acknowledgements

I would like to thank Greg Waite for his comments on a draft of this essay; any remaining errors are my own.

---

[110] Ker 1940, Ker 1957, Torkar, 1981, Waite 2015. CCCC 173 available at https://parker.stanford.edu/parker/catalog/wp146tq7625.

Abbreviations

ASC   *Anglo-Saxon Chronicle*
Corpus   Cambridge, Corpus Christi College MS 173
OEHE   Old English Version of Bede's *Historia ecclesiastica gentis anglorum*
Otho   British Library, MS Cotton Otho B.XI
WSGRL   *West Saxon Genealogical Regnal List*

Bibliography

Manuscripts

Cambridge, Corpus Christi College 41 (SW England, Crediton? s. xi1).
Cambridge, Corpus Christi College MS 173 (Winchester, s. ix/x-xi2).
Cambridge, University Library Kk.3.18 (Worcester, s. xi2).
London, British Library, Additional 34652, fol. 2 (Winchester, s. xi1).
London, British Library, Additional 43703 (1562, Laurence Nowell's transcript of Otho).
London, British Library, Cotton Domitian A.IX, fol. 11 (SE England? s. ixex or in, after 883).
London, British Library, Cotton MS Otho B.XI (Winchester, s. xmed-s. xi1).
Oxford, Bodleian Library Tanner 10 (prov. Thorney, s. x1).
Oxford, Corpus Christi College 279B (Worcester, s. xiin).

Primary Sources

Bately, J. 1986. *The Anglo-Saxon Chronicle: A Collaborative Edition 3 MS A.* Cambridge: D. S. Brewer.
Keynes, S. and Lapidge, M. 1983. *Alfred the Great: Asser's Life of King Alfred and other contemporary sources.* Harmondsworth: Penguin.
Plummer, C. (ed.) 1889. *Two of the Saxon Chronicles Parallel (787-1001 A.D.): with Supplementary Extracts from the Others: A Revised Text.* Oxford: Clarendon Press.
Rowley, S. M. 2011. *The Old English Version of Bede's Historia Ecclesiastica.* Cambridge: D. S. Brewer.
Sweet, H. 1876. *An Anglo-Saxon Reader in Prose and Verse. With Grammatical Introduction, Notes, and Glossary.* Oxford: Clarendon Press.
Wheloc, A. (ed.) 1644. *Historiae ecclesiasticae gentis Anglorum libri V: a Venerabili Beda presbytero scripti.* Cambridge: Roger Daniel.
Winterbottom, M. and Lapidge, M. (eds) 2012. *The early lives of St Dunstan.* Oxford: Clarendon Press.

Secondary Sources

Bahr, A. 2013. *Fragments and Assemblages: Forming Compilations of Medieval London.* Chicago: University of Chicago Press.
Batchelor, K. 2018. *Translation and Paratexts.* London and New York: Routledge.
Bately, J. 1988. Old English Prose Before and during the Reign of Alfred, *Anglo-Saxon England*, 17, 93–138.
Beaven, M. L. R. 1918. King Edmund I and the Danes of York, *English Historical Review*, 33:129, 1–9.
Campbell, J. J. 1951. The Dialect Vocabulary of the Old English Bede, *Journal of English and Germanic Philology*, 50:3, 349–72.
Campbell, J. 2009. Cædwalla, in J. Cannon (ed.), *The Oxford Companion to British History*, revised edition. Oxford: Oxford University Press. Available at: https://www.oxfordreference.com/view/10.1093/acref/9780199567638.001.0001/acref-9780199567638-e-735.
Cubitt, C. 2012. The Politics of Remorse: Penance and Royal Piety in the Reign of Æthelred the Unready, *Historical Research*, 85:228, 179–192.

Dammery, R. J. E. 1990. *The Law-code of King Alfred the Great.* University of Cambridge, PhD Thesis.

Deutschbein, M. 1901. Dialektischte in der ags. Übersetzung von Bedas Kirchengeschichte, *Beiträge zur Geschichte der deutschen Sprache und Literatur*, 26, 169–244.

Dumville, D. N. 1992. *Wessex and England from Alfred to Edgar: Six Essays on Political, Cultural, and Ecclesiastical Revival.* Woodbridge: Boydell Press.

Dumville, D. N. 1994. English Square Minuscule Script: The Mid-Century Phases, *Anglo-Saxon England*, 23, 133–64.

Foot, S. 2008. Where English Becomes British: Rethinking Contexts for Brunanburh, in J. Barrow and A. Wareham (eds), *Myth Rulership Church and Charters: Essays in Honour of Nicholas Brooks*, 127–44. Aldershot: Ashgate.

Foot, S. 2011. *Æthelstan: The First King of England.* New Haven: Yale University Press.

Ford, A. J. 2016. *Marvel and Artefact: The 'Wonders of the East' in its Manuscript Contexts.* Leiden: Brill.

Friedrich, M. and Schwarke, C. (eds) 2016. *One-Volume Libraries: Composite and Multiple-Text Manuscripts.* Berlin: De Gruyter.

Fulk, R. D. 2012. Anglian Features in Late West Saxon, in D. Denison, R. Bermúdez-Otero, C. McCully and E. Moore, with A. Miura (eds), *Analysing Older English*, 63–74. Cambridge: Cambridge University Press.

Gameson, R. 1992a. The Decoration of the Tanner Bede, *Anglo-Saxon England*, 21, 115–159.

Gameson, R. 1992b. The Fabric of the Tanner Bede, *Bodliean Library Record*, 14, 176–206.

Godden, M. 2009. The Alfredian Project and its Aftermath: Rethinking the Literary History of the Ninth and Tenth Centuries, Sir Israel Gollancz Memorial Lecture, *Proceedings of the British Academy*, 162, 93–122.

Goold, P. A. 1999. King Eadred of Wessex, *Somerset Archaeological and Natural History Society*, 142, 317–27.

Gumbert, J. P. 2004. Codicological Units: Towards a Terminology for the Stratigraphy of the Nonhomogenous Codex, *Segno e testo: International Journal of Manuscripts and Text Transmission*, 2, 17–42.

Higgitt, J. 1979. Glastonbury, Dunstan, Monasticism and Manuscripts, *Art History*, 2:3, 275–90.

Hill, D. and Rumble, A. R. (eds) 1996. *The Defence of Wessex: the Burghal Hidage and Anglo-Saxon Fortifications.* Manchester: Manchester University Press.

Johnston, M. and Van Dussen, M. (eds) 2015. *The Medieval Manuscript Book: Cultural Approaches.* Cambridge: Cambridge University Press.

Ker, N. R. 1940. Membra Disiecta, Second Series, *The British Museum Quarterly*, 14:4, 79–86.

Ker, N. R. 1957. *Catalogue of Manuscripts Containing Anglo-Saxon.* Oxford: Clarendon Press.

Keynes, S. 1980. *The Diplomas of King Æthelred 'The Unready' (978-1016): A Study in their Use as Historical Evidence.* Cambridge: Cambridge University Press.

Keynes, S. 2007. An Abbot, an Archbishop, and the Viking Raids of 1006–7 and 1009–12, *Anglo-Saxon England*, 36, 151–220.

Kwakkel, E. (ed.) 2013. *Writing in Context: Insular Manuscript Culture, 500-1200.* Studies in Medieval and Renaissance Book Culture. Leiden: Leiden University Press.

Lapidge, M. 1988. A Frankish Scholar in Tenth-Century England: Frithegod of Canterbury/Fredegaude of Briode, *Anglo-Saxon England*, 17, 45–66.

Lapidge, M. 1996. *Anglo-Latin literature, 600-899.* London: Hambledon Press.

Lavelle, R. 2008. *Aethelred II: King of the English, 978-1016*, revised edition. Stroud: The History Press.

Lees, C. A. and Overing, G. R. 2006. *A Place to Believe in: Locating Medieval Landscapes.* University Park: Pennsylvania State University Press.

Lutz, A. (ed.) 1981. *Die Version G der Angelsächsichen Chronik: Rekonstruktion und Edition.* München: Wilhelm Fink.

Miller, T. (ed. and trans.) 1890-8. *The Old English Version of Bede's Ecclesiastical History of the English People*, Early English Text Society, os, 95, 96, 110, 111. Oxford: Oxford University Press.

Molyneaux, G. 2009. The Old English Bede: English Ideology or Christian Instruction? *English Historical Review*, 124:511, 1289–1323.

Molyneaux, G. 2011. Why were some Tenth-century English Kings Presented as Kings of Britain? *Transactions of the Royal Historical Society*, sixth series, 21, 59–91.

Molyneaux, G. 2015. *The Formation of the English Kingdom in the Tenth Century*. Oxford: Oxford University Press.

Nichols, S. 1990. Introduction: Philology in a Manuscript Culture, *Speculum*, 65:1, 1–10.

Parkes, M. B. 1976. The Palaeography of the Parker Manuscript of the Chronicle, Laws and Sedulius, and Historiography at Winchester in the Late Ninth and Tenth Centuries, *Anglo-Saxon England*, 5, 149–71.

Potter, S. 1931. *On the Relation of the Old English Bede to Werferth's Gregory and to Alfred's translations.* Prague: La Société Royale des Services de Bohême.

Pratt, D. 2014. Kings and books in Anglo-Saxon England, *Anglo-Saxon England*, 43, 297–277.

Richards, M. 1986. The Manuscript Contexts of the Old English Laws: Tradition and Innovation, in P. E. Szarmach (ed.), *Studies in Earlier English Prose,* 171–92. New York: State University of New York Press.

Roach, L. 2014. Apocalypse and Atonement in the Politics of Aethelredian England, *English Studies*, 95:7, 733–57.

Robinson, F. C. 1980. Old English Literature in its Most Immediate Context, in J. D. Niles (ed.), *Old English Literature in Context*, 11–29; 157–61. Cambridge: D.S. Brewer.

Robinson, P. A. 1980. The 'Booklet': A Self-Contained Unit in Composite Manuscripts, in A. Gruys (ed.), *Codicologica 3: Essais typologiques*, 46–69. Leiden: Brill.

Rowley, S. M. 2015. The Long Ninth Century and the Prose of King Alfred's Reign, in J. Simpson (ed.), *Oxford Handbooks Online*, 1–24. Oxford: Oxford University Press. DOI: 10.1093/oxfordhb/9780199935338.013.53.

Shailor, B. 1996. A Cataloger's View, in S. G. Nichols and S. Wenzel. (eds), *The Whole Book: Cultural Perspectives on the Medieval Miscellany*, 153–67. Ann Arbor: University of Michigan Press.

Simpson, J. 2006. Review of Ralph Hanna, *London Literature, 1300–1380, Studies in the Age of Chaucer*, 28, 290–93.

Sisam, K. 1990. Anglo-Saxon Royal Genealogies, in E. G. Stanley (ed.), *British Academy Papers on Anglo-Saxon England*, 145–204. Oxford: Oxford University Press for the British Academy.

Stenton, F. M. 1971. *Anglo-Saxon England*, 3rd edition. Oxford: Oxford University Press.

Stokes, P. A. 2014. *English Vernacular Minuscule from Æthelred to Cnut c. 990–c. 1035*. Cambridge: D. S. Brewer.

Thorman, J. 1997. The Anglo-Saxon Chronicle Poems and the Making of the English Nation, in A. J. Frantzen and J. D. Niles (eds), *Anglo-Saxonism and the Construction of Social Identity*, 60–85. Gainesville: University of Florida Press.

Torkar, R. (ed.) 1981. *Eine altenglische Übersetzung von Alcuins De virtutibus et vitiis, Kap. 20 (Liebermanns Judex): Untersuchungen und Textausgabe : mit einem Anhang: Die Gesetze II und V Aethelstan nach Otho B. xi und Add. 43703*. München: Wilhelm Fink.

Trilling, R. 2013. The Writing of History in the Early Middle Ages: ASC in Context, in C. A. Lees (ed.), *The Cambridge History of Early Medieval English Literature*, 232–56. Cambridge: Cambridge University Press.

Tyler, E. 2017. Writing Universal History in Eleventh-Century England: Cotton Tiberius B. i, German Imperial History-writing and Vernacular Lay Literacy, in M. Campopiano and H. Bainton (eds), *Universal Chronicles in the High Middle Ages*, 65–94. Woodbridge: York Medieval Press.

Waite, G. 2014. Translation Style, Lexical Systems, Dialect Vocabulary, and the Manuscript Transmission of the Old English Bede, *Medium Aevum*, 83:1, 1–48.

Waite, G. 2015. The Preface to the Old English Bede: Authorship, Transmission, and Connection with the West Saxon Genealogical Regnal List, *Anglo-Saxon England*, 44, 31–93.

Whitelock, D. 1962. The Old English Bede, Sir Israel Gollancz Memorial Lecture, in E. G. Stanley (ed.), *British Academy Papers on Anglo-Saxon England*, 227–61. Oxford: Oxford University Press for the British Academy.

Whitelock, D. 1974. The List of Chapter-Headings in the Old English Bede, in R. B. Burlin and E. B. Irving, Jr. (eds), *Old English Studies in Honour of John C. Pope*, 263–84. Toronto: University of Toronto Press.

Williams, A. 2004. Edmund I (920/1–946), in H. C. G. Matthew and B. Harrison (eds), *Oxford Dictionary of National Biography*, vol. 17, 766–8. Oxford: Oxford University Press.

Wormald, P. 1999. BL, Cotton Ms. Otho: A Supplementary Note, in P. Wormald, *Legal Culture in the Early Medieval West: Law as Text, Image, and Experience*. London: Hambledon Press.

Wormald, P. 2004. Living with King Alfred, *Haskins Society Journal*, 15, 1–39.

Yorke, B. 1988. Æthelwold and the Politics of the Tenth Century, in B. Yorke (ed.), *Bishop Æthelwold: His Career and Influence*, 65–88. Cambridge: Boydell and Brewer.

Yorke, B. 1995. *Wessex in the Early Middle Ages*. London: Leicester University Press.

Chapter 6

Winchester, Æthelings and *Clitones*: The Political Significance of the City for Anglo-Saxon Aristocracy and Norman Nobility

David McDermott

The political and symbolic significance of Winchester for kings and queens, and important ecclesiastical figures, has received considerable scholarly attention, but the same degree of academic attention has not been given to the relationship between Winchester and the children of the secular elite. The purpose of this paper is to examine the importance of the city for the younger generation of the Anglo-Saxon aristocracy and the Norman nobility. In addition to being the final resting place of kings and queens, Winchester was considered suitably prestigious to receive the mortal remains of the uncrowned sons of English royalty, and those who could be regarded as royal. In the Anglo-Saxon and Norman periods the city was seen as pivotal in securing the succession of several politically ambitious heirs, male and female. As with the older generation, Winchester and its environs were popular with Anglo-Saxon and Norman youth for its opportunities to hunt, and the consequences of that royal pastime sometimes proved fatal. The significance of Winchester for the offspring of royalty, before and after Hastings, is perhaps exemplified by Edgar Ætheling whose career was connected to the city in dynastic, administrative and litigious contexts.

The early medieval history of Winchester, from its first reference in the *Anglo-Saxon Chronicle* in 641[1] and continuing into the civil war that followed the death of the last Norman king in 1135,[2] is connected inextricably to the lives, deeds and deaths of those who sat on the thrones of Wessex and England. Between the seventh and twelfth centuries Winchester bore witness to the coronation of one king and was the home of two consecrated queens.[3] The royal city was a preferred location for Anglo-Saxon

---

[1] *ASC* 643 A, 26, n. 8.

[2] Henry I died 2 December 1135; *ASC* 1135 E, 263, n. 9.

[3] Edward the Confessor was crowned in Winchester on 3 April 1043; *ASC* MS E, 163; Queen Emma settled in Winchester in 1035; see *ASC* C, 158, n.6; and Biddle 1976, 46 and 342. The Winchester residency of Queen Edith may be inferred from her dying in the city on 18 December 1075; see *ASC* DE, 212 and Stafford 1997, 278.

and Norman kings to hold their Easter court.[4] Monarchs considered Winchester to be an appropriate location for making ecclesiastical appointments.[5] The West Saxon capital also witnessed acts of royal revenge.[6] Two queens passed away in Winchester,[7] and between them the Old Minster and the New Minster interred eleven monarchs.[8] This skeletal account of Winchester may suggest that its early medieval history is the story of the city's relationship with kings and, to a lesser but still important extent, queens. This is a consequence of the centrality of monarchy in the political milieu of the early medieval period.[9] Royals who did not bear the epithet 'king' or 'queen' tend to be marginalised and are referred to only in exceptional circumstances such as rebellion.[10] The history of early medieval Winchester, however, also concerns the children of royalty. More commonly referred to as 'ætheling' but alternatively as '*clito*', the offspring of aristocratic Anglo-Saxons and Normans had connections with the city similar to those of their exalted parents, but they also contributed to the story of the city directly from their status as royal progeny.[11] Kingly transactions conducted in Winchester were sometimes witnessed by æthelings and interment in the city was reserved for a select group of royal sons and senior aristocrats. Winchester, more than any other city in the kingdom, featured significantly in the numerous succession crises of the early medieval period; and for one late-eleventh century scion of Wessex his association with Winchester nearly proved fatal.

---

[4] Æthelred II held his Easter court in Winchester in 1052; William I in 1068 and 1086–7; William II (Rufus) in 1095 and 1100; Henry I in 1108, 1123 and 1132.

[5] In Winchester on 15 August 1114, Henry I appointed his clerk, Thurstan, to the archbishopric of York; *ASC* H, 245 and n. 12. At his Easter court in Winchester, 1132, Henry I appointed Alexander, the nephew of the bishop of Salisbury, to the bishopric of Lincoln; *ASC* E, 252.

[6] In 1035 Harald Harefoot went to Winchester and deprived Queen Emma of the royal treasury, see *ASC* CD, 58–9. In 1043, in an act of revenge for not supporting his claim to the English throne, Edward the Confessor allegedly appropriated all the estates of Queen Emma and robbed her of all her movable wealth (*ASC* CDE, 162–3). William I had Earl Waltheof imprisoned and executed in Winchester in 1076 (*ASC* AE, 212–13; see Lavelle, this volume, p. 125–49). In 1125, Henry I, as punishment for debasing the coinage, had all the guilty moneyers brought to Winchester at Christmas and mutilated; see *ASC* E, 255; and Hollister 2001, 330–40.

[7] Queen Emma died in Winchester on 6 March 1052; see *ASC* D, 176. Queen Edith died in Winchester on 18 December 1075; see *ASC* E, 212. Prior to the consecration of Queen Ælfthryth in 973 it is uncertain if the Latin *regina* or the Old English *cwen* denoted that a king's wife was consecrated but several other kings' wives may have been buried in Winchester. Ealhswith, the widow of King Alfred was buried beside her husband in the New Minster; see Birch 1892, 5. Ælfgifu, the widow and separated wife of King Eadwig, was possibly buried in the Old Minster; see Stafford 2001, 95. n.124; and Whitelock 1930, no. 8. Eadgifu, the third wife of Edward the Elder, may have been buried in the Old Minster; see Stafford 1997, 95. n. 124.

[8] The kings and consecrated queen buried in Winchester are Cynegils, Cynewulf, Egbert, Æthelwulf, Alfred, Edward the Elder, Eadred, Eadwig, Cnut, Harthacnut, Emma and William II. See also Biddle and Kjølbye-Biddle 2016, 212–49.

[9] See Brooks 2011, 43–70; and Nelson 1992, 1–12; Stafford 2006, 99–109; Foot 2011, 6.

[10] Two notable examples of Anglo-Saxon princely rebellion that receive extensive coverage in the *Anglo-Saxon Chronicle* are those of Æthelwold: *ASC* 899 AD, 92–5; and Edmund Ironside: *ASC* 1015 E, 146.

[11] For the constitutional significance of the ætheling see Dumville 1979.

Æthelweard, Ælfweard and Æthelstan

Æthelweard

From the foundation of the Old Minster in the seventh century until 1066 only three æthelings can be identified irrefutably as buried in Winchester, suggesting a particular affinity between those æthelings and the city. Evidence of such a relationship may be the royal transactions witnessed by those æthelings in Winchester. The majority of diplomas witnessed by King Alfred's younger son, Æthelweard, concern grants of land to the community (*familia*) of 'Winchester Cathedral', meaning the Old Minster.[12] Æthelweard also attested a grant from the Old Minster to his brother, King Edward the Elder.[13] Another four diplomas witnessed by Æthelweard relate to Edward's grants of land to the New Minster, Winchester.[14] The most significant piece of royal business witnessed by Æthelweard, it may be argued, was Edward's acquisition of a piece of land that he might 'found a monastery' (*mynster on gestaðolode*) for the salvation of his soul and that of his father, Alfred.[15] When the construction of Winchester's New Minster was completed it received Alfred's remains in accordance with Edward's plans that it become the family mausoleum for the House of Wessex.[16]

Æthelweard's princely status is indicated by two royal styles. In the diplomas he is most commonly referred to as *filius regis* or its variant *filius rex*, both essentially meaning 'a king's son'. From the mid-tenth century kings of Wessex regularly referred to close male relatives as *filius regis* to indicate their eligibility for the throne but also to restrict the status of 'ætheling' to those whose immediate forbears were also a king.[17] The less common title given to Æthelweard, occurring just twice, is that of *frater regis*, identifying him as the brother of the king, Edward the Elder.[18] A special status accorded to Æthelweard may also be inferred from the position of his name in the list of attestations. When Æthelweard and his nephews, the æthelings Ælfweard and Æthelstan, witnessed the same diploma Æthelweard's name usually appeared first. The one exception is an early diploma in which Ælfweard witnessed before his uncle but Æthelweard may be said to retain some seniority by witnessing before his older nephew, the future king Æthelstan.[19]

Ælfweard

Ælfweard was the eldest son of Edward's second wife, Ælfflæd, reputedly the daughter of Ealdorman Æthelhelm (see Fig. 6.1).[20] Ælfweard witnessed six of the diplomas

[12] S 359 (AD 900); S 372–3 (AD 904); S 375–7 (AD 909); S 383 (AD 909).
[13] S 1286 (AD 904).
[14] S 360 (AD 900); S 365–6 (AD 901); S 374 (AD 904).
[15] S 1443 (AD 900).
[16] JW, 352–55; Keynes 1996, 17–18 and 81, fol. 9r.
[17] Dumville 1979, 1.
[18] S 375 (AD 909); 377 (AD 909).
[19] S 366 (AD 901).
[20] ASC 898 [897] A, 9; see also Foot 2011, 37, n. 35.

attested by his uncle Æthelweard[21] and another from which his uncle was absent. On that occasion Ælfweard subscribed after his older half-brother Æthelstan.[22] In the early part of Edward's reign Ælfweard attested before his older sibling[23] but by 909 he regularly witnessed after Æthelstan.[24] Ælfweard's initially high position in the attestations of the æthelings may be related to Edward's intentions for his successor. Ælfweard may have been given prominence to indicate that he was to be regarded as Edward's legitimate progeny and heir apparent.[25] For Ælfweard to have descended to the dubious position of tertiary ætheling suggests a significant shift in Edward's relationship with his sons. The absence of any attestations by Edward's sons from 901 until 909 makes it difficult to define the cause of Ælfweard's apparent decline in popularity but the approach of Æthelstan's political majority may have prompted Edward to give his eldest son greater recognition and a more prominent place in the hierarchy of attestations.[26] Whatever the reason for Ælfweard's putative demotion his princely status and eligibility for the throne were asserted consistently by his diplomatic title of filius regis.

Æthelstan

The ætheling Æthelstan, was the eldest son of King Æthelred II (*i.e.* Æthelred the Unready, 978–1016). Æthelstan's known appearances in Winchester were not as frequent as those of his early tenth-century relatives but they took place over a greater length of time. On three occasions, during the course of nearly twenty years, Æthelstan visited Winchester, attesting Æthelred's diplomas, two of which concern the city directly. The first granted land to the Old Minster,[27] but the second granted a plot in Winchester to Æthelstan's stepmother, Queen Emma.[28] That land became the site of Emma's Winchester property, the location of which is identified today by Godbegot House in the High Street.[29] Emma's residency in Winchester, likely in the Godbegot property, during the succession crisis of 1035, in addition to the city housing the royal treasury, may have influenced the witan's decision that she act as regent for the absent Harthacnut until his return from Denmark, with Winchester functioning as his capital.[30]

---

[21] S 365; S366; S 375; S 377; S378; S 383.

[22] S 381 (AD 909).

[23] S 365; S366.

[24] S 375; S 377; S378; S 381; S 383.

[25] Later in the tenth century King Edgar attempted to forestall a succession dispute by referring to Edmund, the son of his third marriage, as clito legitimus but his son by a previous marriage, Edward, was referred to as clito procreatus; see S 745 (AD 966).

[26] William of Malmesbury asserts that when Æthelstan acceded in 924 he was thirty years old, indicating he was born c. 894; GRA, 11–12.

[27] S 891 (AD 997). An earlier diploma, kept at Winchester but recording a grant to Abingdon Abbey, is S 876 (AD 993).

[28] S 925 (AD 1012).

[29] Biddle 1976, 46, 342.

[30] ASC E, 159–61.

Family of Æthelweard

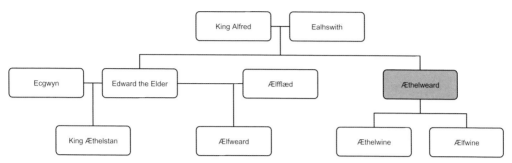

Fig. 6.1: The family of the ætheling Æthelweard. Simplified for illustrative purposes (created using Family Echo, www.familyecho.com).

The Interment of Æthelweard, Ælfweard and Æthelstan

Æthelweard, Ælfweard and Æthelstan were not the only æthelings to be involved with events in Winchester but their burial in the royal city makes them unique. Æthelings not directly in the line of succession, or those who did not accede, were generally interred elsewhere. William of Malmesbury states that King Æthelstan ordered Æthelweard's sons, Æthelwine and Ælfwine, to be buried in Malmesbury where Æthelstan intended himself to be interred.[31] The king may have wished his nephews, who, according to William, had fought alongside him at Brunanburh and were killed in the battle, to accompany him in the afterlife. Æthelstan's strained relationship with Winchester may also explain his decision to bury the æthelings in Malmesbury. Later in the tenth century, Æthelred's elder brother and son of King Edgar, the ætheling Edmund, was buried in Romsey.[32] The burial of æthelings outside Winchester allowed their royalty to be acknowledged but, in some circumstances, it could suggest unsuitability to rule – at least retrospectively. This may be the case with the ætheling Cyneheard whose brother, King Sigeberht of Wessex, was deposed by Cynewulf in 757. In revenge, Cyneheard killed Cynewulf the following year and was himself slain. While Cynewulf was buried at Winchester, the regicidal ætheling was interred at Axminster.[33] Cyneheard's killing of Cynewulf most probably prevented him being buried in Winchester but his æthelinghood was recognised by his interment in a foundation long associated with West Saxon royalty.[34]

---

[31] King Æthelstan commanded that his nephews be buried at the head of the tomb of St Aldhelm; see *GRA*, 220–1.

[32] ASC 971 A, 118.

[33] ASC 755 (for 757) AE, 46–9.

[34] ASC 755 [757] AE, 48–9, n. 8.

In contrast, the æthelings Æthelweard and Ælfweard were laid to rest in the New Minster, Winchester,[35] and Æthelstan in the Old Minster. It is not known if Æthelweard and Ælfweard expressed in life a desire to be buried in Winchester. In death the decision where they were to be interred may well have been taken by Edward the Elder. In having Æthelweard and Ælfweard buried in the New Minster Edward could advance his scheme to make his foundation the centre for commemorating his dynasty. In the case of Æthelstan, it is clear from his will that his donations to the Old Minster were intended to secure his interment by that community.[36] Æthelstan's burial in Winchester may also have been a demonstration of his royal identity and affirmation of his legitimate right to rule.[37] These considerations can also be applied to the interments of Æthelweard and Ælfweard. The burials of the three æthelings may also indicate that interment in Winchester was a privilege reserved for only the most respected scions of the House of Wessex.[38] The possibility that other æthelings were buried in Winchester is suggested by the *Liber Vitae* of the New Minster and Hyde Abbey, which contains not only the names of Æthelweard, Ælfwine and Æthelstan but also, with one exception, the names of Æthelred II's sons for whom there is no contemporary account of their interment.[39] The appearance of the names Ecgbyrht, Eadred, Eadwig and Eadgar is not necessarily evidence of burial in Winchester but their inclusion in the same document that corroborates the interment of Æthelweard, Ælwine and Æthelstan may indicate that Winchester is also their final resting place.[40] If correct, the interment of Æthelstan's brothers in Winchester may enhance the reputation and significance of the city as an early medieval necropolis.

Earl Beorn Estrithson

The immense distinction of burial in Winchester for those of royal blood who never reigned is perhaps best illustrated by the interment of Earl Beorn, the son of Estrith, daughter of King Swein Forkbeard of Denmark (see Fig. 6.2). Beorn was therefore the nephew of Cnut, king of England, Denmark and parts of Norway and Sweden. Beorn's paternal aunt, the Lady Gytha, was married to Earl Godwin of Wessex, and therefore Beorn was also a cousin of the future Queen Edith and King Harold II. In 1049 Beorn was persuaded by his exiled cousin, Swein Godwinson, to accompany him to King Edward at Sandwich to plead for his re-instatement. Beorn agreed but en route Swein had his cousin killed and surreptitiously buried at Dartmouth or Axminster. Beorn's body was eventually translated to Winchester and interred 'with King Cnut,

---

[35] For the burial of Æthelweard see *GRA*, 204–5; for that of Ælfwine see JW, 384–5 and *GRA*, 206–7.
[36] Whitelock 1979, 593–6, at 594.
[37] For recognition of the ætheling Æthelstan's claims to the crown see Stafford 1997, 91.
[38] William of Malmesbury records that Ælfwine was buried with his father because he was thought worthy of interment in Winchester, see *GRA*, 206–7.
[39] Strong circumstantial evidence that King Edmund II Ironside was buried in Winchester is admirably discussed by Biddle and Kjølbye-Biddle 2016, 224–7.
[40] Keynes 1996, fol.14v.

Family of Beorn Estrithson

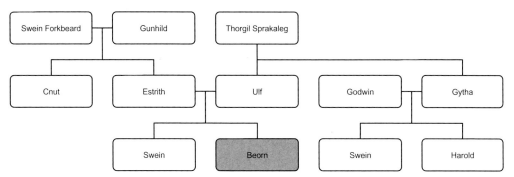

Fig. 6.2: The family of Beorn Estrithson. Simplified for illustrative purposes (created using Family Echo, www.familyecho.com).

his uncle'.[41] Beorn's involvement with state affairs in Winchester cannot account for his burial in the city; only one of the seven diplomas Beorn attested as *Dux* (Duke) concerns the city.[42] Neither can Beorn's final interment be adequately explained by his connections to the Godwinsons. In one recension of the *Anglo-Saxon Chronicle* (C) Harold is responsible for recovering Beorn's body and transporting it to Winchester but it is unlikely that Harold, then only Earl of East Anglia, possessed the influence necessary to have his cousin interred in the city of kings and exalted æthelings. Another recension of the *Chronicle* (E) attributes the translation of Beorn's body to his anonymous friends and the fleet of London.[43] Their collective anonymity suggests insufficient status and the connections necessary to have Beorn buried in Winchester. The earl's final interment may, in part, be explained by his connections to the Danish royal family. The contemporary sources do not identify him as an ætheling, but as the brother and nephew of kings; Beorn Estrithson was probably the highest ranking Dane in England. In burying him alongside his relatives Cnut and Harthacnut, it may be said that Winchester acknowledged Beorn's royalty.[44]

On a superficial level the killing of Beorn by the dispossessed Swein can be seen as the exiled earl exacting his revenge on one of the two men who refused to return to Swein his lost lands. On a more profound level, although we should not overlook the fact that Swein was himself from an Anglo-Danish background, the murder of Beorn

---

[41] *ASC* 1049 CDE, 168–71.
[42] S 1008 (AD 1045).
[43] *ASC* 1049 CE, 168–9.
[44] For the burials of Cnut and Harthacnut see ASC 1035 CDE and 1041 [1042] E, 158–9 and 163, respectively. On the topic of Beorn being the most senior Scandinavian in England, Timothy Bolton (2007) has suggested that Earl Siward of Northumbria was descended from a forgotten branch of the Danish royal family.

could be considered an attack on England's Anglo-Danish community. To assuage the anger and indignation of the prominent Scandinavians in his administration, and elsewhere, King Edward may have thought it judicious to have Beorn buried in Winchester, and possibly ordered Harold to recover the earl's body. Archaeological and onomastic evidence indicates that in the reign of Cnut the greatest concentration of Danes in Wessex was in Winchester, and in the post-Cnut period the city continued to be the centre of Anglo-Danish interests. The re-burial of Beorn, like that of Edward the Martyr who was initially interred in Wareham, may have been an act of appeasement; an attempt to placate the Scandinavian community by giving Beorn a dignified burial and thereby demonstrate that he was considered worthy of interment in the city associated with Danish royalty.[45]

The Norman Ducal family

To be honoured with interment in Winchester it was not essential for an ætheling to have a protracted or significant association with the city, or for him to have died in its vicinity. The final resting place of three members of the Norman ducal family may, however, have been influenced by their exalted status and proximity to the city when they died. All three of these prominent Normans were killed close to Winchester, in the New Forest created by William I, and their deaths can be attributed to the inherent dangers of hunting.[46] The exhilaration and satisfaction to be derived from bringing down big game in a sylvan setting made hunting popular with Anglo-Saxon nobility but for the Normans, with their reliance on cavalry in warfare, the hunt also provided opportunities to perfect their equestrian and military skills. On occasion, however, the perilous nature of hunting sometimes proved fatal with possibly the best known case being William II, better known by his cognomen 'Rufus' (the Red). In addition to the mortal wounding of William II, the treacherous nature of the chase also took the lives of William's older brother, Richard, and their nephew, also called Richard. (see Fig. 6.3)

Richard, Son of Duke William

Richard, the second son of William I, appears to have arrived in England c. 1068 and witnessed three of his father's diplomas. The last diploma, dated 1069, places Richard in 'the monastery of St Swithun' (in monasterio sancti Swiððun), that is to say, the Old Minster, where William I celebrated Easter on 13 April.[47] The year of Richard's

---

[45] For a summary of the archaeological and other evidence for Danes in Winchester, see Yorke 1995, 144. The same evidence also indicates the Danish inhabitants of Winchester belonged to the upper echelons of society, see Kjølbye-Biddle and Page 1975, 390. For the settlement of Danes in Winchester in the post-Cnut period, see Keynes 1996, 39–40. In addition to the possible intervention by King Edward in translating Beorn to Winchester, it is also conceivable that the dowager Queen Emma and the former royal chaplain, Bishop Ælfsige II, may have affected the re-burial of Beorn, see Yorke, this volume.

[46] For the death of William II see ASC 1100 E, 235–6; JW 92–3.

[47] Davis 1913, 8 no. 26.

The Norman Ducal Family

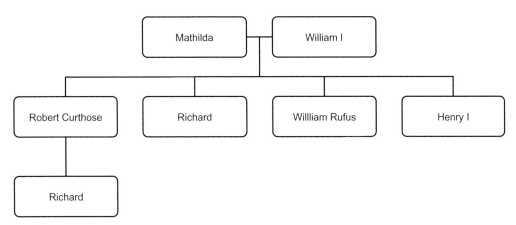

Fig. 6.3: The Norman ducal family. Simplified for illustrative purposes (created using Family Echo, www.familyecho.com).

death is unknown, with estimates extending as late as 1080, but the absence of any attestations by him beyond 1069 suggest that his demise be assigned to the beginning of the 1070s.[48] Neither is it possible to determine Richard's age when he died but the early twelfth-century Anglo-Norman monk Orderic Vitalis, described Richard as a youth who had 'not yet received the belt of knighthood' suggesting he was below the age of 16.[49] Richard may therefore have been born after 1053 and was a juvenile when he met his death.[50] There is no doubt concerning the general area where Richard died but the sources disagree as to the manner of his death. The earliest source on the subject, Orderic Vitalis, records that while Richard galloped through the New Forest in pursuit of fleeing prey he was 'badly crushed between a strong hazel branch and the pommel of his saddle, and mortally injured.' Richard survived his accident for at least a week before succumbing to his fatal wound.[51] Orderic's account of Richard's serious injury is similar to the alleged incident that befell William I in 1087 as he rode through the burning streets of Nantes. His horse, leaping over a ditch, apparently propelled the corpulent king against the pommel of his saddle and William languished for days in ever increasing pain before dying from whatever internal wound he had received.[52] The similarities between the two deaths may invite incredulity but the prominent and unforgiving upholstery of the Norman saddle make injury to a

---

[48] Barlow 1983, 13, n. 37; Douglas 1989, 393; Aird, 2008, 56.
[49] OV, III, 114–15.
[50] See Douglas 1989, 394, for the suggestion that Richard was born before 1056 and died *c.* 1075.
[51] OV, III, 114–15.
[52] GRA, 510–11.

rider, if thrown against it, plausible. A slightly later account of Richard's death, in an epigram by the prior of Winchester, Godfrey of Cambrai, tells how Richard was learning to shoot deer when death 'dared shoot [him] with a strong dart' (ausa est forte figere … jaculo). Godfrey's account may be the product of poetic licence but, if it is read literally, it may indicate that Richard was mortally struck by an arrow. The ambiguity of Godfrey's epigram might not clarify the manner of Richard's death but the author does specify when Richard died, dating his demise to 13 September.[53]

Richard's death in the New Forest is corroborated by William of Malmesbury who also indicates Richard's youth by the describing his death as the promise of 'a springtide flowering' (primeri floris) gone to waste. William's account becomes questionable, however, with the report that Richard died from an unspecified malaise, contracted by breathing 'the foggy and corrupted air' (tabidi eris nebula) of the New Forest. This explanation runs counter to the violent deaths reported in earlier sources, and William of Malmesbury himself issues the caveat that he obtained the tale from an anonymous source.[54] It may be therefore, that Orderic Vitalis has the more reliable account of how Richard died. There is no extant contemporary record of where Richard was buried but the archaeological evidence for his interment in Winchester is convincing. Below a niche in the south screen of the presbytery in Winchester cathedral a tomb covered with a slab of Purbeck marble bears the inscription '+HIC : IACET : RICARDUS : WILL'I SENIORIS : REGIS : FILI' : ET : BEORN : DUX :' (Here lies Richard son of King William the Elder and Duke Beorn). Within the tomb rests a lead coffin which, when examined in 1887, revealed another inscription predating the twelfth-century lettering on the Purbeck slab. The earlier inscription, in late eleventh-century lettering, is a simpler version of the latter and reads 'RICARD' FILI W'LI SENIORIS REGIS ET BEORN DUX'. These discoveries strongly suggest that Richard was initially buried in the Old Minster and later translated to the new Norman cathedral when it was consecrated in 1093.[55] Despite the lack of contemporary documentary evidence for Richard's tomb there is the elegy composed by Godfrey of Cambrai sometime between 1081 and 1107. It is possible that the prior genuinely lamented the premature demise of the untried ætheling but it is also possible that Godfrey's epigram was written to encourage the development of a cult centred around Richard's tomb and thereby increase the revenues of the cathedral.[56] If that was the prior's intention, Richard's tomb failed to attract the multitudes of desired pilgrims.

Richard, Son of Robert Curthose

It is possible that Winchester's post-Conquest cathedral might also contain the remains of Richard, the illegitimate offspring of Robert Curthose, another of Duke William I's sons. Robert, when in rebellion against his father, and raiding Normandy's borders is said, by Orderic Vitalis, to have fallen in love with an old priest's mistress

---

[53] Wright 1872, II, 152.
[54] GRA, 502–5.
[55] Biddle and Kjølbye-Biddle 2016, 224 and n. 54.
[56] For the possible development of nascent cult at Richard's tomb see Mason 2005, 419.

and fathered two bastard sons. Years later, their mother presented the boys at Robert's court and declared him to be their father. She reportedly established the veracity of her allegations by undergoing the ordeal of carrying a hot iron. When Duke Robert left for the First Crusade in 1096, the two youths were acknowledged by their uncle, William Rufus, and admitted to his court.[57] It is not indicated when the two boys were born, but their lack of majority in 1096 suggests that the older son, Richard, was probably born in or just after 1080. Richard met his death, according to Orderic, toward the start of Rogationtide (7–9 May), when he was hunting in the New Forest and a 'tragic event' (*lugubris eventus*) occurred. It is related that as the knights of William Rufus were readying their bows to shoot, one of their company missed his target and the arrow accidentally struck Richard killing him instantly. The unnamed archer is said to have fled immediately and escaped retribution by securing asylum in Lewes Priory where he became a monk. Orderic's comment that many had predicted Richard a promising future underscores the account with a note of irony.[58] Some of Orderic's details invite comparison with the report given for the death of William Rufus. The errant arrow and the immediate departure of the alleged culprit suggest the transference of certain elements from one fatal hunting trip to another but the probability of missing a moving target, and the desire to avoid punishment from vengeful friends, lend credibility to Orderic's account.

Later Anglo-Norman writers embellished the telling of Richard's death. John of Worcester, with a touch of pathos, asserted Richard was shot by one of his own knights.[59] William of Malmesbury provides alternative explanations, first reporting the fatal shaft struck Richard in the neck, then repeating the rumour he was hanged as his horse ran beneath the branch of a tree.[60] The latter account is plausible but its lack of corroboration and late composition suggest Richard was felled by an arrow.[61] At the time of his death, Richard was most probably no more than twenty years of age, and possibly a few years younger. There is no contemporary record that Richard was interred in Winchester but given the location of his death, and the burials of his cousin and uncle in the city's cathedral, it is likely that Richard was also laid to rest there. Recent forensic investigations may support this probability. In 2012 the mortuary chests containing the bones of kings, bishops and a queen were removed from Winchester Cathedral and their contents subjected to intense scientific scrutiny. At the time of writing the full details of the research have yet to be published but amongst the unexpected discoveries were two juvenile skulls belonging to boys aged approximately 10–15, who died *c.* 1050–1150. When the forensic investigations are completed and the results published, we may have the archaeological evidence for Richard's interment in Winchester.[62]

---

[57] OV, V, 282–3; Aird 2008, 96–7.
[58] OV, V, 282–3.
[59] JW, 92–3.
[60] GRA, 504–5.
[61] The similarity between the alleged hanging of Richard and the fate of the Old Testament character Absalom has been noted by Aird 2008, 193.
[62] See Barbara Yorke's comments on this, pp. 61–2.

Succession Disputes

The Æthelings Ælfweard and Æthelstan

In the tenth and eleventh centuries Winchester was the focus of a series of succession crises with consequences that extended beyond Wessex. The first of these dynastic conflicts was between the half-brothers Ælfweard and Æthelstan. The Worcester recension of the *Chronicle* records that upon Edward the Elder's death in 924 Æthelstan was elected king by the Mercians and consecrated at Kingston.[63] Æthelstan's election and his eventual coronation on the borders of Wessex and Mercia suggest his supporters considered him to be king of both regions but it is possible that when news of Edward's death reached Winchester, Ælfweard was elected 'king of the Anglo-Saxons', the title borne by his father and grandfather.[64] Ælfweard's election is not corroborated by contemporary sources but there is documentary evidence to suggest that Ælfweard was regarded as king, at least in Wessex. The *Liber Vitae* of the New Minster records the burials of Æthelweard and Ælfweard, describing one of them as a *clito* and the other as 'crowned with kingly badges' (*regalibis infulis redimitus*).[65] The possibility that the royal regalia adorned Ælfweard is implied by the *Liber Vitae* of Hyde monastery which refers to one 'Elfredus', possibly a Latinised corruption of Ælfweard, who is said to have been crowned in his father's lifetime but who died shortly after.[66] Further evidence for Ælfweard's election in Winchester is the West Saxon regnal list in the twelfth-century *Textus Roffensis* that accords Ælfweard a reign of four weeks.[67] Edward the Elder's sons may have reacted opportunistically to their father's death and had themselves elected king by their respective supporters. When Ælfweard died prematurely Æthelstan became king of Mercia and Wessex in 925 but he may have remained unpopular in Winchester. Æthelstan chose not to be interred in the city and William of Malmesbury relates how a certain Alfred attempted to blind Æthelstan when he visited Winchester.[68] Some of the details in William's account are highly questionable but the assertion that Æthelstan was attacked in Winchester is supported by the claims of Bath and Malmesbury abbeys to Alfred's lands which were allegedly confiscated as punishment for his assault.[69]

Edmund Ætheling and Edward the Martyr

Later in the tenth century King Edgar, hoping to avoid the discord of rival æthelings claiming the throne, nominated Edmund, his son by his third marriage, as his successor. In the re-foundation charter of the New Minster Edmund is described as *clito legitimus* (legitimate ætheling) and his name appears before that of his older half-brother, Edward, who is referred to as *clito procreatus* (a procreated ætheling).[70]

---

[63] ASC 924 D, 105. Æthelstan's coronation did not take place until 4 September 925.
[64] Keynes 1996, 19; Yorke 1988, 69–73.
[65] Keynes 1996, 81.
[66] Edwards 1866, 113.
[67] Dumville 1986, 29.
[68] GRA, 136–7; 222–3; 206–7.
[69] For Bath's claim see S 414; for Malmesbury's claim see S 415; S 434–5. See also Kelly 2005, 216–18.
[70] S 745 (AD 966).

In effect, Edward was denounced as illegitimate and Edmund, the son of Queen Ælfthryth, declared the rightful heir to the throne. The probable architect of the re-foundation charter was one of Ælfthryth's most staunch supporters, Bishop Æthelwold of Winchester.[71] Edgar's efforts to forestall a succession crisis proved ineffective. Edmund died prematurely in 971 and when Edgar passed in 975 his remaining son by Ælfthryth, the future Æthelred II, was a minor. Æthelred and Edward became the nuclei around which powerful factions formed with Æthelred supported by Bishop Æthelwold. Æthelred lost the succession challenge to Edward but secured the crown when the latter was assassinated in 978. Prominent amongst the new king's chief advisors was Bishop Æthelwold.[72] The bishop's drafting of the re-foundation charter, advocacy of Æthelred's succession and position as a chief counsellor to the king illustrate the continuing ability of Winchester's most prestigious representatives to effect the course of political life in Anglo-Saxon England.

Harold Harefoot and Harthacnut

Winchester's involvement in a dynastic dispute also proved crucial in 1035 when Harald Harefoot, the eldest of Cnut's sons by Ælfgifu of Northampton, asserted his claim to the throne by seizing the greater part of the royal treasury in the city (see Fig. 6.4).[73] The absence of Harthacnut, Harald's rival half-brother by Cnut's wife Emma, may have facilitated his pre-emptive action. In response to Harald taking the treasury a meeting of all the royal councillors was held in Oxford, where the country was divided between the rival æthelings. Harald's share was Northumbria and Mercia, and Harthancnut acquired Wessex. In his continued absence, Emma was to reside in Winchester with her son's housecarls and act as Harthacnut's regent until he returned from Denmark.[74] As a solution to the country's succession crisis, partition had the advantage of allowing the rival claimants an opportunity to resolve their differences without recourse to violence but Winchester's status as Harthacnut's capital proved to be ephemeral. In 1037 Harald, whose claim to be king was now said to be universally recognised, expelled Emma from Winchester, and England was re-unified under a son of Cnut not distracted by his overseas territories.[75] The decision to partition the country and make Winchester the capital of an absent king was a plausible strategy. England had been divided, albeit briefly, between rival rulers twice before (between Eadwig and Edgar in 957, and between Edmund Ironside and Cnut in 1016). The re-establishment of Winchester as the chief city of an independent southern England proved to be unsuccessful not because the policy was inherently unsound but because the protracted absence of Harthacnut made the arrangement untenable.

---

[71] Yorke 1988, 82–3.
[72] Yorke 1988, 85; Keynes 1980, 176–7.
[73] *ASC* 1035 C, 158–9. Martin Biddle and Derek Keene discuss the importance of Winchester as the central repository for the king's treasure, in Biddle 1976, 290–1.
[74] ASC 1036 [1035] E, 159–61; Stafford, 1997, 237–8.
[75] ASC 1037 CD, 160–1.

The Family of Cnut

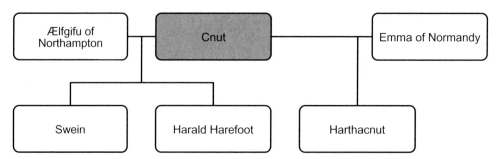

Fig. 6.4: *The family of King Cnut. Simplified for illustrative purposes (created using Family Echo, www.familyecho.com).*

Winchester and the 'Route to Power'

William Rufus and Henry I

Norman *clitones* who wished to gain the English throne also recognised the significance of securing the nation's treasury at Winchester. To assert his claim to the crown William Rufus deserted the bedside of his father, dying at Caen in Normandy, and made straight for Winchester, arriving on 10 or 11 September 1087. Before proceeding to Westminster for his coronation, on 26 September, Rufus is said to have remained in Winchester to oversee the distribution of the dead king's accumulated wealth amongst England's churches and councils.[76] The ability to control the disbursement of the nation's wealth, and his generosity to the Church and nobility, undoubtedly contributed to the acceptance of Rufus as the successor to William I. The pragmatic approach by Rufus to securing the kingdom was emulated by his younger brother, Henry. When William II was pronounced dead in the New Forest, on 2 August 1100, Henry reputedly hastened to Winchester and demanded the keys of the treasury be surrendered to him as his brother's heir. Those loyal to Henry's older brother, Robert Curthose, challenged the young *clito*'s peremptory behaviour but the intercession of those with calmer temperaments resulted in the treasury, and Winchester castle, being transferred to Henry and the assembled nobles recognising him as the new king.[77]

King Stephen

In the protracted succession dispute between Stephen of Blois and the Empress Matilda, the grandchildren of William I, Winchester and its treasury were an integral

---

[76] GRA, 542–5; JW, 46–7; Barlow 1983, 54–5.
[77] OV, V, 290–1; Hollister 2001, 104. For an arrangement between Rufus and Robert Curthose as each other's heirs see *ASC* 1091 [1090] E, 226; Brooke 1978, 165; Hollister 1986, 66.

part of their 'route to power'.[78] When Henry I died in 1135 his nephew, Stephen, was allegedly acclaimed by the magnates of London who elected him unanimously as king.[79] Endorsement by London's most distinguished citizens was not a prerequisite for Stephen's accession but their approval indicates he was supported by the nation's effective capital. More importantly, however, Stephen needed the sanction of the country's ecclesiastical elite which he secured by travelling to Winchester where his full brother, Henry, was bishop and held the highly influential office of Apostolic Legate in England. Stephen was reputedly received at Winchester's gates warmly and escorted by Bishop Henry and the leading citizens into the kingdom's second city. Prior to Stephen's arrival it is alleged Bishop Henry attempted to bribe William Pont de l'Arche, the keeper of the treasury, to relinquish the castle and its treasury. William steadfastly refused the bishop's inducements until he heard of Stephen's approach, whereupon he is said to have presented himself to the future king and surrendered control of the castle and its considerable wealth.[80] The anonymous author of the *Gesta Stephani* may have exaggerated Stephen's reputation for charisma but the episode demonstrates a prospective ruler's need to secure the country's finances stored in the nation's second city. The *Gesta* also credits Bishop Henry as being Stephen's greatest hope for realising his ambitions. Henry might also have persuaded the Archbishop of Canterbury, who had sworn adherence to Stephen's cousin, Matilda, to switch allegiance and crown Stephen on 22 December 1035.[81] Stephen's advancement to the throne was also promoted by the significant figure of Roger, the Bishop of Salisbury, but the impression created by some of the contemporary sources is that Stephen would not have become king without the Bishop of Winchester to champion his cause.[82]

The Empress Matilda

The Empress Matilda, the daughter of Henry I and Matilda, the great granddaughter of Edmund Ironside, employed a methodology similar to that of Stephen. After capturing Stephen at the battle of Lincoln in 1141, Matilda proceeded to Winchester which evidently continued to be seen as a principal city in the kingdom.[83] The city also remained the power base of England's wealthiest and most politically astute prelate, Stephen's brother, Bishop Henry. On 23 February 1141 Matilda met the bishop eight miles outside Winchester, at the nunnery of Wherwell, to discuss her reception by the city. With the arrangements for her entrance satisfactorily concluded the empress and Bishop Henry reconvened outside Winchester on 2 March when he submitted his formal allegiance. Henry's personal motives for apparently deserting Stephen's cause are unknown but the bishop's official justification was his brother's inability

---

[78] Dalton 2012, 86.
[79] *GS*, 8–9; OV, VI, 516.
[80] *GS*, 8–9; Crouch 2000, 36.
[81] *GS*, 8–9; *HN*, 15.
[82] GS, 8–9; *HN*, 15.
[83] King 2010, 45.

to preserve the peace and the alleged alienation of Church property and abuse of ecclesiastical appointments.[84] The following day, accompanied by a procession of the city's dignitaries including the castellan William Pont de l'Arche, Matilda was escorted to Winchester cathedral and formally honoured.

Matilda's acceptance by Winchester marked a significant step towards consecration and her accession was further advanced soon after. On 3 March Matilda issued a diploma which announced her virtual elevation to the throne by referring to her as *Anglorum regina* (queen of the English). The *Gesta Stephani* also reports the assembly in Winchester lauding Matilda as *domina et regina* (lady and queen) and that she exulted in her royal title.[85] Winchester's acclamation of Matilda as queen echoes London's ovation of Stephen as king. The approval of neither city was legally binding, but their endorsement constituted an important symbolic progression on the path to consecration. Despite Stephen's incarceration, and Winchester acknowledging her sovereignty, Matilda did not become queen. Plans for her coronation at Westminster were rudely curtailed when royalist leaders, accompanied by the obligatory angry mob, compelled Matilda and her companions to leave the city in undignified haste.[86] Although Matilda's ambition to be enthroned was unrealised, she could not have reached the cusp of coronation without the support of what was presumably recognised as the kingdom's second city, Winchester. The year 1141 may also be said to have signalled the beginning of the end of Winchester's political significance, and the increasing importance of London and Westminster. In that year a considerable portion of Winchester was sacked by the Londoners and Stephen's troops, and from then on Stephen made increasingly fewer visits to the city.[87] It is also around this time that Stephen is thought to have detached the office of the exchequer from the treasury at Winchester and maintained it, albeit in a lesser form, at London or Westminster.[88]

Edgar the Ætheling

Although the Normans replaced the Anglo-Saxons as rulers of England in 1066 the connection between English royalty and Winchester was maintained by Edgar Ætheling, the grandson of King Edmund II Ironside and great nephew of Edward the Confessor (see Fig. 6.5). In what has been interpreted as the most convincing evidence that Edgar was regarded as Edward's intended heir, the names of Edward, his queen, Edith, and that of Edgar appear together in the *Liber Vitae* of the New Minster, Winchester. Most significantly, Edgar bears the royal title 'Clito'.[89] The association in the document of the king, the queen and the ætheling is a clear indication that at the time the entry was made Edgar was considered to be the heir presumptive, but

---

[84] *HN*, 52–4; Crouch 2000, 169.
[85] Davis *et al.* 1969, 343, 130; GS, 118–19.
[86] *HN*, 56–7; GS, 120–6. See Weikert, this volume, pp. 151–68.
[87] GS, 132–7; see also Tanner 2007, 197.
[88] Round 1889, 80–1; King 1984, 133–53; Yoshitake 1988, 950–9.
[89] Keynes 1996, fol. 29 r. The argument that the *Liber Vitae* provides evidence of Edward's intention that he was to be succeeded by Edgar is made by Baxter 2009, 99.

Family of Edgar Ætheling

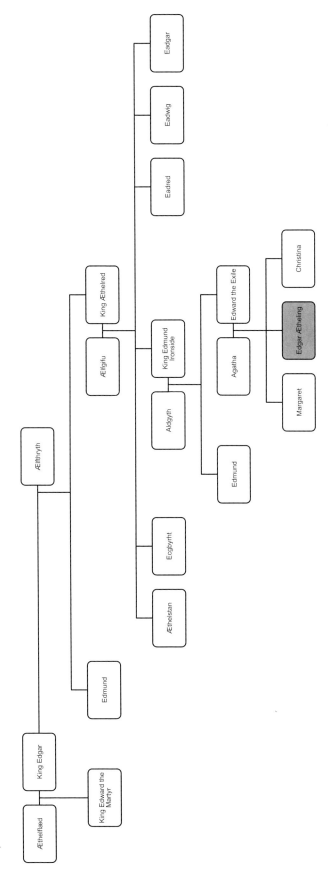

Fig. 6.5: The family of Edgar Ætheling. Simplified for illustrative purposes (created using Family Echo, www.familyecho.com).

in the aftermath of 14 October 1066, Edgar's prospects of becoming the next king of England evaporated when he submitted to William I.[90]

Edgar's long and turbulent career brought him into conflict with William I and William II but he was reconciled to them both and temporarily became a member of their respective courts. When William I held his Easter court in Winchester in 1086 and William Rufus held his Easter court there in 1095, it is reasonable to infer they were accompanied by Edgar as part of their entourage, but the ætheling's association with Winchester surpasses his attendance at court.[91]

In the fourteenth century, John of Fordun recorded that in the reign of William Rufus 'a certain recreant knight' (*miles quidem degener*) named Ordgar, to gain favour with the Norman king falsely accused 'Edgar *Clito*' of treason, and the matter was to be settled by judicial combat.[92]

Edgar's attempts to find a champion to represent him proved unsuccessful until an English knight, called Godwin, came forward to defend the ætheling's honour. Godwin is said to have been 'of Winton', presumably an allusion to Winchester's Anglo-Saxon name *Wintancæstir*. After a heroic and dramatic duel, Godwin defeated Ordgar and was rewarded with the lands and property of his vanquished foe. William Rufus, in acknowledgement of Edgar's now unquestionable innocence, endowed the ætheling with many gifts and honours, and Edgar became the king's 'great friend' (*amicissimus*).[93]

Fordun's tale of late eleventh-century judicial combat in Winchester is, in parts, fantastical but corroborative evidence suggests it may have some foundation in fact. An association between Edgar and a certain 'Godwin' is verified in Domesday Book. The lands owned by Edgar Ætheling in the hundred of 'Edwinstree' (Hertfordshire) identifies a 'Godwin' as his tenant.[94] Domesday also indicates a connection between a 'Godwine' and a certain Ordgar. In 1086 Ordgar possessed land in Lewknor Hundred (Oxfordshire) which he held of the king, but it was previously held freely by one Godwin.[95] The names 'Godwin' and 'Ordgar' were not uncommon in Anglo-Saxon England and therefore the landholders identified in Domesday are not necessarily

---

[90] A tentative dating of the entry in the *Liber Vitae* was initially made by Pauline Stafford who suggested the names were entered by Ælfwig, the abbot of the New Minster, Winchester, who died 14 October 1066; Stafford 1997, 269, n. 61. A slightly narrower dating has been suggested by Tom Licence, who dates the names of Edward, Edith and Edgar in the *Liber Vitae* to c.1063–6; Licence 2017, 113–28. The appearance of Edgar's name alongside that of Edward and Edith is similar to Continental practices of association, and Emily Ward suggests it may reflect Edward's experiences in Normandy during his own youth, Ward 2020, 338. For Edgar's submission to William, see *ASC* 1066 D, 199–200.

[91] *ASC* 1074 DE; *ASC* 1091 E, 210 and 227 respectively.

[92] *John of Fordun's Chronicle*, in Skene 1871 (text), 220 and 1872 (trans.), 210. For an account of judicial combat see *ASC* 1096 [1095] E, 232.

[93] *John of Fordun's Chronicle*, in Skene 1871 (text), 221–2 and 1872 (trans.), 211–12. For the Norman judicial duel see Robertson 1925, 232–3. For the history of judicial combat in Anglo-Saxon and Norman England see Bloomfield 1969, 545–59.

[94] Williams and Martin 2002, 392.

[95] *Ibid.*, 443.

the two combatants named by Fordun. However, Godwin's motive to fight Ordgar may go beyond Fordun's explanation that Godwin was motivated by Edgar's ancient and exalted heritage. The accounts in Domesday and Fordun may be reconciled if Godwin of Winton had lost his manor to Ordgar and seized upon Edgar's trial as an opportunity for revenge. A further connection between Edgar and Godwin is provided by William of Malmesbury. When Edgar left to join the First Crusade he is said to have been accompanied by 'Robert son of Godwin, a most valiant knight.'[96] It is possible Robert was the son of Edgar's tenant in Hertfordshire. The reliability of Fordun's narrative is mitigated by its late composition and melodramatic passages but the references to Godwin in earlier, and closely contemporary sources, lend a veneer of credibility to the story of the honour and the life of Edgar Ætheling being preserved by a knight from Winchester.[97]

Conclusions

The early medieval history of Winchester is inextricably linked to English monarchy, but it is also closely connected to Anglo-Saxon aristocrats and Norman nobles who were not enthroned or whose accession was disputed. A select minority of royal offspring participated in state affairs conducted in Winchester and the privilege of interment in the city was restricted to an elite group of æthelings. The burial in Winchester of royal scions who never ruled argues for its minsters functioning as family mausoleums for West Saxon, Anglo-Danish and Norman dynasties. Strong circumstantial evidence suggests that royal children, for whom there is no documentary or epigraphic evidence of interment in Winchester, may also be buried in the city. Tenth- and eleventh-century claimants to the English throne sought to advance their path to consecration by securing the political, financial and symbolic support of Winchester. The city also provided the means by which one ætheling, who was proclaimed king but abandoned with meretricious alacrity, had his integrity and life preserved. In the early twelfth century Winchester began to be replaced by London as the country's premier city but the West Saxon city, mausoleum of monarchs, sepulchre of princes and guardian of the nation's treasury, continued to exert considerable influence on England's political fortunes.

Abbreviations

ASC   Swanton, M. (ed. and trans.) 2000. *The Anglo-Saxon Chronicles.* London: Phoenix Press.

---

[96] *GRA*, 467. The primary sources give contradictory dates for the presence of Edgar Ætheling in the East. Orderic Vitalis records that Edgar was in Antioch in 1098 but William of Malmesbury dates this event to 1102; OV, V, 270 and n. 2; *GRA*, 466–7. Runciman accepted Orderic's dating but it has been disputed ever since, most recently by Parsons, in favour of William of Malmesbury; Runciman 1968, 227–8; Parsons 2019, 280.

[97] See also Hooper 1985, 210.

GRA   Mynors, R. A. B., Thomson, R. M. and Winterbottom, M. (eds and trans.) 1998. *Gesta Regum Anglorum: The History of the English Kings*, Vol. 1. Oxford: Oxford University Press.

GS   Potter, K. R. (ed. and trans.) 1976. *Gesta Stephani*. London: Thomas Nelson and Sons.

HN   King, E. and Potter, K. R. (ed. and trans.) 1998. William of Malmesbury, *Historia novella*. Oxford: Clarendon Press.

JW   Darlington, R. R. and McGurk, P. (eds) and Bray, J. and McGurk, P. (trans.) 1998. *The Chronicle of John of Worcester*, Vol. 2. Oxford: Oxford University Press.

OV   Chibnall, M. (ed. and trans.) 1968–80. Orderic Vitalis, *The Ecclesiastical History of Orderic Vitalis*, 6 vols. Oxford: Oxford University Press.

S   Sawyer, P. H. 1968. *Anglo-Saxon Charters: an Annotated List and Bibliography*, Royal Historical Society Guides and Handbooks, 8. London: Royal Historical Society.

Bibliography

Primary Sources

Birch, W. de Gray. 1892. *Liber Vitae: Register and Martyrology of New Minster ad Hyde Abbey, Winchester*. London: Simpkin; and Winchester: Warren.

Davis, H. W. C. (ed.) 1913. *Regesta Regum Anglo-Normannorum 1066-1154*. Oxford: Clarendon Press.

Edwards, E. 1866. *Liber Monasterii de Hyda*. London: Longman.

Kelly, S. (ed.) 2005. *Charters of Malmesbury Abbey*. Oxford: Oxford University Press.

Keynes, S. (ed.) 1996. *The Liber Vitae of the New Minster and Hyde Abbey Winchester*, Early English Manuscripts in Facsimile, 26. Copenhagen: Rosenkilde and Bagger.

Robertson, A. J. 1925. *The Laws of the Kings of England from Edmund to Henry I*. Cambridge: Cambridge University Press.

Skene, W. F. (ed.) 1871. *Johannis de Fordun Chronica gentis Scotorum*. Edinburgh: Edmonston and Douglas.

Skene, W. F. (ed.) 1872. *John of Fordun's Chronicle of the Scottish Nation*. Edinburgh: Edmonston and Douglas.

Whitelock, D. (ed.) 1930. *Anglo-Saxon Wills*. Cambridge: Cambridge University Press.

Whitelock, D. (ed.) 1979. *English Historical Documents, c. 500-1042*, 2nd edition. London: Methuen.

Williams, A. and Martin, G. H. (eds) 2002. *Domesday Book: A Complete Translation*. London: Penguin.

Wright, T. (ed.) 1872. *The Anglo-Latin Satirical Poets and Epigrammatists of the Twelfth Century*, Vol. 2. London: Longman.

Secondary Sources

Aird, W. M. 2008. *Robert Curthose Duke of Normandy*. Woodbridge: Boydell & Brewer.

Barlow, F. 1983. *William Rufus*. London: Methuen.

Baxter, S. 2009. Edward the Confessor and the Succession Question, in R. Mortimer (ed.), *Edward the Confessor: The Man and the Legend*, 77–118. Woodbridge: Boydell and Brewer.

Biddle, M. (ed.) 1976. *Winchester in the Early Middle Ages: An Edition and Discussion of the Winton Domesday*. Winchester Excavations Committee 1. Oxford: Clarendon Press.

Biddle, M. and Kjølbye-Biddle, B. 2016. Danish Royal Burials in Winchester: Cnut and his Family, in R. Lavelle and S. Roffey (eds), *Danes in Wessex: The Scandinavian Impact on Southern England, c. 800–c. 1100*, 212–49. Oxford: Oxbow Books.

Bloomfield, M. W. 1969. Beowulf, Byrhtnoth and the Judgement of God: Trial by Combat in Anglo-Saxon England, *Speculum*, 44, 4, 545–59.

Bolton, T. 2007. Was the Family of Earl Siward and Earl Waltheof a Lost Line of the Ancestors of the Danish Royal Family? *Nottingham Medieval Studies*, 51, 41–71.

Brooke, C. N. L. 1978. *The Saxon and Norman Kings*, 2nd edition. London: Fontana.

Brooks, N. 2011. Why is the *Anglo-Saxon Chronicle* about Kings? *Anglo-Saxon England*, 39, 43–70.

Crouch, D. 2000. *The Reign of King Stephen 1135-1154*. Harlow: Longman.

Dalton, P. 2012. The Accession of King Henry I, August 1100, *Viator*, 43, 2, 79–110.

Douglas, D. C. 1989. *William the Conqueror: The Norman Impact on England*, revised edition. New Haven and London: Yale University Press.

Dumville, D. 1979. The Ætheling: A Study in Anglo-Saxon Constitutional History, *Anglo-Saxon England*, 5, 1–33.

Dumville, D. 1986. The West Saxon Genealogical Regnal List: Manuscripts and Texts, *Anglia*, 104, 1–32.

Foot, S. 2011. *Æthelstan: The First King of England*. New Haven and London: Yale University Press.

Hollister, C. W. 1986. *Monarchy, Magnates and Institutions in the Anglo-Norman World*. London: Hambledon Continuum.

Hollister, C. W. 2001. *Henry I*. New Haven and London: Yale University Press.

Hooper, N. 1985. Edgar the Ætheling: Anglo-Saxon Prince, Rebel and Crusader, *Anglo-Saxon England*, 8, 197–214.

Keynes, S. D. 1980. *The Diplomas of King Aethelred 'The Unready', 978-1016: A Study in Their Use as Historical Evidence*. Cambridge; Cambridge University Press.

King. E. 1984. The Anarchy of King Stephen's Reign, *Transactions of the Royal Historical Society*, 5th Series, 34. 133–53.

King, E. 2010. *King Stephen*. New Haven and London: Yale University Press.

Kjølbye-Biddle, B. and Page, R. I. 1975. A Scandinavian Rune-stone from Winchester, *Antiquaries Journal*, 55, 389–94.

Mason, E. 2005. *William II: Rufus, the Red King*. Stroud. Tempus.

Licence, T. 2017. Edward the Confessor and the Succession Question; A Fresh Look at the Sources, *Anglo-Norman Studies*, 39, 13–28

Nelson, J. L. 1992. *Charles the Bald*. Harlow: Longman.

Runciman, S. 1968. *History of the Crusades*, Vol. 1. Cambridge: Cambridge University Press.

Round, J. 1889. *The Commune of London and Other Studies*. London: Archibald Constable.

Stafford, P. 1997. *Queen Emma and Queen Edith: Queenship and Women's Power in Eleventh Century England*. Oxford: Oxford University Press.

Stafford, P. 2006. Writing the Biography of Eleventh-Century Queens, in D. Bates, J. Crick and S. Hamilton (eds), *Writing Medieval Biography, 750-1250: Essays in Honour of Frank Barlow*, 99–109. Woodbridge: Boydell Press.

Tanner, H. 2007. Henry I's Administrative Legacy: The Significance of Place-Data Distribution in the Acta of King Stephen, in D. F. Fleming and J. M. Pope (eds), *Henry I and the Anglo-Norman World: Studies in Memory of C. Warren Hollister*, 183–99. Woodbridge: Boydell Press.

Ward, E. J. 2020. Child Kings and the Norman Conquest: Representations of Association and Succession, in L. Ashe and E. Ward (eds), *Conquests in Eleventh-Century England: 1016, 1066*, 331–52. Woodbridge: Boydell Press.

Yorke, B. 1988. Æthelwold and the Politics of the Tenth Century, in B. Yorke (ed.), *Bishop Æthelwold: His Career and Influence*, 65–88. Woodbridge: Boydell Press.

Yorke, B. 1995. *Wessex in the Early Middle Ages*. London: Leicester University Press.

Yoshitake, K. 1988. The Exchequer in the Reign of Stephen. *English Historical Review*, 103. 950–9.

Chapter 7

The Execution of Earl Waltheof: Public Space and Royal Authority at the Edge of Eleventh-Century Winchester

Ryan Lavelle

This chapter considers the circumstances and the spatial context of the execution in 1076 of Early Waltheof of Northumbria. After examining aspects of the causes and course of the rebellion which led to the arrests of the earl and his co-conspirators in 1075, the chapter addresses the significance of the choice of St Giles' Hill for a public execution as a demonstration of 'hyperlegitimised' royal authority under extraordinary circumstances. This is undertaken by consideration of the other places of execution around the city and by analysis of the urban setting of Waltheof's likely movement through the city to his place of execution. The chapter also addresses the potential significance of Waltheof's position with regard to the royal families of England and Denmark, an issue which may further explain the significance of Winchester as the place of Waltheof's execution.

The execution of the earl of Northumbria, Waltheof, the so-called 'last English Earl', on 31 May 1076 on St Giles' Hill on the eastern edge of the city of Winchester, is a moment which, at first sight, might define the rupture between the old order of pre-Conquest England and the new Anglo-Norman *regnum*. Waltheof's death and his disembodied head's miraculous recitation of the final words of the Lord's Prayer, were recorded in some detail by the early twelfth-century Anglo-Norman historian Orderic Vitalis, who drew on his first-hand knowledge of a Crowland Abbey tradition.[1] The execution marked the final end of a rebellion which had begun in 1075 with Waltheof in league with the Norman Roger de Breteuil, Earl of Hereford and son of William FitzOsbern, and the Breton Roger de Gael, Earl of East Anglia – a conspiracy which Waltheof may himself have betrayed when he confessed to it, perhaps to Archbishop Lanfranc, and threw himself on the king's mercy, probably going to Normandy to do

---

[1] OV, II, 311–25.

so.[2] The moment of Waltheof's execution on St Giles' Hill, overlooking the city of Winchester from the east, is one now largely forgotten in the twenty-first century public memory of the city. However, a small stone memorial commemorating – in a somewhat understated fashion – the earl's death as well as the representation of his trial at 'the Witan Hall' in a civic pageant to celebrate the history of the city in 1908 (Figs. 7.1 and 7.2) indicate the ways in which Victorian and twentieth-century Anglo-Saxonist traditions presented this apparent final tragedy of the Norman Conquest. Waltheof's final words to the court, as imagined for the pageant, resonate with this sense of lamentation:

> That I, the last of Englishmen should fall
> By the churl axe of headsman... for a wife!
> This is the last of Senlac field – my death.
> Harold, great Harold, had I died with thee![3]

In this sense, the execution was part of the standard Victorian and Edwardian representation of the early medieval history of the city. Waltheof's death seems to have been presented as a tragic footnote, a last hurrah of the Anglo-Saxons. As a manifestation of the apparent virtues of Anglo-Saxon England, the subject of the execution of Earl Waltheof attracted the attention of Victorian scholars. Edward Freeman held Waltheof up as a wronged Englishman killed at the merciless hands of William the Conqueror, following Orderic in throwing in some blame for Waltheof's wife Judith, William's niece, for good measure; in the mid-twentieth century, Sir Frank Stenton hinted that he felt similarly: 'it can only be left an open question whether his execution can be justified in morality as well as in law'.[4] More recent readings of Waltheof have, understandably, been less fulsome in praise of Waltheof as a betrayed defender of the old ways, emphasising the establishment of the earl's place in a post-Conquest political order.[5] Most recently, John Hudson's discussion of the execution of the earl emphasised the nature of the punishment as something related to William's kingship and indeed a response to the affront to the king's personal relationship with the earl. The execution was, according to Hudson, an unusual punishment because Waltheof's actions transgressed personal levels of loyalty in a way that the actions

---

[2] Accounts of events written within about half a century of the death of Waltheof, are in *ASC* DE 1075 (Plummer 1892–99, I, 210–12; trans. Swanton 2000, 210–12), John of Worcester, *Chronicon*, s.a. 1074 and 1075 (for 1075 and 1076) (McGurk 1998, 24–9) and William of Malmesbury, *Gesta Regum Anglorum*, chs. 253 and 255 (Mynors *et al.* 1998, 468–73); Thorkell Skallasson's skaldic verse on the betrayal of Waltheof, Thorkell's lord and patron, provides a different perspective (Campbell 1971, 16). A recent and comprehensive treatment of the events is in Bates 2016, 374–88 but from the perspective of the 'English' Waltheof and 'half-English' Ralph, see Williams 1995, 58–66.

[3] Skrine 1908, 31. This was not the first time that the *Tragedy* of Waltheof had been dramatised in England; see Worsley 1843.

[4] Freeman 1867–79, IV, 577–78; 590–96 (Judith's accusation (OV, 320–1) is at 590). Stenton 1971, 610–13 (quotation at 612).

[5] Scott 1952; Williams 1995, 57–65; for a consideration of the post-1076 readings of Waltheof, see Huntington 2009 and Mason 2012.

WINCHESTER PAGEANT : The Trial of Waltheof.   The Wykeham Series, No. D
William the Conqueror pronouncing the Death Sentence.

Fig. 7.1: The Trial of Waltheof, as depicted in the grounds of Wolvesey Castle, at the Winchester pageant of 1908. © Winchester City Council collections. Provided by Hampshire Cultural Trust.

of the Norman Roger and the Breton Ralph did not.[6] Hudson's interpretation makes a lot of sense in the circumstances of the upheaval of post-Conquest England.

While the execution of Earl Waltheof is not a new subject, there is less consideration of its urban and landscape context and it is warranted here in the light of the evidence for other executions around the city of Winchester. This chapter stems from my wider-ranging study of the political and social contestation of space in the early and central Middle Ages, *Places of Contested Power* (2020). In that volume, I consider the significance of the reassertion of authority inherent in the execution of Waltheof in the context of such events as William's victory over an earlier generation of rebel barons at the Norman battle of Val-ès-Dunes (1047).[7] However, the context of the study of the relationship between authority and urban community in Winchester as a 'royal city' provides an opportunity to develop the examination of the significance of the execution of Waltheof. By definition, the topic of rebellion is associated with the authority of rulers, whether royal or ducal, and it is Winchester's royal authority which came into play in what was essentially what might be termed a 'hyperlegitimised' demonstration of power during the later eleventh century, in

---

[6] Hudson 2011.
[7] Lavelle 2020, 124–35.

a manner commensurate with the Conqueror's use of the city.[8]

After a discussion of the context of the 'Earls' Revolt' of 1075 and Waltheof's role in it, this chapter addresses the events of 31 May 1076 and their implications for the projection of royal power in and around the city of Winchester itself. The chapter concludes with a consideration of the context of the death of Queen Edith in Winchester in December 1075,[9] which raises the significance of a set of circumstances and connections which, to my knowledge, have not been previously explored.

The Earls' Revolt: Ambition and Failure

While the nature of the (failed) seizure of power is a dynamic which is often emphasised in readings of the events of 1075,[10] the plotting of this last English earl with his co-conspirators is indicative of the interests of a new generation of post-1066 earls who seem to have perceived themselves as having lost the inheritance of power

Fig. 7.2: A stone commemorating the death of Earl Waltheof, dating from the twentieth century (photographed by the author in 2020). The main text reads 'St Giles' Hill. The great fair of St Giles, granted to Bishop Walkelyn by William Rufus was held for several centuries. Near this spot Waltheof the last Saxon earl was executed on the 31 May 1076 by order of the Conqueror.'

and authority that their fathers – figures belonging to the previous generation – had enjoyed.[11] All the same, the subversion of authority and landscape may well have played a role here. A wedding feast to celebrate the nuptials of Emma, sister of Earl Roger, to Earl Ralph at Exning (Cambs.) in 1075, which Waltheof attended, was a crucial moment in the rebellion. We are reliant on John of Worcester's version of events for the detail that this was Exning – the *Anglo-Saxon Chronicle* relates that the bride-ale (*briydlope*) was in Norwich but, given that Norwich is mentioned with regard to the bringing of

---

[8] For a reassessment of William in Wessex and Winchester, see Bates 2020.

[9] *ASC* D 1075, Plummer 1892–99, I, 212.

[10] *e.g.* Carpenter 2004, 102. Carpenter comments on the 'amnesty' of treason killings that followed Waltheof's death (126–7, 494).

[11] Lewis 1990.

Emma to Norwich, presumably to Ralph's castle there, these details are not necessarily contradictory.[12] The *Anglo-Saxon Chronicle*'s account reads like sedition and, ultimately, tragedy when it is read through a filter of lordship and the subversion of lordship. The poetic judgements of the author indicate the gravity of the occasion:[13]

> there was that bride-ale, which was many man's bale

> *þær wæs þæt brydealo, þæt wæs manegra manna bealo*

and

> some he ordered blinded,
> and some exiled from the land
> and some were reduced to ignominy.
> Thus were traitors to the king laid low.

> *sume hi wurdon geblende,*
> *⁊ sume wrecen of lande,*
> *⁊ sume getawod to scande*
> *þus wurdon þæs kyninges*
> *swican genyðerade*

The *Chronicle*'s sense of language compares to the expectations of tragedy in the four surviving letters of Archbishop Lanfranc of Canterbury to Waltheof's co-conspirator, Earl Roger, son of William FitzOsbern. Lanfranc's words are suggestive of the public nature of rumours of revolt which must have had a bearing on the ways in which Waltheof's own case was received.[14] In his account of the affair, Orderic places emphasis on the refusal of the conspirators to answer the summons to the king's court, though given the evident absence of William himself from an Easter 1075 court, the rebels were evidently absenting themselves from what was a deputed court rather than from the royal presence of the king himself – an important distinction if we bear in mind what Matthew Strickland has noted with regard to rebels' underlying respect for the person of the king in cases of conflict.[15]

Lanfranc's letters to Roger reveal the way in which the crisis escalated, although in the fourth and final known letter, a rather brief communication in which the archbishop quietly advises Roger to 'lie low' (*quiescas*) until Lanfranc has spoken to an evidently furious King William. Lanfranc makes a public declaration in his third letter: 'I have cursed and excommunicated you and all your adherents...' (*te et omnes*

---

[12] John of Worcester, *Chronicon*, s.a. 1074 (for 1075), McGurk 1998, 24–5; *ASC* D 1075, Plummer 1892–99, I, 210–212.

[13] *ASC* D (with variant in MS E) 1075, Plummer 1892–99, 210 and 212. Translation adapted from Swanton 2000, 210 and 212. See Lavelle 2020, 95.

[14] *Ibid.*, 106–7.

[15] *OV*, II, 314–17. Strickland 1994; see discussion in Lavelle 2020, 52–3. For the evidence of William's absence in England in Easter 1075, see Bates 2016, 376.

adiutores tuos maledixi et excommunicaui).[16] This was powerful stuff but there was an obvious contrast with Waltheof's situation here. Roger and Ralph were publicly acting against the king and evidently they continued to do so. The scandal for Waltheof was not necessarily that he was directly acting against the king but that he was implicated in the plot. Here John of Worcester's report of Waltheof's confession to Lanfranc may be relevant.[17] The third of Lanfranc's letters to Earl Roger exasperatedly points out that he had twice given Roger the opportunity to confess his crimes, and indeed the first two letters do offer an opportunity for a meeting, with the second offering safe conduct; the fourth suggests that Roger had indeed requested it but too late. Although Roger's family may have been better-placed to have close connections with Lanfranc, who had once been a Caen-based abbot, as evidenced in the 'quiet word' attitude of Lanfranc's fourth letter to Roger, it is tempting to wonder whether Waltheof had received similar letters from the archbishop. Given Waltheof's eventual fate, it would hardly be surprising that if there had been any letters offering safe conduct to Waltheof, they do not survive as copies in Lanfranc's letterbook.

All the same, notwithstanding whether failing to reveal the plot to the king (or at least failing to reveal the plot early enough) was enough to merit his condemnation to death, Waltheof did exhibit a sense of defiance in events leading to rebellion in 1075. When coupled with participation in rebellious actions in York in 1069–70, for which he had been forgiven by the king, Waltheof had been flexing his muscles in a Northumbrian earldom, which he had been controlling since 1072, by overseeing the murder of a family enemy at a banquet, probably in 1073, and he may have been linked to the Northerners' driving out of a Norman tax collector around the same time. William Kapelle suggested that Waltheof's role in the conspiracy in 1075 was related to his need for support in these endeavours.[18] Perhaps the development of a powerbase for Waltheof in Cambridgeshire – for which the later cult at Crowland is evidence of his patronage of fenland houses, which also included Ely and Thorney – was the added factor here which made the rebellion of 1075 all the more pressing.[19]

John of Worcester notes (adding to the *Anglo-Saxon Chronicle*) that the wedding of Roger's sister Emma to Earl Ralph took place against the king's will, and although knowledge of later events may have influenced John's account, royal cases of unsanctioned marriage in France and England in the ninth and eleventh centuries are suggestive of the ways in which the connections created by marriage could be a touchy subject in early medieval politics.[20] Of course kings might be expected to

---

[16] Lanfranc, nos. 31, 32, 33A and 33B.

[17] John of Worcester, *Chronicon*, s.a. 1074 (for 1075), McGurk 1998, 24–5.

[18] Kapelle 1979, 134–5. Simeon, 2:260.

[19] For a review of Waltheof's lands in Domesday Book and regional patronage, as well a conflict with Peterborough, see Williams 1995, 58–9. An indication of Waltheof's memory in Ely is indicated by *Liber Eliensis* II.107 (Blake 1962, 188; Fairweather 2005, 221), which briefly inserts a positive mention of Waltheof with Ralph's 'Norman' rebellion, conflating events of 1075 with those of Hereward's rebellion in 1071, perhaps deliberately conflating memories of rebellion.

[20] John of Worcester, *Chronicon*, s.a. 1074 (for 1075), see McGurk 1998, 24–5. On the unauthorised marriage

disapprove of certain of the potential marriages of their sons and daughters but there was concern too for the marriage of those who were not directly of the royal kin. It can hardly have escaped William's attention that the son of one of King Edward's household officers, who had himself maintained his father's Breto-Norman connections through his own marriage (and who was apparently not one of William's own Breton contingent), was constructing a powerful alliance through marriage to the daughter of one of William's oldest companions.[21]

Given that the *convivium* of a feast could have had an element of social bonding for those partaking in it, creating new bonds or reinforcing existing ones, this unsanctioned wedding represented an enhancement of the relations between conspirators.[22] Furthermore, the choice of the place of the wedding feast, Exning, put the conspirators at odds with royal power. Exning was within a hundredal unit linked in Domesday Book with the royal farm manor of Soham, which contributed a render of three 'nights' farm' (*de fruento melle ⁊ brasio ⁊ de omnibus aliis*).[23] While no source records the wedding party as occurring in Soham itself, the fact that vills in both Exning and Soham had the same tenant-in-chief in 1066, suggests that there had been some link with the manorial provision in this hundred.[24] The subversion of the wedding feast by the conspirators may have been linked to this royal render, associated with the control of royal territory.[25] Soham's significance is also indicated by the role it had played in supporting the royal forces during the suppression of the siege of Ely, held by an earlier set of rebellious earls (Morcar and Edwin, as well as the elusive Hereward) in 1070–1. Waltheof had remained loyal to William during that affair and had benefited from that. He had nothing to gain from linking himself to a 'lost cause' associated with the pre-1066 order during the events of 1070–1,[26] but in 1075 the choice of the site could not have failed to have some meaning in respect to royal authority in the region, indeed in the kingdom.

The response in 1075 was a violent one but it was also one which was couched in the legitimacy of action. William's agents acted on his behalf during the king's absence, fighting the forces of both Earl Roger and Earl Ralph in western and eastern England respectively,[27] and if it took some time for the decision to be made to execute Waltheof in Winchester, the legitimacy of William's own actions when

---

of the son of Charles the Bald in 862 and Edmund Ironside, the son of King Æthelred II, in the early eleventh century, see Lavelle 2020, 173.

[21] On Ralph's lineage and immediate family, see Williams 1995, 60–2. On Ralph's independence from William, see Keats-Rohan 1991, 167–8. Henry I's control of his nobility's marriages suggests that this was developing into a fine art: see Lavelle 2020, discussing Green 1986, 178–80.

[22] Feasting and rebellion in an Ottonian context is discussed by Leyser 1994, 201–2; see also discussion in Lavelle 2020, 119–24.

[23] GDB Cambs. fol. 189c: Rumble 1981, 1:1.

[24] GDB fols. 189d, 195c–d: Rumble 1981, 1:12; 14:68; 14:73. For East Anglian royal links associated with the estates here, see Lavelle 2020, 120–2.

[25] For *feorm* and royal authority, see Lavelle 2010a, 202–10.

[26] Mason 2012; Hart 1992, 636–47.

[27] For the military campaigns in western and eastern England, see Bates 2016, 381–2.

he returned to England is emphasised by the fact that he made for Westminster, where at least some of the rebels' fates were pronounced (the *Anglo-Saxon Chronicle* specifically mentions the Bretons) and perhaps even enacted.[28] This was a place of crown-wearing associated with William's presence at the funeral of Edith there in December 1075, neatly paired with the role of Winchester, where Edith had died, and where Waltheof was to die in 1076.[29] Thus the royal actions could be seen as legitimate in response to the perceived illegitimacy of the failed rebellion. It is notable that the Norman rebel, Roger de Breteuil, lost land as a result of his actions while the Breton (or part-Breton) Ralph was exiled; the Englishman Waltheof, over whom William was king rather than duke or personal lord, was, as is central to this chapter, imprisoned and eventually executed. The loss of land and its meaning to the personal standing of a lord was hardly negligible of course, but consideration of the circumstances of the execution sheds some light on the response to planned rebellion.[30]

The City and the Condemned Man

The time which elapsed between the end of the abortive rebellion by the autumn of 1075 (probably all over bar the arrival of Danes) and the death of Waltheof, on the last day of May 1076, is notable and will be discussed below, but for the moment discussion needs to focus on execution itself in the context of the city of Winchester. According to Orderic, this took place just outside the city walls, on St Giles' Hill, east of the city.

Orderic, of course, was not averse to making a few things up to suit his narrative and we must entertain the possibility that this could be one of those cases. St Giles, 'abbot and confessor', had heard the confession of a terrible sin of the Emperor Charlemagne, and Orderic's knowledge that a church in Winchester was dedicated to St Giles might give reason for Orderic to draw parallels with William's own sins.[31] However, Orderic does not do so – or at least does not do so with the verve that he was capable of applying to a salutary tale – and we should take seriously the topography of Orderic's account with its inclusion of St Giles' Hill as local details. The cult of St Giles was becoming better known in eleventh-century England, perhaps because of post-Conquest continental connections, and as a cult which spanned the Channel, this was probably appropriate for the functions of the space.[32]

---

[28] On the significance of acts of the mutilation of prisoners captured at a battle at Fagadun (Fawdon in Whaddon, Cambs.), see Lavelle 2020, 129. The specific mention of sparing of mutilation of the surrendered rebel garrison of Norwich castle, mentioned in a letter from Lanfranc to William (Lanfranc, no. 35) is relevant here.

[29] *ASC* DE 1075, Plummer 1892–99, 212; John of Worcester, *Chronicon*, s.a. 1074 (for 1075), McGurk 1998, 26–7; Orderic does not mention Westminster specifically. For discussion of displays of crown-wearing as a response to rebellion, see Lavelle 2020, 134–5. For William's reverence for Edith's burial, 'as England's queen and not as one of Earl Godwine's children', see Bates 2016, 383–4 (quotation at 383).

[30] OV, II, 320–3.

[31] *Ibid.*, 320–3.

[32] For the post-Conquest cult in Old English, see Treharne 1997.

So much for the place of execution in Orderic's account. What of imprisonment? The hill was perhaps already important as the site of an annual fair, whose origins are known by William Rufus's grant of the rights to the fair to the bishop in 1096, a grant which indicates that the church existed by then.[33] Perhaps the origins of the fair lay in royal authority – despite the fair's place under the jurisdiction of the bishop of Winchester. Rufus's reference to the rights of the fair being granted 'as if the fair were his own' suggests that some royal jurisdiction was already at play at the site before 1096. The manner in which public space could be linked to the suppression of rebellion is therefore relevant to this discussion.

The twelfth-century Winton Domesday refers to a *Balchus Regis* as a place of imprisonment in the city, which, judging by its placement in the survey, was probably on the north side of the High Street at the junction with Parchment Street. However, the 'caged' enclosure implied by that name seems to have been a prison specifically for thieves (*latrones*).[34] Orderic's phrase '*in carcere regis*', translated by Marjorie Chibnall, a little misleadingly, as 'in the king's prison', is a reference to royal captivity which matches the imprisonment of his co-conspirator, Earl Roger (a high-status confinement which would normally take place in a castle, not an urban enclosure).[35] If we give credence to John of Worcester's record that Archbishop Lanfranc acted as Earl Waltheof's confessor prior to his execution, the likelihood is that the royal castle in the south-west of the city was the site of imprisonment.[36] Why Winchester and not, say, the Tower of London, may be to do with the likelihood that Waltheof came to William in Normandy. His condemnation related to English law so his imprisonment in England was appropriate. Winchester at this time may have had the nearest – and most secure – royal castle to Waltheof's likely port of entry in England on the south coast, presumably Southampton; though we must admit to the likelihood that some confinement elsewhere preceded that in Winchester, the use of Winchester in these circumstances is an indication of judicial procedure. William may not have dealt with Waltheof in Westminster, a place associated in the *Anglo-Saxon Chronicle*'s 1075 entry with the condemnation of the 'Bretons' at the wedding feast; it is perhaps relevant to this that the *Chronicle* short poem in the 1075 entry mentions blinding, exile and shame, but it does not mention the killing of Waltheof.

Because of the locations of Waltheof's imprisonment and execution, it is possible to consider his execution, as with other executions in the Middle Ages, as an act of public theatre. Claude Gauvard has recently noted the significance of the '*présence*

---

[33] Biddle 1976, 286–7, citing Davis *et al.* 1913–1960, I, no. 377 (William II). The Historic England Research Record of the church, which survived until 1540, is available at: https://www.pastscape.org.uk/hob.aspx?hob_id=230676. I am grateful to Simon Roffey for this reference.

[34] Biddle 1976, 37 (Survey I, no. 19: '*le balche[us] regis, ubi latrones ponebantur in prisone*' ['the king's *balchus* where thieves used to be put in prison']), 75 (Survey II, no. 52), with location and the meaning of a 'balk- or beam-house' discussed at 236, s.v.

[35] OV, II, 318.

[36] John of Worcester, *Chronicon*, s.a. 1075 (for 1076) (McGurk 1998, 28–9).

nécessaire' of the general populace in acts of later medieval executions, and it is likely that this came into play in 1076 too.[37] The condemned man, presumably having confessed his sins (and was apparently guiltless) the night before, was likely to have been roused before dawn, if indeed he had slept. The sun rises just before 4 am on 31 May (by the Julian calendar), St Petronella's Day. This is a point in the year which the ninth-century *Old English Martyrology* recorded as when the month of *Þrimilce*, 'Three Milkings', comes to an end, noting that the night-time equates to one third of the total hours of the day (*i.e.* 8 of the day's 24).[38] There are of course shorter nights in the year, and the calculation is not absolute but at this point in the late spring the sense of hastening daylight must have been very apparent to Waltheof. Orderic relates events happening 'in the early morning' ('*mane*'), so as not to raise public clamour but if he is right on the timing, there may have been other issues at stake. Given the importance of the public witness of what was essentially a judicial execution for treason, the notion of such discretion seems implausible; execution at or just after daybreak – the first point at which dishonourable night killing turned to an honourable act – is less implausible.[39]

The sunrise on 31 May would have originated from an approximately ENE direction (51° from north); although St Giles' Hill is hardly a towering mountain, its position beyond the East Gate means that it is the upper end of the High Street (where the Ordnance Datum is approx. 57 m) which gets the first rays of sunlight, as the sun emerges at that time of year to the northern edge of St Giles' Hill. Thus, whether intentional or not, Waltheof could have been illuminated at his entry point through the West Gate at the upper end of the High Street (presumably opened with the advent of the new day), but if the sun were still low he would have been in relative shadow again once he had progressed a short distance with his guards down the High Street. Here, approximately halfway down the street, the OD height drops by some 20 m on an approx. 1:16 incline over the course of 320 m east to the High Street's junction with Parchment Street. Any early morning shadow would be particularly apparent when the execution party was at the East Gate of the city and while ascending the western slope of St Giles' Hill; then Waltheof would be illuminated once more when atop the hill (see Fig. 7.3).[40]

Of course, we do not know whether Waltheof actually progressed down the High Street but it is a fair bet. Of Winchester's fifty-seven 'lesser' medieval churches, seven were actually on the High Street. Of those seven, we can only really be certain that

[37] Gauvard 2018, 100, 216–22. On the rituals of execution for hanging taking place on a hill outside a city (in the tradition of Golgotha), see Bartlett 2004, 44.

[38] Rauer 2013, 109–12. The calculation of the historical sunrise time of 03:48 UST can be made (admittedly with an anachronistic level of detail) using the NOAA Solar Calculator website, entering an equivalent date of 11 June 1076 in order to allow for a ten-day Gregorian calendar adjustment (which the website does not account for with historical dates) available at: https://gml.noaa.gov/grad/solcalc.

[39] Gauvard 2018, 156–7 highlights the notion of avoiding dishonour in later medieval executions.

[40] The relative heights of archaeological sections (from which the measurements in the text are taken) are in Ottaway 2017, 27, fig. 1.19.

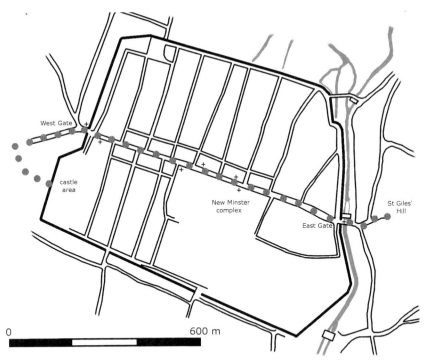

Fig. 7.3: Hypothetical progress of Waltheof's execution party in Winchester, 1076. Simplified map of Winchester drawn after information in Biddle 1976, 329–31 and Biddle and Keene 2017, 29–30 and map 5, with twelfth- and thirteenth-century century High Street churches (marked with crosses) assumed to be present in the eleventh century and an exit from the castle via the west. Locations are approximate.

St Maurice's church, at the entrance to the New Minster complex, and the chapel of St Michael, over the East Gate, were in existence by 1076 but there is direct evidence for most of Winchester's medieval churches from before the end of the twelfth century in a flourishing urban parish system and it is very likely that most of them had been established before the Norman Conquest.[41] It is reasonable to suppose that the journey of a condemned man along the High Street would have been one marked by contemplation of the fates of saints, often martyrs, as he passed by the places dedicated to them.

Whether that contemplation provided succour for Waltheof is open to debate, but a message of royal authority could also be projected through Waltheof and his execution party's journey through a townscape dominated by royally owned property. Royal lordship was extensive over properties on the High Street, which ran (and continues to run) in an almost entirely straight line for some 820m from the West Gate down

---

[41] Martin Biddle and Derek Keene, in their discussion of 'Public Buildings', note the significance of many dedications which 'could all have been made in the Wessex of the tenth and early eleventh centuries.' Biddle 1976, 329–32 (quotation at 330). See also Biddle and Keene 2017, 29–31, and Map 5.

to the East Gate. Assuming that many in the party would go on foot and would not walk particularly quickly, going at something less than a sedate walking speed of 3 mph (4.8 kph, equating to 80 m per minute), this would mean that it would take ten minutes or more for the execution party to progress down the High Street. Although the sun would still not be particularly high in the sky, it would not have taken long for many of the inhabitants of the High Street to be roused, and at the lower part of the street the inhabitants would see the progress of the execution party above them as it progressed in their direction.

Most of the tenements on the High Street owed customs to the king, particularly *landgable*, as part of the tenancy of such high-value urban real estate and their relationship with the king (or at least his agents) was part of the everyday experience of living in a royal city. The High Street was a place in which royal links were evident through the urban landscape, pre-eminent among these links being the location of the urban manor (or manors) of Godbegot and the halls of the *cnichtas*. One of these halls was distinguished by being 'where the *cnichtas* used to drink their guild' (*ubi chenictes potabant gildam suam*) and was held by a likely moneyer of Henry I during the twelfth century.[42] According to a confirmation writ of Edward the Confessor, dated to 1052 x 53, the Godbegot manor – or a substantial chunk of it – was bequeathed to the Old Minster by his mother Queen Emma, who had received it from her husband Æthelred II in 1012, but it was in private hands again on the eve of the Conquest and part of the property, known as '*Domus Emme regine*', which had perhaps been hived off as part of the property deal, was recorded as quit of customs and was probably a royal urban manor.[43] There are also some fifteen pre-Conquest tenement holders in the entries for the first Winton Domesday survey who may be identified with the names of royal agents recorded elsewhere in Hampshire folios of Great Domesday Book, whose service was linked with royal estates.[44] Not all of these tenement-holders were necessarily the same people as those landholders, as names like Ælmær and Ælfric were notoriously common in eleventh-century England but those potential connections are notable nonetheless.[45] The continuity of their service after the Norman Conquest (after all, these were men who were essential for running the royal estates) was part of what King William relied upon to ensure the continuity of his own legitimacy.

Having crossed the River Itchen, the ascent of St Giles' Hill would have required the party and any townspeople to ascend through what became the west gate of

---

[42] Biddle 1976, 34, 39 (Survey I, entries 10 and 34).

[43] S 1153; S 925. Biddle 1976, 37–8, 46 (Survey I, entries 23 and 75) For the interpretation of the Godbegot property, *ibid.*, 37, n.

[44] These are noted briefly in Lavelle 2007, 112, within a broader discussion of lands of royal agents in Domesday Book (104–16; Munby 1982, entries 68:1–11 and 69:1–54).

[45] The early twelfth-century holding of a High Street tenement by 'Cheping the Rich [*dives*]' and Henry of Dummer, held by Godwine son of 'Elmer' (?Ælmær, another pre-Conquest royal agent's name) (Biddle 1976, 48 [Survey I, entry 87]) suggests a link with royal agents associated with land near the royal estate of Basingstoke, at Dummer and Preston Candover; in 1086, the latter was held by 'Cypping' and the former held by a certain 'Oda of Winchester' (Munby 1982, entries 69:7 and 69:8)

the site of the medieval fair. The effects of post-medieval lime quarrying have made for some steep slopes on the western side of the hill, meaning that it is difficult to reconstruct the progress of the execution party and Waltheof's final steps.[46] However, if the slope was gentler in the eleventh century than is the case now, it is reasonable to see that the journey to the top of the hill was part of what could have been a direct route from the west gate of the city, which could take much more than half an hour.

Landscapes of Execution

If St Giles' Hill had significance even before it became the place where Waltheof's life ended, it can really only be fully understood in the context of other execution sites in and around the city (Fig. 7.4). We do not know where the captured Danish pirates were executed who were ordered to be hanged (*ahōn*) after being 'led to Winchester to the king' (*lædde to Winteceastre to þæm cynge*) in 896; perhaps it was not even Winchester but it is reasonable to surmise that it was somewhere public.[47] About a century later, members of what seems to have been a Viking ship's crew, perhaps captured under similar circumstances to those of 896, were decapitated off the coast of Dorset at a point on a hundredal boundary with some of their heads removed for display;[48] in the 896 *Chronicle* entry, the chronicler uses a verb, *ahōn*, which could mean both hanging and, as a term used for crucifixion, suspension in the context of an execution more generally.[49] Although, on balance, it is more likely that the crews in 896 were hanged than beheaded, it is interesting to consider whether the verb might refer to the bodies or heads of the crews *after* their execution.

One known Winchester execution site associated with beheading, excavated in 1990, was at Harestock, at Old Dairy Cottage on the Winchester–Silchester road (now Andover Road). A dozen skeletons were excavated there, of whom some had evidence of decapitation; two were carbon-dated to 770–970 and 890–1020.[50] While a possible link to the Vikings executed in 896 is tempting,[51] what is more significant in the context of the present discussion is the context of the references to 'head stakes' (*heafod-stoccas*) in the bounds of three charters which converge on this point, and the implicit reference to 'head stakes' in the place-name Harestock (from OE *Heafod-stoccas*). As a

---

[46] For the topography of the later medieval properties on the hill and their links to access routes, as well as the effects of lime-quarrying, see Keene 1985, part 2, 1091–113. I am grateful to Mark Allen for discussion on the topography of the hill.

[47] ASC 896, Plummer 1892–99, I, 91.

[48] On the links between the contexts of the later Viking executions and the projection of authority in 896, see Lavelle 2016, 131–4.

[49] Bosworth and Toller 1898, 31–2.

[50] Ottaway 2017, 232–4; Reynolds 2009, 118–20.

[51] Some skeletal tooth enamel from the Old Dairy Cottage excavations shows that there is evidence that at least one individual is an 'incomer' to the site, with marine diets of northern Britain, and northern Germany and southern Scandinavia being posited. Jay 2020, 131–7 (quotation at 134), discusses the Old Dairy Cottage data in comparison to the execution cemetery evidence at Weyhill, near Andover (Hants).

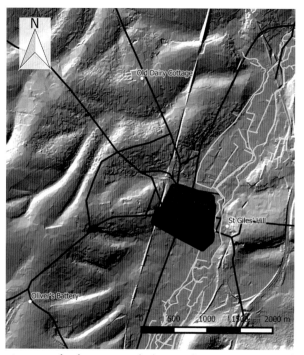

Fig. 7.4: The locations of places of execution around Winchester in their topographical setting. N.B. roads and rivers depicted on the map follow modern routes. Map data © Crown copyright and database rights 2021 Ordnance Survey (licence 1426904).

royal city, Winchester probably had a tradition of judicial beheadings and the display of the victims of such executions may, Andrew Reynolds suggests, even have influenced Ælfric of Eynsham's description of the display of corpses outside the walls of a city in an account of the Seven Sleepers of Ephesus.[52] Martin Biddle and Derek Keene suggested that the early modern gallows on the Silchester (now Andover) road, close to the pre-Conquest execution burial site of Old Dairy Cottage, had been in existence since the thirteenth century, 'and possibly before'.[53] Thus, this north-north-western approach to the city was a landscape in which royal authority was marked by the bodies of those thought to have transgressed that authority and who had been legally punished for those transgressions.[54]

The shackles on two individuals found in an eleventh- or twelfth-century burial site, Oliver's Battery, on the western side of the city, also indicate the likelihood of an extra-urban execution cemetery.[55] Here, the distance from the city was further than that of either St Giles' Hill or Old Dairy Cottage in Harestock, but an executed

---

[52] Reynolds 2009, 118–20, discussing excavations at Old Dairy Cottage (O.S. SU 473314) and the charter bounds for S 309 and 695, which refer to 'head stakes' and S 376, which refers to the 'old killing place', *ealdan cwealmstowe*, at a different site, 'which might suggest that the execution site at Old Dairy Cottage succeeded it during the later ninth century' (119). Reynolds discusses *heafod-stoccan* in general at 223–4 and the influence on Ælfric at 119.

[53] O.S. SU 477304. Biddle 1976, 306.

[54] Cf. Molyneaux 2015, 112–13 for the suggestion that the capital punishment of (perceived) criminals may have been – at least in some cases – a community-led rather than royal action. However, the visual emphasis on royal peace through a link between roads and judicial killing is compelling. Although focused on roads and the notion of royal peace, a useful point is made by Langlands 2019, 185 (discussing Cooper 2002) that royal rights over *herestrete* ('army roads') and *cwealm stowa* can be seen in the early twelfth-century *Leges Henrici Primi*. See also Langlands, this volume, pp. 46–52.

[55] Russel 2016.

body would have been visible to travellers approaching the city from the west.[56] With archaeological evidence of executions on the roads leading to the West Gate and the North Gate, and with the very plausible textual evidence of the execution of the earl at a site which dominated the road leading to the East Gate, it can surely only be a matter of time before the examination of a medieval skeleton provides us with evidence of an execution site dominating the Southampton road and the South Gate's entry to the city.

There is a possibility that, like the site on Oliver's Battery, where there was an early Saxon princely burial near to the Iron Age earthwork on the hill, the use of St Giles' Hill as a site of execution may have been determined by its history as an early Saxon burial site.[57] Unlike the display of 'head stakes' on the Silchester (Andover) Road, but perhaps like the view from Oliver's Battery, much of St Giles' Hill was intervisible with the interior of the city. The tree cover on St Giles' Hill which now obscures it has been a feature of its geography only since the early twentieth century, when the annual fair had ended (see Fig. 7.5).[58] The employment of open space outside the city, appropriate to the performative aspects of execution discussed above, suggests that even at the early hour recorded by Orderic, public viewing was expected. Despite his wish to refer to discretion in the earl's execution, Orderic himself admits to the presence of a small group of clergy and poor, who received the earl's 'rich garments' and who were presumably necessary to witness the miracle reported to have taken place after the execution. If the execution party had indeed processed down the High Street, the crowd were likely to have been somewhat bigger than Orderic's account implies.[59]

Orderic records the disposal of the earl's body in a ditch, where it was quickly covered with turf. It was later exhumed – uncorrupted, naturally – a few years later, so the quiet disposal of a body became linked, in Orderic and his Crowland informants' eyes, with the broader theme of the swift and uncelebrated execution. Only the abbot of Crowland's intervention rescued Waltheof's reputation from oblivion.[60] However, it seems far more likely that the disposal of the body in the

---

[56] See Langlands, this volume, p. 51.

[57] For the Oliver's Battery burial, see Yorke 2010. The Heritage Gateway record for 'at least eleven inhumations' is available at: https://www.pastscape.org.uk/hob.aspx?hob_id=230787. I am grateful to Simon Roffey for this reference and for the suggestion that the evidence of barrows further east along Alresford Road may be suggestive that there were once also barrows stretching west to St Giles' Hill.

[58] The sight-lines associated with the execution of the Welsh rebel William ap Rhys (William Cragh), from the gallows on a hill outside the walls of Swansea in 1290 (Bartlett 2004), are explored in the *City Witness: Place and Perspective in Medieval Swansea* project website available at: www.medievalswansea. ac.uk. I am grateful to Catherine Clarke for discussing this project at different points, which provided inspiration for my own study of Waltheof in Winchester. Discussion in this section develops points raised in Lavelle 2020, 124–8.

[59] See above, p. 136. For a flavour of the complex range of human activity around much later public executions see Gatrell 1996, 56–105.

[60] OV, II, 322–3.

Ryan Lavelle

Fig. 7.5: 'The East Prospect of the City of Winchester', by Samuel and Nathaniel Buck (1736). The engraving shows the hill's intervisibility with the High Street (leading from the West Gate (marked as '22') to the East Gate) and castle (marked as '21'). © Winchester City Council collections. Provided by Hampshire Cultural Trust.

ditch, something that emphasised Waltheof's treachery, was in keeping with the notion of public execution.

The nearest ditch marked the edge of the jurisdiction between what became the site of St Giles' fair and the city,[61] and was a likely place wherein a body might be disposed, with the walls of the city itself near the East Gate being, perhaps, a suitable place where the head of the traitor could be displayed in a show of Anglo-Saxon royal lordship.[62] The urban context of the display of heads of early eleventh-century Scottish enemies – rebels, in effect – on the walls of Durham, recorded in *De Obsessione Dunelmi*, may be compared with the late Anglo-Saxon treatment of the bodies of other perceived deviants.[63]

Orderic, however, was conscious of Waltheof's representation of Englishness. He followed the earl's execution with an account of another Fenland hero, the eighth-century St Guthlac, whose inclusion in '*opusculo nostro*' was made at the request of Wulfwin, the same Crowland prior who had furnished Orderic with material for his account of the death of Waltheof. 'I steadfastly believe that the holy deeds of the overseas Saxons and English [*transmarinorum Saxonum uel Anglorum*] could be no less edifying to northern Christians [*fidelibus Cisalpinis*] than the deeds of Greeks and Egyptians, which devoted scholars have fully recorded in lengthy narratives and give much pleasure,' Orderic declared.[64] Guthlac had little to do with Winchester but just as the sense of place was important in understanding Guthlac's fenland struggles, Orderic's sense of place also played a part in a longer narrative of pre-Conquest England its fate in Orderic's own time.

The Deaths of a Queen and a King – and their Winchester Connections

There is one further set of circumstances which should not go unremarked with regard to Waltheof's death in 1076: that of the death of the widow of Edward the Confessor, Queen Edith, in Winchester. According to the D recension of the *Anglo-Saxon Chronicle*, this took place seven nights before Christmas.[65] If, as Pauline Stafford suggests, Edith spent her final years in Winchester as well as Wilton,[66] it is worth thinking about whether any continuing influence by the queen in Winchester would have been significant for the links between her and Waltheof's family, whose interests in Northumbria had crossed with those of the queen. To this end a pre-Conquest flashback may cast a light on what played out in Winchester in 1075–6. According to

---

[61] On the boundary ditch, see Keene 1985, Part 2, 1092.

[62] Cubitt 2009 and for comparative discussion of the heads of executed Scots on the walls of Durham in 1006, Lavelle 2010b, 30–1.

[63] *Ibid.*, 30–1, citing Simeon, 1:216. For a discussion of the statements of authority (and their limits) in punishment in Anglo-Saxon law (albeit not that of Waltheof, presumably because of its chronological remit), see Rabin 2014.

[64] '*Indubitanter credo quod non minus proderunt fidelibus Cisalpinis sancta gesta transmarinorum Saxonum uel Anglorum, quam Græcorum uel Ægiptiorum de quibus prolixæ sed delectabiles commodæque collationes crebro leguntur congestæ sanctorum sudio doctorum.*' OV, II, 324–5 (Chibnall's translation modified).

[65] *ASC* D 1075, Plummer 1892–99, I, 212.

[66] Stafford 1997, 270–2.

John of Worcester, Edith was guilty of the death of the elder Gospatric, son of Uhtred of Bamburgh, during the 1064 Christmas festival; the ultimate beneficiary of the death, however, was Edith's brother Tostig, who had been Earl of Northumbria since the death of Waltheof's father Siward in 1055.[67] While this, and being passed over for the succession to his father's Northumbrian earldom, might not be *prima faciae* evidence for the link between the queen and the young Northumbrian nobleman, as Chris Lewis remarks, after 1055 '[t]he next ten years are a blank in Waltheof's life. Given his parentage it is likely that he spent part of his childhood at court.'[68]

Lewis's suggestion is a useful one in the consideration of Waltheof. The *Vita Ædwardi Regis* refers to the upbringing of 'boys who were said to be of royal stock' (*ex ipsius regis genere dicebantur*) at court, who Edith 'zealously reared, educated, adorned and showered with motherly love' (*enutrierit, docuerit, ornauerit et omnem maternum affectum eis effuderit*).[69] The ætheling Edgar, who appeared as *Eadgar clito* with the royal couple in the New Minster *Liber Vitae*, suggesting a visit to Winchester around 1063,[70] stands foremost in this context, while Tostig, Gyrth and Leofwine, younger sons of Godwine, were posited as such by Frank Barlow in his 1970 biography of the king.[71]

What if Waltheof had been among such an extended royal family? Noble sons were sent for fosterage at courts, whether the royal court or those of other members of the nobility, as part of the political processes of establishing agreements, and the appearance of the younger Gospatric in Tostig's party during a Roman pilgrimage recorded in the *Vita Ædwardi Regis* suggests that links to the Godwine family were made during the years before the Norman Conquest.[72] A witness list of a charter granting land in Devon to Rouen in 1061 (S 1033) is perhaps relevant in this respect. Waltheof's name is the penultimate among the *duces* whose names are listed at the bottom of this charter, including Harold, Tostig, Ælfgar, Gyrth and Leofwine. In his recent biography of Edward the Confessor, Tom Licence is understandably cautious about accepting the reliability of this charter, noting, alongside the anomalous position of Waltheof, problems with the ecclesiastical hierarchy in the charter, which survives only in the form of later copies.[73] The title of *dux* may not be so problematic for this

---

[67] John of Worcester, *Chronicon*, s.a. 1065 (Darlington *et al.* 1995, 596–9), s.a. 1064. Stafford 1997, 270. On the identification of this Gospatric and the link to the house of Uhtred, see Kapelle 1979, 94–5. On Tostig's elevation to the earldom, *ASC* CDE 1055, Plummer 1892–99, I, 184–5. Note that the death (by beheading) of Tostig and the assumption of the earldom of Huntingdon (*i.e.* Waltheof's post-Conquest earldom) is attributed by legend to Waltheof's father, Siweard in the thirteenth-century *Vita et Passio Waldevi*, see Wright 1939, 131–2.

[68] Lewis 2004.

[69] *Vita Ædwardi Regis*, in Barlow 1992, 24–5.

[70] British Library Stowe MS 944, fol. 29r, available at: www.bl.uk/manuscripts/FullDisplay.aspx?ref=Stowe_MS_944, discussed by Licence 2020, 228–9.

[71] Barlow 1970, 163; in his 1992 edition of the *Vita*, lxvi, he notes the variety of young men of royal stock but highlights the likely implicit reference to Edith's brothers, though see Barlow 2002, 82–3, where he suggests reference to the returned exiled descendants of Edmund Ironside. See Lavelle 2007, 91–2.

[72] Barlow 1992, 54–7.

[73] Licence 2020, 272–3.

charter if it was an acknowledgement of his high familial status in a court context; it may not have required a specific territorial earldom, though Forrest Scott made a case for Waltheof holding an east midland earldom by the early 1060s, even noting a gift by Waltheof at Barnack (Cambs.) dated to 1061 – admittedly recorded by an exceptionally unreliable source, the 'pseudo-Ingulph'.[74]

It certainly seems credible, however, that Waltheof would have been at court in 1061. The Rouen charter dates to the year when Tostig embarked on his journey to Rome taking Waltheof's uncle, the younger Gospatric, with him: as Stafford puts it, 'maybe as follower, as a sworn brother, or as a hostage, because Tostig was afraid of what might happen in the North during his absence; maybe for all these reasons.'[75] In that light, the presence of Waltheof at court and in the hands of Edith (of an age of early adolescence and thus of political value if Waltheof had been born in or just before 1050)[76] would have stood as a counterpoint to the embarcation to Rome of the younger Gospatric in the care of Edith's brother Tostig.

As an heir of Siward, with a claim to lands pertaining to Bamburgh, Waltheof's appointment to the Northumbrian earldom in 1071×2, replacing the younger Gospatric,[77] would certainly have made sense in the context of political connections involving Edith's family which transcended the Norman Conquest (see Fig. 7.6). Pertinent to the execution of the earl was the fact that after Edith's death any residual protection that may have been afforded by the presence of the former queen in Winchester had been lost. Given the difficulties of transcending a febrile political situation related to her being sister of the dead usurper-king Harold II, Edith may not, of course, have had *any* influence in royal affairs in the last year of her life.[78] But as the widow of Edward the Confessor, Edith remained 'the Lady' ('*seo hlæfdie*', as she was in the D *Chronicle*'s record of her death in 1075).[79] If Waltheof's presence in Winchester coincided with the last months of her life, her influence would surely have counted for something.

Furthermore, Timothy Bolton has also postulated, on the basis of the similarities of elements in the thirteenth-century *Vita et Passio Waldevi* to Danish historical traditions that, through his father Siward, Waltheof belonged to a branch of the Danish royal dynasty,[80] a dynasty which William himself may have made some claim to belong to through Winchester cathedral's royal mausoleum.[81] The alliance between

[74] Scott 1952, 163–4.

[75] Stafford 1997, 270, discussing the appearance of Gospatric with the party of pilgrims in the *Vita Ædwardi Regis* (Barlow 1992, 54–7). See also Licence 2020, 197–200.

[76] Scott 1952, 155–6, suggests a date range of 1045×50.

[77] Kapelle 1979, 29–31, 127.

[78] On the problems associated with Edith's position, having 'no clear place', see Stafford 1997, 274–8 (quotation at 277).

[79] *ASC* E 1075, Plummer 1892–99, I, 212.

[80] Bolton 2007 and forthcoming. For a recent assessment of the fantastical elements of the story of Siward, see Parker 2018, 102–38.

[81] Biddle and Kjølbye-Biddle 2016. We might also note that the burial of Beorn (d. 1049) in Winchester kept the dynastic link of descent through Cnut's daughter Estrith a live issue.

Waltheof's Northumbrian descent

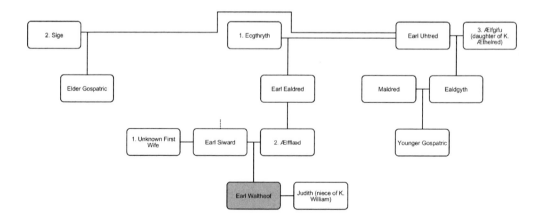

Waltheof's possible Danish royal connection

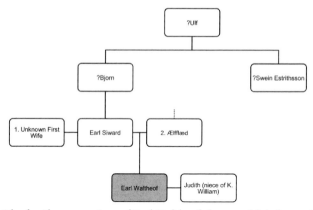

Fig. 7.6: The family connections of Earl Waltheof, drawn with information in Scott 1952, Kapelle 1979, and Bolton 2007. Simplified for illustrative purposes (created using Family Echo, www.familyecho.com).

the revolting earls and King Swein Estrithsson of Denmark may not have manifested itself in so much a well-organised plot as opportunism on the part of Swein's son Cnut (later Cnut II, 'the Holy'), but Cnut's actions in northern England – yet another ravaging, in which property belonging to York Minster was seized[82] – reflected tangible claims to power in England. The claims by Harald Hardrada in 1066 and by

---

[82] ASC D 1075, Plummer 1892–99, I, 211–12. For Lanfranc's letter to Bishop Walcher of Durham warning of the imminent Danish threat, see Lanfranc, no. 36.

Cnut II in 1085–6 tend to get the lion's share of attention in considerations of potential post-1016 Viking conquests of England, but the actions of Cnut, not yet king until after his father's death in 1076 and the death of his brother Harold in 1080, showed that despite William's second coronation in Winchester in 1070, the reign of a man who was spending much of his time in northern France could not be secure even if he could rely on agents acting on his behalf to put down local uprisings.

Exiling Waltheof could have resulted in his departure to Scotland or, more likely, Flanders, places which both presented dangers to William's interests.[83] If the earl had already lost lands, there was little else that could be done beyond continue Waltheof's captivity. Imprisoning Waltheof in a royal castle in Winchester, typical of what would work as the solution to the actions of rebellious earls and kinsmen for the next three hundred years, would only work for so long when Scandinavian fleets were still a clear and present danger, particularly as they now had the additional dimension of activating their links with royal kinsmen to add – as William himself had done – an air of legitimacy to their endeavours.[84]

The connection between Waltheof and the royal family thus mattered, and it would especially matter in Winchester where royal legitimacy could be made an activate factor when it was needed. However, if that were the case, why should five months pass between the news of the Danish attacks in the North and the death of the queen on the one hand, and the execution of Waltheof in May 1076? Perhaps, as Bates suggests, putting paid to Orderic's notion that the earl was executed by jealous lords without the king's consent, William had to undertake 'extensive consultations' before such an act could be undertaken.[85] Waltheof was a kinsman with royal links, after all, and such a killing could not be done lightly. In 1076, William could have expected a second round of Danish attacks following those of late 1075, as might be indicated by the actions taken by William in 1085–6 in response to a threat of invasion in 1085.[86]

In 1086, the death of Cnut put paid to the threat to the English kingdom from Denmark. On 28 April 1076, Cnut's father Swein died.[87] If parallels with the events in the 1080s are anything to go by, Swein's death may have spelled the end of the Danish connection in the earls' revolt but the news either reached Winchester too late to save Waltheof or put an extra imperative on the decision to execute him. Here it is worth noting Tim Bolton's suggestion, developing an idea first posited by L. M. Larson, of a link through Siward to the Danish royal family: the death of Swein could have made Waltheof's Danish royal links more dangerous to William than the threat that he had

---

[83] See the departure of Cnut Sweinsson to Flanders at the end of 1075 (*ASC* E 1075) and the connections between Flanders and Scotland indicated by the account of Edgar 'cild' in *ASC* D and E 1074.

[84] I am grateful to Timothy Bolton for discussion on this issue and for his willingness to let me see a draft version of his paper, 'Earl Siward's Mythical Genealogy and the Death of his Son, Earl Waltheof', currently in preparation.

[85] Bates 2016, 386–7 (quotation at 387).

[86] *ASC* E 1085, Plummer 1892–99, I, 215–16.

[87] *ASC* D 1076, Plummer 1892–99, I, 212. The evidence for the death of Swein, from *Necrologium Lundense*, is discussed by the paper in preparation by Timothy Bolton.

presented in 1075.[88] It may be debatable as to whether, as Bolton suggests, William himself actually panicked on hearing of the death of Swein, but the connection and the timing certainly makes this feasible, and the juxtaposition in the D manuscript of the *Anglo-Saxon Chronicle* of the news of the death of Swein and the execution of Waltheof in Winchester (not to mention the death of Queen Edith in Winchester) takes on an additional dimension in this context.[89]

Conclusions

Ultimately, we cannot be certain what factors resulted in the death of Waltheof, but a great deal was at play in May 1076, and the execution drew on the sense of authority associated with a royal city. Perhaps the queen's presence in part of the period following Waltheof's arrest and imprisonment could have been a factor in ensuring clemency for the rebel earl in 1075 but in 1076 he was surviving on borrowed time. The eyes of those in the royal castle and along Winchester's High Street may have gazed upon Waltheof on the morning of 31 May 1076 but could Waltheof himself have looked toward Winchester with memories of his own place in the royal family – indeed his links to more than one royal family – in his last moments? Whether William himself was there is not recorded. But he did not need to be. For the man who had been English king since 1066 and whose confirmation as king had been made in Winchester in 1070, the message of legitimacy projected in this space outside the royal city was clear enough.

Acknowledgements

I wish to record my thanks to my fellow editors and to Timothy Bolton for reading earlier versions of this paper and for providing helpful comments and criticisms.

Abbreviations

ASC   *Anglo-Saxon Chronicle* (cited by manuscript, where appropriate, and corrected annal year).

GDB   Great Domesday Book (*i.e.* the 'Exchequer' manuscript).

Lanfranc   Clover, H. and Gibson, M. (eds) 1979. *The Letters of Lanfranc, Archbishop of Canterbury*. Oxford: Oxford University Press.

OV   Chibnall, M. (ed.) 1968–80. *Orderici Vitalis Historia Æcclesiastica: The Ecclesiastical History of Orderic Vitalis*, 6 vols. Oxford: Oxford University Press.

---

[88] Bolton forthcoming, discussing Larson 1912, 77–8

[89] ASC D 1076, Plummer 1892–99, I, 212. Although the reader has to turn the folio to follow the event in British Library Cotton MS Tiberius B.IV, fols. 85r–85v, the sense of *mise-en-page* is still notable. For a digitised version of the manuscript, see www.bl.uk/manuscripts/FullDisplay.aspx?ref=Cotton_MS_Tiberius_B_IV.

S   Citation of charter in Sawyer, P. H. (ed.) 1968. *Anglo-Saxon Charters: An Annotated List and Bibliography*. London: Royal Historical Society; revised version available at: *Electronic Sawyer: Online Catalogue of Anglo-Saxon Charters* website, http://www.esawyer.org.uk

Simeon   Arnold, T. (ed.) 1882–5. *Symeonis Monachi Opera Omnia*, 2 vols. Rolls Series. London: Longman.

Bibliography

Manuscripts

British Library Cotton MS Tiberius B.IV
British Library Stowe MS 944

Primary Sources

Barlow, F. (ed.) 1992. *The Life of King Edward Who Rests at Westminster*, 2nd edition. Oxford: Oxford University Press.

Biddle, M. (ed.) 1976. *Winchester in the Early Middle Ages: An Edition and Discussion of the Winton Domesday*. Oxford: Oxford University Press.

Blake, E. O. (ed.) 1962. *Liber Eliensis*, Camden Third Series. London: Royal Historical Society.

Darlington, R. R., McGurk, P. and Bray, J. (eds) 1995. *The Chronicle of John of Worcester: Volume II: The Annals from 450 to 1066*. Oxford: Oxford University Press.

Davis, H. W. C., *et al.* <AQ : please list all editors.> (eds) 1913–1960. *Regesta Regum Anglo-Normannorum*, 4 vols. Oxford: Oxford University Press.

Fairweather, J. (ed.) 2005. *Liber Eliensis: a History of the Book of Ely from the Seventh Century to the Twelfth*. Woodbridge: Boydell Press.

McGurk, P. (ed.) 1998. *The Chronicle of John of Worcester: Volume II: The Annals from 1067-1140 wih the Gloucester Interpolations and the Continuation to 1141*. Oxford: Oxford University Press.

Munby, J. (ed.) 1982. *Domesday Book: Hampshire*. Chichester: Phillimore.

Mynors, R. A. B., Thomson, R. M. and Winterbottom, M. (eds) 1998. *Gesta Regum Anglorum: The History of the English Kings, Volume 1*. Oxford: Oxford University Press.

Plummer, C. (ed.) 1892–99. *Two of the Saxon Chronicles Parallel with Supplementary Extracts from the Others*, 2 vols. Oxford: Oxford University Press.

Rauer, C. (ed.) 2013. *The Old English Martyrology: Edition, Translation and Commentary*. Cambridge: D. S. Brewer.

Rumble, A. (ed.) 1981. *Domesday Book: Cambridgeshire*. Chichester: Phillimore.

Swanton, M. (trans.) 2000. *The Anglo-Saxon Chronicles*, revised edition. London: Phoenix.

Treharne, E. (ed.) 1997. *The Old English Life of St Nicholas with the Old English Life of St Giles*. Leeds: Leeds Texts and Monographs.

Secondary Sources

Barlow, F. 1970. *Edward the Confessor*. London: Methuen.

Barlow, F. 2002. *The Godwins: The Rise and Fall of a Noble Dynasty*. London: Longman.

Bartlett, R. 2004. *The Hanged Man: A Story of Micracle, Memory, and Colonialism in the Middle Ages*. Princeton: Princeton University Press.

Bates, D. 2016. *William the Conqueror*. New Haven and London: Yale University Press.

Bates, D. 2020. William the Conqueror and Wessex, in A. Langlands and R. Lavelle (eds), *The Land of the English Kin: Studies in Wessex and Anglo-Saxon England in Honour of Professor Barbara Yorke*, 517–37. Leiden: Brill.

Biddle, M. and Keene, D. 2017. *Winchester*, British Historic Towns Atlas 6. Oxford: Oxbow Books.

Biddle, M. and Kjølbye-Biddle, B. 2016. Danish Royal Burials in Winchester: Cnut and his Family, in R. Lavelle and S. Roffey (eds), *Danes in Wessex: The Scandinavian Impact on Southern England, c. 800–c. 1100*, 212–49. Oxford: Oxbow Books.

Bolton, T. 2007. Was the Family of Earl Siward and Earl Waltheof a Lost Line of the Ancestors of the Danish Royal Family?, *Nottingham Medieval Studies*, 51, 41–71.

Bosworth, J. and Toller, T. (eds) 1898. *An Anglo-Saxon Dictionary*. Oxford: Clarendon Press.

Campbell, A. 1971. *Skaldic Verse and Anglo-Saxon History: The Dorothea Coke Memorial Lecture in Northern Studies Delivered at University College London, 17 March 1970*. London: University College London.

Carpenter, D. 2004. *The Penguin History of Britain: The Struggle for Mastery: Britain 1066–1284*. London: Penguin.

Cooper, A. 2002. The Rise and Fall of the Anglo-Saxon Law of the Highway, *Haskins Society Journal*, 12, 39–69.

Cubitt, C. 2009. 'As the Lawbook Teaches': Reeves, Lawbooks and Urban Life in the Anonymous Old English Legend of the Seven Sleepers, *English Historical Review*, 124, 1021–49.

Freeman, E. A. 1867–79. *The History of the Norman Conquest of England, its Causes and its Results*, 6 vols. Oxford: Clarendon Press.

Gatrell, V. A. C. 1996. *The Hanging Tree: Execution and the English People, 1770–1868*. Oxford: Oxford University Press.

Gauvard, C. 2018. *Condamner à mort au Moyen Âge: Pratiques d la peine capitale en France XIIIᵉ–XVᵉ siècle*. Paris: Presses Universitaires de France.

Green, J. A. 1986. *The Government of England Under Henry I*. Cambridge: Cambridge University Press.

Hart, C. 1992. *The Danelaw*. London: Hambledon Press.

Heritage Gateway. Available at: https://www.heritagegateway.org.uk/gateway/. (Accessed July 2021).

Hudson, J. 2011. The Fate of Earl Waltheof and the Idea of Personal Law in England after 1066, in D. Crouch and K. Thompson (eds), *Normandy and its Neighbours, 900–1250: Essays for David Bates*, 223–35. Turnhout: Brepols.

Huntington, J. 2009. The Taming of the Laity: Writing Waltheof and Rebellion in the Twelfth Century, *Anglo-Norman Studies*, 32, 79–95.

Kapelle, W. E. 1979. *The Norman Conquest of the North: the Region and its Transformation, 1000–1035*. London: Croom Helm.

Keats-Rohan, K. S. B. 1991. William the Conqueror and the Breton Contingent in the Non-Norman Conquest 1066–1086, *Anglo-Norman Studies*, 13, 157–72.

Keene, D. 1985. *Survey of Medieval Winchester*. Oxford: Oxford University Press.

Jay, M. 2020. Isotope Analysis, in K. E. Walker, S. Clough, and J. Clutterbuck, *A Medieval Punishment Cemetery at Weyhill Road, Andover, Hampshire*, 127–41. Cirencester: Cotswold Archaeology.

Langlands, A. 2019. *The Ancient Ways of Wessex: Travel and Communication in an Early Medieval Landscape*. Oxford: Oxbow Books.

Larson, L. M. 1912. The Efforts of the Danish Kings to Recover the English Crown after the Death of Harthacnut, *Annual Report of the American Historical Association for the year 1910*, 69–81.

Lavelle, R. 2007. *Royal Estates in Anglo-Saxon Wessex: Land, Politics and Family Strategies*, British Archaeological Reports British Series. Oxford: Archaeopress.

Lavelle, R. 2010a. Geographies of Power in the Anglo-Saxon Chronicle: The Royal Estates of Anglo-Saxon Wessex, in A. Jorgensen (ed.), *Reading the Anglo-Saxon Chronicle: Language, Literature, History*, 187–220. Turnhout: Brepols.

Lavelle, R. 2010b. *Alfred's Wars: Sources and Interpretations of Anglo-Saxon Warfare in the Viking Age*. Woodbridge: Boydell Press.

Lavelle, R. 2016. Law, Death and Peacemaking in the 'Second Viking Age': An Ealdorman, his King, and some Danes in Wessex, in R. Lavelle and S. Roffey (eds), *Danes in Wessex: The Scandinavian Impact on Southern England, c. 800–c. 1100*, 122–43. Oxford: Oxbow Books.

Lavelle, R. 2020. *Places of Contested Power: Conflict and Rebellion in England and France, 830–1150*. Woodbridge: Boydell Press.

Lewis, C. P. 1990. The Early Earls of Norman England, *Anglo-Norman Studies*, 13, 207–23.

Lewis, C. P. 2004. Waltheof, Earl of Northumbria (*c.* 1050–1076), in *Oxford Dictionary of National Biography*. Oxford: Oxford University Press. https://doi.org/10.1093/ref:odnb/28646.

Leyser, K. 1994. Ritual, Ceremony and Gesture: Ottonian Germany, in T. Reuter (ed.), *Communications and Power in Medieval Europe: The Carolingian and Ottonian Centuries*, 189–213. London: Hambledon Press.

Licence, T. 2020. *Edward the Confessor: Last of the Royal Blood*. New Haven and London: Yale University Press.

Mason, E. 2012. Invoking Earl Waltheof, in D. Roffe (ed.), *The English and their Legacy, 900–1200: Essays in Honour of Ann Williams*, 185–204. Woodbridge: Boydell Press.

Molyneaux, G. 2015. *The Formation of the English Kingdom in the Tenth Century*. Oxford: Oxford University Press.

NOAA Solar Calculator. Available at: https://gml.noaa.gov/grad/solcalc/. (Accessed July 2021).

Ottaway, P. 2017. *Winchester: Swithun's City of Happiness and Good Fortune: An Archaeological Assessment*. Oxford: Oxbow Books.

Parker, E. 2018. *Dragon Lords: The History and Legends of Viking England*. London: I. B. Tauris.

Rabin, A. 2014. Capital Punishment and the Anglo-Saxon Judicial Apparatus: A Maximum View?, in J. P. Gates and N. Marafioti (eds), *Capital and Corporal Punishment in Anglo-Saxon England*, 181–99. Woodbridge: Boydell Press.

Reynolds, A. J. 2009. *Reynolds, Anglo-Saxon Deviant Burial Customs*. Oxford: Oxford University Press.

Russel, A. D. 2016. Hung in Chains: A Late Saxon Execution Cemetry at Oliver's Battery, Winchester, *Hampshire Studies: Proceedings of the Hampshire Field Club and Archaeological Society*, 71, 89–109.

Scott, F. S. 1952. Earl Waltheof of Northumbria, *Archaeologica Aeliana*, 4th ser., 30, 149–215.

Skrine, J. H. 1908. The Trial of Waltheof, William the Conqueror, in *Winchester National Pageant: To be held in the Grounds of Wolvesey Castle on June 25th and the Five Following Days; The Book of the Words and Music*, 27–31. Winchester: Warren.

Stafford, P. 1997. *Queen Emma and Queen Edith: Queenship and Women's Power in Eleventh-Century England*. Oxford: Blackwell.

Stenton, F. M. 1971. *Anglo-Saxon England*, 3rd edition. Oxford: Oxford University Press.

Strickland, M. 1994. Against the Lord's Anointed: Aspects of Warfare and Baronial Rebellion in England and Normandy, 1075–1265, in G. Garnett (ed.), *Law and Government in Medieval England and Normandy: Essays in Honour of Sir James Holt*, 56–79. Cambridge: Cambridge University Press.

University of Southampton, *City Witness: Place and Perspective in Medieval Swansea*. Available at: https://www.medievalswansea.ac.uk/. (Accessed July 2021).

Williams, A. 1995. *The English and the Norman Conquest*. Woodbridge: Boydell Press.

Worsley, F. 1843. *Waltheof, the Last Saxon Thane. A Tragedy*. London: J. Parkins.

Wright, C. E. 1939. *The Cultivation of Saga in Anglo-Saxon England*. Edinburgh: Oliver & Boyd.

Yorke, B. 2010. The Oliver's Battery Hanging-Bowl from Winchester, and its Place in the Early History of Wessex, in M. Henig and N. Ramsay (eds), *Intersections: The Archaeology and History of Christianity in England, 400–1200: Papers in Honour of Martin Biddle and Birthe Kjølbye-Biddle*, 77–86. Oxford: British Archaeological Reports.

Chapter 8

The Queen, the Countess and the Conflict: Winchester 1141

Katherine Weikert

During the 'Anarchy,' a succession conflict between King Stephen and Empress Matilda 1135–54, both the Empress and Stephen's wife, Matilda of Boulogne, Queen of England, played important parts. This is particularly seen in 1141, as Stephen was imprisoned and the Queen took leadership of the royal faction. This chapter examines aspects of female authority and how gender was used by contemporary writers to connote the appropriateness both the Queen's and the Empress' actions. Two contemporary narratives, the Gesta Stephani *and William of Malmesbury's* Historia novella, *ultimately demonstrate that both women's authority and leadership were accepted as a part of the role they were meant to play as elite women, and gender was a part of casting deeply nuanced meanings to their statuses as Queen, Empress or – potential – king.*

In the height of the Anglo-Norman Civil War of 1135–54, Winchester was the location of a significant turning point in a year filled with turning points, 1141. Following the death of King Henry I in 1135, the throne was taken by his nephew, Stephen of Blois, rather than by his chosen heir, his daughter Matilda (the widow of Emperor Heinrich V, hence her title Empress). As the political dust started to settle with Stephen seemingly in a good position, he lost the confidence of the church in 1139 after arresting bishops over property issues, and in the same year, having already started the reconquest of Normandy under her second husband Geoffrey, Duke of Anjou, the empress moved from Normandy to England to begin her campaign for the throne.

1141 was a year of changes for both the Angevin and the royal factions. The battle of Lincoln in February saw not just an Angevin victory but, importantly, the capture of King Stephen. The empress' star was on the rise, and she acted accordingly, moving to plan her coronation in London the same year. In March, she was received in the city of Winchester by its bishop, Henry of Blois, the brother of King Stephen, who offered her the king's castle and treasury there. He instructed the people of Winchester to declaim her as 'their lady and their queen'.[1] Empress Matilda then went to London. Queen Matilda, Stephen's wife and countess *de jure* of Boulogne, shortly thereafter sent envoys to the empress for the release of her husband from prison, without success. The queen brought troops to the south bank of London and riled the already agitated Londoners; the empress and the Angevins were forced to flee to Oxford without the coronation taking place. The queen treated with the Bishop of Winchester successfully, whilst the Empress returned to Winchester with her army. The bishop and the queen followed, to prepare for what would become a double siege of and in the city. The empress was based in the royal castle on the south-west of town, a key location in case of the need to evacuate the city for points westward, her strongholds; the abbey at Wherwell to the north-west of the city was further fortified by the empress' man, John Marshal. The Angevin forces besieged the bishop's palace, and in turn, the royalist forces under William of Ypres, the queen's kinsman, counter-sieged the city. As the counter-siege tightened, Wherwell and Andover both fell to the royalist forces, and in order to avoid being trapped in an increasingly enclosed city, the Angevin contingency was forced to flee west towards Ludgershall. In an attack at the rear guard at Stockbridge, the empress and Brian fitz Count were able to flee, arriving first at Ludgershall before carrying on to Devizes, whilst many, including her brother Robert, Earl of Gloucester, and her uncle David, King of Scotland, were captured. The queen retook Winchester, and the bishop's alliance was firmly reaffixed to his brother's cause. The empress returned to Oxford for the ensuing negotiation for the release of her brother in exchange for the king; the queen and her son acted as hostages for the safe conduct of the two prisoners back to each other's camps. At the end of 1141, having gone through the twists and turns of a captured king, a government starting to realign to a new regnant queen, and the loss at Winchester, the king, queen and empress all found themselves in the positions they held at the beginning of the year.

In the midst of this hectic year of civil upheaval, we see two women exerting and exacting authority over the political and military spheres against each other, which is unprecedented in the Anglo-Norman world: the empress, in attempting to reclaim her inheritance of the kingdom of England and duchy of Normandy, and the queen, attempting to overturn the state of play whilst her husband was incapacitated from rule by his capture. The extent that these two women acted against each other is surprisingly understudied, though perhaps not so surprising in the face of a historiography that, in the past, has tended to place the spotlight on Stephen (and, further previously, Robert of Gloucester.) It provides a tantalising opportunity to seek to understand what could be considered acceptable or even normative abilities for elite women in the twelfth-century Anglo-Norman sphere. Indeed, neither woman was an exception nor exceptional, but to understand either, they must be placed next to each other.[2]

---

[1] GS 118–19, '*in publise ciutatus et fori audientia dominam et reginam acclamare praecepit*'. Translations from Potter 1976 unless specified.

[2] See Lois Huneycutt, in preparation; Catherine Capel's doctoral study at the University of Winchester will also shed more light on some of these issues.

This is the basis for this chapter: to study writing about Matilda of Boulogne and Matilda of England at the siege of Winchester and surrounding actions to discern contemporary thought about female authority in the Anglo-Norman world but also throughout areas of Europe in the twelfth century.[3] This further links to discourse on biblical women creating a exemplars for female authority as seen through Bernard of Clairvaux and particularly William of Malmesbury, who were acquainted with the queen and empress respectively. Many discussions of the empress in particular are caught up in questions of medieval misogyny, and rather than continue to expound on that line of historiography, I instead wish to try to discern what contemporary medieval writers said about, and wrote about, the authority of the empress and the queen in this pivotal year in light of some of the intellectual climate of the writing to try to seek something in between an interpretation of misogyny in medieval writers, and these women as exceptional women.

In the course of this one year, these two women undertook many of the same actions: they gathered men and troops, commanded (if not led) military action and engaged in diplomacy and negotiation in seeking her own, or her husband's own, reign. As such, contemporary writers had an interest in their actions – not solely as women, but as *women in positions of authority*. In reading these texts together, and these women together, we attempt a better understanding of not only their actions but their ability to wield authority, and the contemporary opinions around women's authority. In order to try to do this, this chapter will create a close read of the two contemporary sources which are strictly dedicated to the war's actions: the anonymous *Gesta Stephani* and William of Malmesbury's *Historia novella*. Whilst both authors were writing contemporaneously to the action – and with their own agendas – a comparative approach of these two is best to see the authors' horizons of understanding of elite female authority in the mid-twelfth century without interlaying our own. The concept of a 'horizon of understanding' is one identified by Jans Robert Jauss in order to seek a dialogue with a text in order to understand it without readerly presentism, though here I will be seeking to place the two texts in dialogue with each other as well.[4] In order to further the dialogue I will be at points working through previous translations in order to offer new nuance to well-trodden texts, illuminating previously understudied aspects of both women's elite authority, and considering particularly meaningful allusions to a literate twelfth-century audience that the writers used to create meaning and understanding of female authority. In order to do this, I will be looking at how each writer is portraying the empress' and queen's actions in 1141 to try to discern an assessment of their comparative perceptions with their abilities and authorities in light of their gender.

---

[3] Through the course of this paper, I shall refer to each Matilda by their given and chosen titles, how they represented themselves: Empress and Queen. I do hope the empress would have forgiven me the use of her lesser title, countess, for the sake of a nicely alliterative title, though I doubt she would.
[4] Jauss 2001.

This, in some sense, is a constructivist exploration as these sources tell us much about the construction of knowledge as well as the creation of the representation of these two women. The construction of the actions of Matilda and Matilda give us significant information in a historical and historiographical sense not only about the Anglo-Norman Civil War, but about how the twelfth-century world was trying to understand female authority, how knowledge was constructed and construed about the female authority and how this has affected our own constructions of the past.

Each text will be taken in turn, the *Gesta* followed by Malmesbury, to see how each woman was written in 1141. Following this, a section will consider aspects of gender seen not just in Matilda or Matilda but throughout the 1141 episodes. Ultimately this chapter will argue that both authors give little sense of problems with female authority and that the actions undertaken by both women were unexceptional for the time, but a combination of authorial political alliance backfilled with gendered expectations, rather than negativity towards female authority, contributed to gendered representations to two individuals. By both using a wider, comparative interpretation of gender in the texts, we find both women accessing authority that was not only available to them, but expected of them, as elite women in the twelfth century.

Gesta Stephani

Whilst the authorship of the *Gesta Stephani* is unknown, the book's contemporaneity to the events, and its favour of King Stephen, are in no doubt. It first came to modern light in 1619 from an 'imperfect and incomplete' manuscript in the possession of the bishop of Laon, according to its first editor Andre Duchesne, who also gave it its title of *Gesta Stephani*. By the mid-nineteenth century this manuscript was lost and editions relied on Duchesne's version, until R. A. B. Mynors' mid-twentieth-century discovery of another manuscript housed in Valenciennes.[5] The 'vividness of the writing'[6] has led to any number of proposals of authorship, none wholly seen as satisfactory or conclusive. R. C. H. Davis suggested Robert of Lewes, Bishop of Bath, on grounds of location and geographic familiarity, though more recently Edmund King proposed a 'monk or canon of one of the London houses, with connections at court and some experience as a confessor' on similar grounds.[7] Although it is possible, as King posits, that the piece was a 'single literary composition,' it is widely accepted that there was likely a break in the writing around the year 1147, and the final book written near or after the close of the war.[8]

Queen Matilda appears infrequently in the *Gesta* despite her significance in the actions of 1141. It is the London episode, rather than the Winchester one, which

---

[5] This manuscript recap comes from King 2006, 195–7.
[6] *Ibid.*, 200.
[7] Davis 1962; King 2006, 206. King also notes Julia Crick's discovery that the Valenciennes manuscript contains materials found in works from Merton and Southward Priories, strengthening a connection to London: 205 n.90.
[8] King 2006, 202–3.

contains more of the queen's role. The queen is firstly described by the author as 'a woman of a subtle heart and a man's resolution'.[9] Her London actions are fully outlined: firstly, she petitioned the empress for Stephen's release and the security of her son's inheritance.[10] In the course of this she was abused by harsh language in seeking insurance for the granting of her son's inheritance from the empress' faction. It was splendidly written that, when that tactic had failed, she 'expect[ed] to obtain by arms what she could not by supplication'.[11] The queen then 'gave orders that they should rage most furiously around the city with plunder and arson, violence and the sword, in sight of the countess and her men'.[12] These actions then moved the Londoners to side with the queen and king, forcing the empress and the Angevin contingency to flee Westminster. Upon the Angevin exit, the queen was then admitted to the city of London, where 'forgetting the weakness of her sex and a woman's softness she bore herself with the valour of a man'.[13] She then 'won over' and 'urged [the barons] persistently to demand their lord back with her' but in contrast, she 'humbly besought' the allegiance of Henry of Blois, Bishop of Winchester.[14] Her 'woman's tearful supplications' were 'pressed on [the bishop] with great earnestness'.[15] In all of this, the queen was successful.

When the queen moves on to Winchester, her actions take more of a backseat, but they are still there. Before reverting to the standard trope of the phrase of 'the king's troops' during the main actions, it is Queen Matilda who brings an army to Winchester and commands them to besiege the besiegers. Although somewhat obfuscated by both the Latin and its translation, the phrase, when broken down to its subject and verb, is '*Et regina... obsidebat*'. This, she does 'with greatest energy and spirit'.[16] From this point the queen again drops out of sight in the Winchester episode.

The queen in the *Gesta* very much plays the role of the queen with the authority of that position: supplications, negotiations, intercessionary actions. However, she also very much plays the role of a leader, too, ordering her men on the Southbank to 'rage most furiously' and taking up the siege in Winchester. The *Gesta* praises her for all of these actions, including the description of her as 'a woman of a subtle heart and a

---

9   GS 123, '*astuti pectoris virilisque constantiae femina*'; Potter's translation differs only slightly as 'a woman of subtlety and a man's resolution'.

10   GS 123, '*nunciis ad comitissam destinatus, pro viro ex carcerali squalore eruendo, filioque illius ex paterno tantum testamento herditando, enixe supplicavit*'; the 'squalor' of the imprisonment is very likely an embellishment based on what would be expected of a king's treatment in captivity and equally in light of Robert of Gloucester's treatment as a prisoner (see below); HN 50, 55.

11   GS 123, '*quod prece non valuit, armis impetrare confidens*'.

12   GS 123, '*...utque raptu et incendio, violentia et gladio in comitissae suorumque prospectu ardentissime circa civitatem desaevirent praecepit.*'

13   GS 126–7, '*sexusque fragilitatis feminineaeque mollitiei oblita, viriliter sese et virtuose continere*'.

14   Ibid., '*invictos ubique coadiutores prece sibi et pretio allicere*'; '*humiliter supplicare*'.

15   Ibid., '*...quidem flexus tum lacrymosis mulieris precibus, qua sei instantissime suggerebat*'.

16   GS 128–31; the full phrase is '*Sed et regina cum eximio militantium robore, cumque invicta Londoniensium caterua, qui fere mille cum galeis et loricis ornatissime instructi convenerant, interius obsidentes vivacissime exterius et ardentissime obsidebat.*'

man's resolution'[17]; the best of both genders, perhaps. She has before been recognised as 'a war leader for her husband';[18] in the *Gesta* this is most obvious.

The empress plays a fuller part in the *Gesta*, unsurprisingly as she is often the focus of the writer's ire as the main contestant against the king. The 1141 episodes with the empress begin after Stephen's defeat and capture at Lincoln. The empress is described as putting on:

> an extremely arrogant demeanour, instead of the modest gait and bearing proper to a gentle woman, began to walk and speak and do all things more stiffly and more haughtily than she had been wont, to such a point that soon, in the capital of the land subject to her, she actually made herself queen of England and gloried in being so called.[19]

Upon being admitted to Winchester with the alliance of Henry of Blois, Matilda is given the king's castle and treasury, and the town was made to solute her 'as their lady and queen'.[20] Upon this, the empress 'began to be arbitrary or rather headstrong', and receiving visitors 'ungraciously and at times with unconcealed annoyance, others she drove from her presence in fury after insulting and threatening them.'[21] With 'extreme haughtiness and insolence', she rebuffs her key advisors David of Scotland, Robert of Gloucester and Henry of Blois.[22]

Upon arrival in Westminster, the empress calls together the men of London to demand taxes from them, 'not with unassuming gentleness, but with a voice of authority'.[23] The empress responds to their denials 'with a grim look, her forehead wrinkled into a frown, every trace of a woman's gentleness removed from her face, blazed into unbearable fury,'[24] and sends them away. The actions were to have significant consequences as the queen's movements with her men and the men of London caused the Angevin faction to flee Westminster. At first, like Nero fiddling over the burning Rome, the empress carries on at dinner while the Londoners pour out of the city gates towards Westminster. But at last the Angevins flee whilst the Londoners pillage the palace. It was, according to the *Gesta*, a disorderly flight.[25]

When the Angevin contingency reaches Winchester, the empress is accompanied by a large fighting retinue. At this point, she begins to plan for the ensuing siege: she 'gathered into a vast army the whole array of those who obeyed her throughout

---

[17] *GS* 123, See n. 9, above.

[18] Crouch 2000, 260.

[19] *GS* 118–19, '*illa statim elastissimum summi fastus induere supercilium nec iam humilem feminae mansuetudinis motum nel incessum, sed solito severius, solito et arrogantius procedere et loqui, et cuncta coepit peragere, adeo ut in ipso mox dominii sui capite reginam se totius Angliae fecerit, et gloriata fuerit appellari*'. A suggested partial retranslation is below.

[20] *GS* 118–19, '*dominam et reginam acclamare*'.

[21] *GS* 120–1: '*cuncta coepit potenter, immo et praecipitanter agere*'; '*inuite et cum aperta quandoque indignation suscipere, alios autem iniuriis et minis afflectos indignando a se abigere*'.

[22] *GS* 120–1: '*supercilii et arrogantiae*'.

[23] *GS* 120–3: '*non simplici cum mansuetudine sed cum ore imperioso*'.

[24] *GS* 123, Latin in n. 64 where it is under further discussion.

[25] *GS*, 124–5.

England, and gave orders for a most rigorous investment both of the bishop's castle...
and of his palace'.[26] At the ultimate failure of the action in Winchester, as the Angevins
flee, the empress is barely seen in the action, though here we see what might have
been a singular compliment or sense of approval from the writer of the *Gesta*. The
empress is described as 'always above feminine softness and had a mind steeled and
unbroken in adversity', a statement that almost sounds admiring in ways that echoes
descriptions of the queen, even while it contrasts it.[27]

William of Malmesbury, *Historia Novella*

The authorial political inclinations are very clear in Malmesbury's *Historia novella*.
Written through the year of 1142, it is long supposed that the text is roughly
contemporaneous to the actions up to that point.[28] The manuscript begins with a
dedication to Robert, Earl of Gloucester; clearly the text will go on to support the
Angevin claim in a larger sense, and Robert in a more particular one. Seen as a 'sequel'
to the *Gesta Regum Anglorum*, all known remaining manuscripts of the *Historia novella*
are found in *GRA* manuscripts.[29] Malmesbury's promise of a fourth book of the *Historia*
was never delivered,[30] hence the reckoning of his death after 1142.

Indeed, the dedication to Robert of Gloucester gives us a clear steer for Malmesbury's
writing. There is a strong, known connection between the two, with Malmesbury
giving Robert (along with the empress and King David of Scotland) copies of the *Gesta
Regum Anglorum* on its completion around 1125. Indeed, the monks at Malmesbury
note in a letter to the Empress that she should use it as a model for instruction from
its own examples of kings and queens,[31] indicative of their assumption of her as heir
apparent to Henry II. As Björn Weiler notes, already by *c.* 1125, David, Robert and
Matilda were thought to likely play significant roles in the growing succession issues
surrounding Henry I.[32] Malmesbury's loyalty to the descendants of Henry I took
priority in his dedication of the *Historia novella,* as did his loyalty to Robert, in whom
he saw much of what a king should be.[33] Malmesbury thus focusses on Robert to an
unsurprising degree in his narrative around the civil war.

This, however, gives a better perspective to view the queen in 1141. Malmesbury
spurns a great deal of adjectival description around both women, but in this, the actions

---

[26] GS 126–7: '*Illa igitur vniversam sibi parentium per Angliam militiam, edicto ubique propenso, in grandem
exercitum convocavit, castellumque episcopi... sed et domum illius, quam ad instar castelli fortiter et
inexpugnabiliter firmarat, validissima obsidione claudere praecepit*'.

[27] GS 134–5: '*femineam semper excedens mollitiem, ferreumque et infractum gerens in adversis animum*'; here,
Potter translates '*excedens*' as 'superior to'.

[28] Potter 1955, xiii.

[29] Mynors 1955, xxxviii–xxxix.

[30] *HN* 77.

[31] Letter from the monks of Malmesbury to Matilda, *Epistolae*, available at: https://epistolae.ctl.columbia.
edu/letter/205.html.

[32] Weiler 2005, 6, n. 13.

[33] *Ibid.,* 13–14.

speak for themselves. To begin with, we have the queen's intercession on behalf of her imprisoned husband following Lincoln. Christian, a clerk of the queen, presents to the papal legate, Henry of Blois, and council a letter from Queen Matilda: 'The queen earnestly begs all the assembled clergy, and especially the Bishop of Winchester, her lord's brother, to restore to the throne that same lord, whom cruel men, who are likewise his own men, have cast into chains'.[34] Here the queen is not only acting as intercessor on behalf of the king, but also utilising her rank as the highest in the land to summon her authority to ask this of the legatine council. The empress at this time had been declared 'lady of England and Normandy'[35] but not only does the queen, no doubt, not recognise this as legitimate, she also had the title and rank of 'queen' at her disposal in the same way that the empress used her imperial title. The queen also utilises her role to convince Henry of Blois to return to his brother's side. At an audience in Guildford, Henry was 'influenced by her tears and offers of amends'.[36] Although this meeting is translated as an 'intimate conference at Guildford',[37] and the queen cast as a tearful supplicant, in actuality this would have been Henry coming to the queen to meet within the confines of the royal residence at Guildford, a significant stage-setting for the scene. The queen's tears – like the king's anger, discussed below – are well-known tropes of royal displays of authority and power so whilst the queen may well have used the trope commonly and effectively available to her, she did so within her royal household: the bishop, in effect, is acted on by the queen's intercession here, within the physical reminder of her status in her own household.

The queen also demonstrates herself to be a valuable manager and keeper of high-ranking prisoners. When Robert of Gloucester is captured at Winchester, his captivity is a genteel one by order of the queen: she, 'though she remembered her husband had been fettered by his orders, never allowed any chains to be put on him or ventured anything that would have dishonoured his rank'.[38] Robert ends up held in Rochester, where the queen is sometimes resident and indeed takes active control over his imprisonment.[39] As with her role in intercession above, her rank and role in the highest available office in the kingdom made her viewed as not only a possible, but perhaps even the best possible candidate to manage Robert's imprisonment.

The queen was adept at negotiations and diplomacy, and she has even been noted as being the saving grace of her husband's 1141 campaigns. Even before 1141, her abilities

---

[34] *HN* 55: '*rogabat regina obnixe omnem clerum congregatum, et nuncupatim episcopum Wintonie fratrem domini sui, ut eundem dominum regno restituerent, quem iniqui viri, qui etiam homines sui essent, in vincula coniecissent.*' Robert of Gloucester had put the king in chains after consistently finding him outside of his area of custody, including at night, *HN* 50.

[35] *HN* 54: '*Anglie Normannieque dominam*'.

[36] *HN* 58: '*eiusque lacrimis et satisfactione infractus ad liberationem germani animum intendit*'.

[37] *HN* 57–8: '*familiare apud Geldeford cum regina*'.

[38] *HN* 66: '*que licet meminisset virum suum eius iussu fuisse compeditum, nichil ei unquam vinculorum inferri permisit, nec quicquam inhonestum de sua maiestate presumpsit*'.

[39] *HN* 66.

at negotiation were well-known with her brokering agreements between Stephen, her husband, and King David of Scotland, her uncle, in 1139; and her negotiations with Robert of Gloucester on behalf of Stephen in 1140; as well as securing the betrothal of her son to the daughter of the king of France.[40] Her abilities as negotiator were noted in more than just the two main contemporary texts under study here: equally, *Liber Eliensis* compares her to the Queen of Sheba in acknowledging her efforts to release her husband during the 1141 campaigns.[41] The queen also acted as a hostage for safe passage in a finite, bilateral agreement for the exchange of Robert for the king. The queen and Eustace were handed over to the earl's men at Bristol in exchange for the king; the king, 'at speed,' went to Winchester and released the earl, who then left his son hostage with the king as he returned 'rapidly' to Bristol and released the queen and Eustace.[42] As further surety to ease Robert's mind, Henry of Blois and the Archbishop of Canterbury were offered as conditional hostages should the king not have kept to the agreements; as the exchange went without hitch, neither were taken into custody by Robert. As with most hostageships that are finite and bilateral for times of truces,[43] there is no indication of distress or constraint but instead the queen, and her son and heir, were not only the best but the most appropriate hostages for someone of the king's rank. In fact, it is unlikely that anyone else would have done, and doubly so seeing as how Robert's concern was for respect of rank when it came to this prisoner exchange between an earl and a king.[44] This was a role that not only could have been, but should only have been enacted by someone of the queen's status.

Vestiges of the queen's authority can be seen throughout her actions in 1141. In the lead-up to the fighting at Winchester, the roads are said to be 'watched by the queen and the earls who had come'[45] to blockade the city. Later, when Robert is in captivity, the royalist earls both try to cajole him to their side, and when he refuses, he is threatened: 'they would send him overseas to Boulogne to be kept in bondage there for life'.[46] Whilst Boulogne is, no doubt, over the sea, it is also, and certainly not coincidentally, the land in which the queen was the ruler in her own right and through the right of her family before her.

Bearing in mind that this all is from the quill of a writer who was pro-empress, or at least pro-Robert and therefore pro-Angevin, the fact that Malmesbury does not demonise the queen or her actions – either as a part of the royalist camp, or as a woman – may come as a surprise. However, Malmesbury gives no indication of dismay either at the queen's actions, or her ability to undertake them. Queen Matilda was acting in the interest of Stephen, but was acting, no doubt, and utilising to her fullest

---

[40] Tanner 2003, 140; Chibnall 1999, 92

[41] *LE* 398.

[42] *HN* 61–2: '*cum festinato*'; '*celeriter igitur permensa via*'

[43] Kosto 2012, 24, 28.

[44] *HN* 67–9; Chibnall 1999, 115.

[45] *HN* 59: '*a regina, et comitibus qui venerant, undique foras muros Wintonie abservate sunt vie*'.

[46] *HN* 68: '*minas intentare ceperunt, quod eum ultra mare in Bononiam mitterent, perpetuis vinculis usque ad mortem innodandum*.'

the authority and power given to her not simply as Queen of England, but countess of Boulogne. It was a right that she knew and deployed well. Through the course of the Anglo-Norman Civil War, her position as countess as much as her role as queen offered her underlying authority to undertake actions, and her presence in Boulogne sporadically throughout the 1140s demonstrates her recognition of the importance of this role, especially after the near-debacle of 1141.[47] Matilda called upon her ability as the countess of Boulogne in a number of ways: by the blockading and capture of Dover from Robert of Gloucester in 1138 with her navy and allies from Boulogne[48] to the issuing of charters whilst in Boulogne around 1148×52. The latter in particular is demonstrative of her continuing and possibly dominating authority as countess *suo jure*: her son Eustace had been endowed count of Boulogne at his coming-of-age in 1147[49] though in the 1148×52 charter Matilda is Queen of England with Eustace merely 'my son from England and Boulogne.'[50] The honour of Boulogne in England was Matilda's by right, and this too she was keenly aware of: 'It was hers, she said – "my manor", in which she exercised "my rights," managed by "my clerks" and household officer, in accordance to her instructions.'[51] Matilda's charters show her awareness of her own rights via her ancestors in Boulogne, and it was an important part of both her access to authority and her extraordinary wealth.[52] In 1141, she used her authority as both queen and countess to act on behalf of Stephen and Eustace.

The empress, as might be expected, receives a better rap here than in the *Gesta Stephani* although it must be noted that, with Robert the centre of Malmesbury's attentions, she does not receive a spotlight. After Lincoln, towards the London episode, 'the most of England respected her rule'.[53] However, after the upset of the Londoners, the Angevins left Westminster with order and discipline, and the empress herself is described as a '*virago*,' a 'woman of masculine spirit' as Potter translates it, or even, simply, a heroine or warrior.[54] This is not the only time that Malmesbury describes the empress as such: when the empress returns to England to take up her fight in 1139, he again calls her an '*eadem virago*'.[55] Here, noting the Empress as a virago in these times specifically of leadership, Malmesbury follows the writing of Isadore of Seville and St Jerome in particular, writers he was both familiar with.[56] Despite modern connotations of the word virago, this was not the insult it sounds. This will be discussed further below.

---

[47] Chibnall 1999, 95–6; Crouch 2000, 202, 248; Crouch 2008, 51; King 2010, 310.
[48] OV vi. 520–1; King 2010, 311.
[49] Crouch 2000, 245.
[50] Crouch 2000, 248n, 261n; partly printed in Davis 1990, 167: '*regina Angl[orum]*'; *Eust[achii] filii mei Angl(ia) et Bolonia*'.
[51] King 2010, 311, citing *RRAN* iii, 301 '*meum manerium*', 541 '*de jure meo et precessorum meorum*', '*mei manerii*', 554; Hubert, the queen's chamberlain issues this '*ex parte regine*'.
[52] King 2010, 311; Tanner 2003, 136; *RRAN* 541, for one example: '*fore de jure meo et predecessorum meorum*'.
[53] *HN* 56: '*Pleraque tunc pars Anglie dominatum eius suspiciebat*', translation my own.
[54] *HN* 56: '*euidem virginis*'. For the empress as a warrior, see Hanley 2019.
[55] *HN* 24.
[56] Thomson 2003, 42, 44 and 210; Sønnesyn 2012, 116–18.

When the Empress ultimately loses support in London, and the support of Henry of Blois, here it is not for the *Gesta*'s reasons of arrogance or anger, but for having broken faith with her barons, 'being unable to show restraint in the enjoyment of what she had gained'.[57] No specific examples are given and indeed Malmesbury places most of the impetus for the empress losing followers as the fault of Henry of Blois.

(En)Gendering Faults

The heart of many questions in the secondary works on the empress and (less so) the queen lies in gender, slander and gendered interpretations, which, probably for the worst, has tended to come from the *Gesta*. Interestingly enough, the *Gesta* uses gender more frequently than Malmesbury does, and it was almost always intended to slander, but it was not exclusively thrown at the empress. For example, in 1141 the author repeatedly calls men who turncoat from Stephen's side to the empress 'effeminate' (discussed below); more specifically, these are in the circumstances after Stephen's capture at Lincoln, and aimed at those who submitted *without* putting up resistance to the Angevins. Those who showed resistance were spared gendered slander. Earl Alan of Cornwall submits only after 'he found his adversaries to be too strong for him and was captured, put in chains and subjected to torment in a filthy dungeon until he assumed the yoke of forced submission and the most degraded servility... and delivered over his castles to [the Earl of Chester's] disposal'.[58] This, clearly, was not a man who willingly handed over his properties to the empress, and so was simply presented as being overpowered. Likewise, Earl Hervey le Breton, husband of Stephen's illegitimate daughter, 'was besieged a very long time in the castle named Devizes by a mob of plain peasants leagued together for his harm' before surrendering and returning to Brittany.[59] Here, too, Hervey mounted significant resistance before his ultimate submission.

But those who did not resist did not fare so well in the eyes of the author of the *Gesta*. Hugh, Earl of Bedford, behaved 'carelessly and slackly (for he was a dissolute and effeminate man)', and simply handed over his castles to Miles de Beauchamp in the wake of the king's imprisonment.[60] Likewise, Robert de Oilli of Oxford, and the Earl of Warwick are derided as 'soft and delicate men' for having 'under no compulsion... transferred their allegiance to the countess'.[61] Clearly, one's masculine respectability relied on one's resistance to submission, according to the author of the *Gesta*. Those

---

[57] *HN* 58: '*set ipsam temerasse, que adquisitis uti modeste nescierit*'.

[58] *GS* 116–17; '*adversariis praevalentibus, captus et catenatus, supliciisque in carcerali squalor fuit addictus; donec coactae humilitatis et vilissimae servitutis induens ceruicem, et hominium comiti Cestriae faceret, et castella sua illius deliberationi permitteret*'.

[59] *Ibid.*, '*in castello, quod Divisa dicitur, a simplici rusticorum plebe in unum se globum in malum illius coniurante*'; King 2010, 129.

[60] *Ibid.*, '*ut vir laxus et effeminatus*'.

[61] *GS* 116–19, '*viri molles et deliciis magis*', translation my own; '*aliis quoque sponte nulloque cogente ad comitissae imperium conversis*'.

who put up a fight were not cast in valourised, masculinised terms, but those who did not resist are very specifically feminised.

But the opposite was used as well. The empress in particular comes under frequent scrutiny in the *Gesta* for losing her feminine qualities. These have been frequently noted, such as the infamous moment in London where she reacts to the Londoners with anger. Immediately after the submission of de Oilli and Warwick, the empress became confident as noted above: 'instead of the gentle and modest bearing of a gentlewoman, she began to walk and speak and do all things more severely and insolently than she usually had'.[62] Here, she is not acting like a gentlewoman but more importantly, she is not acting like a king either. The word '*mansuetudo*' is telling in this case. Equally, in demanding fees from the Londoners, she acts without '*mansuetudo*', without a benevolent kingly manner, but instead acts imperiously or commandingly – with the word '*imperioso*' literally coming from the word '*imperium*', empire, a not-so-subtle reminder of the empress' status.[63] In the same scene, she 'with a grim look, her forehead wrinkled into a frown, every trace of a woman's gentleness removed from her face, flared with impatient displeasure'.[64] With both statements, in her bearing after the submission of de Oilli and Warwick and in the infamous episode with the furrowed brow, the combination of '*mansuetudo*' and '*mulier*' or '*feminiae*' certainly weight a gendered interpretation of Matilda's lack of feminine gentleness. However, the third, when she is acting without '*mansuetudo*' and with '*imperiositas*', is more specifically a comment on a lack of kingly behaviour.[65] This sense of 'ease of manners and civility in the action of good kings... politeness, but above all a concern for the honour status and standing of a ruler's subjects' implied by '*mansuetudo*'[66] is lacking with Matilda's actions here. She is not acting with a king's ease or concern for her nobility in these episodes; she is not acting like a proper king.

Additionally, there remains the issue of her anger. Rather than Potter's translation of 'fury,' I would suggest as above, 'impatient displeasure'. The alternative meanings of '*indignatio*' allows this, but the further indication of a lack of '*mansuetudo*' and kingly behaviour is noted by the lack of either '*furor*' or '*ira*' in the phrase. A king's anger could be either righteous – *ira* – or evil, unrighteous – *furor* - as was frequently written.[67] Potter's translation of 'fury' is also seen in the scene where the empress is admitted to Winchester the first time in that 'others she drove from her presence in fury after insulting and threatening them': '*alios autem iniuriis et minis afflictos indignando*

---

[62] *GS* 118–19, Latin above in footnote 20; translation my own.

[63] *GS* 120–1, '*illa, ditioribus quibusque mandatis, infinitae copiae pecuniam, non simplici cum mansuetudine sed cum ore imperioso, ab eis exegit*', translated by Potter as 'she sent for the richest men and demanded from them a huge sum of money, not with unassuming gentleness, but with a voice of authority.'

[64] *GS* 122–3, '*illa, torua oculos, crispata in rugam frontem, totam mulierbris mansuetudinis eversa faciem, in intolerabilem indignationem exarsit*'. Potter translates the last clause as 'blazed into unbearable fury'. McGrath further notes the association of anger with not only heat or fire, but with physical distortion of one's expression, 2019, 25–6.

[65] Weiler 2005, 20–1.

[66] *Ibid.*, 9–10.

[67] Barton 1998, 156–7; McGrath 2019, 24–7.

a se abigere'.[68] Again, neither *'furor'* or *'ira'* are used here but instead *'indignando'* – scorn or indignation, not regal anger or anger enforced by violence.[69] Similar to the empress' lack of kingly behaviour as noted with *'non simplici cum mansuetudine'*,[70] here, the empress' emotions, whether rage or displeasure, were again not that which would mark her out as a king, neither *ira* nor *furor*. This is no surprise; to the *Gesta,* the empress was certainly not the rightful ruler, but here her anger marks her out as not a *king* as well.

The queen's praise for being a 'woman of a subtle heart and a man's resolution' should also hardly be seen as exceptional for the writer of the *Gesta*. Although this writer criticises the empress for failure to behave as a king, praising the queen for acting like a man falls in line with contemporary thoughts about female authority. Bernard of Clairvaux famously instructed Melisende of Jerusalem to 'put your hand to strong things and show a man in a woman'.[71] The queen had met Bernard in Boulogne and was in occasional correspondence with him;[72] it is not impossible that he may have counselled her similarly as Melisende. Additionally, the queen's calling on her own resources in Boulogne are well within the sphere of activities of a female authority figure. As noted above, the queen was very actively aware of her role leading Boulogne and consistently used resources from her own patrimony to assist the king, from calling in Flemish soldiers and sailors to using Boulogne as a negotiating piece for prisoners to go over the sea. Although lost in most Latin texts, but near-contemporaneous to the Anarchy, Queen Morphia of Melitene, wife of King Baldwin II acted similarly to Matilda of Boulogne within Morphia's reign in Jerusalem. Morphia commissioned soldiers from her native Armenia to rescue her husband from his 1123 captivity in Khartpert, as well as assisted negotiating his ransom in exchange for hostages including her youngest daughter Ioveta, in another example of a woman's bellicose activity in support of a husband with a habit of being captured.[73] Similarly to Morphia's drawing on her patrimony in Armenia, Queen Matilda thoroughly involved Boulogne and her sources in the Anarchy. Neither the *Anonymous Syriac Chronicle* nor Orderic Vitalis make anything of Morphia's involvement; the same should be expected of Queen Matilda in 1141.

Malmesbury is somewhat more tempered in his gendered casting of characters. The *Historia novella* is not a text prone to windy adjectival phrases, so the ones Malmesbury does use stand out. The queen's actions may be implicitly gendered, but they are ones that are gendered for a woman who is a queen. The actions taken by the queen are ones that are indeed female, but that of an elite woman who holds specific and

---

[68] *GS* 120–1.

[69] McGrath 2019, 25.

[70] *Ibid.*

[71] *'Opus est ut manum tuam mittas ad fortia et in muliere exhibeas virum'*, Bernard ep. 354.

[72] Bernard ep. 534 and 315 with the latter indicating a meeting at some time in Boulogne *c.* 1130–37.

[73] Tritton and Gibb 1933, *Anonymous Syriac Chronicle*, 92; OV iv, 114–15; Harari 2007, 78; Hamilton 1978, 148. Baldwin II had allied with Gabriel of Malatia with his marriage to his daughter Morphia and had Armenia within his sphere, but that these actions stemmed from Morphia should not be overlooked.

particular authority: her tears, her supplication are not signs of submission but signals of wielding her official authority, as discussed above.

Malmesbury does, however, use more specifically gendered terms for the empress, most particularly of the term '*virago*'. Translated by Potter as variations of 'a masculine woman', not badly, the term has a much deeper connotation than that. Kirsten Fenton points out that Malmesbury uses the term *virago* to 'defeminise' women in authority, make them 'honorary men in the process', but this use is restrained to women he admires. Gender is defined by Malmesbury as 'by men in relation to women'.[74] This is no surprise, as this concept of two binary sexes seen in relation to one another is as old as Aristotle and Malmesbury might have learned this, for example, from Ælfric's late tenth-century *Grammar* amongst other writings.[75] But I am not certain that a status of honorary man is solely what Malmesbury was seeking for the empress, as using *virago* casts another precedent and another version of man. *Virago* is not only a gendered term, it may be *the* gendered term. *Virago* is used in the Vulgate Bible at Gen. II:23 for the creation of woman from man's rib. It is the only instance *virago* is used in the Vulgate Bible, and Jerome's commentary explains his use of this word as an important translation from the Hebrew from the Latin to maintain the alliteration and the etymology from '*iš* to '*iššāh* – from *vir* to *virago*: 'This one shall be called *virago*, because she was taken from *vir*'.[76]

Eve may not seem an obvious reference for Malmesbury to use with the empress. The biblical model for earlier medieval queens were often Judith and Esther. Although Malmesbury was writing about the miracles of the Blessed Virgin Mary in the late 1130s,[77] he appeared not to draw upon Mary for either the queen or the empress in his *Historia Novella*. The *Miracula Sanctae Mariae Virginis* is a 'work of deep personal devotion' written to 'kindle the same ardent devotion in its readership'[78] rather than a commentary on history, politics, or any sense of it being a model for earthly behaviour. Indeed, the Marian exemplar for queenship had not yet reached great influence, with its main proponent, Bernard of Clairvaux, contemporaneously preaching the Marian form of intercession during the period of the Anglo-Norman Civil War.[79] But in pre-lapsarian Eden, Eve represents a translation of Adam, a version of man, and one who disrupted and shared Adam's unique power.[80] With the empress as a *virago*, following Jerome and the Vulgate, perhaps Malmesbury is referring to the empress as *a* first woman in the way that Eve was *the* first woman: in the empress' case, potentially the first queen regnant in England.

Virago has significant meaning in bellicose situations as well. *Virago* has the classical denotation of a female warrior, and the influential *Etymologies* of Isidore of Seville notes this:

---

[74] Fenton 2008, 51–2.
[75] Thomson 2003, 45–6; Monk 2011, 15; Lochrie 2011.
[76] Dutripon 1868, 1460; Hayward 1995, 32, 113–14.
[77] Thomson and Winterbottom 2015, xv; Sønnesyn 2012, 60.
[78] Sønnesyn 2012, 68.
[79] Pranger 2012, 194.
[80] Bloch 1987, 11; Campbell 2019.

A *virago* is so named because she does manly things, *virgum agere*, that is, she does a man's work, and her strength is masculine. The ancients thus named strong women. But a virgin is not properly called a *virago* if she does not exercise the office of a man, although if a woman really does a man's work, as an Amazon, she is rightly called a *virago*.[81]

Virago was occasionally, and effectively, used to describe elite women in leadership positions in the period under bellicose situations. Matilda of Tuscany, for example, was referred to as a *virago* by Hugh of Flavigny for her support of Pope Gregory VII's reforms, of which she was, until her death, 'the military arm of the reformers'.[82] Hugh of Flavigny was, at that time, himself a supporter of the reforms[83] and so this should not be, and has not been, taken as slander. Malmesbury too was familiar with Isidore's writings[84] and, although he used the term very sparingly, this sense of the empress being a *virago* should not be taken as insult but, instead, compliment and a gendered one at that. Malmesbury, at least, saw little wrong with the empress enacting leadership in situations such as the return to England in 1139, and the orderly retreat from Winchester in 1141. His use of *virago* only emphasises this when in comparison to other women leaders at the time, doubly so in light of his clever allusion to the Empress as the potential first ruling queen of England.

Conclusions

Very frequently, whilst we tend to ignore the queen for the perhaps more colourful character of the empress, we have dismissed many of these contemporary constructions particularly of the empress as pure bias in the writer, and societal misogyny overall, rather than trying to approach it with what Jans Robert Jauss has called the horizons of understanding.[85] When this relationship between reader and text is dialogical, interactive rather than passive, we come closer to the worldview of the writers and the societies. Too often we've taken a singular rather than a comparative approach to these texts and these women; too often scholarship has neglected to create a dialogic discourse between them. What appears to be gendered, negative or misogynist, should be tempered as there is no real consistency between the two texts and their display of aspects of gendered authority. Malmesbury's *Historia novella* by and large talks about the queen's queenly virtues and praises the empress' masculine qualities for leadership in war; the *Gesta Stephani* both phrases the queen's womanly aspects but also her masculine behaviours whilst denigrates the empress for behaving like a man but not a king. Both the queen and the empress are active leaders in both texts, undergoing negotiation and diplomacy, leading in war, and undertaking duties of elite people in the period. The queen acts as a queen, and the empress attempts to

---

[81] Sharpe 1964, 50.
[82] Cassagnes-Brouquet 2014, 41.
[83] Cassagnes-Brouquet 2014, 41; Thomas and Mallet 2011, 301–6.
[84] Thomson 2003, 42, 44 and 210; Sønnesyn 2012, 116–18.
[85] Jauss 2001.

act like a king (unsuccessfully, as the *Gesta* would have it.) To some degree, both texts give a sense of elite people taking up the business and roles that they were literally born to do, as the uppermost echelon of Anglo-Norman society. Queen Matilda is undertaking actions bestowed to her by coronation; 'she was expected to rule with the king.'[86] The queen as queen is undertaking a gender role that could almost be called a queenly gender, reflective of both her gender and her status, and going through all the actions and motions both as a queen and, when necessary, in place of the king. The empress attempts to act like a king, with her father's spectre over her and her lessons with Heinrich V in the courts of the Holy Roman Empire the exemplars she knew best, which no doubt fostered her strong will and determination not to be a 'passive cipher,' but may have hindered her ability to *be* a king.[87]

But how this has been constructed in the past and the present has had a profound effect on our understanding of gender, authority and activity in the past. Scholarship is fortunately beyond the phase of thinking that women who held power were exceptional, or that status within a highly hierarchical society did not affect gender and authority.[88] Clearly the queen and the empress were of the highest social class that could exist in secular society in the Anglo-Norman world in the twelfth century. It should come as no surprise that they enacted secular and military authority during the Anglo-Norman Civil War, particularly at the turning of events in Winchester. When we impose readerly presentism onto the texts of the war, we impose our own constructions of knowledge onto the twelfth-century writers who were writing with their own understanding of their world. In a very real sense, both Malmesbury and the anonymous writer of the *Gesta Stephani*, in the case of the queen and the empress, perfectly accepted female authority within the boundaries of their roles in the societal hierarchy, including both secular rule and military leadership, as something inherent to the class of people to which the two women belonged. Gender then served as a backfill to highlight or denigrate as needed, according to political inclinations. This can be seen through careful consideration of translation to nuance gendered understanding of the writing, considering aspects of the women's authority which have been understudied, and examining clever allusions which gave very particular meaning and connotations of elite female authority to the readers of these twelfth-century texts. Beyond this, we can see some aspects of the intellectual climate of the twelfth century which both sees this wider acceptance of elite female authority in other contexts, with historical and biblical comparatives to draw from and allude to in the writers' works, particularly from Malmesbury. With a comparative approach to the two main contemporary sources to the Anglo-Norman Civil War, we can better see what authority looked like to the queen and the empress, and how the queen and the empress could enact (unexceptional) roles of authority within the political and intellectual climate of the Anglo-Norman sphere of the twelfth century.

---

[86] Tanner 2003, 135.
[87] Chibnall 1999, 206.
[88] Tanner 2019; Weikert 2020.

Abbreviations

Bernard   LeClercq, J. and Rochais, H. (eds) 1979. Bernard of Clairvaux, *Sancti Bernardi opera*, Rome: Eds. Cisterciennes, Volume 8, cited by ep. number. Translations from *Epistolae*, available at: https://epistolae.ctl.columbia.edu/.

GS   Potter, K. R. (trans. and ed.) 1976. *Gesta Stephani*. London: Thomas Nelson and Sons Ltd.

HN   Potter, K. R. (ed. and trans.) 1955. William of Malmesbury, *Historia novella*. London: Thomas Nelson and Sons Ltd.

LE   Fairweather, J. (ed. and trans.) 2005. *Liber Eliensis*. Woodbridge: Boydell Press.

OV   Chibnall, M. (ed. and trans.) 1978. Orderic Vitalis, *The Ecclesiastical History of Orderic Vitalis, Volume 6*. Oxford: Oxford University Press.

RRAN   Cronne, H. A. and David, R. H. C. 1968. *Regesta Regum Anglo-Normannorum, 1066-1154*, vol. 3. Oxford: Clarendon Press.

Bibliography

Primary Sources

Dutripon, F. P. 1868. *Biblorum Sacrorum Concordantiae*, 2nd edition. Paris.

Hayward, C. T. R. (ed. and trans.) 1995. *Saint Jerome's Hebrew Questions on Genesis*. Oxford: Clarendon Press.

Monks of Malmesbury. Letter to Empress Matilda. *Epistolae*. Available at: https://epistolae.ctl.columbia.edu/letter/205.html. (Accessed 19 November 2020).

Sharpe, W. D. (ed. and trans.) 1964. Isidore of Seville: The Medical Writings. An English Translation with an Introduction and Commentary, *Transactions of the American Philosophical Society*, 54:2, 1–75.

Tritton, A. S. and Gibb, H. A. R. (trans.) 1933. The First and Second Crusades from an Anonymous Syriac Chronicle, *Journal of the Royal Asiatic Society of Great Britain and Ireland*, 1, 69–101.

Secondary Sources

Barton, R. 1998. Zealous Anger and the Renegotiation of Aristocratic Relationships in Eleventh- and Twelfth-Century France, in B. H. Rosenwein (ed.), *Anger's Past: The Social Uses of an Emotion in the Middle Ages*, 153–70. Ithaca: Cornell University Press.

Bloch, R. H. 1987. Medieval Misogyny, *Representations*, 20, 1–24.

Campbell, L. C. 2019. Power and Authority in Late Medieval Translations of Genesis, unpublished paper.

Cassagnes-Brouquet, S. 2014. In the Service of Just War: Matilda of Tuscany (Eleventh-Twelfth Centuries), *Clio*, 39, 35–52.

Chibnall, M. 1999. *The Empress Matilda: Queen Consort, Queen Mother and Lady of the English*. Oxford: Blackwell.

Crouch, D. 2000. *The Reign of King Stephen 1135-1154*. London: Pearson Educational.

Crouch, D. 2008. King Stephen and Northern France, in P. Dalton and G. J. White (eds), *King Stephen's Reign (1135-1154)*, 44–57. Woodbridge: Boydell Press.

Davis, R. H. C. 1962. The Authorship of the Gesta Stephani, *English Historical Review*, 77:303, 209–232.

Davis, R. H. C. 1990. *King Stephen*. 3rd edition. London: Routledge.

Fenton, K. 2008. *Gender, Nation and Conquest in the Works of William of Malmesbury*. Woodbridge: Boydell Press.

Hamilton, B. 1978. Women in the Crusader States: The Queens of Jerusalem (1100–1190), *Studies in Church History Subsidia*, 1, 143–74.

Hanley, C. 2019. *Matilda: Empress, Queen, Warrior*. New Haven: Yale University Press.

Harari, Y. N. 2007. *Special Operations in the Age of Chivalry, 1100-1550*. Woodbridge: Boydell Press.

Jauss, J. R. 2001. The Identity of the Poetic Text in the Changing Horizon of Understanding, in J. L. Machor and P. Goldstein (eds), *Reception Study: From Theory to Cultural Studies*, 7–28. Abington: Psychology Press.

King, E. 2006. The Gesta Stephani, in D. Bates, J. Crick and S. Hamilton (eds), *Writing Medieval Biography 750-1250: Essays in Honour of Frank Barlow*, 195–206. Woodbridge: Boydell Press.

King, E. 2010. *King Stephen*. New Haven: Yale University Press.

Kosto, A. 2012. *Hostages in the Middle Ages*. Oxford: Oxford University Press.

Lochrie, K. 2011. Heterosexuality, in R. Evans (ed.), *A Cultural History of Sexuality in the Middle Ages, Volume 2*, 37–56. London: Bloomsbury.

McGrath, K. 2019. *Royal Rage and the Construction of Anglo-Norman Authority, c. 1000-1250*. New York: Palgrave Macmillan.

Mynors, R. A. B. 1955. The Text, in K. R. Potter (trans. and ed.), *Gesta Stephani*, xxxviii-xliii. London: Thomas Nelson and Sons Ltd.

Monk, C. 2011. Defending the Rihthæmed: The Normalizing of Marital Sexuality in the Anglo-Saxon Penitentials, *SELIM: Journal of the Spanish Society for Medieval English Language and Literature*, 18, 7–48.

Potter, K. R. 1955. Introduction, in Potter, K. R. (ed. and trans.) William of Malmesbury, *Historia novella* , xi-xliii. London: Thomas Nelson and Sons Ltd.

Pranger, M. B. 2012. Bernard of Clairvaux: Work and Self, in M. Birkedal Bruun (ed.), *The Cambridge Companion to the Cistercian Order*, Cambridge Companions to Religion, Cambridge: Cambridge University Press. doi:10.1017/CCO9780511735899.

Sønnesyn, S. O. 2012. *William of Malmesbury and the Ethics of History*. Woodbridge: Boydell Press.

Tanner, H. J. 2003. Queenship – Office, Custom or Ad Hoc? The Case of Queen Matilda III of England (1136–52), in J. Carmi Parsons and B. Wheeler (eds), *Eleanor of Aquitaine: Lady and Lord*, 133–58. London: St Martin's Press.

Tanner, H. J. (ed.) 2019. *Medieval Elite Women and the Exercise of Power, 1100-1400: Moving Beyond the Exceptionalist Debate*. London: Palgrave Macmillan.

Thomas, D. and Mallett, A. 2011. Hugh of Flavigny, in D. Thomas and A. Mallet (eds), *Christian-Muslim Relations: A Bibliographical History, Volume 3 (1050-1200)*, 301–6. Leiden: Brill.

Thomson, R. M. 2003. *William of Malmesbury* revised edition. Woodbridge: Boydell Press.

Thomson, R. M. and Winterbottom, M. 2015. Introduction, in R. M. Thomson and M. Winterbottom (ed. and trans.) William of Malmesbury, *The Miracles of the Blessed Virgin Mary*, xiii-lxiv. Woodbridge: Boydell.

Weikert, K. 2020. *Authority, Gender and Space in the Anglo-Norman World, 900-1200*. Woodbridge: Boydell Press.

Weiler, B. 2005. William of Malmesbury on Kingship, *History*, 90:1, 3–22.

Chapter 9

Lantfred and Local Life in Winchester in the 960s and 970s

Mark Atherton

This chapter explores the text and context of Translatio et miracula S. Swithuni *(Translation and Miracles of St Swithun) by the Frankish author Lantfred, an outsider figure commissioned by the monks of the Old Minster to write the earliest hagiography of this Winchester saint. This is a story of the discovery of Swithun's saintliness through dreams and visions, the translation of his relics into the Old Minster and the miracles that accompanied his cult, which drew people from all over King Edgar's England and abroad. Lantfred is revealed as an enthusiast for the city, a supporter of religious and political unity, but at the same time also a critic of the harsh rule and injustices perpetrated by the king's men. As a writer he has a good investigative flair, an ear for dialogue and an eye for vivid detail, all of which he applies to his task, painting a picture of everyday material existence - buildings, artefacts, the quality of life - and portraying many of the lively and colourful characters from all social classes (from ealdorman to smith to moneyer to servant) that he encounters on his journeys round the city.*

> St Swithun's day if thou dost rain:
> For forty days it will remain:
> If on St Swithun's day it really pours:
> You're better off to stay indoors.

St Swithun's Day is celebrated on 15 July, commemorating the day of the translation of the relics of that holy man into the Old Minster in Winchester in the year 971. The present chapter takes a renewed look at the hagiography associated with the first promotion in the 960s and 970s of the cult of Winchester's patron saint. I will focus mostly on the text *Translatio et miracula S. Swithuni*, the original treatment of that narrative by the Frankish author Lantfred, who was the contemporary recorder and witness to the events at first hand. Since much of the narrative is anecdotal, a literary approach will be taken, using the techniques of close reading to assess selected stories and anecdotes in the context of the work as a whole. But because of his close familiarity with both the people and the place, Lantfred's work has an added historical value. I will discuss the extent to which Lantfred as an outsider living in Winchester was able to observe and comment on local customs and ways of life of the citizens: the details of ordinary living, including everyday objects and artefacts, travel and communication, everyday talk and conversation, housing and architecture, the workings of the law and the keeping of the peace and public order.

The Author

Lantfred, or Lantfred of Fleury, as he is sometimes called, was the author of the *Translatio et miracula S. Swithuni*,[1] which he wrote at Winchester probably around the year 975. Of the writer himself little is known other than some autobiographical references within his oeuvre, the exception being – as Michael Lapidge, the editor of the *Translatio* points out – a letter to Archbishop Dunstan from the period 974–985 signed 'L.' and sent from the abbey of Fleury (the important Benedictine centre, now St Benoît-sur-Loire near Orléans in France). 'L.' may well be our author, since he wishes to recover a book he had lent to Osgar, one of the more prominent of the Benedictine reformers during the reign of King Edgar (ruled 959–75). Osgar had become abbot of Abingdon in 964, and previously had also spent a period of stay at Fleury.[2] The evidence points therefore to Lantfred being L., a Frankish monk from Fleury. A close study of his *Translatio et miracula* indicates that the author spent a number of periods in residence at the monastic precinct of the Old Minster in Winchester in the years around 970. Apparently Lantfred felt at home in Winchester. And as he describes himself in chapter 32 of his *Translatio*, entitled '*De muliere quae in Gallia sanata est*' ('Concerning the woman who was cured in France'), he was also a priest (*sacerdos*). Perhaps for reasons of modesty to be associated with the genre of hagiography, he presents himself in a distanced mode of description, using the third-person pronoun:

> *Accidit autem ut sacerdos quidam nomine Lantfredus de Anglorum finibus, dum pergeret ad Galliam in illis temporibus, hospitaretur in eadem ciuitatula in qua intolerabili dolore egrotat mulier pretaxata.*
> Now it happened that while a certain priest from England named Lantfred was travelling in France at that time, he was put up as a guest in the same village in which the aforementioned woman lay sick in unbearable pain.[3]

Lantfred's actual formulation – literally 'a certain priest named Lantfred from the land of the English' – almost suggests that he has 'gone native': England has become his home, and on this occasion he is only temporarily visiting France. Elsewhere in the text, however, there are expressions which suggest that he is still an outsider in England, a more distanced observer commenting, for instance, on the place-names

---

[1] *The Translation and Miracles of St Swithun*, Lapidge 2003.
[2] Lapidge and Winterbottom 1991, 36–7; Atherton 2017, 230.
[3] Text and translation in Lapidge 2003, 320–1.

that the English give to certain regions '*eorum lingua*', 'in their language'.[4] With one exception he accurately reproduces the Old English names of shires such as *Bedefordscir* (ch. 6) or place-names like *Wincelcumbe* (Winchcombe; ch. 1), though Winchester, as the chief royal city of the realm – and indeed the main location of the action – is consistently given its then current and widely-used Latin name of Wintonia, for example in the Prefatory Letter to the monks of the Old Minster at the very beginning of the work.[5]

The reasons for Lantfred's stay at Winchester are not wholly clear: it may have been to exercise his function as a priest, but in addition we assume he must have served as a consultant on Benedictine customs and practices at Fleury, perhaps to advise the relatively recently appointed monks from Abingdon, who, since the expulsion of the secular canons and married clerics in 964, now served as the clergy in the city. His main task, however, was to write his account of St Swithun: the Prefatory Letter states that Lantfred was commissioned by the monks of the Old Minster in Winchester – perhaps with the approval of the new monastic bishop, Æthelwold, though this is not explicitly stated – to write a biography of Swithun, the obscure ninth-century bishop of the city.[6] This was a burning issue at the time, for in the period from 968 to 971 Swithun was 'invented', which here means essentially that he was rediscovered, as the patron saint of Winchester and moved or 'translated' from a tomb in the churchyard into a shrine within the seventh-century Old Minster (which at the time was still a two-cell structure, much smaller than the adjacent, early-tenth century royal foundation of the New Minster). According to Lapidge, the rise to prominence of Swithun as a saint was part of Bishop Æthelwold's plan of reconciliation with his kinsman Eadsige, who had been a prominent churchman at Winchester until he lost his position when the clerics were ejected from the city's churches during the Benedictine takeover in 964. As we will see when we come to examine Lantfred's narrative, Eadsige later had a change of heart and decided to join the monks at Winchester, and in return he was appointed as sacrist to the Old Minster, with particular duties as warden of the new tomb of St Swithun.

Of course, a newly established saint requires a new hagiography – to be written in Latin, naturally, in order to reach a wide and international audience. And there were precedents for giving such writing commissions to an outsider. Continental or foreign scholars were often been employed for literary purposes in the long tenth century: one need think only of the Welsh cleric Asser, who wrote *The Life of King Alfred*, while others include Frithegod at Canterbury, who wrote his *Breuiloquium uitae Wilfridi* to record the move of St Wilfrid's relics from Ripon to Canterbury in the year 948, and the prolific Goscelin of Saint-Bertin at Sherborne, author of many hagiograhical works in the eleventh century, or even the foreign-trained cleric B., who wrote the

---

[4] Lantfred, *Translatio et miracula*, chs. 6 and 7, in Lapidge 2003, 290–1.
[5] Lapidge 2003, 252–3. Hereafter all references to Lantfred's *Translatio et miracula* will be by chapter number in Lapidge's edition.
[6] The issue of who commissioned the work is discussed in Lapidge 2003, 253, n. 8.

Vita S. Dunstani in the 990s.[7] A likely if straightforward reason for this practice is that these writers were skilled Latinists, not only because of their training and education elsewhere but in many cases also because they were speakers of the cognate romance language, French, which at the time was still regarded as a colloquial form of Latin rather than as a separate language.[8]

The end product of Lantfred's commission was his *Translatio et miracula S. Swithuni*, or the *Translation and Miracles of St Swithun*, which is essentially a Latin prose narrative, but one that includes a prosimetric element, in that some chapters include summarising poems and/or verse prayers. To sum up the plot, we may say that Lantfred tells an exciting tale of how Swithun the saint was rediscovered in various dream visions by three prominent Winchester citizens over a period of three years (chapters 1–3), and thereafter was celebrated as a posthumous healer and worker of miracles (chapters 4–39).[9] In terms of its plot in the first three chapters, there is a tension in the narrative: the reader or listener is allowed to wonder whether Swithun will actually be discovered and given his due. Or will he be prevented by human weakness and prevarication (as told in chapter 1)? Or even by evil creatures (chapter 3)? And as the account of the saint's posthumous miracles unfolds in the later chapters, the reader engages with stories of human folly and injustice, all put right in the end by St Swithun's curative and salutary influence as a man of God. Additional literary value is provided by vivid characterisation, dramatic dialogue and local colour, for Lantfred's work centres on Winchester and its environs but includes a whole array of characters from all walks of life and from all parts of the new and unified realm of the 'renowned and unconquerable king', Edgar the Peaceable.[10] A recurring motif is the constant movement of people into Winchester in order to experience healing and renewal, after which they return to their home regions praising the works of the omnipotent Creator. Lantfred's purpose is to be all-inclusive, for example in the Prefatory Letter to the Monks of Winchester which opens the whole work, he speaks of 'the miracles, which the omnipotent author of miracles has deigned to bestow on all the peoples of England through the merit of most holy Swithun'.[11] The multi-ethnic emphasis is telling: England is referred to by its peoples in the plural, reflecting the fact that it had only recently been unified as one kingdom (by Æthelstan in 937, again by Eadred in 954, then by Edgar in 959). It is often argued that the Benedictine emphasis on unity of practice fitted well with Edgar's unificatory aims, and Winchester in its role as a kind of proto-capital was an ideal location to promote such ideals.[12]

It is clear that Lantfred's *Translatio et miracula* achieved its aims over the next decade. Undoubtedly the promotion of Swithun as a healing saint had economic and

---

[7] Keynes 2014 on Asser; Lapidge 1988 on Frithegod; Love 1996, xl–xliv on Goscelin; Winterbottom and Lapidge 2012 on 'B'.

[8] Wright 1982. See also Jansson 1991 and Richter 1983.

[9] See also the chapter by Karl Alvestad in this volume, pp. 257–74.

[10] Lantfred, Preface in Lapidge 2003, 259.

[11] Lapidge 2003, 253.

[12] Molyneaux 2015, 215.

political repercussions for the city, which became a goal for pilgrims and visitors. In October 980 a new and much grander Old Minster was eventually opened and dedicated by Æthelwold, 'one of the largest and most magnificent churches in the Europe of his day'.[13] Thereafter, in the 990s, Lantfred's hagiography was revisited by two Winchester writers of the next generation: Wulfstan of Winchester writing in Anglo-Latin verse and Ælfric of Cerne Abbas (later abbot of Eynsham) writing in Old English.[14]

Earlier Research

I have discussed the story of Lantfred's *Translatio et miracula* in a previous publication, *The Making of England*, which in scope and coverage is a survey of the period.[15] For reasons of space, it was not possible there to cover all the features and ramifications of the narrative. I propose here, therefore, to briefly survey the cultural context and then to summarise my previous findings.

In terms of its cultural and political context and significance, Winchester had become the chief city of England, a position it was to hold until at least the time of King Cnut (1016–1035), when, after a hiatus in the Viking period, London as city and port redeveloped and was able to reassert its significance. With Æthelwold in place from the year 964 as bishop and monastic reformer, Winchester became the powerhouse of a Benedictine Reform that affected not only the spiritual life but also the political power relations, education, culture and arts of the newly refounded kingdom of England.[16] Æthelwold and the other reformers provided an ideology, an agenda and an impetus for unity in the kingdom, for developments in education, for the standardisation of the English language, for governance of the country and the making of laws, for the regulation of urban markets and the reform of coinage.[17] Though still part of a rural economy, nevertheless Winchester was a model for the new kind of town or city that had developed in Edgar's reign.[18] Radical changes had taken place in the city, only some of which may be mentioned here: the growth in trade along the market street, *i.e.* the (formerly Roman) high street (Latin *forum*) that runs from the east gate to the west gate across the middle of the city, the building of the royal palace in the south of the city, the clearance of the south-east corner of the city to make way for the new monastic precincts based on the Old Minster, the New Minster and the Nunnaminster.[19] This is the background to Lantfred's account of the rise to prominence of the new patron saint of the city.

---

[13] Lapidge and Winterbottom 1991, li.
[14] For Wulfstan, also known as Wulfstan Cantor, see Lapidge and Winterbottom 1991 and Lapidge 2003; for Ælfric's perspective on Swithun as a saint 'of our days' see Gretsch 2006, 157–231.
[15] Atherton 2017, 255–76.
[16] Biddle 1975.
[17] Yorke 1988; Hofstetter 1988; Molyneaux 2015; Wormald 1999; Jonsson 1987.
[18] Biddle and Hill 1971.
[19] Rumble 2002.

In my previous discussion of Lantfred's *Translatio*, I focussed mainly on the political interest of three of the chapters: ch. 1, the story of the smith and the ejected cleric Eadsige; ch. 20, the stolen enslaved girl and Eadsige, now the sacrist; ch. 25, the foreign merchant Flodoald and his unjustly arrested enslaved man who has to undergo the judicial ordeal; the latter discussion led to a brief exploration of the other two 'legal' chapters (26 and 27) which also narrate the cases of men unjustly accused of theft and of handling stolen property. The key issue turned out to be the question of whether Lantfred had a hidden agenda as a critic of some of the practices he observed. In particular, what was his attitude to monastic bishops? And what was his view of the severities of Edgar's royal rule, particularly when implemented by the ministers and agents of royal government?

At first sight, Lantfred's Preface offers straightforward ideological support for the combined policy of unification as expressed in Edgar's royal rule and the Benedictine Reform. The English in particular are singled out for praise. Accordingly, the Preface begins with an outline of biblical salvation history until the moment when the disciples are sent out 'into the whole world and preach the gospel to every creature'[20]; here the English – or 'Anglo-Saxons' (Latin *Anglisaxones*) as they are called here – are singled out for their welcome of the new faith, which they accepted without any bloodshed or violence against the foreign missionaries who preached to them. As elsewhere in the *Translatio et miracula*, there is an emphasis on the various 'peoples' (Latin plural *gentes*) who make up the nation of the English, as well as the devotion of their ruling classes that included 'not only bishops, monks and abbots, but even kings, queens and nobles'.[21] For these reasons the Lord has bestowed such grace ('*tantam gratiam*') 'on the aforesaid nation' so that it would produce from its ranks vast numbers of saints who demonstate the Lord's power through their healing miracles.[22] The 'glorious bishop Swithun', it is implied, is one such saint, and his sanctity is discovered during the reign of Edgar, king of several peoples in Britain:

> *Eadgaro regnante, basileo igsigni atque inuictissimo, prepotente ac clementissimo necnon gloriosissimo sceptrigera ditione et feliciter gentibus imperante compluribus habitu distantibus, uoce atque moribus, diffuse in insula commorantibus quae 'Albio' nuncupata legitur ab Anglorum fore ueteribus...*

> ...with Edgar reigning, that renowned and unconquerable king, powerful and most merciful and fully glorious in his sceptre-bearing sovereignty, blessedly commanding several peoples distinct in appearance, speech and custom, dwelling widely scattered in the island which was reportedly called 'Albion' by the early English...[23]

Edgar, 'powerful and most merciful and fully glorious' as Lantfred describes him here, is untouchable in his power. In brief, he is beyond criticism.

---

[20] Lapidge 2003, 256–7.
[21] Lapidge 2003, 256–7.
[22] Lapidge 2003, 256–7.
[23] Lapidge 2003, 258–9; in his note 33, Lapidge cites S 841, a charter of the year 982, for a near-contemporary use of the name Albion, which is also found in Bede, *Historia ecclesiastica* I.1.

The same cannot be asserted for the agents of royal power who feature in *Translatio et miracula*, for it seems that Lantfred is not comfortable, not entirely at ease, with the manner in which they exercise their power. As already intimated, Lantfred's discomfort is not immediately apparent, but support for this interpretation may be found by extensive reading in the stories of the *miracula* and sometimes also with some judicious close reading or probing of the implications of Lantfred's statements (especially in chs. 20, 25–7). But the first oddity, as it were, in Lantfred's narrative is that he has been commissioned to write his work not by Bishop Æthelwold but by the monks of the Old Minster: the work is not, then, quite the official hagiography that one might have expected. And Æthelwold himself does not feature very prominently in the narrative, nor does Lantfred appear to have had much contact with him. The focus instead is on the local people of Winchester who witness or experience the miracles: this makes the work less a mouthpiece of the Reform party and more of a sociological study, a kind of snapshot of Winchester society around the year 970.

As Lapidge has demonstrated in his edition, Lantfred follows some standard hagiographic models for his account of the *inventio* and *miracula*, notably the classic account of the finding and translation of St Stephen and then the more recent story of the translation of St Benedict from Montecassino in Italy to Fleury in France during the Langobard invasion of Italy.[24] What is perhaps surprising is that Swithun manifests himself first not to a monk but to a smith, not always by reputation the most reputable of medieval citizens, and so Lantfred takes the trouble to state that this was a 'trustworthy smith' (ch. 1). Also suprising, perhaps, is that the new saint is not obviously of the monastic persuasion, for he is a local bishop, whose earthly career – as Lantfred cheerfully acknowledges in his Prefatory Letter to the Monks of the Old Minster – is obscure and little known. Swithun, then, is more of a local hero rather than a monastic reformer. This is perhaps why the smith is instructed to deliver his message first to Eadsige, the disgraced cleric, who is now living in Winchcombe; as Lapidge points out, we learn elsewhere that Eadsige was a kinsman of Æthelwold, and perhaps a story of a compromise and reconciliation lies behind the rediscovery and translation of St Swithun. Later in Lantfred's account (chs. 5 and 20) we realise that Eadsige has now returned to Winchester and been appointed as sacrist of the Old Minster, with particular duties at the new shrine of St Swithun within the Old Minster itself. But here is another oddity in Lantfred's work, for Eadsige is not presented with much sympathy either, even after he has rejoined the reformed community; perhaps Lantfred's aim is to include some intentional humour, but in the dialogue the new sacrist comes across as arrogant and authoritarian, though the other characters involved in the incident also bicker and squabble in less than exemplary ways.[25]

What emerges from chapter 20 is that Lantfred evokes sympathy for the predicament of the enslaved girl. She has after all been stolen from her owner in

---

[24] Atherton 2017, 266–7, and further references 317; Lapidge 2003, 13–14, 252–4; Head 1990.

[25] Lapidge 2003, 302–5; for an interpretation of the rather truculent character of Eadsige in chapter 20, see Atherton 2017, 271–2.

the north of England, abducted and brought to Winchester '*ab auidis mangonibus*', 'by greedy traders'.[26] The disapproval of the oppressors here is entirely typical of Lantfred's approach, as is his sympathy for the oppressed. The reader is made to feel interest and concern, for the enslaved girl quite by chance meets her former owner on the market street of Winchester (the *forum* or High Street) and attempts to speak to him, but to prevent further contact the enraged owners have her bound in shackles and left in the house for the day. It is now that Swithun intervenes, and he miraculously spirits her away in an instant to the sanctified area of the Old Minster where Swithun's shrine is located and it is here that the incident with Eadsige takes place. Clearly the saint is on the side of the disadvantaged enslaved girl in this narrative.

A similar if even clearer sympathy for an enslaved person is found in the anecdote about the ordeal found in ch. 25, in which the king's reeve is singled out for his injustice, overbearing arrogance and undue pride.[27] And the same holds for other episodes in which the agents of royal authority are seen as too strict, too zealous and even cruel in the exercise of their power. So ch. 26 deals with Edgar's 'law of great severity' which stipulated blinding and mutilation as a deterrent for robbery and as a means of establishing law and order, a punishment that churchmen of the next generation were willing to support as 'merciful', despite its cruelty, because it allegedly gave the condemned prisoner time to repent.[28] But Swithun by contrast shows greater mercy, and heals and restores the sight of the blinded prisoner. Similarly, ch. 27 tells of a man condemned to death for accepting a few sheaves of royally owned wheat from the king's reapers. But in a scene not unlike the escape from the Château d'If in Dumas' *The Count of Monte Christo*, Swithun helps the condemned man to free himself undetected from his stocks with a (hopelessly inadequate) small knife, and then to escape from his imprisonment, and even to turn the tables on his captors by locking them into the building with a conveniently placed wagon wheel. Such sympathies for victims of unjust law-enforcement add a nuance to Lantfred's political stance and detract noticeably from the all-out praise heaped upon King Edgar in the opening pages of the *Translatio et miracula*.

With these features in mind, we turn now to some other episodes from the work not hitherto discussed. The emphasis, as already intimated, will be on close reading in context, and the ultimate aim is to show how such an approach may illuminate the source and enrich our knowledge of the social conditions of the tenth-century city.

The Crippled Cleric (*Translatio et miracula*, Chapter 2)

In his story of the cleric Æthelsige, who suffers from curvature of the spine, Lantfred narrates the events leading up to the first healing miracle that Swithun performs (in chapter 2 of *Translatio et miracula*).[29] Stylistically, and in terms of length and quality

---

[26] Lapidge 2003, 302–3.
[27] Lapidge 2003, 308–11; there is further discussion in Atherton 2017, 273–4.
[28] Keynes 1986, 212; O'Brien O'Keeffe 1998, 225–8; Wormald 1999, 125–8; 370, 414–15.
[29] Lapidge 2003, 266–74.

of narrative, we are dealing with a short story rather than simply a brief anecdote, and the profuse details of plot, dialogue and local colour allow us to identify Lantfred's characteristic techniques and to explore some of his themes and motifs as a hagiographer.

To begin with, we may note that Lantfred is a careful observer and recorder of extraneous detail, since he is after all collecting evidence for the sanctity of his subject; the corollary is that his writing must be seen to be reliable and accurate. He therefore provides a date for these events, namely 4 July in the year 969, in fact two years before Bishop Æthelwold actually allows the ceremony of Swithun's translation to take place. In chapter 2, the focus is on Æthelsige, and Lantfred takes care to locate his home and his origins precisely. We are informed that Æthelsige has suffered from his condition of roundback since the day of his birth; that he lives at the royal estate of Alderbury: and it is noteworthy that our Frankish writer Lantfred, despite being a non-native speaker of English, nevertheless spells this name in a corrrect manner as *Aþeluuarabyrig*. Apparently there was a group of monks in residence there, and Æthelsige has been made a cleric so that he may be permitted to live in their community. As Lapidge, editor of the scholarly edition of *Translatio et miracula* implies in a footnote, at least some of this information can be seen as accurate.[30] There was indeed a royal estate at this location, confirmed by a charter in which King Edgar granted four hides of land at *Afene* (Avon, now Avon Farm at Little Durnford, in Stratford-sub-Castle, Wiltshire) to Wynstan, his *cubicularius*, that is, as the text subsequently states, his *burthegn* or chamberlain.[31]

This charter repays extensive quoting since the king's grant is precisely datable from the wording of the charter to the year 972: '*Anno dominice incarnationis DCCCC LXXII*', which makes it exactly contemporary with Lantfred's writing of his *Translatio et miracula*. And appropriately enough, the bounds of this charter include Alderbury, in a very similar spelling to that used by Lantfred:

> Þis synd þara feower hida land gemæra æt afene þe Eadgar cyning gebocade Wynstan his burðene on ece yrfe . Ærest of afene on þa ealdan burhdic on þæne weg . ofer ðæne weg east swa Wulfsige hit gemærsode oð hit cymð to ðæm wege þe scæt fram hambres buruh to Æþelware byrig oð hit cymð to þam wege þe scæt eastan fram winter burnan west to billan cumbe to þæm ealdan wuduforda . þonan up on midne stream oþ hit cymð eft fornangean þa ealdan burh dic.

> These are the four hides of land at Avon which King Edgar booked to his burthegn Wynstan as a perpetual inheritance. First from Avon to the old fortress ditch on the way; over the way eastwards, as Wulfsige marked it out, until it reaches the way that leads from Hambres burh to Æthelwarebyrig [Alderbury] until it reaches the way which leads from the east from the winterbourne westwards to Billancombe to the old wood ford; from there up the middle of the stream until it again reaches the old fortress ditch.[32]

---

[30] Lapidge 2003, 266, n. 71.
[31] S 789.
[32] Text available in S 789, KCD 572, BCS 1286. My translation.

Æthelwarebyrig is to be interpreted as 'Æthelwaru's fortified place or manor', and Lapidge suggests a link to St Peter Street, Winchester, the late Old English name of which was Alarnestret, which may also be named after the lady Æthelwaru.[33] As he further points out, there is no mention in any other source of a community of monks at Alderbury, though Domesday Book records a church as owning property there in the year 1066. If, as this chapter argues, Lantfred is to be regarded as a reliable historical source, then this data should be accepted: it seems likely that Lantfred had access to information about a (presumably small) community of monks that is otherwise unknown.

The very same charter is relevant also for its witness list, a snapshot of those currently in power at the time that Lantfred was actively engaged in writing his hagiography at Winchester. The list follows the usual hierarchy of bishops, secular rulers, abbots, ealdormen and thegns, in that order:

> *Anno dominice incarnationis . DCCCC . LXXII . Scripta est hæc carta his testibus consentientibus quorum inferius nomina caraxantur . Ego Eadgar . rex prefatam donationem concessi . Ego Dunstan Dorovernensis ecclesie archiepiscopus consignavi . Ego Oswold archiepiscopus confirmavi . Ego Æþelwold episcopus corroboravi . Ego Ælfstan episcopus consolidavi . Ego Ælfwold episcopus confirmavi . Ego Ælfstan episcopus concessi . Ego Ælfðryð regina . Ego Æscwig abbas . Ego Osgar abbas . Ego Æðelgar abbas . Ego Ælfhere dux . Ego Æðelwine dux . Ego Byrhtnoð dux . Ego Oslac dux . Ego Æðelweard minister . Ego Ælfweard minister . Ego Ælfsige minister . Ego Heanric minister . Ego Leofa minister . Ego Leofwine minister.*

> In the year of the Incarnation of our Lord 972, this charter was written with the agreement of the following witnesses whose names are inscribed below. I, King Edgar, granted the aforesaid gift; I, Archbishop Dunstan, of the church at Canterbury, signed it; I, Archbishop Oswald, confirmed it; I, Bishop Æthelwold, corroborated this; I, Bishop Ælfstan, supported this; I, Bishop Ælfwold, confirmed it; I, Bishop Ælfstan, conceded this; I, Queen Ælfthryth; I, Abbot Æscwig; I, Abbot Osgar; I, Abbot Æthelgar; I, Ealdorman Ælfhere; I, Ealdorman Æthelwine; I, Ealdorman Byrhtnoth; I, Earl Oslac; I, Æthelweard, thegn; I, Ælfweard, thegn; I, Ælfsige, thegn; I, Heanric, thegn; I, Leofa, thegn; I, Leofwine, thegn.[34]

Most of the people listed may be identified from their activities elsewhere.[35] Here, conveniently gathered for the occasion, are Dunstan, Oswald and Æthelwold, *i.e.* the three principal Benedictine reformers later celebrated as saints, with fully fledged contemporary biographies devoted to them; King Edgar and his queen also attend; and among the other prominent churchmen at the meeting are the names of Osgar (the above-mentioned abbot of Abingdon) and Æthelgar (abbot of the rival institution of the New Minster in Winchester at the time of the translation of St Swithun).

Only four ealdormen are mentioned in the witness-list, and this appears to represent the full quota of these high-ranking princely figures at this point in Edgar's reign. Two of them, Æthelwine and Byrhtnoth (the later hero of Maldon), held power

---

[33] Watts 2004, 6; Lapidge 2003, 266, n. 71.
[34] S 789.
[35] Scragg 2008 provides an authoritative study.

in East Anglia and Essex respectively, where they were both active as administrators, and they do not appear to have been very active in Wessex or Hampshire; both feature prominently in the *Vita S. Oswaldi* by 'B.' The fourth name is Oslac, that is, the northern earl, with Danish connections, who found himself demoted and a landless exile after the sudden demise of Edgar in 975.

This leaves only one other ealdorman, Ælfhere, whose jurisdiction was Mercia, and who seems to have been a close associate of Bishop Æthelwold.[36] By a process of elimination, it is probably this ealdorman who is alluded to in ch. 9 and who features in '*De puero qui de equo cecidit*' ('Concerning the boy who fell from a horse'), one of the shorter miracle stories in Lantfred's *Translatio et miracula* (ch. 31):

> At the very same time as well a certain much beloved ealdorman of the king, who was very influential in secular affairs, set off quickly with a huge retinue – as is the custom among the Anglo-Saxons – for a particular estate in which a mighty preparation for the necessary customs of entertainment had been sumptuously set up for him.[37]

The interest here lies in Lantfred's obvious wish as an outsider to observe and record the customs of the tenth-century Anglo-Saxon nobility: their love of festivals, as implied here, or their attendance at long wedding celebrations that last several days (ch. 9). In both narratives, horse-riding features prominently, and in chapter 9 much is made of the horse-trappings with which the horses are decked out, a feature that is referred to in the near-contemporary poem *The Battle of Maldon*, as well as in various tenth-century wills.[38] Lantfred's chapter 31 by contrast records the flip side, the ever-present hazard of riding accidents, though in this case – through the prayers of the ealdorman (further evidence for the piety of the tenth-century elite) and through the sanctity of Bishop Swithun whose aid the ealdorman petitions – the young man recovers consciousness quickly, despite a broken arm and leg, and – so it is implied – is able to proceed on his journey.

With this plausible detail in mind, let us return to the account of the cleric and the moneyer with which we began this section. Given the circumstantial evidence, Æthelsige is probably to be seen as a real character, another historical personage. Hearing in a dream (here termed a '*somnium*' or 'prophetic dream') that he would meet a '*medicum peritissimum*' ('a highly-skilled physician'), Æthelsige bids farewell to his community of monks at Alderbury and heads off to Winchester, where he finds lodgings with a friendly local moneyer. Again, Lantfred provides some intriguing if unconfirmed information. Who is this moneyer? Unfortunately the author neglects to name him, but Lapidge suggests he is one of the four moneyers named on the coinage of King Edgar: Æthelstan, Deal, Ealstan or Wynsige.[39] Again Lantfred's choice of word for the moneyer's profession

---

[36] Lapidge 2003, 292, n. 184; Williams 1982; Roach 2016, 85–6.
[37] Lapidge 2003, 318–21. *Eadem quoque tempestate quidam consul regis nimium dilectus, in caducis prepotens rebus, cum ingenti comitatu – sicut mos est Anglosaxonum – properanter equitabat ad quendam uicum, in quo grandis apparatus ad necessarios conuiuandi usus erat illi opipare constructus.*
[38] Atherton 2021, 35–9.
[39] Lapidge 2003, 267, n. 73.

is illuminating: *trapezeta* is a Greek-derived term, typical of the elaborate 'Hermeneutic' diction that was popular with other Winchester writers in this period, and Lantfred is no exception in making such lexical choices, though he also refers to the moneyer using other, more mainstream Latin terms such as *argentarius, nummularius, opifex*. This moneyer, so Lantfred asserts, is kindly and hospitable and willing to extend his love of God, 'the creator of all things' as he is called here, to his neighbour, *i.e.* he takes the injunction to 'love your neighbour' seriously – to such an extent that he even allows his unexpected guest to lodge with him for six months, looking after him and taking him on horseback if he attends a *conuiuium* or banquet (note again the theme of feasting), since he is reluctant to leave the hunchback behind alone and unattended.

It will be seen that dreams play a large part in this narrative, for in chapters 1–3 and 10, and again in the mystical vision of ch. 35, this is how the heavenly world of the saint communicates with the world of human beings in Winchester. Various types of dream seem to be in play, as often in medieval literature, deriving as they do from long-standing traditions of dream theory going back to such writers as Macrobius and his *Commentary on Scipio's Dream*.[40] Accordingly we find the *somnium* or enigmatic dream, as in the dream telling Æthelsige that he will meet a 'skilled physician' in Winchester; *visio, i.e.* the more straightforwardly prophetic dream that 'actually comes true', and the *oraculum* 'in which a parent, or a pious or revered man, or a priest, or even a god clearly reveals what will or will not transpire, and what action to take or avoid': this latter category is obviously relevant to the appearances of Swithun in the dreams of various characters in the *Translatio*. Macrobius's other two categories are the *insomnium* or nightmare, caused by anxious or hopeful thinking on the future, and the *visum* or apparition of hostile forces, of which there may be an example in chapter 3, when the mule-owner falls asleep under a tree in the heat of the day outside the city and experiences an attack by three strange and hostile Furies.[41]

The dreams that the cleric dreams in the moneyer's house may thus be seen as falling under the categories of *visio* and *oraculum*, though it remains uncertain how precisely Lantfred is using such terms. Initially, in fact, Æthelsige's dream is called a *somnium*, and is narrated as follows:

> *Contemplatus est geminos adulescentes per somnium ad se uenientes, miro candore fulgentes dulcibusque eius aures affaminibus complentes, ac tali sermone egrum alloquentes: 'Dormisne an uigilas?'*

> In a dream [he] saw two youths coming towards him, shining with a marvellous brightness and filling his ears with sweet speech, and speaking to him in these words: Are you asleep or are you awake?[42]

The question 'Are you asleep or are you awake?' is delivered not without a trace of humour. Like the smith when asked the same question in chapter 1, Æthelsige

---

[40] Stahl 1990, 87–90.
[41] For this incident with the Furies, see further discussion in this volume by Eric Lacey, pp. 191–214.
[42] Lapidge 2003, 266–7

replies that he was asleep but now he is awake, and the conversation continues in this apparent waking state (we will consider further below the partly jockeying partly serious colloquial style in which these conversations take place). The two youths now depart to the light of heavenly bliss after telling the cleric to visit the churchyard at dawn and lie down there between Swithun's tomb and a stone cross; if he follows these directions, they declare, he will receive healing in both body and soul. Æthelsige immediately wakes up the moneyer to tell him of what he has seen in his dreams. Understandably his host is 'greatly surprised as to why the sick man had awakened him at that hour' – such ironic asides suggest a concern for psychological plausibility in Lantfred's narration – but once the moneyer has learned the reason, his joy at the news seems genuine.[43]

A kind of parenthesis or non-sequitur now ensues: the moneyer starts to discuss a short sword of his that has gone missing: he hasn't seen it for more than two weeks and wonders if it has been stolen. Michael Lapidge, editor of the text, comments on the 'largely irrelevant' nature of this scene.[44] But to give Lantfred his due, in relating this scene he in fact adds further authentication and plausibility to the story: it is probably true to say of human interaction that even in times of crisis the topics of conversation can become utterly banal. And so, in the middle of the night, the tired moneyer changes the subject and talks of another issue still on his mind, his lost *scramaseax* and scabbard (and it need hardly be emphasised that such weapons were of great value). But the moneyer suddenly recovers himself, realising that his guest needs to get as much rest as he can before his early start at dawn. '*Sed te quid uerbis detineo plurimis?*' he blurts out, 'But why do I detain you with so many words?' (my translation), and he sends the sick man to get some sleep.[45] Again the narrative gains a little depth, and we will see below that through these touches of colloquial language, presented in a realistic manner, the text gains added value as a source for the *Alltag*, the everyday social life and interaction of tenth-century Winchester.

Back in his bed, the cleric has another dream of the two shining youths, apparently '*in quiete soporis*' ('in the quiet of his sleep'), but once again the boundary between the sleeping and waking state is blurred.[46] The youths lead the cleric to a wooden chest, unlock it with a key and show him the missing sword (which must have been there all along), then place the key under the pillow of the sleeping moneyer. At dawn the cleric meets the moneyer but is greeted with derision when he suggests that the sword is not lost: the moneyer however changes his tone when he is sent back to his bed to check his pillow, only to find the key to the chest and discover that his lost treasure is now found. The efficacy of the dream experience is confirmed.

---

[43] For the details of this part of the narrative see Lapidge 2003, 268–9.
[44] Lapidge 2003, 14.
[45] Lapidge 2003, 270–1.
[46] Lapidge 2003, 270–1.

'Enlightened on the Journey' (Lantfred, *Translatio et Miracula*, Chapter 29)

Such is the interest of the *inventio* part of Lantfred's narrative, which we have seen forms one of three substantial chapters that cover the story in vivid and even superfluous detail. I turn now to the main section, 36 chapters of varying length and quality on the *miracula*, in order also to demonstrate their interest as a literary and historical source. And to fulfil this aim I will take a seemingly ordinary but nevertheless characteristic chapter from the *Translatio* and consider briefly its style, structure and themes.[47] Like many such chapters in a medieval *vita*, chapter 29 is not long (barely two thirds of a page in Lapidge's edition), and in terms of genre it resembles an anecdote, in that it focusses on one single incident. This is headed '*De ceco in itinere illuminato*', which Lapidge renders clearly and formally as 'Concerning the blind man who received his eyesight on a journey', but when translated word-for-word the participle *illuminato* is seen to take on symbolic connotation: 'The Blind Man Enlightened on the Journey', a translation which perhaps better suits Lantfred's theological purpose.

The first feature worth noting about this narrative is the context: the fact that Lantfred tends to arrange similar stories into groups in his work, and this anecdote is no exception, for it belongs to a group of three broadly similar stories. The subsequent story for example tells of a man on crutches who is healed at the shrine in the Old Minster (ch. 30) and immediately beats a hasty retreat, leaving his crutches behind as tangible evidence that the miracle had happened just as the 'crowds of onlookers' remembered it, and just as Lantfred recorded it '*in hac pagina*' 'on this page', adding a stamp of authenticity to his narrative. The emphasis on objects of proof, tangible things that aid the memory and authenticate the deed is characteristic.[48] A similar theme pertains to the earlier story in this group of three (ch. 28), which focusses on a cautery iron. This narrative is also about a blind man, in this case a prior of the monastery at Abingdon. (Although Lantfred does not draw his readers' attention to it, Abingdon was the monastery where Æthelwold had been abbot before he began his rise into royal politics as Bishop of Winchester in 964, and where Osgar was now abbot; the personal contacts are probably an added reason for Lantfred to include this story). The blind prior, otherwise unknown in the sources, is called Byrhtferth, and Lantfred tells us that he had survived the pains and indignities of no less than twelve treatments with the cautery iron, which 'did him no good, but rather did a good deal of harm' (Lantfred clearly has no truck with some of the medical practices of his day). Perhaps as an act of penance for the state of his soul, Byrthferth had walked barefoot to Winchester, prayed at Swithun's tomb and then kept vigil there all night, with the result that he 'was found worthy to see the daylight with his eyes'. Lantfred concludes his chapter (which in fact is little more than a brief report of eight lines of text) with a suitable coda following a pattern found in many of his chapters:

---

[47] Lantfred, *Translatio et miracula*, ch. 29 in Lapidge 2003, 316–19.

[48] The focus on objects as proof and as an aid to memory of an event is well attested in medieval culture, see Carruthers 2008 and Clanchy 2013.

'*atque sospes domum rediens, omnipotentem Dominum glorificare studuit*' ('and returning home in sound health, he took care to glorify the omnipotent Lord'). Connecting this event with the next anecdote by an adverbial connector 'in that same year' Lantfred then continues the narrative as chapter 29. The link is in the theme: both stories are about a man of impaired vision receiving light on a journey, and both motifs – light and journeying – are frequent in Lantfred's writing.

In chapter 29 Lantfred again tells the story of a healing from blindness. The sick man has heard rumours of the miracles and, like many of the characters in this work, he hurries to the city of Winchester, though he lives far away and the journey is long and arduous. Since his sight is so impaired he has a young boy (apparently his son) with him to act as a guide. Events now happen thick and fast. First, as they approach within a few miles of Winchester they sit down to rest near a large stone cross – in Wulfstan of Winchester's later version of this story it is named appropriately as the King's Cross. Since the Latin wording itself is so clearly relevant here, I give Lantfred's text:

> *Qui dum appropinquaret ciuitatem Wintoniam, uenit ad locum quendam in quo, fatigatus ex itinere, cepit paululum requiescere. Erat autem ubi repausabant ingens crux lapidea, tria passuum milia pene distans a prefata urbe.*

> As he was approaching the city of Winchester he came to a certain place in which, tired out from his journey, he began to rest a little. Now in the place where they were resting, nearly three miles distance from the aforementioned city, there was a large stone cross.

The verb *repausare*, here in the imperfect tense '*repausabant*' ('they rested') is a minor error that only a francophone writer would make: Lantfred, as we noted above, reveals his mother tongue through his writing. Probably he needed a synonym for *requiescere* in order to vary his style, and in the process he inadvertently made up a Latin verb based on his native French *repauser* ('to rest'). So the passage has some documentary value in helping to identify our author. Leaving that aside, there is the topographical fact of the stone cross, described a little later by the boy to his father as '*staurus hic est saxea fulgens grandis altissima, ad laudem Christi posita*'.[49] Here is a further benefit for more study of Lantfred, for the scattered details of material culture that he adds to these miracle stories – objects such as a stone cross, crutches, manacles, a knife, a wooden chest, a key – provide information on ordinary everyday living in contemporary Winchester. But the detail is necessary and not extraneous to the plot: the father (being of course blind) needs to know where exactly he is located, and the boy's description of the Christian cross (perhaps they thought of it in their native vernacular as a *Cristes mæl*, a cross of Christ) prompts him to pray to Christ in particular 'so that he might be divinely healed through the merit of the great man [*i.e.* Swithun]'.

---

[49] 'There is a large, tall shining cross here, put up to the glory of Christ.' Lapidge 2003, 316–17. See Alex Langlands, above, pp. 41–58, for further discussion.

Also worthy of note is the gospel echo. Though medieval Latin authors were steeped in the language of the Bible and sometimes echoed its wording in their own writing subconsciously, the biblical allusion to 'being wearied with his journey' here seems singularly appropriate, and is probably deliberate:

> *Venit ergo in civitatem Samariae quae dicitur Sychar iuxta praedium quod dedit Iacob Ioseph filio suo. Erat autem ibi fons Iacob. Iesus ergo fatigatus ex itinere sedebat sic super fontem. Hora erat quasi sexta.*

> He cometh therefore to a city of Samaria, which is called Sichar, near the land which Jacob gave to his son Joseph. Now Jacob's well was there. Jesus therefore, being wearied with his journey, sat thus on the well. It was about the sixth hour.[50]

Both Lantfred's narrative and the gospel passage describe the approach to a city and the pause for rest at an ancient landmark, during which there is a crucial development in the narrative. In fact, Lantfred has prepared us already for his biblical echo in the phrase *'in itinere illuminato'* of his chapter title; the blind man who at the end of this time of rest is going to be 'enlightened on the journey' is still – at this point in the narrative – 'wearied with the journey'. Interestingly, this is the second time that Lantfred has employed the phrase *fatigatus ex itinere*, the first being in chapter 3, when again the scene takes place outside the city, at the conspicuous landmark of a shady tree under which the owner of the mule pasture falls asleep. This is a significant place, as we noted above, since the plot at that point is also about to take an unexpected turn.[51]

In terms of its literary genre chapter 29 may be characterised as an *anecdote*, which sense 2a of the Oxford English Dictionary defines as 'a short account of an amusing, interesting, or telling incident or experience'. Such a definition fits in a number of ways with the narrative that now ensues in the *Translatio*: a lively dialogue, on the time-honoured theme of a hungry child's need for food on a journey, here given in Lapidge's translation:

> And while they were resting there briefly, the hungry lad said to the blind old man: 'Let us eat something, father, since I am now suffering from great hunger, and we are near the city. When we get to it, we shall not have any chance of eating.'
> The blind man said, 'My son, it is not yet the appropriate time.'
> The boy said, 'Yes it is, father. Lunchtime has passed!'
> The blind man replied: 'How much of the trip is still left, from here to the city?'
> The boy says to the sick man: 'We shall soon come to the saint; therefore let us take some food before we enter the city wall, since there is a huge crowd there.'
> The sick man replied to the boy: 'Nones have not yet sounded. Let us wait, therefore, until nones, I beg you; and after we have arrived at the body of the man of God, there let us break our fast with the blessing of Christ the Lord.'
> The naughty young guide spoke again: 'But it *is* nones; you ought not to fast any longer.'

---

[50] John 4.5–6.
[51] See the beginning of Lantfred's chapter 3, in Lapidge 2003, 274–5.

The family argument breaks off when the father hears the footsteps of some passers-by – they turn out to be pilgrims heading for the shrine of St Swithun – and he asks the boy to describe the surroundings of the locality. This of course leads to the cure, and even as the healed man hurries to the Old Minster to honour the relics and report his healing to the monks the narrator adds, in a humorous aside, that he went in haste 'without having lunch – just as he wished'.[52]

Apart from the entertainment value of this conversation, several points of interest may strike the historically minded reader: the practice of timekeeping in the medieval city by listening out for the sound of bells marking the monastic hours; the mention of the crowds that the cult of St Swithun was by this time attracting; the need to fast before the hour of nones and before attending the shrine of the saint (perhaps a rule for penitents on pilgrimage?). But there is also a linguistic interest in the many colloquial dialogues that Lantfred reports. It is clear that Lantfred has an ear for such conversations: the author frequently succeeds in capturing the register of the dialogues through the choice of a (mostly) appropriate colloquial vocabulary, through the quickfire repartee and the question-and-answer style. All this is of course mediated through the Latin language rather than the original Old English; nevertheless, it is clear that the Frenchman Lantfred had mastered the local vernacular to the extent that he could translate it, rework it and present it convincingly in Latin.

Once the blind man realises he is standing by a cross dedicated to Christ, this become the impetus for his prayer: '[he] implored Christ in his prayers... that he might be divinely healed through the merit of the great man, saying: "Omnipotent Lord God, hear my prayers; restore the light to my eyes with the merits of St Swithun the bishop assisting"'. As often in these miracle stories, his prayer is the culmination of the anecdote, encapsulated in the subsequent sentences; again I give the Latin text, to be compared with Lapidge's elegant and idiomatic translation in the note:

> *Cumque cecus ille talem cum gemitu fudisset orationem, illuminatus est ibidem per sacri sacerdotis interuentionem.*[53]

A few comments on the Latin are necessary in order that the imagery of light and enlightenment may be fully appreciated. The telling phrase is *'illuminatus est ibidem'*, meaning literally, 'he was enlightened there in that place': here the sanctity of place becomes significant, and enlightenment comes to the man on the journey at the very moment when he reaches the desired location:

> *Moxque ut glaucoma ab eius oculis cecidit, suspiciens haud longe Wintoniam conspexit, quam tot mentis ardore paululum ante desiderabat uidere.*

---

[52] Lapidge 2003, 318–19.
[53] Lapidge's translation reads: 'And when the blind man had poured out this prayer in lamentation, he received his eyesight in that place through the intercession of the holy bishop.' Lapidge 2003, 319.

> And as soon as the glaucoma receded from his eyes, he looked up and saw Winchester not
> far off, which he desired to see with all his heart a short while before.

The phrasing 'he looked up and saw Winchester not far off, which he desired to see with all his heart a short while before' is characteristic and could almost serve as the concluding sentence of many of these stories. The key to these miracles is the moment of light and vision: even when the events take place elsewhere or outside the city, Winchester remains literally in focus, and remains so for most of the narrated time in the story.

The Structure of Lantfred's *Translatio et Miracula*, and Some Conclusions

It is appropriate at this point to summarise what has been argued on the structure and style of Lantfred's *Translatio et miracula S. Swithuni* (see Table 9.1). Basically, the text consists of two prefaces; a set of three chapters which might be called, in hagiographic terms, an *inventio* (*i.e.* the 'discovery' of the saint); 36 chapters of *miracula* forming the bulk of the narrative which demonstrate the sanctity of the holy person now discovered; finally, a brief coda or conclusion to round off the work. The chapters differ in style and treatment. There are detailed narratives that tell of a particular person in detail, sometimes with a symbolically significant object like a cross or ring forming one or more focal points. Here the narrative includes description, narration of plot, dialogues and monologues (including prayers), all of which allow it to resemble a modern short story in terms of literary value and fullness of treatment. But there are also brief summaries that merely report the event, with few if any concrete details; such brief reports are only a few lines long and lack much literary or cultural-historical interest. In the middle ground between these two extremes there are anecdotes that summarise a single point in a larger narrative or focus solely on one detail such as a prayer, a conversation or a single significant object. In the list below, therefore, I will use the following abbreviations (in round brackets) to categorise the stories according to their length and style of narration: **ss** = short story, **a** = anecdote; **sa** = short anecdote; **r** = brief report. Items within square brackets record significant objects, customs and practices, or architectural features which also figure within the story.

It will be seen that dreams occur prominently, especially in the opening three chapters and in the long anecdote that describes the mystical vision of the nobleman on the Isle of Wight. As noted above, the stories are otherwise only rather loosely connected together. Criteria for the groupings tend to be the following:

(1) geographical location, in particular the Winchester area, but also southern England, London, France – all areas with which the author was presumably familiar.
(2) types of ailment, with lameness or blindness being the most common.
(3) enslaved people and prisoners, often bound in chains or manacles of some sort.

Table 9.1: Outline of the chapter and themes of Lantfred's Translatio et miracula S. Swithuni.

Outline of the chapter and themes of Lantfred's *Translatio et miracula S. Swithuni*

Prefatory Letter to the Monks of the Old Minster

General Preface

1. the smith's dream and his message for Eadsige (**ss**) [metal ring on tombstone; churchyard; market street]
2. the cleric with curvature of the spine (**ss**) [short sword, chest, key; smithy; house with separate chambers]
3. a land-owning citizen of Winchester and the translation of Bishop Swithun; the three Furies (**ss**) [sleeve of tunic, spear, shoe; mule-pasture, town walls, gate, river Itchen, churchyard, tower]
4. countless miracles (**r**) [small crowded church]
5. three blind women and a young mute on Isle of Wight – the sacrist (**sa**)
6. enslaved girl (Lat. *ancilla*) owned by Teoðic the bell-founder (**r**) [shackles; punishments for enslaved persons,]
7. paralytic in *Hamne, i.e.* Hampshire (**r**) [horse-trappings]
8. powerful lady (*matrona*) in Bedefordscire, cured of blindness (**r**) [placed a present of cloth on the altar at Winchester]
9. *materfamilias*, another land-owning lady – her ride to a wedding (**a**) [horse-trappings; feasting; ealdormen]
10. a dream dreamed by 'a certain lady' (*matrona*) on Æthelwold's directive to report miracles to the monks as soon as they happened (**a**)
11. paralysed man from London, taken to Winchester (**r**)
12. 16 blind people from London, came to Winchester, returned *uidentes* (**r**)
13. another lame man from London – went to Winchester (**r**)
14. 25 people from various regions; went to Winchester (**r**)
15. boy aged 10, blind for 5 years, spent the night in OM with mother and retainers (**r**) [son of a rich ealdorman]
16. blind man who went to Rome (**r**) [pilgrimage to Rome]
17. paralysed man from Hrofeceaster (**sa**) [prayer]
18. blind man abandoned by an angry guide (**a**)
19. 4 people from Essex (**r**)
20. the enslaved girl (*seruula*) from the north – meets the sacrist Eadsige (**a**) [shackles; market; slavery; locked shrine area in Old Minster]
21. 2 women and a mute (**r**)
22. 26 in Winchester (**r**)
23. 124 sick people (**r**)
24. a chained murderer from Europe on pentitential pilgrimage (**sa**) [iron rings on body as penance; one metal band left in the Old Minster as proof of the miracle]
25. Flodoald's enslaved man (Latin *famulus* and *seruus*) – the practice of the ordeal (**a**) [iron bar; king's reeve; merchants]
26. the man accused of robbery and blinded by the enforcers of King Edgar's 'law of great severity' (**a**)
27. the prisoner who escaped with a small knife (theft of sheaves) (**a**) [knife, punishment stocks; royal steward and king's estate]
28. blind Prior Byrhtferth of Abingdon (**r**)
29. blind man on a journey with boy as guide, vivid argument about lunch on the journey (**a**) [stone cross]
30. lame man (**r**)
31. the ealdorman (perhaps Ælfhere of Mercia?) and the youth who fell from his horse (**a**) [feasting, horsemanship]
32. woman in France (**r**) [prayer inscribed on candle]
33. another French woman (**r**) [yawning and demon possession]
34. overseas thief, long prayer (**a**) [prison, torture on rack]
35. vision of nobleman on Isle of Wight (**la**) [dream vision; vigil in church]
36. blind man from Collingbourne (*Colungaburna*) (**r**)
37. cripple from Somerset (**a**)
38. washerwoman, lost clothes and arrested and bound in manacles (**a**)
39. enslaved man (*seruus*) in chains (**r**)
40. short exordium

(4) social class: Lantfred treats the full hierarchy of society from ealdormen and/or powerful ladies and their households to working smiths and merchants, ranging down to enslaved persons, though it is noteworthy that only one of the visions or miracles occurs among the clergy (the prior of Abingdon in ch. 28).

In short, the work is mainly concerned with the influence of the saint and former bishop on secular society. A common feature in the miracle stories is the prayer that the oppressed person prays in the moment of crisis, which is granted through the power of the saint. Lantfred seems to have been given free rein to explore the city of Winchester and the region and talk to whoever he wished. Like an investigative journalist, he uncovers interesting 'unofficial' information, meets some interesting characters and records some vivid conversations, all of which, without the unique witness of this somewhat neglected text, would have been lost to posterity.

Abbreviations

BCS   Birch, W de G. 1885–93. *Cartularium Saxonicum*, 3 vols. London: Charles J. Clarke.

KCD   Kemble, J. M. 1839–48. *Codex Diplomaticus Aevi Saxonici*, 6 vols. London: Sumptibus Societatis.

S   Sawyer, P. H. 1968. *Anglo-Saxon Charters: an Annotated List and Bibliography*, Royal Historical Society Guides and Handbooks, 8. London: Royal Historical Society.

Bibliography

Primary Sources

Lapidge, M. 2003. *The Cult of St Swithun*, Winchester Studies, 4.ii. Oxford: Clarendon Press.

Lapidge, M. and Winterbottom, M. (ed. and trans.) 1991. *Wulfstan of Winchester: The Life of St Æthelwold*. Oxford: Clarendon Press.

Love, R. C. (ed. and trans.) 1996. *Three Eleventh-Century Anglo-Latin Saints' Lives*. Oxford: Clarendon Press.

Stahl, W. H. (trans.) 1990. *Commentary on the Dream of Scipio by Macrobius*. New York: Columbia University Press.

Winterbottom, M., and Lapidge, M. (ed. and trans.) 2012. *The Earliest Lives of St Dunstan*. Oxford: Clarendon Press.

Secondary Sources

Atherton, M. 2017. *The Making of England: A New History of the Anglo-Saxon World*. London: I. B. Tauris.

Atherton, M. 2021. *The Battle of Maldon: War and Peace in Tenth-Century England*. London: Bloomsbury.

Biddle, M. 1975. *Felix urbs Winthonia*: Winchester in the Age of Monastic Reform, in D. Parsons (ed.), *Tenth-Century Studies*, 123–40. London: Phillimore.

Biddle, M. and Hill, D. 1971. Late Saxon Planned Towns, *Antiquaries Journal*, 51, 70–85.

Carruthers, M. 2008. *The Book of Memory: A Study of Memory in Medieval Culture*. Cambridge: Cambridge University Press.

Clanchy, M. 2013. *From Memory to Written Record: England 1066-1307*, 3rd edition. Chichester and Malden: Wiley-Blackwell.

Gretsch, M. 2006. *Ælfric and the Cult of Saints in Late Anglo-Saxon England*. Cambridge: Cambridge University Press.

Head, T. 1990. *Hagiography and the Cult of the Saints: The Diocese of Orléans 800-1200*. Cambridge: Cambridge University Press.

Hofstetter, W. 1988. Winchester and the Standardization of Old English Vocabulary, *Anglo-Saxon England*, 17, 139–161.

Jansson, T. 1991. Language Change and Metalinguistic Change: Latin to Romance and Other Cases, in R. Wright (ed.), *Latin and the Romance Languages in the Early Middle Ages*, 19–28. London: Routledge.

Jonsson, K. 1987. *The New Era: The Reformation of the Late Anglo-Saxon Coinage*. London: Spink and Son.

Keynes, S. 1986. A Tale of Two Kings: Alfred the Great and Æthelred the Unready, *Transactions of the Royal Historical Society*, fifth series, 36, 195–217.

Keynes, S. 2014. Asser, in M. Lapidge, J. Blair, S. Keynes and D. Scragg (eds), *The Wiley Blackwell Encyclopedia of Anglo-Saxon England*, 2nd edition, 51–2. Chichester: John Wiley.

Lapidge, M. 1988. A Frankish Scholar in Tenth-century England: Frithegod of Canterbury / Fredegaud of Brioude, *Anglo-Saxon England*, 17, 45–65.

Molyneaux, G. 2015. *The Formation of the English Kingdon in the Tenth Century*. Oxford: Clarendon Press.

O'Brien O'Keeffe, K. 1998. Body and Law in Late Anglo-Saxon England, *Anglo-Saxon England*, 27, 209–32.

Richter, M. 1983. A quelle époque a-t-on cessé de parler latin en Gaule? A propos d'une question mal posée, *Annales: Économies, sociétés, civilisations*, 38, 439–48.

Roach, L. 2016. *Æthelred the Unready*. New Haven and London: Yale University Press.

Rumble, A. R. 2002. *Property and Piety in Early Medieval Winchester*. Oxford: Clarendon Press.

Scragg, D. (ed.) 2008. *Edgar, King of the English, 959-975*. Woodbridge: Boydell Press.

Watts, V. 2004. *The Cambridge Dictionary of Place-Names*. Cambridge: Cambridge University Press.

Williams, A. 1982. *Princeps Merciorum gentis*: The Family, Career and Connections of Ælfhere, Ealdorman of Mercia, 956–83, *Anglo-Saxon England*, 10, 143–72.

Wormald, P. 1999. *The Making of English Law: King Alfred to the Twelfth Century*. Oxford: Blackwell.

Wright, R. 1982. *Late Latin and Early Romance in Spain and Carolingian France*. Liverpool: Cairns.

Yorke, B. (ed.) 1988. *Bishop Æthelwold: His Career and Influence*. Woodbridge: Boydell Press.

Chapter 10

Wælcyrian in the Water Meadows:
Lantfred's Furies

Eric Lacey

In chapter 3 of Lantfred's Translatio et miracula S. Swithuni (*The Translation and Miracles of St Swithun*) *we have a detailed account of a supernatural female figure from early medieval English popular belief. Lantfred preserved a variety of details that resonate with supernatural women we find elsewhere in Old English literature, leading previous commentators to suggest he was describing a creature known as the* hægtesse. *In the present chapter, I argue that Lantfred supplies us with our only narrative account of the Old English* wælcyrge, *the lesser-known cognate of the Old Norse valkyrie. In doing so, I offer the most complete discussion to date of what we can recover about two Old English supernatural entities: the* wælcyrge (*nominally 'chooser of the slain'*) *and the* hægtesse (*nominally 'hag'*).

In chapter 3 of Lantfred's *Translatio et miracula S. Swithuni* (The Translation and Miracles of St Swithun) we have what is perhaps the most detailed account of some kind of supernatural female figure from early medieval English popular belief. Lantfred, a Frankish monk from Fleury, had collected this account from his perambulations through and around the city of Winchester, and he is careful to avoid identifying them too closely with any specific classical entity. In this way, he preserves a variety of intriguing details that resonate with supernatural women we find elsewhere in Old English and Anglo-Latin literature. In the present chapter, I propose a new interpretation of what these women represent and argue that Lantfred supplies us with our only narrative account of the Old English *wælcyrge*, the lesser known cognate of the Old Norse valkyrie (*valkyrja*). In doing so, I bring together both the narrative and glossary evidence for the entities in Old English known as *hægtesse* (nominally 'hag') and *wælcyrge* (nominally 'chooser of the slain') to draw attention to hitherto underappreciated features of them and offer the most complete discussion of them to date. As Lantfred initially likened these women to the furies of classical myth, for convenience I shall refer to them as Lantfred's Furies throughout.

Background and Texts

Lantfred had probably arrived in Winchester in the 960s during Bishop Æthelwold's programme of reform.[1] The text itself was composed sometime in the early 970s in order to commemorate 15 July, 971, the date when Swithun's relics were moved from his tomb into the Old Minster. Rather than recount the life of the ninth-century saint (which Lantfred laments not really knowing) the *Translatio* collects testimonies of various miracles that happened posthumously, with the first three chapters covering miracles before the translation of Swithun's relics and the rest of the *Translatio* devoted to miracles which happened afterwards.[2] Later, over the course of the 990s, a monk named Wulfstan (sometimes known as either Wulfstan of Winchester or Wulfstan the Cantor) versified Lantfred's account. This *Narratio metrica de S. Swithuno* (The Metrical Narrative of St Swithun) stays faithful to his source material, frequently re-using Lantfred's very words, but does impart his own knowledge or impose his own views.[3] In preserving even the folkloric elements of Lantfred's *Translatio*, Wulfstan's treatment stands in stark comparison with that of Ælfric of Eynsham, who excised episodes, including Lantfred's Furies, from his Old English translation of the saint's life and is probably also responsible for omitting the same episodes in the Latin *Epitome translationis et miraculorum S. Swithuni* (The Epitome of the translation and miracles of St Swithun) on which the Old English was based.[4]

Both Lantfred and Wulfstan were intimately familiar with Winchester and its environs and conveyed this intimate connection in their works. Mark Atherton has shown how Lantfred sought much of his information through verbal inquiry with the residents of Winchester as evidenced through the idiom, tone and specific details of his reports – despite the injunction against fraternising with citizens in the New Minster Charter of 964.[5] While we cannot be sure that Wulfstan was also able to flout such rules, he furnishes Lantfred's account with his own details, such as the dedication to St Michael at the East Gate (I.573–4). He seems to have had seen the translation of Swithun's relics first-hand, and he implies in his *Narratio* that he was a child oblate at Winchester (I.899; II.259–63).[6] Because Wulfstan's *Narratio* is so close to Lantfred's *Translatio*, I will only quote from it in the subsequent discussion when it elaborates or deviates from Lantfred.

It is convenient to think about Lantfred's account in three sections: the backdrop, the appearance of two raven-like Furies and its culmination in a tall white figure that delivers a paralysing attack. The backdrop comprises how a certain citizen who was a

---

[1] Lapidge 2003, 223–4. What little we know about Lantfred is summarised therein.
[2] Koopmans 2011, 51–9.
[3] Lapidge 2003, 247; for some examples of alterations see, for example Foxhall-Forbes 2013, 170 and Atherton 2017, 276.
[4] The case for Ælfric's authorship is made in Lapidge 2003, 553–7 and is generally accepted. Lapidge also edits and translates the *Epitome* (564–74) and Ælfric's *Life of St Swithun* (590–610). On Ælfric's generally critical attitude towards miracles see Godden 1985.
[5] Atherton 2017, 256, 266–76. See also his chapter in this volume and Sigal 1987, 153–54, 168–71.
[6] Lapidge and Winterbottom 1991, xiv.

native of Winchester ('*ciues Wintoniensis natiuitate*') went to tend to his mules, which were grazing by a river which ran past the city (presumably the Itchen).[7] Although it is never articulated where, exactly, this grazing spot was, it is attractive to think of it taking place in what is known as the Water Meadows today, an area of verdant flood plains to the south-east of the city of Winchester immortalised in Keats' *Ode to Autumn*. He falls asleep in the midday sun and after some time wakes up, wishing to go home. It is at this point that he encounters the two black Furies:

> *Qui dum euigilaretur a somni grauedine, prospectis burdonibus, desiderans domum redire nil mali sperans posse ei contingere in tam uicino itinere, is, dum propter amnem praefatum caperet itineris incessum, haud procul prospiciens geminas ante se conspexit mulierculas, haud ullo cultu preditas nullisque uestibus septas, uerum teterrimo corpora nudas ac furuis crinibus horrendas, Tysiphoneisque uultibus infectas atque infernali nequitia ac ueneno armadas super ripam fluuii considentes, quasi bine ex tribus Furiarum sorores. Quae ilico ut uirum coram sese uentientem conspexerunt, surgentes contra eum partier concordi uoce dixerunt, 'Frater, huc ueni, quoniam indubitanter uolumus tibi perpauca colloqui.' Qui perterritus ac nimium stupefactus, contemplans Ethiopissas fuligineis coloribus inopertas, nudis corporibus, nullum eis uerbum penitus quiuit respondere; sed primum ab ipsis pedetemptim cepit secedere et postmodum prepete cursu fugere. Quem illae contemplantes fugientem et earum iussionibus obtemperare nolentem, ueloci eum gradu insequentes dicebant ad hominem, 'Cur, insane, fugis? Quo, moriture, abis? Non, ut estimas, nos effigies indempnis, nostris confabulationibus spretis. Nequaquam euades periculum nostrae feritatis. Licet nostra floccipendas imperia, non te liberabit pernix fuga. Haud hinc abibis ulla ratione incolomis, neglectis astute sententiis nostre sermocinationis.' Vir autem ille haec audiens, magno terrore concussus inquiens, 'Miserere mei, Domine Deus omnipotens'; qui interim in quantum quibat fugiens, uicinam properabat ad urbem.*

When he had awakened from a deep sleep and had looked over his mules, he wishes to return home hoping that nothing unfortunate could happen to him in such a nearby journey; this man, while choosing the route of his journey along the previously mentioned river, observed not far away in front of him two female-like things – not adorned in any finery nor covered with any clothing, but rather stripped naked to their foul bodies and terrifying with their dark hair, corrupted/stained with faces like Tisiphone and armed with infernal wickedness and venom – who were sitting down on the river bank, just as if they were two of the three Furies. Immediately when they saw the man coming towards them, they rose to meet him and spoke together in a joint voice: 'Brother, come here, because, without a doubt, we would like to converse with you a little bit.' The man, terrified and greatly overcome, staring at these undressed Ethiopians with their soot-black colour and their naked bodies, was utterly unable to say any word to them in reply; but he at first drew away from them one step at a time and afterwards fled at a swift pace. Observing the man fleeing and not willing to comply with their bidding, they pursued him at a swift pace, and said to the man: 'Why, fool, do you flee? Where, doomed man, are you going? You shall not, as you suppose, escape from us unharmed after having spurned our conversation. By no means shall you evade the danger of our savagery. Although you ignored our commands, swift flight shall not free you. You shall on no account get away from here unharmed, given that you have craftily disregarded the purpose of our conversation.' The man, hearing these things and

---

[7] Lapidge 2003, 274.

struck with great fear, said, 'Have mercy on me, omnipotent Lord God!' – and, fleeing as quickly as he could, hurried towards the nearby city.[8]

The two figures here speak to the citizen in couched euphemisms. Christopher Jones has pointed out how Lantfred portrays the women as 'tempters of sexual sin', not in the least in their loaded characterisation as '*Ethiopissas*', let alone the way that they beckon him over for a few intimate words.[9] Whether because of virtue or cowardice, he flees, and just as it looks like he will escape from these two creatures, they are joined by a third supernatural female figure, quite different in appearance but similar in disposition. Where the two black Furies were unsuccessful in assailing the Winchester citizen, this tall and pale one ambushes him and paralyses him with an unusual attack:

> *Verum cum a coruinis (quas humana cohibebat statura) mulierculas uir ille non posset comprehendi nec aliqua offensione retardari, accessit tertia mirae proceritatis quae instar turris eminebat ceteris, candido tamen prioribus colore dissimilis ac decenter niueis ornate induuiis. Haec etenim fraude nacta retro collem latitabat iuxta uiam per quam homo transire disponebat, quatinus eum comprehenderet si a furuis intactus existeret. Quae consurgens de latibulo, ad se furuas conuocauit ilico quibus dixit sermon infesto: 'Huc ad meum commigrate ocius contubernium et ulterius desinite persequi homuncionem istum. Non hic a meis periculum effugiet manibus, quod se euasisse estimauit funditus, uobis more anserum perstrepentibus.' Quae protinus ad uiatorem conuersa fugacem, haud illum concito prosequintur uestigio ut furue, uerum fixa in predicti perseuerans collis cacumine, ingentem manicam ter plicauit in rugam; quam cum ingenti collisione sursum eleuans eumque toto uirtutis conamine desiderans percutere, Deo largiente (quem inuocobat mente, quamuis non posset ore) non preualuit ipsum contingere. Sed uentus ex stridore ipsius manice procreatus super eum uenit, quem paulisper dextro in latere tetigit. Et mox cum nigro comitatu ab eodem discedens, in amnis gurgite saltu eximio se dedit precipitem.*
>
> *Vir autem ille, percussus dirae uestis spiramine, confestim pronus corruit in faciem ceu cadauer exanime, immobilis iacens pene per interuallum unius horae...*

When the man could not be seized nor slowed down by any interference from these two raven-like females who appeared in human form, a third one of remarkable height approached who stood out like a tower over the others, and who was dissimilar to the others, being of a bright white colour and being pleasingly adorned in snowy-white garments. She, however, relying on deception, was hiding behind a hill next to the road along which the man was set to travel, where she might seize him if he appeared untouched by the dark ones. Rising up from her hiding-place, she called the dark ones over to her and spoke to them in poisonous words: 'Come over here quickly to my look-out spot, and give up pursuing this little man any further. He shall not escape from destruction at my hands – which he reckons he can completely avoid with you two honking after him like geese.' Turning immediately to the fleeing traveller, she does not follow behind him with rapid steps as the dark ones did, but rather, remaining stationary on the top of the aforementioned hill, she folded over the sleeve of her tunic three times into a plait; lifting it up with a mighty commotion and desiring to strike him with the whole power of her strength, she was unable to touch

---

[8] The edition used is Lapidge 2003, 274–7 and the translation is my own based on Lapidge 2003, 275–7.
[9] Jones, 2014, 419–25.

him, since God was granting his protection – whom the man was invoking with his heart, because he could not with his mouth. But the wind created by the whistling of her sleeve came over him, and briefly touched him on his right side. And then, departing from him with her black company, she sent herself into the stream of the river with a great headlong dive.

The man, however, struck by the gust from the foul garment, fell suddenly on his face like a lifeless corpse, lying thus immobilised for the space of nearly an hour...[10]

Afterwards, though paralysed entirely on his right side, the citizen is able to limp back to the city, and Wulfstan tells us that he entered through the East Gate (a detail consistent with the attack taking place in the area of the Water Meadows). Although he collapses once more after he arrives there, he is eventually healed through the assistance of St Swithun.

There have only been two extended discussions of the nature of these 'Furies' before, from Michael Lapidge and Christopher A. Jones, and it is worth revisiting their arguments in brief here. In his edition, Lapidge proposed that these were the creatures known as *hægtessan* in Old English (roughly 'witch', 'sorceress' or 'hag') based on two things. Firstly, Lapidge notes that in the Latin-Old English glossaries, the word *hægtesse* (sing., *hægtessan* pl.) glosses the Latin words *Furia*, *Eumenides* and *erenis*, a garbled form of *Erinyes* – all names for the Furies.[11] Secondly, he notes the parallels between the paralysing attack of Lantfred's tall white female figure, which renders the victim unable to move anything on the right side of his body, and the medical affliction known as the *stiċe* ('stitch') in Old English and draws attention to a charm preserved in a manuscript roughly contemporary to Lantfred's account[12] known as *Wið færstiċe* ('Against a sudden stitch').[13] We will return to this charm in detail below, but for now it is sufficient to note that part of its narrative reports that the 'stitch' is caused by the assault of women who ride over a hill (OE *hlæw*), and among the agents explicitly identified as causing the stitch are *hægtessan*. Lantfred's tall white Fury hides behind a hill (*collis*) before assaulting the man, too, and there are some vaguer parallels between the projectile force that Lantfred's tall white Fury injures the man with and the spear- and arrow-like *gescot* that features in *Wið færstiċe*.

Jones' highly nuanced argument approaches Lantfred's Furies not merely as vestiges of pre-Christian belief, but as aspects of folklore which arose from the intermingling of Christian thought and popular belief. He demonstrates how both Lantfred and Wulfstan understood the three Fury-figures within a framework comprising Classical, Christian, and folkloric knowledge in order to 'build a surprisingly roomy imaginative space that accommodates the existence of otherworldly beings without assigning them to fixed categories as human or simply (Christian) demonic.'[14] Jones points out

---

[10] Lapidge 2003, 276–7. My translation here is based on Lapidge 2003, 277.
[11] Lapidge 2003, 275, n. 118.
[12] London, British Library Harley 585, *c.* 1000.
[13] Lapidge 2003, 277–8, n. 125.
[14] Jones 2014, 442.

how Vergilian and Christian literary echoes underpin the episode without going so far as to define the nature of beings, and thus, for example, 'the two dark pursuers resemble but are not actually Furies, and they display attributes of 'Ethiopian' demons without being simply reducible to that stereotype.'[15] In an extension of the same argument, he criticises Lapidge's identification of Lantfred's 'Furies' with *hægtessan*, noting that in his principle source of evidence, the *Wið færstiċe* charm, the capability to inflict a 'stitch' is ascribed to several entities: the charm presents itself as not only the remedy for *hægtessan gescot* ('the harm of *hægtessan*'), but also the cure for *ylfa gescot* ('the harm of elves') and *esa gescot* ('the harm of **ese*', a problematic word that is probably cognate with Old Norse *Æsir*, the name for a group of gods).[16] Moreover, Jones draws attention to the complexities surrounding the glossaries. We will return to this below, but for now the issues here can be summarised as relating to the complex nature of interpreting glosses in early medieval England, particularly the intricate network of gloss (*lemma*) and interpretation (*interpretamentum*), which means that Latin words are rendered by a motley assemblage of different words. Thus, while, as Lapidge notes, Latin words for the Furies may be translated by *hægtessan*, there are several terms which also translate it. Jones aligns the overlapping occurrence of the Furies, *hægtessan* and figures associated with fate in the glossaries with a general intersection of these figures elsewhere in Old English and Latin and interprets this as an example of folklore: book-learning which has escaped the confines of the medieval schoolroom and merged with popular superstition. His piece finishes by suggesting that this episode benefits from being read comparatively with later folkloric accounts, and that such readings help illuminate some of the more unusual details of the text, such as Lantfred's tall, white Fury using her sleeve to beat the Winchester resident.[17]

Defining Old English *Hægtesse*

Jones is correct to query Lapidge's identification of the Furies with *hægtessan*, which we know very little about. Including their appearance in *Wið færstiċe*, where the word appears three times, it is attested only 22 times in the extant corpus of Old English (see Tables 10.1 and 10.2). Most of these (16, Table 10.2) are in the Old English glosses, discussed below, which require considerable work to interpret, leaving only 6 attestations in narrative sources.

In *Wið færstiċe*, we are presented with an outline of the potential causes of the titular affliction.[18] It begins by describing some women riding over a burial mound and an instruction for the charm's recipient to '*scyld ðu ðe nu þu ðysne nið genesan mote*'

---

[15] *Ibid.*, 425.

[16] It is beyond the scope of this chapter to go into the complexities of OE **ese* and its semantics; see North 1997, 107–8; Hall 2007, 60–3, 108–10, 112–16; Simek 1993, 3–4.

[17] Jones 2014, 439–40, notes that in analogous episodes a rod is usually used by the otherworldly assailant, and raises the possibility that it arose from misinterpretation of Lantfred's French, where *menche/ manche* ('rod, hilt, flail') was construed as *manche* ('sleeve').

[18] See Hall 2007, 110–12.

Table 10.1: Old English narrative sources featuring hægtesse.

Attestations in narrative sources	
Wið færstiċe	3
Durham proverbs	1
Ælfric's Dei Auguriis	1
Ælfric's Book of Kings	1

Table 10.2: Old English glosses featuring hægtesse.

Attestations in glosses	
London-Antwerp glossary	2
First Cotton Cleopatra Glossary	4
Third Cotton Cleopatra Glossary	1
Cotton Otho E.i	1
Corpus Glossary	4
Épinal-Erfurt	1
Leiden Glossary	2
Interlinear gloss in Aldhelm's verse De virginitate (CCCC 326)	1

('shield yourself now, you can survive this strife', l. 3). These '*mihtigan wif*' ('mighty women', l. 6), who are '*anmode*' ('fierce', l. 2), then unleash an assault of flying spears, which the charm seeks to shield and fight back against, all the while commanding any projectiles which might have landed to get out of the patient. It then shifts away from this narrative to an enigmatic passage about one smith forging a '*seax*' ('a knife', l. 11), and then six smiths forging '*wælspera*' ('slaughter spears', l. 14), before iterating in some detail what this charm can remedy: '*gif ðu wære on fell scoten oðða wære on flæsc scoten/ oðða wære on blod scoten/ oðða wære on lið scoten*' ('if you were afflicted in the skin or afflicted in the flesh or were afflicted in the blood or were afflicted in the limb', ll. 18–20). It closes with a similarly detailed litany of what afflictions it can remedy, and this is where the *hægtessan* are mentioned alongside the other potential culprits: the elves and the **ese*. The *hægtessan* are mentioned one more time than the others, as earlier in the charm, after the cryptic mention of the smiths, it proclaims that '*gif her inne sy isernes dæl,/ hægtessan geweorc hit sceal gemyltan*' ('if there be in here any portion of iron, the work of a *hægtesse*, it shall melt', ll. 16–17). While this might suggest a stronger association between the *hægtessan* and the pains inflicted in the charm, it is not clear if the 'mighty women' who ride over the burial mound are meant to be *hægtessan* (or even elves or **ese*). Moreover, Alaric Hall has convincingly demonstrated that the afflictions mentioned by the charm – whether the *færstiċe* or the *gescot* – were potentially enduring stabbing pains rather than paralysis.[19] An examination of *hægtessan* elsewhere in Old English confirms that whatever characteristics it did have, they do not seem to overlap substantially with Lantfred's Furies.

Ælfric uses the word rather generically. In his homily *Dei Auguriis* ('On Auguries'), he uses the variant form *hætse* to encompass women guilty of an orgy of debaucheries (ll. 147–61) and contrast these with Christian men (ll. 162–6); in his homily on the Book of Kings he has Jezebel's slayer, the king Jehu, refer to her as a *hætse* as he bids his servants retrieve and bury her horse-trampled corpse (l. 350).[20] There are connotations

---

[19] Hall 2007, 110–12.
[20] The edition consulted here is Skeat 1881, vol. 1.

of magic and licentiousness which might seem to resonate with Lantfred's Furies in both cases: evil fornication (*manfulla forligr*) and magical practices reckon amongst the catalogue of depravities practiced by *hætse* in *Dei Auguriis*, and before Jezebel's death Jehu remarks on her '*manfullan forligr and fela unlybban*' ('wicked fornication and many witchcrafts', ll.332–3). However, the sort of magic here does not seem comparable with Lantfred's Furies. *Unlybban* is customarily used of magic achieved specifically through potions (*e.g.* in *Scriftboc* §14), and many of the activities Ælfric lists in the passage in *Dei Auguriis* seem to be potion-based too, such as 'drinks for their wooers' (*heora wogerum drencas*) that can make men 'take them as wives' (*to wife habbon*, ll. 157–8).[21] It may be, of course, that this merely reflects Ælfric's interpretation of *hægtesse*, as Ælfric departs from his sources here and there seems to be little in common with the features observed in *Wið færstiċe*, which features brazen attacks, not potions, and which lacks any implications of lustiness.[22] The gloss evidence seems to concur with Ælfric's understanding rather than the mighty women at the opening of *Wið færstiċe*, however, which raises questions not only about the security of Lapidge's identification but also about the longstanding identification of these women as *hægtessan*.

Before turning to those, however, there is one more narrative source to account for. The eleventh-century *Durham Proverbs* furnish us with a particularly inscrutable example of an *hægtesse*. The text is a collection of forty-six maxims in both Old English and Latin, with the Latin text generally being a translation from the Old English.[23] The eleventh proverb in the collection reads:

> *Neque confiderem liceat bene ambulasset dixit qui vidit strigas capite pregredientes*
> *Ne swa þeah treowde þeah þu teala eode cwæþ se þe geseah hægtessan æfter heafde geongan.*[24]

We may translate both languages identically: '"I would not trust [you] anyway, even if you walked properly" said the one who saw a *hægtesse/striga* [a witch] walking past by means of her head'. This mode of capital locomotion is recorded nowhere else, and one has to wonder if it is intended merely as some extreme hyperbole for stressing the treachery of the *hægtesse*. Recognising this profound untrustworthiness, in any case, is the core of the proverb's wisdom, and thus must have been a characteristic central to eleventh-century clerical understanding of these women. The use of Latin *striga* to describe this creature almost certainly derives from the glossary tradition, wherein Latin *striga* is always rendered by *hægtesse*, and so cannot be interpreted without recourse to this broader glossary tradition.

Patrizia Lendinara and Alaric Hall have stressed the importance of properly evaluating glosses and glossary evidence.[25] The relationship between these words is

---

[21] Bosworth and Toller 1898, s.v. 'un-lybba'. For the *Scriftboc* see Frantzen 2003–2021, and for more on philtres and the sorts of magic implied here, see Filotas 2005, 295–305.

[22] For *Dei Auguriis* see Meaney 1985, 489. I am unable to find any source for Ælfric's description of Jezebel and it is notable that the text, as a whole, is absent from *Fontes Anglo-Saxonici*.

[23] Arngart 1956 §11; 1981, 292.

[24] *Ibid.*, 292.

[25] Lendinara 1999a, 8; Hall 2007, 77.

not a case of straightforward lexical equivalence: it is a one-way relationship, with the glossing word (the *interpretamentum*) seeking to articulate what the glossed word (the *lemma*) meant in its context. As Hall notes, glosses do not 'attempt to "define" their lemmata: they gloss them'.[26] This is easier for marginal or interlinear glosses, where the context is apparent, but is more difficult in the case of glossaries, where the glosses have been assembled, and in the process abstracted, from multiple glossed texts. Accordingly, interpretation of glossary items requires tracking down these original contexts and reading the *interpretamentum* against the motives, artistry and purposes of their sources. Another potential pitfall is that multiple surviving glossary texts might repeat glosses derived from the same source, and in such cases we need to be mindful that they are not, then, independent witnesses for a specific interpretation or line of reasoning. This is the case for the *hægtesse–striga* equivalence in the *Durham Proverbs*, where the Latin translator must have been rehearsing a gloss-interpretation combination they had seen before, whether in independent study or in a classroom.[27] *Striga* is glossed with some spelling of *hægtesse* in the Second Corpus Glossary (S.528), the Épinal-Erfurt glossary (l. 913), the Leiden Glossary (§47.80), and in Cotton Otho E.i (l. 81), though all of these probably derive from the same source.[28] J. D. Pheifer tentatively identified the so-called Philoxenus Glossary as this source. This Classical Latin-Greek glossary is the source of a number of other glosses, and here Latin *striga* is glossed by the garbled λωστυγων and the more comprehensible γυνή φαρμακίς (*gyné pharmakis*, 'female sorceress'). [29] The specific word for sorceress, φαρμακίς (*pharmakis*) is readily identifiable as derived from φάρμακον (*pharmakon*, 'drug', 'potion'), and the form of magic they were known for was brewing potions, particularly love potions and poisons.[30] If this is indeed the source for the glosses noted above, then this correlates with the Ælfrician evidence in characterising the *hægtessan* as workers of philtre-based magic, both for amorous and poisonous purposes.

The more common glosses featuring *hægtessan* are those which Lapidge pointed to in his interpretation of Lantfred's Furies, where it glosses both specific furies and the furies generally. For ease of reference, all the glossary headwords (lemmata) featuring *hægtessan* in the interpretametum are tabulated in Table 10.3.

While a discussion of all these glosses is beyond the scope of this chapter, they nevertheless indicate a broader issue underpinning any exploration such as this. There is, as Alaric Hall and Christopher Jones have drawn attention to, a sprawling and intricately inter-related network of terms in the glosses: *hægtesse* glosses 'Pythonissa' alongside the even more cryptic *hellerune* in the Sixth Antwerp Glossary, but elsewhere

---

[26] Hall 2007, 77.

[27] For the potential use of glosses and glossaries in scholastic education contexts, see Lendinara 1999a, 5–6.

[28] The editions consulted for each of these texts is as follows. *Corpus*, Hessels 1890; *Épinal-Erfurt*, Pheifer 1974; *Leiden*, Hessels 1906; Cotton Otho E.i: Voss, 1996.

[29] Pheifer 1974, 121, see also Lindsay 1917.

[30] Beekes 2010, 2, 1554; Faraone 1999, 23, 110–18.

Table 10.3: Lemmata glossed by hægtesse.

Lemmata	Witnesses	Other interpretemantum (if applicable)
Furia(rum), 'Furies'	First Cotton Cleopatra (2536, 2537), Third Cotton Cleopatra (2076), Second Corpus (F.434)	First Cotton Cleopatra 2537: *hægtessa uel wedenheotra synna* ('of *hægtessan* or of mad-hearted misdeeds')
Furiis, 'fury, insanity', '?Fury'	Gloss on Aldhelm's prose *De laude virginitatis* (CCCC MS 326)	
Eumenides, 'Furies'	First Cotton Cleopatra (2039), Second Corpus (E.354), Leiden Glossary (§43.53)	Leiden Glossary: eumenides filie noctis hegitissę (Eumindes, daughters of the night: *hægtesse*)
Erinyes, 'Furies'	First Cotton Cleopatra (2038), Second Corpus (E.283)	
Striga, 'witch'	Second Corpus (S.528), the Épinal-Erfurt glossary (l. 913), Leiden Glossary (§47.80), Cotton Otho E.i (l. 81)	
Pythonissa	Sixth Antwerp Glossary (730)	*Phinotissa hellerune uel haegtesse* ('Pythonissa: *helrune* or *hægtesse*)
Parca, 'Fate'	Sixth Antwerp Glossary (748)	

it is glossed by *wicce* ('witch'), which itself also glosses *Parca*, and *Parca* in turn is glossed by *gewyrd* ('fate') and *burgrune* (some sort of practitioner of magic) alongside *wicce* and *hægtesse*.[31] We must be mindful that it is not only the original contexts of the gloss that might motivate certain interpretations, but that processes such as folk etymology or recognising 'false friends' between languages may come into play too. *Pythonissa*, sometimes spelled *phitonissa*, as Bernadette Filotas has shown, variously denoted necromancers or soothsayers in medieval texts.[32] In Old English it is always glossed with some variation of *helrunan* (a sort of magic user) and or *wiccan* ('witch') outside of the Sixth Antwerp Glossary.[33] Without going into the details of the sources for these glosses, the unique inclusion of *hægtesse* here seems to be motivated by the unusual spelling of *pythonissa* as *phinotissa*, where the end of the word resembles an apparent Old English word *tessa*, found not only the end of *hægtesse* but also in a

---

[31] Hall 2007, 86, charts these relationships succinctly, see also Jones, 2014, 430–5.

[32] Filotas 2005, 234–6.

[33] Ælfric's Glossary l. 10, in Zupitza 1880, 303, and some interlinear glosses in Aldhelm's prose *Virginitate* in London, British Library MS Royal 5.E.xi, (Napier 1900, no. 8, l. 106), Oxford, Bodleian Library MS Digby 146 (Napier 1900, no. 1, ll. 1926, 4192), London, British Library MS Royal 6.B.vii (Napier 1900, no. 2, l. 60), London, British Library MS Royal 6.A.vi (Napier 1900, no. 7, l. 107) and Brussels, Bibliothèque Royale MS 1650 (Goossens 1974, l. 1902).

gloss in the Third Cotton Cleopatra Glossary: *Allecto wælcyrge, tessa* ('Allecto: *wælcyrge* [discussed below], *tessa* l. 2080).[34]

Rather than attempt to exhaustively examine the glosses in order to articulate the recoverable facets of *hægtesse*, I will here only briefly point out issues with using the gloss evidence to suggest that there is some especially meaningful connection between *hægtesse* and the Furies, especially when so many other vernacular terms gloss these terms too.

***

We have the most context for the gloss in the mid-tenth- to early eleventh-century Corpus Christi College, Cambridge MS 326 copy of Aldhelm's prose *De laudibus virginitatis*, where there are occasional interlinear glosses to the Latin text in both Latin and in Old English.[35] In chapter 50, the guard Dulcitius, stationed to watch over the imprisoned sisters Chionia, Irene and Agape before their martyrdom, is incited by lust and tries to break into the girls' room. This room happens to be where all the cooking paraphernalia is kept, and for some reason, he insanely ends up embracing and kissing the sooty kitchenware instead of the girls. At this point in MS 326, on p. 108, just above line 19, the glossator has added *hegitesum* ('by the *hægtessan*') above the words *furiis uesaniae* ('by the fury of insanity'):[36]

> *Mox furiis vesaniae correptus coepit quasi limphaticus vel freniticus denigratos lebetes etfurviores fuligiae caccabos complecti tetrasque sartagines basiare.*[37]

Lapidge translates this: 'Straightaway, carried away by the fury of his insanity, he began like a madman or a lunatic to embrace blackened pots and cauldrons darker than soot.'[38] This does not seem to be how the glossator understood this, however. Despite the gloss sitting above the word '*uesaniae*' (genitive singular of *vesania*, 'insanity'), it was certainly glossing '*furiis*' (here an ablative plural of *furia*, 'fury') with '*hegitesum*' (dative plural of *hægtesse*) because of the alignment of case and number, and thus they read Dulcitius' actions as being caused 'by the *hægtessan*', perhaps incited to do so by misreading '*correptus*' (the third person singular perfect passive of *corripio* 'to seize') as *corruptus* ('he was corrupted' or 'he was debauched').[39] They may have also taken '*uesaniae*' as a dative, thus explaining Dulcitius' behaviour because 'he was corrupted by the *hægtesse* to madness'. However *uesaniae* was read, the glossator reasoned that Dulcitius was compelled to amorous madness by an entity that they equated with a *hægtesse*, and this aligns with both Ælfric's understanding and the gloss interpreting

---

[34] For another example of glossators being influenced by their own intuition, see Lacey, 2016, 93–7.

[35] Ker 1957, no. 61 at 107.

[36] The manuscript is available online at *Parker on the Web*, https://parker.stanford.edu/parker/catalog/bp151fr4113.

[37] Ehwald 1919, 305–6.

[38] *Aldhelm Prose*, 117.

[39] See *DMLBS* s.v. '*corrumpere*' for other instances of this word in Aldhelm's writings.

striga ... φαρμακίς (*pharmakis*). The *hægtesse* is not a Fury in this case, but the instigator of a particular type of frenzy.

There does seem to be a consistent understanding of *hægtesse* causing insanity, at least by the glossators of Aldhelm's works. A collection of Aldhelm glosses made their way into the contents of the Cotton Cleopatra glossaries, and the gloss *Furiarum. hægtessa uel wedenheotra synna* ('of the furies': 'of *hægtessan* or of mad-hearted misdeeds') in the First Cotton Cleopatra Glossary l. 2537 originates with Aldhelm's *Carmen de virginitate* l. 2634. The context is a battle between the personifications of virtues and vices. Anger has gathered a company and faces Patience, who silences Anger's loquacious incitement to war and conflict:

> *Sed moderata gestat cetram Patientia contra*
> *Atque cruentatum ferro fractura cerebrum*
> *Irae bacchantis strepitum compescit inormem,*
> *Vincere ne valeat furiarum maxima mentes*
> (2631–4)

> Yet temperate patience carries a small shield in opposition and, prepared to fracture the skull of rampaging Anger made bloody by the sword, she silences the loud cry lest the greatest of furies be able to conquer minds.[40]

The gloss offers a double interpretation to account for the literal and allegorical meanings here. On a literal level, *hægtessan* glosses the entities Patience silences, who are able to afflict minds, and on an allegorical level patience assuages those bellicose 'mad-hearted misdeeds' that can consume minds. In neither of the Aldhelmian glosses is there any clear connection with philtres, though there are passionate nuances. In the *Carmen de virginitate* this passion is not just pugnacious either, as the language Aldhelm uses of Anger's incitement is embedded in sexual euphemism. Lapidge's translation does justice to these: Anger 'lusts (*'cupit'*) for the perils of war and arouses (*'ciet'*) by means of her contentiousness the hearts of brothers to conflict, as she breaks treatises joined (*'copulata'*) for righteous peace' (ll. 2625–8).[41] The choice of *hægtesse* to gloss *furiarum* here cannot be divorced from these – as all of these connotations informed the glossator's choice – and the resonances it bears coincide with nuances in the other examples we have examined.

Taking all of this together, a *hægtesse* has erotic and mind-altering characteristics, and is employed as a gloss for Furies because of specific correspondences, rather than because they embody the general characteristics of them; in connection with this it is notable that *hægtesse* never glosses any individual Furies. There is a strong association with philtres in the Ælrician tradition and in some of the glosses too, though any clearer a picture of them eludes us. There are some overlaps between *hægtessan* and Lantfred's Furies, such as the carnal nuances (in their nakedness, and

---

[40] The text is Ehwald 1919, 459; the translation is from *Aldhelm Poetic*, 161.
[41] *Aldhelm Poetic*, 161. See *DMLBS* s.v.v. 'cupere', 'ciere' and 'copulare'.

in their euphemistic request to have a 'conversation' with him), deception (if we can compare the tall white Fury's use of *'fraude'*, 'trickery', with the caution in the *Durham Proverbs*), and the two black Furies being *'ueneno armatas'* ('armed with poison'). There are, however, key differences between Lantfred's Furies and *hægtessan*, two of whom are compared with Tisiphone specifically, and whose assault leaves the Winchester citizen immobilised rather than afflicted with any sort of madness. Lantfred's Furies are twice compared with birds (firstly ravens and then geese), and there are no avian connotations of *hægtessan*. There is an underappreciated prophetic aspect to them too, as the two black furies ask the citizen *'quo, moriture, abis?'* (translated by Lapidge as 'where, doomed man, are you going?'); *'moriture'* is based on *moriturus* the future active participle of *morior* ('to die'), and so the Furies, whether truthfully or not, are implying that they can foresee the man's death. Such connotations are especially present if we may assume that Lantfred assays to faithfully translates the vernacular term in the account he heard, as the only Old English word which fits is *fæge* 'doomed, fated to die'.[42]

Moreover, especially given that it is not clear that the 'mighty women' in *Wið færstiċe* are actually *hægtessan*, Lantfred's Furies also have topographical associations with hill and stream which are unaccounted for if we identify them with *hægtessan*. This partial correlation seems to favour Jones' argument that Lantfred's Furies do not represent any single vernacular construct, comprising instead a complex composite of various elements, but I am unsatisfied with leaving it at that, as we have every reason to believe that Lantfred's account was not a literary confection but a story he had heard, collected from conversational circulation, and some of the extra details provided by Wulfstan in his account suggest that he was adding to Lantfred's account from his own knowledge of the episode, such as specifying some extra details where the citizen's pastures were (*Narratio* l.497), and that he was *'vir... locuples'* ('a wealthy man', *Narratio* l.494). While Lantfred furnished the account with his classical and patristic learning, at its core there is some foundation in the living lore of tenth-century Winchester, and in what follows I propose that there is enough evidence to recover what was thought to have attacked the citizen outside Winchester's city walls: a *wælcyrge*.

Defining Old English *Wælcyrge*

The Old English *wælcyrge* (sing., *wælcyrian* pl.) has frequently been discussed in relation to its better-known Norse cognate, the *valkyrja* ('valkyrie'). This has been as much a bane for scholarship as a boon: the availability of a rich assemblage of Old Norse material allows for fruitful comparative readings of the words, but comparative reading frequently impose what is known of the Old Norse onto the Old English material.[43] The reasons for this overreliance on Old Norse material are the complexities

---

[42] *DOE*, s.v. *'fæge'*.
[43] Damico 1984; Damico 1990.

of interpreting the extant Old English attestations, many of which are in glossaries, and nowhere are there detailed narratives of valkyries and their exploits like we find in Old Norse.[44] There is certainly some shared foundation underpinning the Old English *wælcyrge* and the Old Norse *valkyrja*, as they both derive from Common Germanic **wala-kuzjōn*.[45] What this means in practice is difficult to say other than the original entities seem to have had some jurisdiction over choosing the slain (**wala* is the etymon of OE *wæl*, 'corpse', 'slain', and ON *valr*, 'slain'; **-kuzjōn* is presumably connected to OE *ceosan* and ON *kjósa*, 'to choose'). It is fallacious to merely read the Old Norse material into the Old English, as the languages, cultures, and beliefs had been separated and developing divergently for centuries, even though there is the potential for both languages to have preserved some facets of the original.[46] There is also the possibility of direct influence from Old Norse during the Viking Age, when Scandinavian settlers and raiders were in high intensity contact with Old English speakers.[47] We must remain open to the possibility of Norse influence, then, but proceed cautiously, by evaluating the Old English on its own terms before seeking comparison with the Norse.

Wælcyrge occurs five times outside of the glossaries, in two homilies by Archbishop Wulfstan of York (*Sermo Lupi ad Anglos*, 'The Wolf's Sermon to the English', and *Sermo ad populum dominicis diebus* 'Sermon to the people on Sundays'), Cnut's First Letter to the English people and twice in *The Wonders of the East*, a prose survey of some marvellous and bizarre creatures purported to dwell in the near East. To this we may add a passage in the Old English *Exodus* poem, which at the very least strongly alludes to the *wælcyrge* if it does not indeed comprise an attestation of sorts to it. The use of *wælcyrge* in Wulfstan's homilies and in Cnut's First Letter to the English (which Wulfstan at least partially authored) is identical.[48] Each time it features in a list of disreputable deeds and reprehensible people in an alliterative stock phrase, '*wiccan and wælcyrian*', ('witches and *wælcyrian*').[49] The near-synonymous nature of many of the items makes inferring much untenable besides the *wælcyrge* being something unchristian and many commentators have left it at that.[50] The instances in *The Wonders of the East* have been overlooked because they do not immediately seem relevant for decoding aspects of a female folkloric entity, but, as we will see, they yield valuable information. The first occurrence is in §4, describing unusual wild beasts in a place called Lentibelsinea. These beasts have '*eahta fet, 7 wælkyrian eagan, 7 twa heafda*' ('eight feet, and *wælcyrge*'s eyes, and two heads').[51] This unusual detail makes more sense

---

[44] Cf. Lionarons 2005, 288–9 and Mitchell 2001, 70.

[45] Kroonen 2013, s.v.. '**wala-*'; Orel 2003, s.v '**wala-kuzjōn*'.

[46] Instructive here is the methodology outlined in North 1991, especially 10–13, and North 1997, 3–11.

[47] For some examples of this see Frank 1987 and Dance 2003.

[48] Treharne 2012, 24–28.

[49] Cnut's First Letter: §15, in Liebermann, 1903–16, 1, 274; *Sermo Lupi*: l. 164, in Bethurum 1957, 267–75; *Sermo ad populum* in Napier 1883, 291–9, at 298, l. 18.

[50] Lionarons 2005, 288; Simek 1993, 349.

[51] Orchard 2003, 186.

when we compare the Old English with the Latin it translates: the beasts '*pedes habent octenos, oculos habent gorgoneos, bina capita habent*' ('have eight feet, they have the eyes of Gorgons, and they have two heads').[52] Indeed, *the Wonders of the East* consistently translates Latin *gorgo* ('Gorgon') with *wælcyrge*, as later, in §9, a river which in the Latin is called *Gorgoneus* ('Gorgon-like') is translated and explicated in the Old English as '*haten Gorgoneus, þæt is Wælcyrginc*' ('called *Gorgoneus*, that is *wælcyrge*-like').[53] The implication is that the *wælcyrge* had analogous paralysing abilities to the Gorgon, and in equating the Gorgon with *wælcyrge* the Old English translator also seems to have had in mind the information on Gorgons in the *Liber Monstrorum* ('Book of Monsters') I.38, which says:

> *Gorgones quoque in monstruosa mulierum natura tres, quae dicebantur Stheno, Euryale, Medusa, iuxta montem Atlantem fuisse et in finibus Libiae describuntur, quae suo uisu homines conuertebant in lapides. Quarum unam Perseus scuto uitreo defensus interficit, quae absciso capite suos oculos ita uertisse fertur ut uiua.*

> Three Gorgons are also described with the monstrous nature of women, Stheno, Euryale, and Medusa, who are said to have lived on the borders of Libya next to Mount Atlas, who used to turn men to stone by their sight. Perseus slew one of them, protected by a glassy shield, and she is said, when her head was cut off, to have moved her eyes as though alive.[54]

This must be a distinctive feature of the *wælcyrge*, as there is nothing quite like this said of valkyries in Old Norse, although in the poem known variously as *Hrafnsmál* ('The lay of the raven') or *Haraldskvæði* ('Poem about Harald') ascribed to Þorbjǫrn Hornklofi and typically dated to *c.* 900, a valkyrie is described as having '*glæhvarma*' ('glowing eyes', st. 2.6), and in '*Guðrúnarkviða in fyrsta*' ('The first lay of Guðrún'), the valkyrie Brynhild has '*eldr ór augom*' ('fire blaze from her eyes', st. 27.5) when she sees her lover, Sigurð, dead by her own hand.[55] We might also note here that in Wulfstan of Winchester's metrical account of the Furies episode, he elaborates on Lantfred's account of the two black furies being '*ueneno armatas*', 'armed with poison', saying instead that they are '*armatas gelido serpentinoque ueneno*', 'armed with cold snake's venom' (l. 500).[56] Jones articulates how this serpentine allusion evokes the Gorgon by drawing attention to verbal parallels between Lantfred's description of the two Furies *Tysiphoneisque uultibus infectas* ('blackened with faces like Tisiphone') and the *Aeneid* VII.341, where Alecto is described as '*Gorgoneis... infecta uenenis*' ('tainted with the Gorgon's poison'), as well as their 'dark hair' ('*furuis crinibus*') being reminiscent of *Aeneid* VII.329, 'where Alecto's blackness is associated with the vipers sprouting

---

[52] *Ibid.*, 176.
[53] *Ibid.*, 177,190.
[54] Text and translation from Orchard 2003, 278–9, which discusses the *Liber Monstrorum* in early medieval England throughout. See also Lendinara 1999b.
[55] Fulk 2012, 91; *Edda*, 206.
[56] Lapidge 2003, 274 (Lantfred) and 436 (Wulfstan).

from her head ('*pullulat atra colubris*').[57] We will see more Gorgon similarities when we discuss Alecto in the glossary evidence, below.

Before moving onto the glossary evidence, there is one more narrative source that might inform our understanding of *wælcyrge*. The poem *Exodus* reframes the Old Testament account of Moses and the Israelites fleeing Egypt and crossing the Red Sea in traditional Old English heroic style, both in form, by shaping it into alliterative poetry, and in content, by characterising Moses and the Israelites as an army. At several points the poem presents the precursor to a battle, complete with the customary beasts of battle, though with one notable idiosyncrasy in its description of the raven:

> *Onhwæl þa on heofonum hyrnednebba,*
> *(hreopon herefugolas, hilde grædige)*
> *deawigfeðere ofer drihtneum,*
> *wonn wælceasega. Wulfas sungon*
> *atol æfenleoð ætes on wenan,*
> *carleasan deor, cwyldrof, beodan*
> *on laðra last leodmægnes fyl.*
> *Hreopon mearcweardas middun nihtum,*
> *fleah fæge gast, folc wæs gehæged.*
> (ll.161–69)

> The horny-beaked cried to the heavens,
> (battle-birds clamoured, greedy for war)
> over the troops of corpses, the dark chooser-of-the-slain,
> dewy-feathered. Wolves sang
> terrible evening songs in anticipation of feasting,
> reckless beasts, dedicated to slaughter, waiting in the
> tracks of the hateful ones for the destruction of peoples.
> The border-guards clamoured in the middle of the night
> the fated soul flies away, the population was diminished.[58]

It is not uncommon for the raven to appear before battle in Old English verse, nor is it uncommon for it to identify or presage which particular individuals might fall.[59] Referring to the bird as a *wælceasega* is unparalleled, however. The semantic composition of the word is identical to *wælcyrge*, and its function of selecting which individuals will die in the coming slaughter is shared by valkyries in Old Norse, a parallel also noticed by Joseph Harris.[60] Moreover, valkyries in Old Norse are associated with ravens and other birds in various ways. Sometimes they literally associate with ravens, as in the aforementioned *Hrafnsmál/Haraldskvæði*, where the poem takes the form of a dialogue between raven and valkyrie, or in Úlfr Uggason's *Húsdrápa*

---

[57] Lapidge 2003, 274; Jones 2014, 414. Jones also observes, in n. 27, that the characterisation of poison as 'cold' can be found in Isidore's *Etymologiae* XII.iv.42.

[58] Lucas 1994, 102. Translation here is my own.

[59] For a discussion of this, as well as an overview of the beasts of battle, see Lacey 2014, 99–135.

[60] Harris 2007, 14.

('Eulogy on the house'), a skaldic poem from the early 990s which observes raven and valkyrie jointly following Óðinn to Baldr's funeral pyre (st. 10).[61] Sometimes this connection is transformative, as has been noted by Jóhanna Katrín Friðriksdóttir, Charles Donahue and Matthias Egeler.[62] Sometimes they are ravens or crows (*e.g.* the *óskmey* 'wish-maiden' who delivers a child-bearing apple from Óðinn to Vǫlsung's father in *Vǫlsunga saga* ch. 1) and sometimes swans (*e.g.* in the introductory prose of *Vǫlundarqviða*).[63] The association can even be more subtle, as when valkyries are aligned linguistically with birds. In *Helgaqviða Hundingsbana ǫnnur* st. 43, the valkyrie Sigrún rides into Helgi's burial mound so she may be reunited with him after his death, and on seeing him again says '*nú em ec svá fegin fundi ocrom/ sem átfrekir Óðins haucar / er val vito*' ('now I am as glad at our meeting as Óðin's food-hungry hawks', *i.e.* ravens, 'when they know of slaughter'), and in *Vǫlsunga saga* chap. 29, the armour-clad valkyrie Brynhild is described sitting in her throne '*sem alpt af báru*' (like a swan on the waves').[64] Their affinity with birds can even be denoted in the similarity of features, such as their ability to fly (*e.g. Helgaqviða Hiǫrvarðzsonar* prose between st. 9–10, *Helgakviða Hundingsbana ǫnnur*, prose between st. 4–5).[65] In light of the Old Norse comparative evidence, it is reasonable to conclude that the *wælceasega* in *Exodus* attests to some similar matrix of ideas connecting ravens and *wælcyrge* in Old English, and this connection would explain Lantfred's characterisation of the two black Furies as '*coruinis (quas humana cohibebat statura)*' ('raven-like women, who were in human form', III.26–7).[66]

What we have seen so far, then, is that the *wælcyrge* in early medieval England seem to have had some capacity to paralyse their victims, that they could possess corvid forms (or at least possessed corvid affinities), and they had some potential to either select or foretell those to die – all of which correspond, in one way or another, to aspects of Lantfred's Furies. We now turn to the glossary evidence. Due to considerations of space, however, it is not possible to exhaustively discuss each of the glossary occurrences, and so it is appropriate here to focus on articulating what some of the glosses can tell us about the Old English *wælcyrge* (see Table 10.4).

The MS Digby 146 copy of Aldhelm's prose *De virginitate* is heavily glossed and annotated with both dry-point and ink glosses; the latter are in a single hand. Many of its glosses are shared with other Aldhelm prose *De virginitate* manuscripts, but our gloss of *ueneris* ('of Venus') is unique.[67] The gloss occurs during chapter 47, at the point where the father of the martyr Christina finds out that his daughter has rejected him and his pagan ways:

---

[61] Marold 2017, 420.

[62] Friðriksdóttir 2020, 7–8, 68–9; Donahue 1941, 4; Egeler 2008, 9–10.

[63] Finch 1965, 1–4; *Edda*, 116.

[64] *Edda*, 158; Finch 1965, 49. For more on this see Bek-Pedersen 2011, 126.

[65] *Edda*, 143, 151.

[66] Lapidge 2003, 276.

[67] For a discussion of the relationship of the different groups of glosses, see Ker 1957, no. 320, 381–3 and Gwara 1998, especially 141–6.

Table 10.4: Lemmata glossed by wælcyrge.

Lemmata	Witnesses	Other interpretamentum (if applicable)
Allecto	First Cotton Cleopatra (l.299) Third Cotton Cleopatra (l. 2080)	Third Cotton Cleopatra (l. 2080): Allecto wælcyrge, tessa. ('Allecto: wælcyrge, *tessa*') The latter element may be part of *hægtesse*, see above
Bellona	First Cotton Cleopatra (l. 754) Third Cotton Cleopatra (l. 1847)	
Tisiphona	Sixth Antwerp Glossary (l. 741)	
Herinis (for 'Erinyes')	First Cotton Cleopatra (l. 2983) Second Corpus glossary (H.87)	
Ueneris (genitive singular 'of Venus')	Gloss on Aldhelm's prose *De virginitate* (Oxford, Bodleian, MS Digby 146)[1]	Ueneris. gydene wælcyrie ('goddess', *wælcyrge*)
Eurynis (for Erinyes? Corruption of *Euryale*?)	Second Corpus glossary (E.351)	

[1] Napier 1883, no. 1, l. 4449.

...sed cum se ab unica filia merito spretum comperisset et deauratas simulacrorum effigies, Iovis scilicet et Apollinis simulque Veneris, stuprorum amatricis, minutatim in frusta confractas animadverteret, ilico diversa tormentorum genera eandem filiam nexatura cruentus carnifex et truculentus parricida potius quam pius pater crudeliter machinatur.

When he learned that he had been – deservedly! – rejected by his only daughter, and when he discovered that (his) gilded statues of the pagan gods, that is, of Jupiter and Apollo and also Venus, the lover of debauchery, had been smashed to tiny pieces, this blood-thirsty butcher and savage infanticide rather than affectionate father cruelly devised on the spot various sorts of torture to harness his daughter.[68]

From the other glosses it is clear that the glossator knew this text and their Latin well enough to not make an interpretive mistake of the sort we saw in CCCC 326, above. This glossing of 'Venus' is evidence, then, that *wælcyrge* possessed sexual connotations, and this also receives support from the comparative Norse evidence, where valkyrie-lovers are numerous.[69] This sordid amorousness also lurks in the background of the source for the *allecto. wælcyrge* glosses in the First and Third Cotton Cleopatra glossaries. We have already seen this in our discussion of the gloss *furiarum. hægtessa uel wedenheotra synna*, above: it is the clash between Patience and Anger in Aldhelm's *Carmen de virginitate*, where Anger's love of conflict was simmering with euphemism.

---

[68] Text, Ehwald 1919, 1288. Translation, *Aldhelm Prose*, 114.
[69] See, for example, the valkyries at the beginning of *Vǫlundarqviða*, Sigrún and Helgi in *Helgaqviða Hundingsbana in fyrri*, and Sigurð and Brynhild in the *Vǫlsung* materal, such as *Vǫlsunga saga*, *Sigurðarqviða in scamma*, *Helreið Brynhildar*, in *Edda* 1983.

The specific portion of the passage which informs the gloss follows immediately from Patience quelling the loud noise that would allow the 'greatest of furies' to 'conquer minds', and is underlined here:

> Quamvis Gorgoneo stridat maculata cruore
> Atque venenatis mordendo sibilet ydris,
> Dum caput ex herebo nigrantis filia Noctis
> Tollit et in mundum Stygiis emersa latebris
> Suscitat Allecto scaevas ad scandala mentes
> Haec solet ad bellum ferratos ducere contos
> Horrida facturos animabus vulnera sanctis,
> Nostras ni dominus mentes defendat inermes.
> 2635-

> Even though this fury, stained with Gorgon blood, hisses and gnashes, biting with her poisoned snakes, as his daughter of black Night raises her head from the infernal regions and so rising out of murky Styx into the world <u>Allecto incites stupid minds to sin</u>. She is accustomed to bring to the battle iron spears which would inflict grievous wounds on holy souls, were it not that the Lord protects our defenceless breasts.[70]

Although *scandalum* was, generally, not overtly sexual in this period, it could be sexual in terms of the types of sin or immorality denoted.[71] After the euphemisms barely 10 lines before, and the clear divisions Aldhelm sews in this extended battle scene, with virginity and purity on one side and various vices in opposition to it, these sexual connotations must have been nevertheless present here. More interestingly, however, is the presence of several features which might have motivated glossing *Allecto* with *wælcyrge* which are present in Lantfred's Furies: Alecto's rising from the waters of the Styx mirrors Lantfred's Furies plunging into the stream of the river at the end of her encounter with the Winchester citizen (III.39–40); she preys upon stupid minds (and Lantfred's Furies call the Winchester citizen *insane*, 'fool', III.29); and she attacks with poison, which is a feature of the Furies noted both by Lantfred and Wulfstan (Lantfred III.14; Wulfstan l.510, *uirus ab ore uomunt*, 'vomit poison from their mouths', l. 527).[72] We also find once more the foregrounding of Alecto's Gorgon nature, and the brandishing of a weapon (where the latter resonates particularly with the Norse analogues). Either some collection of these or the cumulative total of these motivated the gloss, and the consistent presence of Gorgon associations with *wælcyrge* should not be overlooked.

Conclusion: The Case for *Wælcyrge*

There are more general conclusions to be drawn here than just the identity of Lantfred's Furies. In addition to charting out the close-knit association between

---

[70] Text, Ehwald 1919, 460. Translation, *Aldhelm Poetic*, 161.
[71] DMLBS, s.v. 'scandalum'.
[72] Lapidge 2003, 274 (Lantfred) and 436 (Wulfstan).

wælcyrge and Gorgons in Old English, I have also articulated aspects of the *hægtesse*, such as its association with the form of magic known as *lybban* in Old English, which comprised both philtres and poisons, and its intimate connection with amorous magic.

I have argued that Lantfred's Furies are based on the entity known as the *wælcyrge*, and by way of conclusion will rehearse how it aligns with the defining features of Lantfred's Furies:

- They are likened to the Classical furies ('*quasi bine ex tribus Furiarum sorores*'; '*… accessit tertia*').
- They have sexual connotations (*Ethiopissas*, '*corpora nudas*'; '*nudis corporibus*'; "*huc ueni, quoniam indubitanter uolumus tibi perpauca colloqui*").
- They have topographical associations with rivers and mounds (*amnem*, '*in amnis*'; *collem, collis*).
- Two of them are raven-like, one is white ('*coruinis (quas humana cohibebat statura)*', '*candido tamen prioribus colore dissimilis ac decenter niueis ornate induuiis*').
- They are deceptive (*fraude*).
- One uses an unusual attack involving the thrice-folded tunic.
- The effect of the attack is paralysis.
- There is the implication of prophesying or causing death ('*quo, moriture, abis?*'; *wælcyrge* as literally 'chooser of the slain').

In this chapter, I have tried to show how *wælcyrge* potentially addresses all of these – and at the very least, that it corresponds more of these features than *hægtesse*. We have seen how the *wælcyrge* glosses the furies, and that there are sexual connotations in both the passages glossed and in the Old Norse cognates. A topographical association between *wælcyrge* and rivers can be inferred from the gloss on Aldhelm's *Carmen de virginitate*, and especially if the waterway is seen, like the Styx, as demarcating a boundary between different domains. The use of *wælcyrginc* to name a river in *The Wonders of the East* §9 may have reinforced this fluvial connection if it was not indeed responsible for it. The association with mounds is patchier, however, and requires either interpreting the *mihtigan wif* of *Wið færstiċe* as *wælcyrian* or reading the association of Old Norse *valkyrjur* with mounds (attested in, for example *Helgaqviða Hundingsbana ǫnnur*). *Exodus* evidences the ravenlike nature of the *wælcyrge* in Old English and is supported by the Old Norse analogues, though there is, admittedly, not very much evidence in Old English for a *wælcyrge* being white. In Old Norse *hvít* ('white') is both a name element and an attribute of beauty for valkyries, but this connection is tenuous; on the other hand, there is no evidence for *hægtesse* being associated with whiteness either. Finally, a central argument of this chapter was that *wælcyrge* was used to translate and gloss Gorgon words because the paralysing attack of the *wælcyrge* was so characteristic of it. This leaves only the unusual use of the tunic attack unexplained, and my suspicion here is that this is perhaps meant to draw upon a not uncommon experience of disciplinary beating of children (where the consistency of a folded sleeve is not unlike a rolled-up towel). Proving this is another matter, however, as Shulamith Shahar laments: '[i]t is difficult to locate direct testimony on the beating of small children, since, as long as it did not cause death or severe bodily injury, it was considered a private matter.'[73] It is fortunate for our Winchester citizen that Swithun was able to remedy against any long-lasting harm from Lantfred's Furies, and it is fortunate for us that his ordeal at their hands was not a private matter.

Abbreviations

Aldhelm Poetic	Lapidge, M. and Rosier, J. (eds and trans.) 1985. *Aldhelm: The Poetic Works*. Cambridge: D. S. Brewer.
Aldhelm Prose	Lapidge, M. and Herren, M. (eds and trans.) 1979. *Aldhelm: The Prose Works*, Cambridge: D. S. Brewer.
DMLBS	Latham, R. E., Howlett, D. and Ashdowne, R. (eds) 1975–2013. *Dictionary of Medieval Latin from British Sources*. 17 vols. Oxford: Oxford University Press. Available at: http://www.dmlbs.ox.ac.uk/web/online.html.
DOE	Getz, R. and Pelle, S. (eds) 2018. *Dictionary of Old English: A-I*. Available at: https://tapor.library.utoronto.ca/doe/.
Edda	Neckel, G. and Kuhn, H. (eds) 1983. *Edda: die Lieder des Codex Regius nebst verwandten Denmälern*. 5th edition., 2 vols. Heidelberg: Winter.
OE	Old English
ON	Old Norse
Parker	Stanford University, Parker Library on the Web. Available at: https://parker.stanford.edu/parker/. (Accessed 21 July 2021).

Bibliography

Manuscripts

Brussels, Bibliothèque Royale MS 1650.
Cambridge, Corpus Christi College MS 326.
Épinal, Bibliothèque municipale MS 72(2).
Erfurt, Wissenschaftliche Bibliothek MS Amplonianus MS 2° 42.
Leiden, Leiden University Library MS Voss. Q0 Lat. N0. 69.
London, British Library Cotton MS Cleopatra A.iii.
London, British Library Cotton MS Otho E.i.
London, British Library MS Harley 585.
London, British Library MS Royal 5.E.xi.
London, British Library MS Royal 6.A.vi.
London, British Library MS Royal 6.B.vii.
Oxford, Bodleian Library MS Digby 146.

---

[73] Shahar 1990, 111.

Primary Sources

Arngart, O. (ed.) 1956. *The Durham Proverbs: An Eleventh Century Collection of Anglo-Saxon Proverbs.* Lunds Universitets årsskrift, N.F., Avd.1, Lunds Universitet. 52. Lund: Gleerup.

Arngart, O. 1981. The Durham Proverbs, *Speculum,* 56:2, 288–300.

Bethurum, D. (ed.) 1957. *The Homilies of Wulfstan.* Oxford: Oxford University Press.

Ehwald, R. (ed.) 1919. *Alhelmi Opera.* MGH 15. Berlin: Weidmann.

Finch, R. G. 1965. *The Saga of the Volsungs.* London: Nelson.

Frantzen, A. (ed.) 2003–2021. *The Anglo-Saxon Penitentials: A Cultural Database.* Available at: http://www.anglo-saxon.net/penance/. (Accessed 21 July 2021)

Fulk, R. (ed.) 2012. Þorbjǫrn hornklofi, Haraldskvæði (Hrafnsmál), in D. Whaley (ed.) *Poetry from the Kings' Sagas 1: From Mythical Times to c. 1035.* Skaldic Poetry of the Scandinavian Middle Ages 1. Turnhout: Brepols. Available at: https://skaldic.abdn.ac.uk/m.php?p=text&i=1436.

Goossens, L. (ed.) 1974. *The Old English Glosses of MS Brussels, Royal Library 1650 (Aldhelm's 'De laudibus virginitatis').* Brussels: Paleis der Academien.

Hessels, J. H. (ed.) 1890. *An Eighth-century Latin-Anglo-Saxon Glossary preserved in the Library of Corpus Christi College, Cambridge.* Cambridge: Cambridge University Press.

Hessels, J. H. (ed.) 1906. *A Late Eighth-century Latin-Anglo-Saxon Glossary preserved in the Library of the Leiden University.* Cambridge: Cambridge University Press.

Lapidge, M. (ed.) 2003. *The Cult of St Swithun,* Winchester Studies, 4.ii. Oxford: Clarendon Press.

Lapidge, M. and Winterbottom, M. (eds.) 1991. *Wulfstan of Winchester: The Life of St Æthelwold.* Oxford Medieval Texts. Oxford: Oxford University Press.

Lieberman, F. (ed.) 1903–1916. *Die Gesetze der Angelsachsen.* 3 vols. Leipzig: Niemeyer.

Lucas, P. (ed.) 1994. *Exodus.* Exeter: Exeter University Press.

Marold, E., (ed.) 2017. Úlfr Uggason, Húsdrápa, in K. E. Gade and E. Marold (eds) *Poetry from Treatises on Poetics.* Skaldic Poetry of the Scandinavian Middle Ages 3. Turnhout: Brepols. Available at: https://skaldic.abdn.ac.uk/m.php?p=text&i=1492.

Napier, A. (ed.) 1883. *Wulfstan.* Berlin: Weidmann.

Napier, A. (ed.) 1900. *Old English Glosses.* Oxford: Clarendon Press.

Pheifer, J. D. 1974. *Old English Glosses in the Épinal-Erfurt Glossary.* Oxford: Oxford University Press.

Skeat, W. (ed.) 1881–1900. *Ælfric's Lives of Saints.* 2 vols. London: Trubner.

Voss, M. 1996. Altenglische Glossen aus MS British Library, Cotton Otho E. i, *AAA: Arbeiten aus Anglistik und Amerikanistik,* 21:2, 179–203.

Zupitza, J. (ed.) 1880. *Ælfrics Grammatik und Glossar.* Berlin: Weidmann.

Secondary Sources

Atherton, M. 2017. *The Making of England: A New History of the Anglo-Saxon World.* London: I. B. Tauris.

Beekes, R. 2010. *Etymological Dictionary of Greek,* 2 vols. Leiden: Brill.

Bek-Pedersen, K. 2011. *Norns in Old Norse Mythology.* Edinburgh: Dunedin.

Bosworth, J. and Toller, T. 1898. *An Anglo-Saxon Dictionary.* London: Oxford University Press.

Damico, H. 1984. *Beowulf's Wealtheow and the Valkyrie Tradition.* Madison: University of Wisconsin Press.

Damico, H. 1990. The Valkyrie Reflex in Old English Literature, in H. Damico and A. H. Olsen (eds) *New Readings on Women in Old English Literature,* 176–89. Bloomington: Indiana University Press.

Dance, R. 2003. North Sea Currents: Old English-Old Norse Relations, Literary and Linguistic, *Literature Compass,* 1, 1–10.

Donahue, C. 1941. The Valkyries and the Irish War-Goddesses, *PMLA: Publications of the Modern Language Association of America,* 56:1, 1–12.

Egeler, M. 2008. Death, Wings, and Divine Devouring: Possible Mediterranean Affinities of Irish Battlefield Demons and Norse Valkyries, *Studia Celtica Fennica,* 5, 5–26.

Faraone, C. 1999. *Ancient Greek Love Magic*. Harvard: Harvard University Press.

Filotas, B. 2005. *Pagan Survivals, Superstitions and Popular Cultures in Early Medieval Pastoral Literature*. Toronto: Pontifical Institute of Medieval Studies.

Fontes Anglo-Saxonici: A Register of Written Sources Used by Anglo-Saxon Authors. Available at: https://www.st-andrews.ac.uk/~cr30/Mercian/Fontes. (Accessed 21 July 2021).

Foxhall-Forbes, H. 2013. *Heaven and Earth in Anglo-Saxon England: Theology and Society in the Age of Bede*. London: Routledge.

Frank, R. 1987. Did Anglo-Saxon Audiences Have a Skaldic Tooth?, *Scandinavian Studies*, 59:3, 338–55.

Friðriksdóttir, J. K. 2020. *Valkyrie: The Women of the Viking World*. London: Bloomsbury Press.

Godden, M. 1985. Ælfric's Saints' Lives and the Problem of Miracles, *Leeds Studies in English*, 16, 83–100.

Gwara, S. 1998. The Transmission of the 'Digby' Corpus of Bilingual Glosses to Aldhelm's *Prosa de virginitate*, *Anglo-Saxon England*, 27, 139–68.

Hall, A. 2007. *Elves in Anglo-Saxon England*. Woodbridge: Boydell Press.

Harris, J. 2007. Beasts of Battle, South and North, in C. D. Wright, F. M. Biggs and T. N. Hall (eds), *Source of Wisdom: Old English and Early Medieval Latin Studies in Honour of Thomas D. Hill*, 3–25. Toronto: University of Toronto Press.

Jones, C. 2014. Furies, Monks, and Folklore in the Earliest *Miracula* of Saint Swithun, *Journal of English and Germanic Philology*, 113:4, 407–442.

Ker, N. 1957. *Catalogue of Manuscripts Containing Anglo-Saxon*. Oxford: Clarendon Press.

Koopmans, R. 2011. *Wonderful to Relate. Miracle Stories and Miracle Collecting in High Medieval England*. Philadelphia: University of Pennsylvania Press.

Kroonen, G. 2013. *Etymological Dictionary of Proto-Germanic*. Leiden: Brill.

Lacey, E. 2014. Birds and Bird-lore in the Literature of Anglo-Saxon England, unpublished PhD thesis, University College London.

Lacey, E. 2016. Birds and Words: Aurality, Semantics and Species in Anglo-Saxon England, in S. Thomson and M. Bintley (eds), *Sensory Perception in the Medieval World: Manuscripts, Texts, and Other Material Matters*. Utrecht Studies in Medieval Literacy 34, 75–98. Turnhout: Brepols.

Lendinara, P. 1999a. Anglo-Saxon Glosses and Glossaries: an Introduction, in P. Lendinara, *Anglo-Saxon Glosses and Glossaries*, 1–26. Aldershot: Variorum.

Lendinara, P. 1999b. The *Liber monstrorum* and Anglo-Saxon Glossaries, in P. Lendinara, *Anglo-Saxon Glosses and Glossaries*, 113–38. Aldershot: Variorum.

Lindsay, W. M. 1917. The Philoxenus Glossary, *The Classical Review*, 31:7, 158–63.

Lionarons, J. T. 2005. Dísir, Valkyries, Völur, and Norns: The *Weise Frauen* of the *Deutsche Mythologie*, in T. Shippey (ed.), *The Shadow-Walkers: Jacob Grimm's Mythology of the Monstrous*, 271–98. Turnhout: Brepols.

Meaney, A. 1985. Ælfric's use of his Sources in his Homily on Auguries, *English Studies*, 66, 477–95.

Mitchell, S. 2001. Warlocks, Valkyries and Varlets: A Prolegomenon to the Development of North Sea Witchcraft Terminology, *Cosmos*, 17, 59–81.

North, R. 1991. *Pagan Words and Christian Meanings*. Costerus New Series 81. Amsterdam: Rodopi.

North, R. 1997. *Heathen Gods in Old English Literature*. Cambridge: Cambridge University Press.

Orchard, A. 2003. *Pride and Prodigies*. Toronto: University of Toronto Press.

Orel, V. 2003. *A Handbook of Germanic Etymology*. Leiden: Brill.

Shahar, S. 1990. *Childhood in the Middle Ages*. London: Routledge.

Sigal, P. A. 1987. Le travail des hagiographes aux XIe et XIIe siècles: sources d'information et méthodes de rédaction, *Francia*, 15, 149–82.

Simek, R. 1993. *Dictionary of Northern Mythology*. Woodbridge: Boydell Press.

Treharne, E. 2012. *Living Through Conquest: The Politics of Early English, 1020 to 1220*. Oxford: Oxford University Press.

Chapter 11

SK27, Or a Winchester Pilgrim's Tale

Simon Roffey

This paper investigates evidence for an early twelfth-century pilgrim burial, designated SK27, from the medieval leprosy hospital of St Mary Magdalen, Winchester. The study presents an archaeological investigation of the remains and interprets them in their wider historical and religious context, revealing the broader human story behind the archaeology.

Perhaps in this neglected spot is laid
Some heart once pregnant with celestial fire;
Hands that the rod of empire might have swayed,
Or waked to ecstasy the living lyre.
Thomas Gray, *An Elegy Wrote in a Country Church Yard* (London, 1751)

This world is but a thoroughfare full of woe,
And we being pilgrims, passing to and fro...
Geoffrey Chaucer, *The Canterbury Tales* (late fourteenth century)

For the archaeologist, one of the most important considerations behind the excavation of human remains lies in the striking of a balance between the advancement of scientific knowledge, and the ethical implications behind the effective disinterment of the dead. Thus, in practice, where official permission has been acquired and subsequent burial licence is in hand, the bodies are dutifully roused from their slumber and scientific knowledge dutifully advanced. In this light we may get to learn much about the individual's, age, health and circumstances of death. But their life – their 'story'– the years and decades leading up to their demise, often remains hidden, or at worst ignored. Unless history decides they are someone of particular significance, in the vast majority of cases the lives of the dead remain invisible. Almost as if they hadn't lived them. It is therefore beholden on the archaeologist, in fact an ethical responsibility, wherever possible to bring the dead back to life. Metaphorically speaking, of course. We must justify our excavation wherever possible by shedding light on the existence, life, works and deeds of the dead. The purpose of this paper is to attempt to shed light on one single individual known as SK27 (or skeleton '27', in order of excavation). No documents survive, or in all likelihood were ever written, about this individual. Yet, by piecing together the evidence from scientific analysis of the remains and interpreting them in the light of context, much can be revealed about SK27, a Winchester pilgrim.

Circumstance of Excavation

Burial SK27 was excavated in 2011 from the cemetery of the medieval leprosy hospital of St Mary Magdalen, Winchester.[1] The hospital was founded sometime in the last few decades of the eleventh century and was an institution, at its outset, that specialised in the care of individuals affected by leprosy, a disease that was widespread in England from the late eleventh to early fourteenth centuries. The dates for the origins of the hospital place it as one of the earliest excavated leprosy hospitals in western Europe.[2] Excavations at Winchester revealed evidence for an initial phase of occupation consisting of a small chapel, timber structures, a large storage cellar and a well organised cemetery comprising a number of anthropomorphic graves. It was in one of these graves, just to the north of the chapel, that the burial SK27 was found.

The Burial

The burial SK27 was found parallel and external to the north wall of the medieval chapel. The grave was of anthropomorphic shape, with head niche, and cut directly into the chalk (Fig. 11.1). A ledge ran along the lip of the grave suggesting that a ledger or 'lid' had once been placed over the grave. The fact that this grave and the others in the surrounding cemetery were not truncated suggest that they were marked, possibly by the placement of the ledgers or alternatively, stones or wooden crosses. This was a practice that was not uncommon in the medieval period. However the use of anthropomorphic graves is unusual to hospitals and is more normally found in the context of monastic burials.[3] The burial was accompanied by a scallop shell, the traditional symbol of pilgrimage and therefore led to the identification of SK27 as a medieval pilgrim. Samples taken from the skeleton were subsequently radiocarbon dated to AD 1020–1162 cal AD. This, together with other dates from the cemetery and stratigraphic evidence, suggests a likely date for the burial as sometime in the early twelfth century, a period that also coincided with an increased popularity in pilgrimage.

Osteological analysis concluded that the individual was a young adult male (25–35 years) with a stature of 168.9 ± 2.99 cm (calculated from measuring the femur plus tibia). This is within the expected range of average male stature for the period of 171 cm or 5'6".[4] Ancient DNA analysis revealed high levels of *Mycobacterium leprae* DNA

---

[1] Roffey *et al.* 2017.
[2] Roffey 2012.
[3] See Roffey 2020.
[4] Roffey *et al.* 2017.

Fig 11.1: SK27, St Mary Magdalen, Winchester (author).

in various skeletal elements, suggesting that the pilgrim suffered from lepromatous leprosy, a type of leprosy that particularly affects the skeleton, and the individual would probably have displayed soft-tissue lesions in life. This meant that the effects of leprosy would have been visible, including possible facial paralysis as a result of nerve damage associated with the disease. Genotyping showed he was infected with a type 2F isolate of *M. leprae*, nowadays associated with cases of leprosy from south-central and western Asia.[5] The individual also displayed evidence consistent with *ante-mortem* dental trauma, as well as degenerative and entheseal changes (ligaments and tendons). The cranial morphology and metrics suggested an unusual appearance that showed no affinity with northern European samples but that *might* share some possible physical characteristics with populations in southern Europe or northern Africa.[6] However, we should be cautious as to the limitations of the data. The strontium and oxygen isotope analysis of the individual certainly suggests that they were not local to the chalk geology found in the Winchester region, but the signature could match other parts of southern England.[7] The scientific analysis of carbon and nitrogen isotope from the pilgrim's bone collagen also suggested consumption of a diet rich in animal protein, with some possible marine input. The implications of all of this will be discussed below.

The Pilgrim Token

The burial was accompanied by a scallop shell that was found on the left side of the pelvis and represents the only example of a pilgrim burial with accompanying scallop shell token a British medieval leprosy hospital cemetery though there are a small number of Continental examples for example at Moissac, Bernay and Aachen.[8] The two small holes pierced through the shell (Fig. 11.2) were presumably for attachment to a scrip or pilgrim's bag which no longer survives. Together with the pilgrim's staff and hat, the scrip, which in appearance would have resembled a pouch or wallet, had a symbolic as well as practical function and was often blessed before pilgrimage. The pilgrim badge was one of the three traditional accoutrements of pilgrimage, though in the case of the shell only on the return journey, which also included a staff and a bag, or scrip, such as those excavated from Lichfield and Worcester Cathedrals and Hulton Abbey.[9]

The scallop shell become synonymous with pilgrimage more universally up until the Reformation. However, since 1130, if not earlier, the scallop shell was primarily associated with pilgrimage to the shrine of St James the Great at the Cathedral of Santiago de Compostela, Galicia, Spain.[10] During this period historical documents report that pilgrims from England were increasingly travelling to Compostela to visit

---

[5] Taylor et al. 2013.
[6] Roffey *et al.* 2017.
[7] *Ibid.*
[8] Köster 1985, 129, 132.
[9] Gilchrist 2008, 127.
[10] Cherry 2007, 40.

Fig. 11.2: Scallop Shell from St Mary Magdalen, Winchester. Note small holes for attachment to bag or 'scrip' (author).

the shrine.[11] According to tradition, St James the Great was martyred in Jerusalem in AD 44. In around AD 830 Theodomir, the Bishop of Iria Flavia in Galicia, north-western Spain, allegedly discovered the relics on the banks of the Ulla river and they have been housed in Compostela ever since. According to one legend a vessel carrying the apostle's body to Spain was shipwrecked and when it was washed ashore it was found to be covered in scallop shells. However, the scallop shell's ready availability, via the Galician coastline, and its durability, made it an otherwise suitable token.

Burials with *pierced* scallop shells are generally rare, although a thirteenth-century example was excavated from Winchester Cathedral Green in the 1960s. Other examples of scallop shell burials from England include two individuals from the East Kirk, Aberdeen,[12] Fishergate House, York, dating to the twelfth century, and an example from Wallingford, Oxfordshire, which has been dated to the eleventh century.[13] Further afield, examples have been found at Saint-Denis, France[14] and at Montagne (Gironde, France) in the district called the Libournais, close to Saint-Emilion, which is on the pilgrim route from Paris, and a number of individuals from cemeteries along

[11] Yeoman, 1999, 115.
[12] Roffey *et al.* 2017.
[13] Booth *et al.* 2000, 269.
[14] Wyss and Meyer-Rodrigues 2012.

the pilgrimage route in Spain.[15] Andersson listed forty-one Scandinavian graves that included pilgrim badges, largely comprising scallop shells from Compostela, placed on the chest or arms of males buried in monasteries before *c.* 1400.[16] In Germany, twenty-four examples of scallop shells are recorded from male graves in Baden-Württemberg, dated *c.* 1200.[17]

Context: A Pilgrim's Tale

It is clear from the analysis presented about that the Winchester pilgrim was a young adult male who had some point contracted leprosy, and had seen out the last phase of his life as a resident of the leprosy hospital of St Mary Magdalen, Winchester. We now attempt to fill in the rather large gap concerning his life as a pilgrim and what this may have been like. In this sense it is much like trying to finish a jigsaw puzzle where many of the pieces are not only missing, but they will never be found. We can only guess at the bigger picture from the fragmented pieces that remain. Nonetheless some possibilities can be advanced.

The shrine at Santiago was the only place permitted to distribute scallop shells under pain of excommunication, although 'fake' shells were also thought to have been sold during the medieval period.[18] The scallop shell buried with the Winchester individual can been identified as a specimen of *Pecten maximus*, which is found in Atlantic waters, including along the Galician coast. It is therefore the correct species of shell that would be expected to have been given to a pilgrim who had indeed completed the pilgrimage to Santiago. This veracity of the pilgrim's badge is tangible proof that the individual had conducted the arduous pilgrimage to Santiago. Evidence from the skeleton for degenerative and entheseal changes (ligaments and tendons) suggest trauma caused by intensive physical activity and may further point to a life of pilgrimage and the physical impact of prolonged and intensive periods of long-distance walking. Similar physical injuries can be found today, for example, in certain athletes.

The presence of the scallop shell in the grave also gives us an insight into the pilgrim's religious life and beliefs concerning the afterlife. In light of the relative absence of grave goods in later medieval contexts, the presence of the scallop shell would have a particular eschatological resonance which extended into the afterlife. Importantly it may have also been part of a package including other pilgrim paraphernalia, such as bag, hat and staff, which being organic would not have survived in the archaeological record. This would have been seen as the pilgrim's 'passport to paradise', physical proof of his spiritual endeavour and a potent and powerful symbol of personal salvation.

---

[15] Simonena *et al.* 2010.
[16] Andersson 1989, 141–54.
[17] Haasis-Berner 2003, 274.
[18] Yeoman 1999, 1.

The next question is why Winchester? If the pilgrim was from southern Spain, or Moorish *Al-Andalus* as it was then known (Andalucia), he may have left to avoid religious persecution. However, we must be careful not to go too far beyond the limits of the evidence. Regardless of his origins, and his presence in England, Winchester had one of only handful of leprosy hospitals at this period and we know the pilgrim had the disease. However, by the mid-twelfth century, England had at least 100 leprosy hospitals, if not more. Certainly, if the pilgrim was from the region the hospital at Winchester would have made a practical choice. However, scientific analysis of the skeleton suggests that the individual may not have been of northern European descent and may have had Spanish or North African origins.[19] Furthermore, the presence of the scallop shell indicates that he had made the pilgrimage to Santiago de Compostela and the shrine of St James. Many pilgrims travelled to Compostela in the hope of a cure. Santiago had a documented list of such miracles as mentioned in the *Liber miraculorum*, *Liber Sancti Jacobi* II.[20] It may be possible that the pilgrim had visited Spain in search of a cure. Otherwise, his presence in southern England would not necessarily have been too remarkable. Although the most popular shrines in later medieval England were at Canterbury and Walsingham, Winchester was an important and popular pilgrim centre in its own right, particularly before the early twelfth century during the lifetime of our pilgrim. Indeed, it may possible that the pilgrim was in southern England for this reason. Winchester at this time was a busy and cosmopolitan city. Shrines, religious institutions and hospitals peppered its townscape with the city representing a central place in a pilgrimage landscape.[21] Winchester accommodated important holy relics including those of the saints Birinus, Judoc and Grimbald.

Preeminent of the saints was Swithun, an Anglo-Saxon former bishop of Winchester whose containing popularity in the Anglo-Norman period was evidenced by his reliquary, which by the early twelfth century would have had principal place in the new Norman cathedral. Swithun's relics were contained within the silver-gilt reliquary or *scrinium* that had been given to Old Minster by King Edgar *c.* 973. This sat initially on the high altar and from the 1150s on a special shrine altar at the head of the Romanesque apse. Winchester was only 19 km (12 miles) from the bustling port of Southampton to the south where many pilgrims would have arrived or embarked on pilgrimages overseas. To the north, some two days' journey away was the newly built shrine and mausoleum church of Edward the Confessor in Westminster. A similar journey would bring one to Reading Abbey, which was one of the most important pilgrimage sites in western Europe. By the twelfth century Reading had acquired the hand of St James from the German Imperial Treasury and brought to England by Matilda, daughter of Henry I.[22] Such an acquisition would have been a major draw for pilgrims in the region more widely. Winchester, served by its own important shrines,

---

[19] Roffey *et al.* 2017
[20] Coffey *et al.* 1996.
[21] Roffey 2020.
[22] Cherry 2007, 40.

was thus a key focal point in a wider pilgrim network and consequently would have been an important focus for pilgrim activity. It may be a further possibility that the pilgrim was in southern England to seek healing. The shrines of medieval saints were often associated with miraculous cures and healing, including leprosy. This may have included some of the shrines of southern England. For example, in the mid-twelfth century, the Benedictine monk, Reginald of Durham, writes of a nobleman in southern England who conducted an experiment to determine which of England's main cults would be most likely to cure him of the disease.[23]

Other details of the pilgrim's life can be revealed by the carbon and nitrogen isotope analysis. The high values from a diet rich in animal and some marine protein, suggests that the individual enjoyed a rich diet, which may indicate perhaps that he had a level of social status and means, at least in the years before he arrived at the hospital.[24] Certainly, his relatively young age and the fact that he had the time and support to conduct a pilgrimage may point to this certain status in life. His burial, close to the wall of the chapel, points to a level at a status at a time when proximity to the church was viewed, eschatologically, as spiritually efficacious. One other small detail is that the scallop shell was placed on the left of the pilgrim and was probably attached to a bag that hung here. This would suggest he was right-handed.

Whatever the origins of the pilgrim we know that he had contracted leprosy and that the evidence suggests it was at a fairly advanced stage and would have precipitated physical and likely visual manifestations. Our final question concerns where the pilgrim might have contracted leprosy. The evidence presented above indicates that the pilgrim had suffered from the early onset of the disease, although the disease was probably not the direct cause of death. His pilgrim status may point to the fact that he was a religious man and he therefore might have volunteered his time by working at the hospital and caring for the community. One of traditional Seven Acts of Mercy was caring for the sick, and as a religious man he would have been keenly aware of this and its practical implications. However, due to his age and the fact that the incubation period of the disease can be between 3 to 5 years, it is more likely that the pilgrim had contracted the disease before coming to Winchester. As a pilgrim this further raises the possibility that he had come into contact with a carrier of the disease, possibly asymptomatic, during his travels. Leprosy is only contracted by those who had a predisposing genetic susceptibility, and shrines and pilgrim routes would have attracted a huge and diverse range of people. The shrines and interiors of churches would have busy places and, at times, densely packed with pilgrims and visitors. For example, at Santiago de Compostela, during the eleventh to twelfth centuries, it is estimated that between half a million and two million people visited every year.[25] This could amount to over five thousand pilgrims a day. It is therefore likely that the St Mary Magdalen pilgrim contracted the disease at some point during

[23] Crook 2011, 145.
[24] Roffey *et al.* 2017.
[25] Rahtz and Watts 1986, 52.

his travels before finally coming to Winchester. If he was of Spanish origin, it maybe that his intention was to visit the newly installed relic of St James at Reading, or one of the southern English pilgrimage centres, before the recognition of the disease heralded a more static, albeit short, life within the *leprosarium* at Winchester.

In the end, of course, we will never know the full story of the Winchester pilgrim. However, through a study of the archaeology, in context, we are able to make some conjectures as to how that life *may* have been. Fragments of the pilgrim's life; his status, religious beliefs, travels, illness and death can help create a broad picture. But more than this perhaps – and dare one say more importantly – they pay reverence to a life beyond the science. Rather than a studied death, a commemoration of a life lived.

Acknowledgements

I am grateful to Dr John Crook, Dr Heidi Dawson-Hobbis, Dr Alex Langlands and Dr Kate Weikert for comments on initial drafts. Thanks also go to David Ashby, Phil Marter and Katie Tucker for their work on the excavations of St Mary Magdalen. Special thanks to Greg Campbell for his help in providing research material for this paper.

Bibliography

Andersson, L. 1989. Pilgrimsmärken och Vallfart: medeltida pilgrimskultur i Skandinavien, in *Lund Studies in Medieval Archaeology*, 7. Stockholm: Almqvist and Wiksell International.

Booth, P., Dodd, A., Robinson, M. and Smith, A. 2000. The Archaeology of the Gravel Terraces of the Upper and Middle Thames Valley: AD43–AD1000. Oxford: Oxford University School of Archaeology.

Cherry, J. 2007. The Depiction of St James Compostela on Seals, in S. Blick (ed.), *Beyond Pilgrim Souvenirs and Secular Badges: Essays in Honour of Brian Spencer*, 37–47. Oxford: Oxbow Books.

Coffey, T. F., Davidson, L. K. and Dunn, M. J. 1996. *The Miracles of Saint James: Translations from the Liber Sancti Jacobi*. New York: Italica Press.

Coghill, N. (trans.) 2003. *The Canterbury Tales. Geoffrey Chaucer*. London: Penguin Classics.

Crook, J. 2011. *English Medieval Shrines*. Woodbridge: Boydell Press.

Gilchrist, R. 2008. Magic for the Dead? The Archaeology of Magic in Later Medieval Burials, *Medieval Archaeology*, 52, 119–59.

Gray, T. 1751. *Elegy Wrote in a Country Churchyard*. Facsimile edition, Oxford: Clarendon Press 1927.

Haasis-Berner, A. 2003. *Pilgerzeichen des Hochmittelalters,* Würzburg: F. Konstroffer

Köster, K. 1983. *Pilgerzeichen und Pilgermuscheln von mittelalterlichen Santiagostraßen*. Neumünster: Karl Wachholtz.

Rahtz, P. and Watts, L. 1986. The Archaeologist on the Road to Lourdes and Santiago de Compostela, in L. A. S. Butler and R. K. Morris (eds), The Anglo-Saxon Church: Papers on History, Architecture and Archaeology in Honour of Dr HM Taylor, 51–73. London: Council for British Archaeology.

Roffey, S. 2012. Medieval Leper Hospitals in England: An Archaeological Perspective from St Mary Magdalen, Winchester, *Medieval Archaeology*, 56, 170–180.

Roffey, S. 2020. Charity and Conquest: *Leprosaria* in Early Norman England, in D. M. Hadley and C. Dyer (eds), *The Archaeology of the 11th Century: Continuities and Transformations*, 170–180, Society for Medieval Archaeology Monograph, 38. London: Routledge.

Roffey, S. and Tucker, K. 2012. A Contextual Study of the Medieval Hospital and Cemetery of St Mary Magdalen, Winchester, England, International Journal of Paleopathology, 2, 170–180.

Roffey, S., Tucker, K., Filipek-Ogden, K., Montgomery, J., Cameron, J., O'Connell, T., Evans, J., Marter, P. and Taylor, G. M. 2017. Investigation of a Medieval Pilgrim Burial Excavated from the Leprosarium of St Mary Magdalen Winchester, UK, *PLOS Neglected Tropical Diseases*, January 11:1.

Simonena, C. J., Urmeneta, M. U. and Unzu M. G.-B. 2010. Evidencias arqueológicas sobre la muerte en el Camino de Santiago, *Trabajos de Arqueologia Navarra*, 22, 195–248.

Taylor, G. M., Tucker, K., Butler, R., Pike, A. W. G., Lewis, J., Roffey, S., Marter, P., Lee, O. Y.-C., Wu, H. H. T., Minnikin, D. E., Besra, G. S., Singh, P., Cole, S. T. and Stewart, G. R. 2013. Detection and Strain Typing of Ancient Mycobacterium Leprae from a Medieval Leprosy Hospital, *PLoS ONE*, 8:4, e62406, Available at: doi:10.1371/journal.pone.0062406. (Accessed 26 July 2021).

Wyss, M. and Meyer-Rodrigues, N. 2012. *Saint Denis, A Town in the Middle Ages*. Available at: http://www.saint-denis.culture.fr/en/2_6_pelerin.htm. (Accessed 16 April 2021).

Yeoman, P. 1999. Pilgrimage in Medieval Scotland. London: Historic Scotland/Batsford Ltd.

Chapter 12

The Early Jewish Community in Twelfth-Century Winchester: An Interdisciplinary View

Toni Griffiths

The histories of England's medieval Jewish communities from c. 1066–1290 are significant, both in their own right and as part of the understanding of the political and social history of the region of the time. This chapter focuses on the early Jewish community in Winchester as a substantial element of the communities that made up the city's population during the twelfth century. It highlights the challenges of tracing medieval Jewish settlements in this period and considers what is known about the city's Jews. The following addresses the heritage representation of twelfth-century Jews in Winchester and identifies the impact of interdisciplinary research has contributed valuable insights into this aspect of local history, including archaeology and literary studies. The focus of this chapter on the twelfth century and surrounding periods brings together the evidence for the early Jewish community in Winchester, where other studies of the city have focused on the more materially rich thirteenth century and contextualises it within the wider landscape of Jewish communities in England.

The first medieval Jewish community in England was established in London following the Norman Conquest in 1066. The Jews were granted royal protection in 1070 and other settlements were set up in towns and cities across England from 1130s.[1] Just over two centuries later in 1290, the entire community was expelled by King Edward I and formal Jewish settlements remained absent from England until the mid-1600s. The histories of these communities are significant, both in their own right and as part of the understanding of the political and social history of the region of the time. This chapter focuses on the early Jewish community in Winchester as a substantial element of the communities that made up the city's population during the twelfth century. It highlights the challenges of tracing medieval Jewish settlements in this

---

[1] Mundill 2010, 5.

period and considers what is known about the city's Jews. The following addresses the heritage representation of twelfth century Jews in Winchester and highlights the impact of interdisciplinary research has contributed valuable insights into this aspect of local history, including archaeology and literary studies.[2]

The Jewish communities of England were extensively documented by the state and England was the only country to have set up a separate governmental department specifically designed to control Jewish affairs. Called the Exchequer of the Jews, its intensive record keeping from the late 1190s until the expulsion of England's Jews in 1290 resulted in substantial documentation of the community and its financial and legal dealings.[3] In contrast to this large quantity of documentary evidence, there is a relative lack of built heritage and evidence detailing the everyday life of communities. The impact of this deficit in material evidence is exacerbated by a paucity of written sources for the late eleventh and twelfth centuries, meaning that the intricacies of the footprint of early Jewish settlements remain partially hidden. Thus, the focus of this chapter on the twelfth century and surrounding periods is significant because it brings together the evidence for the early Jewish community in Winchester, where other studies of the city have focused on the more materially rich thirteenth century and contextualises it within the wider landscape of Jewish communities in England.

In recent decades there has been a paradigm shift in the study of medieval Jewish history in England which has enriched the field through increased dialogue between History and other disciplines such as Archaeology, Theology, Art and Literature. This new approach has seen the introduction of new methodologies, collaborative working and a focus on previously underutilised sources to provide new insights into the everyday life, finance and culture of England's medieval Jewish communities.[4] Another contribution to this new approach includes the transition from omission to recognition of previously forgotten narratives within the public sphere, including heritage sites, tourist literature and museums.

Since the publication of the Medieval Jewish Trail walking tour for Winchester in 2015 there has been growing recognition of medieval Jewish history in the public sphere.[5] Before the publication of the trail, Winchester's medieval Jewish history was characterised by many decades of silence. However, the trail provided the impetus for other public-facing initiatives in the city and there have been several projects which have focused on the Jews of Winchester. In 2018 a show called 'Winchester! The First 100,000,000 Years' by the Blue Apple Production Company included the medieval Jews and the Expulsion (1290) in a 'a whistle-stop tour of the city we call "home"'[6] and in the same year *The Licoricia of Winchester Appeal* was established. The latter has since

---

[2] For more on heritage representation of medieval Jewish history in Winchester, see Griffiths and Welch forthcoming.
[3] Mundill 2010, 28.
[4] For example, see Skinner 2003; Rees Jones and Watson 2013.
[5] Welch 2019.
[6] Theatre Royal Winchester 2018.

been crowd funding to raise money to erect a statue outside the Discovery Centre on Jewry Street of the thirteenth-century Jew, Licoricia of Winchester (d. 1277) and her son Asher.[7]

Winchester was a significant centre for trade and finance; it was a major location for the minting of coins and hosted the annual St Giles's fair (31 August–2 September), one of England's largest international markets until the mid-thirteenth century.[8] As such, it was an important location for the establishment of a Jewish settlement, which was one of the earliest Jewish communities outside of London. The first reference to Jews in Winchester was in 1148 in the Winton Domesday Survey II, a survey of the city conducted for Bishop Henry of Blois recorded in the Winton Domesday manuscript. The survey mentions two Jews, Urselin and Deulecreise, with properties in *Scowrtene* Street, now Jewry Street.[9] In 1159 a *donum* was assessed on the Jews of London and ten other provincial communities; all were located in towns in the king's hands and the levy was used to pay for Henry II's campaign in Toulouse (1159–61).[10] From the communities listed, Winchester's Jews now ranked fourth in terms of wealth, equal with Cambridge, after London, Norwich and Lincoln.[11] From 1148 to 1159 the community grew in wealth and status, reflecting the beginning of the significant expansion of Jewish settlements during the reign of Henry II (1154–89), amongst the longest period of relative peace and prosperity for Jews in England. Further indication of Winchester's wealthier Jews during the twelfth century was recorded in 1160, when Gentil, a Jew living in the city, was recorded as having paid a considerable sum of £15 so as not to wed.[12]

As one of the earliest Anglo-Jewish settlements, Winchester was also the location of one of the first Anglo-Jewish cemeteries, after a royal edict was issued by King Henry II in 1177 granting permission for Jews to have burial grounds outside of London.[13] The royal edict was reflective of the longest period of relative peace and prosperity for the Jews, which in turn saw a significant expansion of Jewish settlements. In the same year as the edict a large plot of land was rented from the Priory of St Swithun's in Winchester in the area that is now called Crowder Terrace.[14] It is one of only a few medieval Jewish cemeteries to have been discovered in England and is one of three to have been excavated; the other two were in London and York.[15] Crowder Terrace was excavated in 1974–5 and 1995, and the human remains discovered there were recovered and studied.[16]

---

[7] The Licoricia of Winchester Appeal 2021.
[8] Letters 2013.
[9] Biddle 1976, 101.
[10] Hillaby and Hillaby 2013, 3.
[11] Hillaby 2003, 21; PR 5 Henry II, 3, 12, 17, 24, 28, 35, 46, 53 and 65.
[12] PR 6 Henry II, 50.
[13] Riley 1853, 457.
[14] Keene 1985, 1034.
[15] For London, see Honeybourne 1964 and Grimes 1968. For York, see Lilley *et al.* 1994.
[16] Ottaway and Qualmann 2018.

The human skeletal remains from the site of Winchester's medieval Jewish cemetery were handed over for reburial in March 1996, after 'strong representations from the Jewish authorities'.[17] Prior to reburial preliminary tests and studies were carried out on remains and archaeological reports from the excavations reveal some insight into life during the twelfth and thirteenth centuries.[18] Many of the bones showed signs of rickets (caused by a lack of vitamin D and calcium) and one skeleton shows evidence of a violent encounter; the skull of one man showed two deep cuts to the back of his head from a sharp weapon, possibly a sword. Evidence shows that the man survived for a short while after the attack.[19] The excavations also revealed some unexpected contradictions between medieval and traditional burial customs based on Jewish law; this is also a trend also found in the excavations at York, thus demonstrating that some medieval communities did not conform to standardised practice.[20] Traditional death customs and rituals based on Jewish Law assert that burials should not have any identifying factors of an individual's wealth or status and that all Jews are equal in death.[21] The deceased is expected to be wrapped in 'a simple linen vestment'[22] and placed in a plain coffin 'made of wood, and wooden pegs'.[23] Caskets are buried in consecrated burial grounds, facing west to east,[24] as per the biblical imperative in *Bereishit* 3:19 which states 'For dust thou art, and unto dust shalt thou return'. However, the medieval graves in Winchester demonstrate signs of adaptation to Jewish law and tradition as some were found with metal coffin fixings, rather than wooden pegs. [25] Other graves did not conform to the expected simplicity advocated by Jewish law and contained grave goods including a metal pin and a sea urchin, or echinoid, which was found in one of the graves reserved for children.[26]

In accordance with the royal stipulation that Jewish cemeteries should remain outside of city walls,[27] the burial ground in Winchester was outside the West Gate, bordering the far side of the castle ditch. The location and presence of the castle was significant for protection of the cemetery and for the Jewish community. In many instances, the castle enabled 'the Jews to protect their lives and enable the royal government to protect to protect its investment in those lives'.[28] Originally built by William the Conqueror in 1067, the castle had eight or nine towers, including one in

---

[17] Qualmann 2018a, 221. The human skeletal remains were interred in the Rainsough Jewish Cemetery in Manchester which mainly houses graves of Eastern European Jews from the nineteenth century and their descendants. See Kushner 2009, 107.
[18] Qualmann 2018b, 203.
[19] Strongman 2018, 241.
[20] Discussed further in Griffiths forthcoming.
[21] Lamm 2000, 11.
[22] Kertzer and Hoffman 1996, 257.
[23] Witty 2001, 467.
[24] Heilman 2002, 96.
[25] Qualmann 2018c, 227–32.
[26] *Ibid.*
[27] Riley 1853, 457.
[28] Dobson 2010, 5.

the southern section of the compound known as the Jews' Tower.[29] The tower was integral to the everyday life of medieval Jews in the city and its purpose was multi-faceted, acting as both a place of imprisonment and protection.[30] Zefira Entin Rokéah suggests that the tower was also the place where 'the local archa was kept, and where local cases involving Jews were heard'.[31] However, Vivian Lipman's asserts that the Jews would not have gone into the castle 'for the business of the *archa*, since the latter was not normally kept there'.[32] Indeed, Dean Irwin highlights that this was not the case and 'the *archae* were... physically separate from the royal jurisdiction'.[33] An archa was an official chest with three locks and seals in which Jews were to deposit all deeds and contracts along with a counterpart in order to preserve the records. For every archa there were 'two Christian chirographers and two Jewish chirographers plus one or two clerks'.[34] Winchester was one of the first towns in England to have an archa and it remained in the city until the Jews were expelled from the country in 1290;[35] at the height of the archa system there were twenty-six towns and cities in England with archae/an archa.[36]

The role of the tower as a prison for Jews in Winchester can be seen in an example from 1211 when a Jew known as Isaac the chirographer (of the archa) was incarcerated there for not paying the full amount of a tax, known as the Bristol tallage, imposed on all Jews by King John in 1210.[37] Isaac and his wife (and business partner) Chera were ordered to pay a sum of 5100 marks, over £3340, which was the largest amount for any individual family in the country. This amount demonstrates the significance, wealth and thus importance of Jews such as Isaac and Chera at this time.[38] In 1213 the couple were separated and Isaac was incarcerated in Winchester Castle, whilst Chera was imprisoned in Bristol.[39]

In May 1287 the whole of England's Jewish population was imprisoned to ensure they paid a the large tallage imposed on them by King Edward I. A Jew named Asher or Sweteman, son of the prominent businesswoman, Licoricia of Winchester, left an inscription on the wall of Winchester Castle as a testament to the imprisonment of the Winchester community at this. The caption read 'Day six of Emor were imprisoned all

---

[29] Biddle and Clayre 1983, 15.

[30] Kushner 2009, 101.

[31] Rokeah 2000, 77–8.

[32] Lipman 1981–2, 12.

[33] Irwin 2021.

[34] Brand 2003, 73.

[35] The contents of the archa have largely not survived, the second earliest extant acknowledgement of debt comes from Winchester *c.* 1208: Oxford, Magdalen College Misc. 284. I am grateful to Dean Irwin for his discussions and bringing this to my attention.

[36] Mundill 2013, 148–9.

[37] PR 13 John, 105. For a parallel example of the interconnections between town, castle and Jews in Gloucester, see Hillaby 2001. I am grateful to Emma Cavell for her discussions and for bringing this to my attention.

[38] Bartlet 2009, 28–9.

[39] Hillaby and Hillaby 2013, 389.

the Jews of the land of the isle, in year 47 of the sixth thousand, I Asher inscribed this'.[40] Emor relates to the part of the *Torah* that was read on that Sabbath eve, constituting *Vayikra*, or Leviticus 21:1–24:23 and means the inscription was written on Friday 2 May, 1287. The incarceration of England's entire Jewry is noted by Robin Mundill as representative of 'the last decade of Edward's reign [which] meant confinement or worse' for most Jews[41] and can be understood in retrospect as a potent signal that the King was readying for mass expulsion. An alternative role of Winchester Castle and Jews' Tower as a place of protection during the medieval period can be found in 1265 when only those members of the Winchester Jewish community who managed to reach the safety of the castle survived the attacks on the Jews led by Simon de Montfort the Younger and his men.[42]

Although the Jews' Tower in Winchester Castle was significant for its role as a prison and refuge, no tangible evidence remains of it, and thus mapping its exact location is problematic. In 1251 reference was made in the Close Rolls 'to the door of the Jews' tower' and in 1249 the Sheriff of Hampshire was ordered 'to furnish the Jews' Tower there with a watch-tower and leaden roof... and make a fireplace therein'.[43] Further, the Jews' tower is discussed in academic and public history texts,[44] including a map with the tower's location in the 1983 edition of *Winchester Castle and the Great Hall*, alongside a brief reference in the same text to the relationship between royal authority and the medieval Jewish community as expressed through the castle.[45] However, in 2000 the second edition of the text was published with a smaller plan of the castle. The reduction in size resulted in insufficient space for the names of the castle towers and all medieval buildings; thus they were removed.[46] Beatrice Clayre notes that the forthcoming publication in the Winchester Studies series, *Winchester Castle: Fortress, Palace, Garrison and County Seat*, will once again include mention of the Jews' Tower.[47]

The dual roles of Winchester Castle reflect the complex relationship between Christians and Jews in the city in the period. As was common in medieval England, the Jewish community was not restricted to a ghetto, but clustered in one specific area and lived alongside Christian neighbours, in what Elisheva Baumgarten, Ruth Mazo Karras and Katelyn Mesler describe as a 'near-paradox of simultaneous connection and separation'.[48] Jews in Winchester largely dwelled within close proximity of the castle

---

[40] 'ו. אמר היו תפיסים כל יהודי ארץ האי שנ(ת) מז לפ(רט) לאלף ששי אני אשר הקקתי'. Selden 1640, 215; Tovey 1738, 150; for the original Hebrew see Hillaby and Sermon 2007, 106.

[41] Mundill 2003, 61.

[42] Hillaby and Hillaby 2013, 275.

[43] CLR III, 369 and CLR III, 235–6.

[44] For examples, see Biddle and Clayre 1983, 15; Kushner 2009, 100–2; Mundill 2003, 61; Rokeah 2000, 77–8.

[45] Biddle and Clayre 1983, 15.

[46] Beatrice Clayre 2021, email to Toni Griffiths, 4 January.

[47] Publication forthcoming; Beatrice Clayre 2021, email to Toni Griffiths, 4 January. For the Winchester Studies series, see Martin Biddle's chapter in this volume, pp. 38–9.

[48] Baumgarten *et al.* 2017, 4.

in and around *Scowrtenestret*, or Shoemakers Street.[49] After the expulsion of the Jews in 1290, this street became known as Jewry Street and with the exception of a 'brief [period] from the mid-eighteenth century until 1830 as Gaol Street'[50], it has remained Jewry Street until the present day. There is evidence of Jews living side by side and in occasional close interaction with Christians in the city, for example, the Bishop of Winchester Peter de Roches (d. 1238) entertained some Jews at his castle and Licoricia had a Christian maid servant.[51] Further, during 1189–90 Winchester was among a small number of towns in the south and West where Jewish inhabitants remained unharmed as crusade riots swept across the country, following the coronation of Richard I. The resulting violence led to the murder of many Jews, including the infamous massacre/martyrdom of over 150 members of the Jewish community of York at Clifford's Tower in 1190.

At least one resident of the city, Richard of Devizes, took exception to the presence of the Jewish population in Winchester. Devizes was a monk at St Swithun's Priory and his monastic chronicle covers the early part of King Richard's reign until October 1192. In his narrative of the 1189–90 violence, he seemingly suggests that Winchester was a place of distinct difference in how it treated its Jews, describing it as 'the Jerusalem of Jews in which they enjoyed perpetual peace'.[52] Literal interpretations of Devizes' work, such as those found in some public-facing interpretations of the relationship between Christians and Jews of medieval Winchester, focus on the city as an exceptional place in its role as a safe haven for Jews. For example, Barbara Carpenter Turner notes that one city tour guide, incorrectly, spoke of the 'tolerant religious policy [which] allowed the Winchester Jews in their unenclosed ghetto to live peacefully with their fellow citizens'.[53] However, as Anthony Bale's close reading of Devizes' text reveals, the description of Winchester as the Jerusalem of Jews is not what it at first appears. Bale notes:

> The idea of Winchester being 'the Jerusalem of the Jews' not only teases the city's large Jewish population (and perhaps mocks the financial dealings between churchmen and the Jews) but ironises the body-text, which at this point follows Richard I's lame progress in his journey to Jerusalem. The Jerusalem of the Jews is Jerusalem, whilst Winchester was an ecclesiastical and royal centre for Christians.[54]

Richard of Devizes' *Chronicle* is now commonly accepted as a work of satire 'directed at many aspects of contemporary society'[55] and not as a historical account of

---

[49] For a list of houses owned by Jews, compiled after the Expulsion in Winchester, see The National Archives E 101/249/30.

[50] Kushner 2009, 58.

[51] Bartlet 2009, 16 and 109.

[52] Appleby 1963, 67.

[53] Carpenter Turner 1970, 10.

[54] Bale 2000, 62.

[55] Hillaby and Hillaby 2013, 388.

Winchester's Jewish community. Indeed, utilising the account for such purposes has attracted academic warning; Patricia Skinner highlights the dangers of 'searching for the truth about Jewish life' in literary sources and the need for historians to be 'wary of trying to find the literal in the literary'.[56] The same caution is advised by Bale in the context of interpreting Jewish-Christian relations based on tropes of persecution and victimisation more generally, as he notes that 'Christian narratives of persecution by Jews did not translate simply or seamlessly into the Christian persecution of Jews'.[57] Indeed, Richard of Devizes writes that in 1192 the Jews of Winchester were accused of ritually murdering a child; however, the account is described by Anna Sapri Abulafia as 'an elaborate tale' and is interpreted by Bale as a piece of literary fiction.[58] The Jews of Winchester suffered further and increasingly severe accusations of ritual murder in 1225 and 1232.[59] In total there were 'at least a dozen' such cases in England, the first was in 1144 with the case of William of Norwich.[60]

In Winchester, one of the four Jews accused of ritual murder in 1225 was Abraham Pinch. In 1232 he was charged with another crime and was hanged in 1236 for petty theft.[61] The gallows were erected in Jewry Street, nearby to the synagogue, which was owned by Pinch.[62] Besides its location, little else is known about the synagogue, though its ownership by a patron of the community and placement in the centre of town was typical for the time.[63] There are no architectural remnants of the synagogue. However, in 1968 during excavations at Lower Brook Street, a small lead token or counter was discovered and is described by experts as likely a coin substitute with some commercial or attendance-recording function such as going to the synagogue.[64] The token has been dated between 1180 and 1247 which makes it one of the earliest of its kind.[65] Later lead discs, such as those held in the British Museum (and recently displayed at the London Jewish Museum for the Jews, Money, Myth exhibition in 2019)[66] were used to designate kosher food items, *i.e.* food that conforms to Jewish dietary requirements. The Winchester token is shaped like a short-cross penny with a Hebrew inscription and eleven-pointed star on the front and is one of the very few remaining artefacts relating to Winchester's medieval Jewish community.

The other material remnants of the medieval Jewish community in Winchester are in the form of painted images in the city's cathedral, which has a potent

---

[56] Skinner 2003, 9. For more on the text as satire see Bale 2000.
[57] Bale 2010a, 26.
[58] Abulafia 2014, 177.
[59] Vincent 1992, 128–9.
[60] Stacey 2007, 61.
[61] Hillaby and Hillaby 2013, 399.
[62] Keene 1985, 666.
[63] Mundill 2010, 51.
[64] Archibald and Biddle 2012, 700.
[65] *Ibid.*
[66] British Museum and Jewish Museum London 2019.

connection to the city's medieval heritage, largely through the Christian Church's antisemitic narrative that was at its most vehement in the medieval period.[67] The images in the cathedral's Holy Sepulchre Chapel date from the twelfth century and depict a fresco of Jesus' entombment after his crucifixion and feature a number of Jews in a sensitive manner. The images include a man washing Jesus' legs, wearing a Jewish hat, likely to be Joseph of Arimathea; several portraits of Jews on the archway into the chapel wearing a Jewish cap including one in a blue conical hat (Fig. 12.1); and at least one other portrait of a Jew in a roundel inside the chapel. Christina Welch asserts that the images are not specifically antisemitic in nature and do not portray the Jewish figures negatively.[68] Welch argues that the paintings are either of Church patriarchs or figures central to the resurrection story and are therefore part of the Biblical narrative, which is consistent with the Easter resurrection theme of the chapel.

Welch identifies that each painting in the Holy Sepulchre Chapel depicts the Jewish characters in the same manner as non-Jews, except that the Jews are identifiable by their hats.[69] Conversely, Bale describes them as 'anti-semitic grotesques'.[70] However, there are several arguments employed by Welch and evident elsewhere that support the non-negative nature of the paintings. Firstly, associations with the hat as antisemitic can be discounted, at least during the period that the Holy Sepulchre Chapel images were painted. Leslie Ross notes that the hat was not compulsory for Jews until the Fourth Lateran Council of 1215, when the '*Judenhut* (*pileus cornutus*, pointed hat) ... was specified among the required identifying badges for Jews'; Ross notes that until this point it was a voluntary fashion.[71] Secondly, and perhaps most importantly, Ross highlights that 'the directive of distinguishing Jews by dress was interpreted with some variation in different regions and in England this was a badge of yellow cloth',[72] not a hat as instructed elsewhere in Europe. Thirdly, as Sara Lipton points out, 'the sign of the "Jewish hat" was not inescapably negative and did not necessarily enshrine a sense of utter difference'.[73] Finally, in the twenty-first century, the Cathedral image of the Jew wearing the blue conical hat in the Holy Sepulchre Chapel (see Fig. 12.1) has been adapted and reproduced in cartoon form by a contemporary Jewish community and features as part of the header for the Oxford Jewish Heritage website.[74] The website was established in 2006 by the Oxford Jewish Congregation and one presumes the image would not have been used if the modern group thought or believed it was antisemitic in nature.

---

[67] Ruether 1996.
[68] Welch 2016, 10.
[69] *Ibid.*
[70] Bale 2012, 65.
[71] Ross 1996, 135.
[72] *Ibid.*
[73] Lipton 2014, 45.
[74] Oxford Jewish Heritage 2019.

Fig. 12.1: Wall painting of a Jew wearing a blue conical hat in the Holy Sepulchre Chapel, Winchester Cathedral (photograph © John Crook).

There are two further images of Jews by the Winchester Cathedral community, and these can be found in the Winchester Bible from the twelfth century.[75] These images, though, differ significantly in the representation of the Jewish community than those of the Holy Sepulchre Chapel paintings. The Bible is significant in its size and quality and at the time of writing one volume is on public display in the north transept. Welch highlights that unlike the Holy Sepulchre wall-paintings, the Winchester Bible illustrations depict Jews negatively as Jews are depicted without beards.[76] Welch also asserts that the difference in how the Jews are presented in each example problematises earlier interpretations by Larry Ayres that the images were all produced by the same artist.[77] The presence (or not) of a beard is significant in both Jewish and non-Jewish contexts. In Judaism the beard is seen as a sign of maturity and is described in the Talmud as 'the glory of the face'.[78] Similarly in medieval England it 'could signify maturity and masculinity, nobility and power'.[79] Therefore, Welch asserts that the Jews in the Winchester Bible can be understood as demonstrating both subordination and immaturity; they have, in effect, yet to come to Christ.

[75] Winchester Cathedral Library, Winchester Bible, fol. 131, and Pierpont Morgan Library MS M.619.
[76] Welch 2016, 10.
[77] Ayres 1974, 213.
[78] Babylonian Talmud, Shabbat 152a.
[79] Lipton 1999, 20.

The images of Jews in the Holy Sepulchre Chapel and the Winchester Bible are not mentioned on the Cathedral's website. There is, however, an article on the Cathedral website about the series of images in the Lady Chapel, which features one painting of a Jewish boy on the south wall.[80] The collection of images in the Lady Chapel date from the early sixteenth century and depict the *Legenda Aurea*, or *Lives of Saints*, 'a thirteenth-century compendium of stories that became the standard source of information about saints in the two centuries that followed'.[81] The Jewish boy is portrayed as having been shielded and saved from the flames by the Virgin Mary, after he was thrown into the oven by his father for attending a Christian mass.[82] Such images are not unusual of the time and are similar to those at Eton Chapel.[83] Julie Adams' article on the Lady Chapel paintings acknowledges the image of the Jewish boy in an informative and detailed manner; however, there is no explanation regarding the antisemitic rhetoric of the image itself or the story that accompanies it. The absence of such additional information is complicated by historic insensitivities concerning how the painting was described to the public by cathedral tour guides; the term 'Jew-boy' was used until 1985 and was widely criticised, for example by Jewish visitors, *The Jewish Chronicle* and a Labour MP.[84]

Public access to the Lady Chapel has been intermittent across the years. In 1538, the images were white-washed during the Reformation, but after many years they began to show through again as the white-wash flaked off. In 1901 they were covered with fabric which was removed in 1929 and, finally, they were covered over with wooden hinged boards that now display a copy of the images. It is this version of its history that is available to the public and Adams notes that behind the hinged boards 'there is very little left of the original paint work'.[85] The chapel is open to the public but does not feature in regular tour guides of the Cathedral, although Former Tour Guide Training Manager Phil Ferris notes 'some guides may try to fit it in'.[86] However, Ferris also notes that guides 'are unlikely to home in on such a specific detail' as the image of the Jewish boy.[87]

Another representation of the medieval Jewish communities found in Winchester is in the Retrochoir at the far end of the Cathedral where there is a thirteenth-century sculpture, thought to represent Ecclesia, or the Christian Church. If the identification is correct, this is one half of a pair of statues known as Ecclesia and Synagoga that were placed in cities with thriving Jewish communities to symbolise the superiority of Christianity over Judaism.[88] The statue on display is described on the Cathedral

---

[80] Adams 2017, 12.
[81] Witmore 2007, 29.
[82] Mundill 1998, 53.
[83] Rubin 1999, 18.
[84] Kushner 2009, 98.
[85] Adams 2017, 14.
[86] Phil Ferris, Former Tour Guide Training Manager 2021, email to Toni Griffiths, 1 April.
[87] *Ibid.*
[88] Rowe 2014, 1.

website as having been excavated from the 'grounds headless, armless, and weather beaten' but makes no reference to the other half of the pair, Synagoga.[89] To discuss only one half of the sculpture in this way removes the meaning of the sculptures in the context of the thirteenth century when they were erected, which is described by Joe Hillaby as 'one of violent confrontation'.[90] Further, the importance of discussing the statues as a pair is highlighted by Bale who asserts that 'Ecclesia and Synagoga only gain meaning in relation to each other, and through their mutual likeness'.[91] The absence of a full description was complicated further in 2012 at the annual Lovell Interfaith Lecture held at the Cathedral, by the assertion of Jewish Chaplain Alexander Goldberg that the statue currently on display as 'Ecclesia' could in fact be Synagoga. Goldberg notes that due to its current state, as '[d]ecapitated and armless it is difficult to tell whether the remaining statue is Ecclesia or Synagoga, the two becoming indistinguishable from the other in its current state'.[92] Regardless of if this statue is Synagoga or Ecclesia, its very existence indicates tension between the Jewish and Christian communities in Winchester in the thirteenth century.

In conclusion, tracing the medieval Jewish history of twelfth-century Winchester is not without its challenges. However, the Jews of Winchester were a substantial element of the communities that made up the city's population from the Conquest until 1290. The role of interdisciplinary research, including literary studies, art history and archaeology, has provided crucial glimpses into this aspect of history, revealing the complexities of Jewish and Christian relations, as well as additional insights that have aided new interpretations and impacted how the Jews of Winchester are remembered. Further, public-facing interpretations and projects have played a crucial role in reversing the previous silence surrounding this chapter of history and now have a critical part to play in preserving the local memory of medieval Jewish history in Winchester, whilst highlighting the potential for future research and work in this area.

Abbreviations

CLR   *Calendar of the Liberate Rolls, III: Henry III, 1245–51.* 1937. London: HMSO; Digital General Collection, University of Michigan. Available at: https://quod.lib. umich.edu/cgi/t/text/text-idx c=genpub;idno=ABH6499.0003.001. (Accessed 10 December 2020).

PR   Pipe Rolls Society volumes: *The Great Roll of the Pipe for the 5th Year of the Reign of Henry II*. London: Pipe Roll Society, 1884, repr. 1966; *The Great Roll of the Pipe for the 6th Year of the Reign of Henry II*. London: Pipe Roll Society, 1884, repr. 1966; D. M. Stenton (ed.), *The Great Roll of the Pipe for the 13th Year of the Reign of King John*. London: Pipe Roll Society, 1953.

---

[89] Winchester Cathedral 2020.
[90] Hillaby and Hillaby 2013, 346.
[91] Bale 2010b, 1.
[92] Goldberg 2012.

Bibliography

Manuscripts
London, The National Archives E 101/249/30.
New York, Pierpont Morgan Library MS M.619.
Oxford, Magdalen College Misc. 284.
Winchester, Winchester Cathedral Library Winchester Bible.

Primary sources
Appleby, J. T. 1963. *The Chronicle of Richard of Devizes of the Time of King Richard the First*. London: T. Nelson.
Epstein, I., Kirzner, E. W., Daiches, S., Freedman, H., Simon, M., Slotki, I. W., Shachter, J., Mishcon, A., Cohen, A., Silverstone, A., Lazarus, H., Segal, M., Israelstam, J. and Slotki, J. 1935. *The Babylonian Talmud*; seder Nizikin, translated into English with notes, glossary and indices under the editorship of Rabbi Dr. I. Epstein. London: Soncino Press.
Riley, H. T. 1853. *The Annals of Roger de Hoveden; Comprising the History of England, and of Other Countries of Europe, from A.D. 732 to A.D. 1201*. London: H. G. Bohn.
Selden, J. 1640. *De Jure Naturali et Gentium Juxta Disciplinam Ebraeorum, Libri Septum*. London: Excudebat Richardus Bishopius.
Tovey, D. 1738. *Anglia Judaica or the History and Antiquities of the Jews in England*. Oxford: Oxford Fletcher.

Secondary sources
Abulafia, A. 2014. *Christian-Jewish Relations 1000–1300*. New York: Routledge.
Adams, J. 2017. The Wall Paintings in the Lady Chapel. Available at: http://www.winchester-cathedral.org.uk/wp-content/uploads/The-Wall-Paintings-of-the-Lady-Chapel-second-version.pdf. (Accessed 10 December 2020).
Archibald, M. and Biddle, M. 2012. A Jewish Counter or Token, in M. Biddle (ed.), *The Winchester Mint: and Coins and Related Finds from the Excavations of 1961–71*, 699–704 Oxford: Oxford University Press.
Ayres, L. 1974. The Work of the Morgan Master at Winchester and English Painting of the Early Gothic Period, *The Art Bulletin*, 56:2, 201–23.
Bale, A. 2000. Richard of Devizes and Fictions of Judaism, *Jewish Culture and History*, 3:2, 55–72.
Bale, A. 2010a. *Feeling Persecuted: Christians, Jews and Images of Violence in the Middle Ages*. London: Reaktion Books.
Bale, A. 2010b. *The Jew in the Medieval Book: English Antisemitisms 1350–1500*. Cambridge: Cambridge University Press.
Bale, A. (2012) Richard of Devizes and Fictions of Judaism, *Jewish Culture and History*, 3, (2), 55–72.
Bartlet, S. 2009. *Licoricia of Winchester: Marriage, Motherhood and Murder in the Medieval Anglo-Jewish Community*. London: Vallentine Mitchell.
Baumgarten, E., Mazo Karras, R. and Mesler, K. 2017. Introduction, in E. Baumgarten, R. Mazo Karras and K. Mesler (eds) *Entangled Histories: Knowledge, Authority, and Jewish Culture in the Thirteenth Century*, 1–22. Philadelphia: University of Pennsylvania Press.
Biddle, M. (ed.) 1976. *Winchester in the Early Middle Ages: an edition and discussion of the Winton Domesday*, Winchester Studies, 1. Oxford: Clarendon Press.
Biddle, M. and Clayre, B. 1983. *Winchester Castle and the Great Hall*. Winchester: Hampshire County Council.
Brand, P. 2003. The Jewish Community of England in the Records of English Royal Government, in P. Skinner (ed.), *Jews in Medieval Britain: Historical, Literary and Archaeological Perspectives*, 73–84. Woodbridge: Boydell Press.
British Museum. n.d. Kosher seal; food label. S.44. Available at: https://www.britishmuseum.org/collection/object/H_S-44_1. (Accessed 19 November 2020).

Carpenter Turner, B. 1970. *The Pictorial History of Winchester: In Ancient Times the Royal Capital of England*. London: Pitkin Pictorials.

Dobson, R. B. 2010. *The Jewish Communities of Medieval England: The collected essays of R. B. Dobson*. York: The Borthwick Institute, University of York.

Goldberg, A. 2012. *Lovell Interfaith Lecture, Winchester Cathedral: From Disputation to Dialogue*. Available at: https://web.archive.org/web/20170502173029/http://www.alexgoldberg.eu/wpblog/?p=231. (Accessed 10 December 2020).

Grimes, W. F. 1968. *The Excavation of Roman and Medieval London*. London: Routledge and Kegan Paul.

Heilman, S. C. 2002. *When a Jew dies: The Ethnography of a Bereaved Son*. Berkeley: University of California Press.

Hillaby, J. 2001. Testimony from the Margin: The Gloucester Jewry and its Neighbours, *c.* 1159–1290, *Jewish Historical Studies*, 37, 41–112.

Hillaby, J. 2003. Jewish Colonisation in the Twelfth Century, in P. Skinner (ed.), *The Jews in Medieval Britain: Historical, Literary, and Archaeological Perspectives*, 15–39. Rochester, New York: Boydell Press.

Hillaby, J. and Hillaby, C. 2013. *The Palgrave Dictionary of Medieval Anglo-Jewish History*. London: Palgrave Macmillan.

Hillaby, J. and Sermon, R. 2007. Jacob's Well, Bristol: Further Research, *Bristol & Avon Archaeology*, 22, 97–105.

Honeybourne, M. 1964. The Pre-Expulsion Cemetery of the Jews of London, *Transaction of the Jewish Historical Society*, 20, 145–59.

Irwin, D. A. 2021. Acknowledging Debt in Medieval England: A Study of Medieval Anglo-Jewish Moneylending Activities, 1194–1276, unpublished thesis, Canterbury Christ Church University.

Jewish Museum London 2019. *Jews, Money, Myth*. Available at: https://jewishmuseum.org.uk/exhibitions/jews-money-myth/. (Accessed 19 November 2020).

Keene, D. 1985. *Survey of Medieval Winchester. Parts 1, 2 and 3*. Oxford: Clarendon Press.

Kertzer, M. N. and Hoffman, L. A. 1996. *What is a Jew?* New York: Touchstone.

Kushner, T. 2009. *Anglo-Jewry Since 1066: Place, Locality and Memory*. Oxford: Manchester University Press.

Lamm, M. 2000. *The Jewish Way in Death and Mourning*. New York: Jonathan David Publishers.

Letters, S. 2013. *Online Gazetteer of Markets and Fairs in England and Wales to 1516*. Available at: https://archives.history.ac.uk/gazetteer/gazweb2.html. (Accessed 10 December 2020).

Lilley, J. M., Stroud, G., Brothwell, D. R. and Williamson, M. H. 1994. *Archaeology of York: V.12: The Medieval Cemeteries: Fasc. 3: The Jewish Burial Ground at Jewbury*. York: Council for British Archaeology.

Lipman, V. D. 1981–82. Jews and Castles in Medieval England, *Transactions of the Jewish Historical Society of England*, 28, 1–19.

Lipton, S. 1999. *Images of Intolerance: The Representation of Jews and Judaism in the Bible Moralisée*. London: University of California Press.

Lipton, S. 2014. *Dark Mirror: The Medieval Origins of Anti-Jewish Iconography*. New York: Metropolitan Book/Henry Holt and Company.

Mundill, R. R. 1998. *England's Jewish Solution: Experiment and Expulsion, 1262–1290*. Cambridge: Cambridge University Press.

Mundill, R. R. 2003. Edward I and the Final Phase of Anglo-Jewry, in P. Skinner (ed.), *Jews in Medieval Britain: Historical, Literary and Archaeological Perspectives*, 55–72. Woodbridge: Boydell Press.

Mundill, R. R. 2010. *The King's Jews: Money, Massacre and Exodus in Medieval England*. London: Continuum.

Mundill, R. R. 2013. The 'Archa System' and its Legacy after 1194, in S. Rees Jones, and S. C. Watson (eds), *Christians and Jews in Angevin England: The York Massacre of 1190, Narratives and Contexts*, 148–62. York: York Medieval Press.

Ottaway, P. and Qualmann, K. (eds) 2018. *Winchester's Anglo-Saxon, Medieval and Later Suburbs: Excavations 1971-86*. Winchester: Hampshire Cultural Trust.

Oxford Jewish Heritage 2019. *The Jewish Pointed Hat*. Available at: https://www.oxfordjewishheritage. co.uk/news-events/news/330-the-jewish-pointed-hat. (Accessed 10 December 2020).

Qualmann, K. 2018a. Mews Lane, in P. Ottaway and K. Qualmann (eds), *Winchester's Anglo-Saxon, Medieval and Later Suburbs: Excavations 1971–86*, 218–23. Winchester: Hampshire Cultural Trust.

Qualmann, K. 2018b. Crowder Terrace, in Ottaway, P. and Qualmann, K. (eds) *Winchester's Anglo-Saxon, Medieval and Later Suburbs: Excavations 1971–86*, 203–17. Winchester: Hampshire Cultural Trust.

Qualmann, K. 2018c. The Jewish Cemetery: Grave Catalogue, in P. Ottaway and K. Qualmann (eds) *Winchester's Anglo-Saxon, Medieval and Later Suburbs: Excavations 1971–86*, 227-32. Winchester: Hampshire Cultural Trust.

Rees Jones, S. and Watson, S. C. (eds) 2013. *Christians and Jews in Angevin England: The York Massacre of 1190, Narratives and Contexts*. York: York Medieval Press.

Rokeah, Z. E. (ed.) 2000. *Medieval English Jews and Royal Officials: Entries of Jewish Interest in the English Memoranda Rolls, 1266–1293*. Jerusalem: Magnes Press.

Ross, L. 1996. *Medieval Art: A Topical Dictionary*. London: Greenwood Publishing Group.

Rowe, N. 2014. *The Jew, the Cathedral and the Medieval City: Synagoga and Ecclesia in the Thirteenth Century*. Cambridge: Cambridge University Press.

Rubin, M. 1999. *Gentile Tales: The Narrative Assault on Late Medieval Jews*. New Haven: Yale University Press.

Ruether, R. 1996. *Faith and Fratricide: The Theological Roots of Anti-Semitism*. Eugene, OR: Wipf and Stock.

Skinner, P. (ed.) 2003. *Jews in Medieval Britain: Historical, Literary and Archaeological Perspectives*. Woodbridge: Boydell Press.

Stacey, R. 2007. 'Adam of Bristol' and Tales of Ritual Crucifixion in Medieval England, in B. Weiler, J. Burton and P. Schofield (eds), *Thirteenth Century England XI: Proceedings of the Gregynog Conference, 2005*, 1–15. Woodbridge: Boydell Press.

Strongman, S. 2018. Assessment of Human Remains from Mews Lane, in P. Ottaway and K. Qualmann (eds), *Winchester's Anglo-Saxon, Medieval and Later Suburbs: Excavations 1971–86*, 239–241. Winchester: Hampshire Cultural Trust.

The Licoricia of Winchester Appeal 2021. *The Licoricia of Winchester Appeal.* Available at: https:// licoricia.org/. (Accessed 10 March 2021).

Theatre Royal Winchester 2018. *Winchester! The First 100,000,000 Years.* Available at: http:// blueappletheatre.com/winchester-the-first-years. (Accessed 26 November 2020).

Vincent, N. 1992. Jews, Poitevins, and the Bishop of Winchester, 1231–1234, in D. Wood (ed.), *Christianity and Judaism*, 119–132. Oxford: Blackwell.

Welch, C. 2016. Putting Jewish Medieval Winchester on the Tourist Map, *Shemot: The Jewish Genealogical Society of Great Britain*, 24:1, 8–11.

Welch, C. 2019. *Medieval Jewish Winchester*. 2nd edition. Available at: https://www.visitwinchester. co.uk/listing/medieval-jewish-trail/#download. (Accessed 6 November 2020).

Winchester Cathedral. 2020. Medieval Sculpture: Ecclesia. Available at: https://www.winchester-cathedral.org.uk/our-heritage/art-architecture/medieval-sculpture-ecclesia/. (Accessed 22 May 2021).

Witmore, M. 2007. *Pretty Creatures: Children and Fiction in the English Renaissance*. New York: Cornell University Press.

Witty, R. 2001. *Exploring Jewish Tradition: A Transliterated Guide to Everyday Practice and Observance*. New York: Toronto Doubleday.

Chapter 13

Henry of Blois and an Archbishopric of Winchester: Medieval Rationale and Anglo-Saxon Sources

Alexander R. Rumble

There were two failed attempts by Bishop Henry of Blois (1129–71) to raise Winchester to metropolitan status. While Henry had personal reasons for trying, the fifteenth-century historian Thomas Rudborne gave a cogent argument upon which such a claim might be made: Birinus, first bishop of the West Saxons, had been commissioned by the pope and had a better claim to be the second archbishop in England than Paulinus of York who was appointed by Augustine. Bishop Henry could well have used the same argument. A portfolio of evidence to support the claim would have probably included extracts not only from hagiographical sources but also from certain forged Anglo-Saxon charters which describe Birinus's role in the conversion of Wessex and refer to Winchester as the capud *of its church. Copies of these charters are prominent in the* Codex Wintoniensis, *the cartulary produced for Bishop Henry. Two other documents therein concern the status of Canterbury and York and record the division of the West Saxon sees by Edward the Elder. Discussion of the make-up of the projected archbishopric and its possible effects conclude the chapter.*

According to slightly later written sources, Bishop Henry of Blois (1129–71) tried on two occasions to gain papal approval for the raising of the diocese of Winchester to metropolitan status, that is, to make Winchester into an archbishopric with authority over a number of dioceses in the south of England. A fifteenth-century Winchester monk also contemplated such a promotion and gave a cogent reason to support it. The same reason may well have been the basis of the twelfth-century case, though unrecorded at that time and hitherto not surmised by modern commentators.[1] The present paper will discuss both the possible rationale behind Bishop Henry's claim

---

[1] Cf. Morey and Brooke 1965, 159: 'We do not know what was the basis of Henry's plan that Winchester should become the seat of an archbishop'. I owe this quotation and some other pertinent references to the anonymous reviewer of this chapter.

for the promotion of his see and his probable use of Anglo-Saxon texts as evidence. It will also briefly consider some likely effects on the geography and politics of the English church had the claim succeeded.

Context and Chronology

The general historical context in which Bishop Henry's promotional attempts occurred was one of fluidity and controversy. There were frequent changes of pope at Rome with much interference by the Holy Roman Emperors and there was dissension within the church between the Cluniacs and the Cistercians. In the political sphere in England, this was the period of the so-called Anarchy, with civil war between Henry's brother King Stephen and his cousin the Empress Matilda and the latter's son Henry (subsequently Henry II). There were also several ongoing disputes over the authority of the archbishop of Canterbury (relating to York, London and the Welsh sees), as part of a wider debate about the power and status of metropolitans within the church in Britain and Ireland,[2] a somewhat similar debate to that which also occurred in other parts of western Europe at this time (see below). Against this background, two separate attempts appear to have been made by Bishop Henry to persuade the papacy to change the see of Winchester into an archdiocese. Both entailed journeys to Rome to pursue his case in person in the papal curia. However, despite his efforts, his metropolitan ambitions ended in failure.

Bishop Henry's first bout of lobbying occurred in a visit to Rome between 1143 and 1145. What is known of his itinerary places him at Cluny in the winter of 1143–4 but back in London in the summer of 1145.[3] His mission was made difficult by the high turnover of popes at this particular time, there being four in office between 24 September, 1143 and 15 February, 1145 (Innocent II, Celestine II, Lucius II and Eugenius III).[4] Although in the late-twelfth-century *Abbreviationes chronicorum* of Ralph de Diceto, dean of St Paul's in London, Lucius II is reported to have sent Henry a pallium via the legate Ymar of Tusculum, it was yet to be handed over when Lucius died in February 1145 and so was invalidated.[5] According to the same source, Henry was to have had seven bishops below him.[6] This visit to Rome was recorded too (under the year 1143) in the thirteenth-century Winchester Annals, which claimed both that the abbey of Hyde was to be made into a bishopric and that the diocese of Chichester was to be subject to Henry.[7] The annalist was also of the opinion that

---

[2] Haddan and Stubbs 1869–79, Vol. 1, 302–452; Knowles 1951, 47–8, 160–2; Southern 1958; Richter 1973, lviii–xcvi.

[3] Winchester Acta, 218–19.

[4] Kelly 1986, 167–73.

[5] Diceto, Vol. 1, 255. Similar invalidation was applied in 1145 to the pallium sent for the archbishop of York: Cronne 1970, 58.

[6] Diceto, Vol. 1, 255.

[7] Luard 1865, 53. It may be significant in connection with this annal that in 1145 Bishop Seffrid of Chichester was deprived for unknown reasons: Knowles 1951, 25. Note that Knowles (1966, 288) was mistaken in saying that there were intended to be only six suffragans.

the scheme grew out of dissension between Bishop Henry and the Archbishop of Canterbury. In the fifteenth century, the Winchester chronicler Thomas Rudborne stated that Pope Lucius had sent a pallium in 1142. In a significant aside, he claimed that the seven proposed subordinate bishops had formerly belonged to the kingdom of the West Saxons.[8]

Bishop Henry's second attempt at an archdiocese was also unsuccessful. This was in 1149–50, during the papacy of Eugenius III, but was subsequently reported in the Winchester Annals under the year 1151.[9] Henry's mission was doomed on this occasion because of the opposition to him at Rome from the Cistercian faction there, his time being eroded by the necessity first to clear himself of accusations made against him by his rivals (including the abbot of Hyde), and to explain his non-attendance at a papal synod.[10] Otherwise, it is a distinct possibility that Henry's case for a metropolitan, if backed by the right faction in the church, might have been accepted at this time. Eugenius III (1145–53) divided Ireland between four metropolitan sees.[11] His legate Nicholas Breakspear (afterwards Hadrian IV, the only English pope to date) reformed the church in Scandinavia, establishing Trondheim as the metropolitan see for Norway.[12] On the other hand, the bishop of Dol's attempt to acquire metropolitan status over Brittany had been stopped by Lucius II in 1144 who restored authority over the region to the archbishop of Tours.[13]

Bishop Henry's Purpose

There can be no doubt that Henry of Blois had strong personal reasons for trying to increase the authority of Winchester within the English church. It is unsurprising that he sought higher ecclesiastical status for himself through the elevation of his see. Born *c.* 1090, his royal blood made him part of the European elite. He was the grandson of William I (through the latter's daughter Adela), the nephew of William Rufus and Henry I, the brother of Stephen and the cousin of Matilda.[14] He had already enjoyed varied ecclesiastical positions in plurality. He may have been prior of Montacute in 1120,[15] before being made abbot of Glastonbury from 1126 and bishop of Winchester from 1129 (both until his death). He was the dean of St Martin le Grand in London from 1139 to *c.* 1160[16] and dean of Waltham Abbey (perhaps from 1141 to

---

[8]   Wharton 1691, I, 285–6.
[9]   Luard 1865, 54–5.
[10] Luard 1865, 54–5; Chibnall 1956, 79 (lacking dates: but see discussion, *ibid.* app. 1, at 91–4); Winchester Acta, xlv–xlvii.
[11] Kelly 1986, 173.
[12] *Ibid.*, 174.
[13] *Ibid.*, 171.
[14] For accounts of his life, see Knowles 1966, 286–93 and Winchester Acta, xxxv–xlix; also Voss 1932.
[15] Winchester Acta, xxxv.
[16] *Ibid.*, nos. 68–78.

1144).[17] He founded St Cross hospital outside Winchester[18] and endowed the hospital of St Mary Magdalen,[19] and at times administered the vacant sees of London, Salisbury and Chichester. Although a professed monk of Cluny, his career was entirely set in England, firstly at the court of Henry I, subsequently (until the break in 1139) at that of Stephen and later at that of Henry II. He acted as vicar at Canterbury during the vacancy of 1136–8.[20] He was reported by Orderic Vitalis to have been the successful (but papally vetoed) candidate for the primacy in 1136.[21] Subsequently he often found himself in disagreement with the actual appointee, Archbishop Theobald of Bec (1138/9–61); to his satisfaction though, Henry held the higher authority while he was papal legate (between 1 March, 1139 and 24 September, 1143).[22] Significantly, his first attempt at archiepiscopal status for Winchester was begun directly after the lapse of his legatine authority on the death of Innocent II. It cannot be denied that such status would have given him, and his successors in office, a considerable amount of exemption from the direct jurisdiction of the archbishop of Canterbury. Nevertheless, another aspect of his plan for a metropolitan see may have been a real desire to impose a tighter structure upon the church in southern England for the greater efficiency of its spiritual mission. By all accounts, Henry possessed a very forceful personality – note his political and military actions during the civil war, particularly during 1141, the year of the siege of Winchester[23] – but in addition was someone with a consistent appreciation of both administrative detail and the value of written records. This interest in administration is reflected in surviving documents relating to most of the major churches with which he had a connection,[24] besides in the commissioning of the 1148–9 survey of property and rents in the city of Winchester.[25] His actions resulted in the improved management and defence of church property,[26] as well as in precisely defined or reformed rules for particular institutions. A *libellus* of *c.* 1140 describes his abbatial rescue of Glastonbury from financial distress,[27] while *Cod.Wint. I* (1129×39), the earliest section of the *Codex Wintoniensis*, survives as a contemporary testimony to his efforts as recently-appointed bishop of Winchester to investigate the pre-conquest archives of his diocesan church in order to safeguard

---

[17] *Ibid.*, xxxv–vi and no. 122.

[18] *Ibid.*, nos. 133–4.

[19] See above, p. 215–24.

[20] Knowles 1966, 288.

[21] OV, VI, 479.

[22] Knowles 1966, 288.

[23] Cronne 1970, 118–34; Winchester Acta, xlv. For discussion of the amount of damage caused during the siege, see Biddle and Keene 1976, 297–9, 318–19, 322–3.

[24] As noted by Knowles 1966, 290.

[25] Survey II (13v–32v) in the *Liber Wintoniensis* (London, Society of Antiquaries 154; Winchester, s. xiimed); Barlow 1976, 18, 69–141.

[26] He was instrumental in forcing his brother King Stephen to grant to the English church the 1136 charter of liberties (*RRAN*, no. 271); Cronne 1970, 125–8; Rumble 1982, 157–8.

[27] Winchester Acta, 204–13.

its ancient territorial endowment.[28] A constitution was created for the hospital of St Cross founded by him in 1129×32,[29] and that of St Martin le Grand was reformed by him in 1158.[30] During visits to his *alma mater* of Cluny he organised a survey of rents[31] and also loaned sums of money from his personal wealth.[32] A partial reorganisation of urban parishes within Winchester in 1142 suggests an appreciation of the geographical aspects of the Christian mission,[33] evident on a larger scale in his scheme for a new archdiocese discussed in the present chapter.

The Rationale of Winchester's Archiepiscopal Claim

Although mainly fuelled in the twelfth century by Bishop Henry's personal ambition and goals, his claim for enhanced status for the see of Winchester can still, it seems to me, be accorded a high degree of justification. In the fifteenth-century, Thomas Rudborne, a monk of St Swithun's,[34] put forward a coherent argument upon which a Winchester case might be made, in book two, chapter two of his *Historia maior Wintoniensis*.[35] I translate this as follows:

> We respectfully pose a most worthy question to readers, with the tolerance of those who hear it, so that ill will does not reprove the thoughts and understanding of the questioner but that the respectful proposition of the questioner might crave indulgence. Since the primate of any province is said by Florence [in 'Flowers of History', book 2, chapter 18][36] to be the

---

[28] London, British Library Add. 15350 (Winchester, s. xii1–s. xivmed); Davis 2010, no. 1042. For a full analysis, see Rumble 1980. For the date and purpose of *Cod.Wint. I*, see Rumble 1982, 153–62.

[29] Winchester Acta, nos. 133–4.

[30] *Ibid.*, no. 76.

[31] Bernard and Bruel 1894, no. 4143 (1149×56, ?1155).

[32] Winchester Acta, no. 38 (31 December, 1148 × 25 March, 1150). See also Voss 1932, 108–19.

[33] Biddle and Keene 1976, 300 and 493.

[34] Greatrex 1997, 731. For Rudborne's historical works, see Gransden 1982, 394–8; Crook 2003.

[35] 'Quæstionem dignissimam piè legentibus proponimus cum supportatione eorum qui audiunt, ut non invidia mentes intellectusque objurget moventis, sed pia motio indulgentiam postulat interrogantis. Numquid cum Primas alicujus Provinciæ dicatur per Florentium in Florario historiali lib. 2. cap. 18. eo quod primitus Provinciam illam per Regnum illud vel Provinciam aliquam in Regno ad fidem convertit Christianam; sedes Wyntoniensis Ecclesiæ sedes sit Angliæ primaria? Augustinus primus Anglorum Apostolus immediatè à beato Gregorio in Angliam missus pro tunc adhuc Britanniam dictam nec immeritò Primas totius Angliæ dicitur, quia partem aliquotam Gentis illius in propriâ personâ salutaris undæ lavacro perfudit, & primus, anno Domini DXCIV. Ad Eboracensem verò Provinciam ipse Augustinus Monachus Paulinum, unum ex suis commonachis, destinavit; qui Gentem illam convertit ad Fidem; & ille Paulinus, quamvis non immediatè à Papa, sed mediatè summi Pontificis Legato, fuerit directus, ipse tamen propter causam prætactam & successores sui in sede Eboracensi nomine & dignitate Primatis, ac Apostolicæ Sedis Legati funguntur. Cur ergo Wyntoniensis Episcopus eodem non gaudet Privilegio? Nam beatus Birinus primus Gewyseorum Episcopus non mediante Papæ Legato, sed immediatè .XLI. anno post adventum beati Augustini missus est à beato Papâ Honorio, ut residuam Angliæ partem permaximam quidem, quam Augustinus inconversam reliquerat, Fidei signaculo insigniret. Mirum ergo videtur hanc moventi quæstiunculam, cur non Primatis nomine & dignitate cum privilegio Wentani Pontifices sicut & cæteri Anglorum Primates quàm gloriosè præpolleant.' Wharton 1691, I, 190–1. A brief note of Rudborne's argument was made by Gransden 1982, 398.

[36] If this refers to Florence (*i.e.* John) of Worcester as quoted by Matthew of Westminster (Matthew Paris),

first who converted to the Christian faith this or that province in a particular kingdom, should not the see of the church of Winchester be a primatial see of England? Augustine, the first apostle of the English, having been sent to England [then called Britain] directly by the blessed Gregory, is worthily called the primate of all England, because in A.D. 594 he himself first bathed a certain part of that race with the baptism of healing water. The same monk Augustine indeed chose Paulinus, one of his fellow monks, for the province of York, who converted that people to the faith; and this Paulinus and his successors in the see of York, although not appointed directly by the pope but through the mediation of a legate of the supreme pontiff, because of the aforementioned reason have operated with the name and dignity of a primate and a legate of the apostolic see. Why therefore does the bishop of Winchester not enjoy the same privilege? Assuredly the blessed Birinus, first bishop of the Gewisse[37] was sent, not through the mediation of the pope's legate, but directly by the blessed Pope Honorius in the forty-first year after the arrival of the blessed Augustine, so that he might mark with the sign of the faith the remaining part of England, the great part indeed of which Augustine had left unconverted. It seems extraordinary to the one posing this simple question: why are the bishops of Winchester not distinguished with the name, dignity and privilege of a primate as the other primates of the English so gloriously are?

Rudborne's reasonable contention was that, since Birinus, the first bishop of the West Saxons, had been sent to Britain as a missionary bishop direct from the pope, Winchester had a better claim to be second archbishopric in England rather than York whose first bishop Paulinus had been sent by the pope simply as a minister, with others, to assist Augustine of Canterbury. As Bede records,[38] Paulinus was only consecrated as a bishop after some time in England, by Augustine's successor Archbishop Justus in 625, before journeying to Northumbria with the Kentish princess Æthelburh who was to marry King Edwin. In contrast, Birinus had been consecrated at Genoa in Italy by Archbishop Asterius of Milan and had arrived in England in 634/5 already possessing episcopal status.[39] I suggest that Bishop Henry may well have used the same argument about Birinus as was later employed by Rudborne, though specific details of his case for an archdiocese of Winchester are not recorded in twelfth-century sources.

The spiritual authority of Birinus as the founder of Christianity among the West Saxons was very soon appropriated by the church of Winchester from the primary foundation at Dorchester-on-Thames. After his death in c. 650, his relics were taken from Dorchester to Winchester Cathedral by Bishop Hædde in c. 690.[40] According to William of Malmesbury, Birinus was subsequently accounted the patron of the city (after God).[41] The relics in Winchester Cathedral were translated again (perhaps on 4 September, 980) by Æthelwold and once more (with others including those of

---

Rudborne may have made use of the manuscript which is now Oxford, Bodleian Library Laud Misc. 572 (Winchester cathedral priory, s. xiv); Ker 1964, 201.

[37] For the etymology of the name Gewisse, used of the West Saxons, see Coates 1991, 1–3.

[38] Bede, *HE*, ii.9, 164–5.

[39] Bede, *HE*, iii.7, 232–3; Love 1996, 10–11 (§ 5).

[40] Bede, *HE*, iii.7, 232–3; Love 1996, 44–5 (§ 21).

[41] *patronus ciuitatis post Deum habetur*: *Gesta pontificum*, ii. 75.7, vol. 1, 250.

Hædde) in 1150.[42] A life of Birinus (the *Vita S. Birini*) was composed at Winchester at the end of the eleventh century.[43] It was a work of hagiography with no factual information other than that already disseminated by Bede. It added an account of two miracles said to have been performed by Birinus: one of them where he walked on water (§§11–12) and the other the curing of a woman who was both blind and deaf (§§15–16).[44] Michael Lapidge agreed with Rosalind Love that the *Vita S. Birini* was most probably composed by the same anonymous author as both the *Vita S. Swithuni* and the *Miracula S. Swithuni*,[45] but dated it slightly more precisely to between 984 and *c.* 1100.[46] As Lapidge demonstrated in detail, there appears to have been a specific linking of the cults of Birinus and Swithun at Winchester in the late Anglo-Saxon period, Bishop Æthelwold having translated the relics of Swithun in 971 and those of Birinus *c.* 980. The *Narratio metrica de S. Swithuno*, composed by Wulfstan the Cantor in the 990s, links the relics of the two saints when describing the second dedication of the Old Minster on 20 October 980: 'Here lies that holy apostle Birinus, who washed these western peoples with baptism. Mighty in miracles, Swithun too rests here in body; he brings relief to the entire populace with his prayers'.[47] The same Wulfstan created a hymn honouring Birinus.[48] In a joint prayer possibly composed by Bishop Æthelwold, Birinus is referred to as having provided a foundation for Christian belief, while Swithun added 'the fiery building-stones of his miracles'.[49] A Winchester troper, from *c.* 1000, includes a sequence with a joint commemoration.[50]

Reconstructing the Twelfth-century Portfolio of Evidence

I suggest that Bishop Henry's portfolio of written evidence to take to Rome in support of his argument for an archbishopric of Winchester would have contained at least three different elements: extracts from hagiographical narratives, quotations from Anglo-Saxon title-deeds and references to English synodal decrees. Copies of apposite material (translated from the vernacular into Latin where necessary) would have been worked up into a formal legal brief in order to pursue the case in the papal curia.

---

[42] Lapidge 2003, 272, n. 99; Love 1996, lxi; Luard 1865, 54. Nevertheless, the Augustinian canons of Dorchester claimed still to have the saint's relics in 1224 and a marble shrine was erected there in 1320: Love 1996, lxxiii–iv; Crook 2016, 227–8 and 266–7.

[43] For edition and translation, see Love 1996. For the date, see *ibid.*, l and lvi–lx.

[44] *Ibid.*, lii–liii, lxv–lxvi, 20–7, 30–5.

[45] *Ibid.*, liv–lviii; Lapidge 2003, 611–12, 641–2.

[46] Lapidge 2003, 612.

[47] *Ibid.*, 392–3 (lines 265–6):

> *Qua uir apostolicus iacet almus et ille Birinus*
> > *has lauacro gentes qui lauit occiduas.*
> *Signipotens in ea pausat quoque demate Suuiðhun*
> > *qui precibus cunctum subleuat hunc populum.*

[48] Love 1996, lxix–lxx; Lapidge 2003, 340.

[49] *eiusdem ... igneos miraculorum lapides*: Lapidge 2003, 135–6.

[50] Cambridge, Corpus Christi College 473, 130rv (Winchester, Old Minster, s. x/xi); Lapidge 2003, 94–6.

Hagiography

A careful selection of extracts from Bede's *Historia ecclesiastica* would have formed the essential starting-point for the portfolio, to remind (or inform, in some cases) those at Rome of the reported facts about Augustine's mission to England in the late sixth century and his foundation of the primatial see of Canterbury.[51] A suitably edited version of Bede's account of the later mission of Birinus to the West Saxons would also be required, stressing both the encouragement received from Pope Honorius I and his episcopal status before arrival in England.[52] Bede's representation of him as the first bishop of the whole kingdom of Wessex and (a modified) reference to the deposition of his body at the church of SS Peter and Paul in Winchester could also have been shown to be very relevant to the metropolitan claim. It is likely, however, that in addition to Bede, use would have been made of the more recent and particular *Vita S. Birini*, which described his life in hagiographical style and formulation and alluded both to the saint's two miracles and to the continued location of his relics at Winchester.[53] The extra importance of Winchester Cathedral as the site of many miracles associated with the resting-place of the relics of Swithun, a saint of international significance, would certainly have been stated in the portfolio. While there were in existence the extensive and scholarly tenth-century works composed by Lantfred and Wulfstan,[54] it may be more likely that the two abbreviated texts about Swithun composed by the same author as the *Vita S. Birini* would have been preferred for the purpose of the portfolio, particularly if they all happened to be in the same manuscript.[55] The congruence of literary style between the three texts would surely have been a factor in favour of their joint employment.[56]

Quotations from Anglo-Saxon Title-deeds

Anglo-Saxon title-deeds forged at Winchester Cathedral in late tenth or early eleventh century, in the time of Bishop Ælfheah II, portrayed Birinus as the missionary who had converted the seventh-century West Saxon kings Cynegils and Cenwealh in the early days of Christianity amongst the English. The origin of the very basic information provided in these passages was probably a manuscript of Bede's *Historia ecclesiastica* (see above), but it was modified both to imply that Cenwealh was converted by Birinus, rather than while in exile among the East Angles, and to exclude Dorchester from the account while highlighting the importance of the church of Winchester. Thus, one of these charters refers to Winchester as the 'chief-place' ('*capud*') of the West Saxon

---

[51] It is not possible to say whether the manuscript of the *Historia ecclesiastica* used in this regard was Winchester Cathedral 1 (?Old Minster, s.x/xi; Bede, *HE*, l–li; Ker and Piper 1992, 578–9). The marginal reference (45v) to the acquisition of the relics of Birinus is fourteenth century.

[52] Bede, *HE*, iii.7, 232–3.

[53] Love 1996, 20–7 (§§ 11–12), 30–5 (§§ 15–16) and 44–7 (§ 21).

[54] Lapidge 2003, *passim*.

[55] Such a manuscript is not recorded, but two from *c.* 1100 contain both the *Vita S. Birini* and the *Vita S. Swithuni*, see *ibid.*, 612.

[56] On the style of the anonymous author, see Love 1996, l–lx; Lapidge 2003, 611–12, 641–2.

church and none mentions Dorchester. S 376, a forgery recording Edward the Elder's alleged renewal in 909 of the cathedral's tenure of Chilcomb, includes the following passage: '…just as formerly by my ancestors Cynegils and Cenwealh and many of their successors was devoutly granted and restored, in confirming I renew… the estate which surrounds the city, which was granted to the blessed Peter and his coapostle Paul *in the beginning of the Christian religion when the venerable Bishop Birinus was preaching*'.[57] S 821, Edgar's alleged confirmation of Downton (in Wiltshire) and Chilcomb, is much more expansive about the period of the conversion, but was probably influenced in its agricultural imagery by Bede's reference to Birinus as having, in the presence of the pope, 'promised that he would scatter the seeds of the holy faith in the remotest regions of England':[58]

> Which freedom indeed, spread by apostles through the whole world, was directed by the grant of the Lord's indulgence to the West Saxons through the preaching of *St Birinus*. The aforementioned bishop indeed first caused the king called Cynegils to be reborn in the font of baptism, then [the king called] Cenwealh, [each] having been instructed in the rudiments of faith; which [latter] king indeed nobly built a church in the place Winchester and had it dedicated to the venerable Trinity and the indivisible Unity and also to the blessed Peter, the foremost of the apostles, and his fellow apostle Paul; and, founding an episcopal see therein, he enriched it with goods given him by God. From that beginning therefore, the plentiful cornfield of faith having been watered by the bathing of baptism, the tares of paganism gradually disappearing, it sprouted and grew; which [faith], swelling as corn in the Lord's granary, accumulates ceaselessly to this day by the grace of the Lord with an extensive return for the Church's labourers throughout Wessex. Wherefore I, Edgar… desiring to renew, enrich with the same freedom… so that *the chief-place of our church of the West Saxons and the starting-place of our religion* should in no way be deprived of any substance of its share.[59]

Two other charters in the name of Edgar continue the pseudo-history. Thus S 817, concerning Chilcomb: 'I have also ordered that this renewal should endure to the

---

[57] …*uti olim ab antecessoribus meis Cynegislo atque Cynepalho. multisque eorum successoribus deuote tradita atque restaurata fuerant confirmans renouarem… terram quæ undique adiacet ciuitati quæ in exordio Christianæ religionis Birino uenerabili episcopo predicante. beato Petro eiusque coapostolo Paulo concessa fuerat.* OMW 50, CW 190: quoted here from the single-sheet (in an imitative script) which was the exemplar for the cartulary-copy: London, British Library Harley Charter 43. C. 1, s. x/xi.

[58] *promittens… se… in intimis ultra Anglorum partibus… sanctae fidei semina esse sparsurum*: Bede, *HE*, iii.7, 232–3.

[59] *Quę uidelicet libertas, in totum per apostolos dilata\ta/ orbem, Domini annuente clementia ad Uuest Seaxan sancto predicante Birino directa est. Prefatus equidem pontifex primo regem Cynegislo, deinde Cynepealh, nuncupatum, fidei rudimentis imbutum, baptismatis fonte regenerauit, qui uidelicet rex ęcclesiam Uuintonia ilico pulchrę edidit reuerendeque Trinitati ac indiuiduę Unitati necnon beato Petro apostolorum principi eiusque coapostolo Paulo dedicare fecit, cathedramque episcopalem inibi constituens, bonis a Deo sibi collatis locupletans uberrime ditauit. Inde itaque primum copiosa fidei seges paulatim pereunte gentilitatis lolio baptismatis lauacro irrigata, pu\l/lulans secreuit, quę Domini gratia per totam Occidentalem Saxoniam ęcclesię cultoribus sata granaria Domini multiplici reditu repplendo, usque in hodiernum diem incessabiliter accumulat… Hinc ego Eadgar… renouare cupiens eadem dito libertate… ut nostrę Occidentalium Saxonum ęcclesię capud nostręque religionis exordium nullatenus \aliqua/ suę portionis priuaretur substantia.* Rumble 2002, 106–7: OMW 142, CW 26.

end in that same freedom in which I have learnt it was given by my ancestors and forefathers and by all my antecedent kings, of whom the first were King Cynegils and his son King Cenwealh who granted possession of the same estate to the aforesaid minster of the holy place, *when the holy Bishop Birinus was preaching the Word of God at the beginning of the Christian faith.'*[60] Similarly, S 814, relating to Alresford: 'Indeed the pious king called Cenwealh, having been instructed in the sacraments of faith by *Bishop Birinus*, granted the same estate with great devotion of spirit to the aforementioned church of God *at the beginning of the Christian religion.'*[61]

Reading the text of these charters of Edgar in particular may have been the trigger for Bishop Henry's plan for the promotion of his see to an archbishopric which would serve the former kingdom of Wessex. Transcripts of them are prominent in *Cod.Wint. I*, S 821 being the first document in this primary section of the *Codex Wintoniensis*. As such, it was supplied with a notable inhabited initial and a long rubric. It would definitely have caught the bishop's attention on even a cursory inspection of the cartulary which he had almost certainly commissioned. It headed the transcription of a pre-existing dossier of charters, probably put together in the time of Bishop Ælfheah II to commemorate the Edgarian refoundation of the Old Minster, that included S 814 and 817.[62] Charters forged in the name of other kings, including both Edward the Elder (S 376, above) and Æthelstan, may have been used for the twelfth-century portfolio of evidence, but S 821 is very unlikely to have been omitted. Two alleged charters of Æthelstan, whose texts were the work of one individual in the first half of the eleventh century,[63] may have been included if a link were thought needed between the time of Edward the Elder and that of Edgar. S 393, concerning Downton, used the phrase 'even as King Cenwealh established and strengthened, *whom St Birinus the first bishop of the Saxons baptized'.*[64] S 443, confirming two appurtenances belonging to the estate of Taunton (in Somerset, which had probably been acquired in 904),[65] included a quotable affirmation of the status of the church of Winchester: it claimed to have been issued so that 'for the peace of the kingdom and the salvation of the nation, the church of Winchester which is justly *the chief of the churches built in the provinces of the West Saxons* should possess eternal freedom, respect and foremost lordship for ever'.[66]

---

[60] *Hanc quoque renouationem in ipsa eademque libertate fine tenus perdurare iussi qua illam ab auis et atauis et ab omnibus regibus antecessoribus meis donatam esse comperi, quorum primi extiterunt Cynegils rex et filius eius Cynepalh rex, qui in exordio Christianę fidei sancto Birino episcopo uerbum Dei predicante concesserunt eiusdem ruris possessionem ad prefatum sancti loci monasterium.* Rumble 2002, 110; OMW 143a, CW 27. The vernacular version of this (OMW 143b, CW 28) mentions Cynegils and Cenwealh, but not Birinus.

[61] *Nam rex religiosus Cynepalh nuncupatus, a Birino pontifice fidei sacramentis imbutus, idem rus in Christiane religionis exordio prefatę Dei ęcclesię magna animi largitus est deuotione.* Rumble 2002, 117; OMW 145, CW 30.

[62] Rumble 2002, no. 5; OMW 142–54; CW 26–39.

[63] Both were composed by the same draftsman as S 439 (OMW 64, CW 228), Æthelstan's alleged renewal of the beneficial hidation of Chilcomb.

[64] *quemadmodum Cyneuualh rex, quem sanctus Byrinus primus Saxonum episcopus baptizauit, instituit et corroborauit.* OMW 62, CW 42.

[65] S 373 and 1286; OMW 44–5, CW 118 and 62.

[66] *pro pace regni et gentis salute ęcclesia Uuentana quæ caput est ecclesiarum ęquæ in Occidentalium Saxonum*

Synodal Documents

Two other documents in the *Codex Wintoniensis*, of a different diplomatic category, are certainly of direct relevance to the metropolitan claim and may well have been acquired specifically to support it. These occur one after the other within the first part of *Cod.Wint. II*, being (from the date of the script of the copyists) additions to the *Codex* effected during the episcopate of Bishop Henry.[67] They are two of the only three documents in the cartulary as a whole which are not relevant to the cathedral landholdings.[68] They both claim to record decisions made at church synods which had a significant effect on the number and organisation of dioceses in Anglo-Saxon England. The first of these synodal records was forged at Canterbury in the ninth century but claims to emanate from the council of Hatfield under Archbishop Theodore in AD 680. This text concerns the respective status of the archbishops of Canterbury and York and the number of English bishops (twelve) intended to be under the authority of each.[69] The cartulary's exemplar may possibly have been taken or copied from the Canterbury archive during the vacancy in 1136–9 when Henry of Blois had control of the archdiocese as vicar.[70] The second document is a record of the division of the kingdom of Wessex, by Edward the Elder in 909, into five sees (where previously had been only two)[71] and the consecration by Archbishop Plegmund of Canterbury of seven bishops in one day (for the West Saxon sees of *Winchester, Ramsbury, Sherborne, Wells, Crediton* as well as for those of *Dorchester* and the *South Saxons*).[72] Although this text contains several serious anachronisms, most of its core information may be true. Of its content, we may particularly note the reference to Plegmund's visit to Rome to gain prior approval from Pope Formosus. Compare also the consecration of seven bishops here with the assertion made by Thomas Rudborne (and earlier Ralph de Diceto) that seven bishops were proposed to be put under Henry of Blois as archbishop,[73] Rudborne stating that they had formerly belonged to the kingdom of the West Saxons.[74] There are two principal later recensions of this record, which was probably forged at Crediton in the second half

---

prouinciis construuntur eternam libertatem et reuerentiam et dominationem principalem sine fine possideat. OMW 67, *CW* 56: quoted here from the single-sheet (in an imitative script) which was the exemplar for the cartulary-copy: London, British Library Cotton Charter viii. 17, ? s. xi1.

[67] They were copied on 112r by scribes *d,e* and *f*: Rumble 1982, 164–5.

[68] The third being Eadwine's testimony describing an agreement between the Old and New Minsters (S 1428: Rumble forthcoming, appendix 2.3; *CW* 232).

[69] The 'Pseudo-Hatfield' (S 1428a: Rumble forthcoming, appendix 2.1; *CW* 213). For analysis and dating, see Cubitt 1999, 1244–88.

[70] Knowles 1966, 288.

[71] The diocese of the West Saxons had been divided between Winchester and Sherborne *c.* 705: Bede, *HE*, v. 18, 514–15. Some reference would presumably also have been made to this in the portfolio.

[72] The Plegmund Narrative, dated 905 for 909 (S 1451a: Rumble forthcoming, appendix 2.2; *CW* 214). See Rumble 2001, 238–44; with translation, *ibid.*, 238–9.

[73] Diceto, Vol. 1, 255; Wharton 1691, I, 285.

[74] Note that John of Salisbury's contemporary statement that Henry wished to become 'archbishop of western England' (Chibnall 1956, 78) had merely described the area in geographical rather than historical terms.

of the tenth century,[75] and the Winchester version differs from that of Canterbury.[76] It is possible that the Winchester text was brought to the area in the mid-eleventh century by Bishop Lyfing of Cornwall and Devon and was later appropriated from Hyde Abbey by Bishop Henry, who administered the abbey during a prolonged vacancy after the death of Abbot Osbert in 1135.[77]

Although most of the documents here suggested to have been contained in Bishop Henry's portfolio can in modern times be demonstrated to be forgeries created in the Anglo-Saxon period, it is unlikely that this would have been discernible in the twelfth century and, all in all, his case could have been a strong one in contemporary terms – stronger still if indeed it had anticipated the argument which was later put forward by Rudborne. A stress on the status of Birinus as the successful papal missionary to the West Saxons would doubtless have been gratifying to the papacy, as would reference to the seeking of papal authority for past diocesan reforms.

The Projected Archbishopric of Winchester

The new archbishopric was, it appears, envisaged as one intended to have jurisdiction over, and to serve the needs of, central southern and south-western England (*i.e.* the former West Saxon kingdom, together with sees serving the South Saxons and Cornwall).[78] Besides *Winchester* itself (covering most of Hampshire, Surrey and the Isle of Wight), there were plans for seven subordinate bishoprics to be included within a potential archdiocese. These might have comprised the following: *Salisbury* (for Wiltshire); *Bath* (for Somerset); *Exeter* (for Devon); *St Germans* (for Cornwall); *Sherborne* (for Dorset, if retrieved from Salisbury); also *Chichester* (for Sussex);[79] in addition, according to the Winchester Annals,[80] a new diocese for the lands of the abbey of *Hyde*. The last one would have excluded these lands from the diocese of Winchester and may have been proposed by Bishop Henry in order to circumvent expected opposition to his plan from the abbot of Hyde. As with the arrangement instituted by Edward the Elder, there seems to have been a close, but not absolute, congruity with secular, shire boundaries. We may note that some changes within these bishoprics had already been made in the eleventh century, entailing the moving of particular cathedrals to nearby major urban centres. Thus, the episcopal centre for Crediton moved to Exeter (1050); Selsey to Chichester (1075); Ramsbury to Sherborne

---

[75] London, British Library Add. 7138, s. x2, is a single-sheet text of the record whose origin is probably Exeter or Crediton: Rumble 2001, 241.

[76] Rumble forthcoming, commentary to appendix 2.2.

[77] Knowles *et al.* 1972, 82; Biddle and Keene 1976, 319. Note King Cnut's grant of Abbots Worthy, near Winchester, to Lyfing in 1026 (S 962: OMW 186, *CW* 175). Lyfing's personal archive is discussed in the introduction to Rumble forthcoming.

[78] For the geographical context, cf. Hill 1981, maps 238 and 240.

[79] This diocese may have been annexed by the bishops of Winchester at one point in the pre-conquest period, see Kelly 1998, 90–1. It was quite a poor benefice and had been held in plurality with the abbacy of the New Minster by Bishop Æthelgar (980–8).

[80] Luard 1865, 53 (s.a. 1143).

(1058), then to Salisbury (*i.e.* Old Sarum, 1078); and Wells to Bath (between 1088 and 1090).[81] However, these changes probably did not affect the diocesan boundaries as established in the early tenth century.

Had Bishop Henry's scheme been successful it would have had a number of lasting effects on both the internal politics of the English church and the status of the city. For example, the creation of a new diocesan boundary between Winchester and Hyde would have decreased the size and revenue of the former. There would also have been a considerable diminution in both the size and direct jurisdiction of the archdiocese of Canterbury, though it would still have had overall primacy in England and Wales. A further consequence would have been a relative reduction in the status of the archbishop of York. On the other hand, alongside its existing significance as the centre of the cult of St Swithun, the city of Winchester could have enjoyed an even greater symbolic position for the people of southern England resulting from the continual advertisement of its alleged central role in the conversion of Wessex to Christianity by Birinus. This would have attracted more visitors and trade, with some compensation for the ever-growing dominance of London.

Conclusion

Aspects of Henry of Blois's claim for metropolitan status may be illuminated by referring both to Anglo-Saxon documents copied in the twelfth century and to the opinion of Thomas Rudborne in the fifteenth. Employment by Bishop Henry of pre-conquest documents to support his case would be a good example of the pragmatic use of historical records in the twelfth century.[82] Although anachronism needs always to be avoided, I hope to have illustrated that study of an historical event may sometimes be helped by widening the date-range of texts consulted and thus avoiding too narrow a temporal focus. The opinions of later medieval chroniclers such as Rudborne, though often biased in favour of their own institutions, might either reflect their knowledge of earlier records which have not survived or indicate a lasting oral tradition within a community, founded at least partly on fact.

Abbreviations

Bede, *HE*   Colgrave, B. and Mynors, R. A. B. (eds) 1969. *Bede's Ecclesiastical History of the English People*, OMT. Oxford: Clarendon Press.

CW   Number of charter in Rumble, A. R. 1980. The structure and reliability of the *Codex Wintoniensis* (British Museum Addition MS 15350: the cartulary of Winchester cathedral priory), 2 vols., unpublished PhD thesis, University of London.

---

[81] Crosby 1994, 32–3.
[82] Southern 1970, 160–2; Gransden 1974, 273–4.

Diceto   Stubbs, W. (ed.) 1876. *Radulphi de Diceto, decani Lundoniensis, Opera
                           historica: The Historical Works of Master Ralph de Diceto, dean of London*,
                           RS 68. London: HMSO.
Gesta pontificum   Winterbottom, M. (ed. with the assistance of R. M. Thomson) 2007.
                           William of Malmesbury, Gesta pontificum Anglorum: *The History of
                           the English Bishops*, OMT. Oxford: Clarendon Press.
OMT   Oxford Medieval Texts
OMW   Number of charter in Rumble, A.R. (ed.) forthcoming. *Charters of
                           the Old Minster, Winchester*, Anglo-Saxon Charters. London: British
                           Academy, Oxford University Press.
OV   Chibnall, M. (ed.) 1968–80. *The Ecclesiastical History of Orderic Vitalis*,
                           6 vols., OMT. Oxford: Clarendon Press.
RRAN   Cronne, H. A. and Davis, R. H. C. 1968. *Regesta Regum Anglo
                           Normannorum, 1066–1154*, vol. 3. Oxford: Clarendon Press.
RS   Rolls Series
S   Sawyer, P. H. 1968. *Anglo-Saxon Charters: an Annotated List and
                           Bibliography*, Royal Historical Society Guides and Handbooks, 8.
                           London: Royal Historical Society. Updated version available at
                           https://esawyer.lib.cam.ac.uk. (Accessed 23 July 2021).
Winchester Acta   Franklin, M. J. (ed.) 1993. *Winchester 1070–1204*, English Episcopal
                           Acta, 8. London: British Academy, Oxford University Press.

Bibliography

Manuscripts

Cambridge, Corpus Christi College 473.
London, British Library Add. 7138.
London, British Library Add. 15350.
London, British Library Cotton Charter viii. 17.
London, British Library Harley Charter 43. C. 1.
London, Society of Antiquaries 154.
Oxford, Bodleian Library Laud Misc. 572.
Winchester, Winchester Cathedral 1.

Primary Sources

Barlow, F. (ed. and trans.) 1976. The Winton Domesday, in M. Biddle (ed.), *Winchester in the Early
    Middle Ages: An Edition and Discussion of the Winton Domesday*, Winchester Studies, 1, 1–141. Oxford:
    Clarendon Press.
Bernard, A. and Bruel, A. (eds) 1894. *Recueil des chartes de l'abbaye de Cluny*, Vol. 5, *1091–1210*, Collection
    des documents inédits sur l'histoire de France. Paris: Imprimerie Nationale.
Chibnall, M. (ed. and trans.) 1956. *The Historia pontificalis of John of Salisbury*, Nelson's Medieval
    Texts. London: Thomas Nelson and Sons.
Greatrex, J. 1997. *Biographical Register of the English Cathedral Priories of the Province of Canterbury c.
    1066 to 1540*. Oxford: Clarendon Press.
Haddan, A. W. and Stubbs, W. (eds) 1869–79. *Councils and Ecclesiastical Documents relating to Great
    Britain and Ireland*, 3 vols. Oxford: Clarendon Press.

Kelly, S. E. (ed.) 1998. *Charters of Selsey*, Anglo-Saxon Charters, 6. London: British Academy, Oxford University Press.

Lapidge, M. 2003. *The Cult of St Swithun*, Winchester Studies, 4:ii. Oxford: Clarendon Press.

Love, R. (ed. and trans.) 1996. *Three Eleventh-Century Anglo-Latin Saints' Lives: Vita S. Birini, Vita et miracula S. Kenelmi, Vita S. Rumwoldi*, OMT. Oxford: Clarendon Press.

Luard, H. R. (ed.) 1865. *Annales monasterii de Wintonia (AD 519-1277)*, Annales monastici, RS 36:2, 1–125. London: HMSO.

Morey, A. and Brooke, C. N. L. 1965. *Gilbert Foliot and his Letters*. Cambridge: Cambridge University Press.

Richter, M. (ed.) 1973. *Canterbury Professions*, Canterbury and York Society, 67. Torquay: The Devonshire Press.

Rumble, A. R. 1980. The Structure and Reliability of the *Codex Wintoniensis* (British Museum Addition MS 15350: The Cartulary of Winchester Cathedral Priory), 2 vols., unpublished PhD thesis, University of London.

Rumble, A. R. 2002. *Property and Piety in Early Medieval Winchester: Documents relating to the Topography of the Anglo-Norman City and its Minsters*, Winchester Studies 4:iii. Oxford: Clarendon Press.

Rumble, A. R. (ed.) forthcoming. *Charters of the Old Minster, Winchester*, Anglo-Saxon Charters. London: British Academy, Oxford University Press.

Wharton, H. (ed.) 1691. *Anglia sacra, sive Collectio historiarum ..., de archiepiscopis et episcopis Angliæ, a prima fidei Christianæ susceptione ad annum MDXL nunc primum in lucem editarum*, 2 vols. London: Richard Chiswell.

Secondary Sources

Biddle, M. and Keene, D. J. 1976. Winchester in the Eleventh and Twelfth Centuries, in Biddle, M. (ed.) 1976. *Winchester in the Early Middle Ages: An Edition and Discussion of the Winton Domesday*, Winchester Studies, 1 , 241–448. Oxford: Clarendon Press.

Coates, R. 1991. On Some Controversy Surrounding *Gewissae / Gewissei, Cerdic* and *Ceawlin, Nomina*, 13 (for 1989–90), 1–11.

Cronne, H. A. 1970. *The Reign of Stephen: Anarchy in England 1135-54*. London: Weidenfeld and Nicolson.

Crook, J. 2003. Thomas Rudborne, in Lapidge, M. *The Cult of St Swithun*, Winchester Studies, 4:ii, 165–76. Oxford: Clarendon Press.

Crook, J. 2016. *English Medieval Shrines*. Woodbridge: Boydell Press.

Crosby, E. U. 1994. *Bishop and Chapter in Twelfth-Century England: A Study of the* Mensa Episcopalis. Cambridge: Cambridge University Press.

Cubitt, C. R. E. 1999. Finding the Forger: an Alleged Decree of the 679 Council of Hatfield, *English Historical Review*, 114, 1217–18.

Davis, G. R. C. 2010. *Medieval Cartularies of Great Britain and Ireland*, revised by C. Breay, J. Harrison and D. M. Smith. London: The British Library.

Gransden, A. 1974. *Historical Writing in England, i: c. 550-c. 1307*. London: Routledge and Kegan Paul.

Gransden, A. 1982. *Historical Writing in England, ii: c. 1307 to the Early Sixteenth Century*. London: Routledge and Kegan Paul.

Hill, D. 1981. *An Atlas of Anglo-Saxon England*. Oxford: Basil Blackwell.

Kelly, J. N. D. 1986. *The Oxford Dictionary of Popes*. Oxford: Oxford University Press.

Ker, N. R. 1964. *Medieval Libraries of Great Britain: A List of Surviving Books*, second edition, Royal Historical Society Guides and Handbooks, 3. London: Royal Historical Society.

Ker, N. R. and Piper, A. J. 1992. *Paisley–York*, Medieval Manuscripts in British Libraries, 4. Oxford: Clarendon Press.

Knowles, D. 1951. *The Episcopal Colleagues of Archbishop Thomas Becket*, Ford Lectures (Oxford, 1949). Cambridge: Cambridge University Press.

Knowles, D. 1966. *The Monastic Order in England: A History of its Development from the times of St Dunstan to the Fourth Lateran Council 940-1216*, 2nd edition. Cambridge: Cambridge University Press.

Knowles, D., Brooke, C. N. L. and London, V. C. M. (eds) 1972. *The Heads of Religious Houses: England and Wales 940-1216*. Cambridge: Cambridge University Press.

Rumble, A. R. 1982. The Purposes of the *Codex Wintoniensis*, in R. A. Brown (ed.), *Proceedings of the Battle Conference on Anglo-Norman Studies 1981*, 4, 153–66, 224–32. Woodbridge: Boydell Press.

Rumble, A. R. 2001. Edward the Elder and the Churches of Winchester and Wessex, in N. J. Higham and D. H. Hill (eds), *Edward the Elder 899-924*, 230–47. London: Routledge.

Southern, R. 1958. The Canterbury Forgeries, *English Historical Review*, 73, 193–226.

Southern, R. 1970. The Place of England in the Twelfth-Century Renaissance, in *Medieval Humanism and Other Studies*, 158–80. Oxford: Basil Blackwell.

Voss, L. 1932. *Heinrich von Blois, Bischof von Winchester (1129-71)*, *Historische Studien*, 210. Berlin: Emil Ebering.

Chapter 14

Swithun in the North: A Winchester Saint in Norway

Karl Christian Alvestad

This paper briefly examines the veneration of the ninth-century Winchester bishop St Swithun in Norway throughout the centuries. By taking a chronological and at times historiographical view, this paper demonstrates that there is still some uncertainty surrounding the establishment of the cult of St Swithun in Norway. Among the competing origin points of the veneration is both an eleventh-century context where English bishops and missionaries were active in Norway, as well as the more traditional view of Bishop Reinald of Stavanger as the person who introduced the saint from Winchester. Beyond this, the paper has highlighted that St Swithun's mass 'Syftesok' on 2 July was an important date in the agricultural calendar throughout Norway from the fifteenth to the eighteenth century. The modern re-discovery of Swithun in the nineteenth century caused the saint became both a religious and civic symbol in Stavanger, demonstrating the longevity and change in Swithun's role in Norway.

Introduction

As the twentieth century dawned in Norway, the Norwegian state and church, as well as significant aspects of the Norwegian cultural landscape, continued its late nineteenth century trend of revisiting the medieval past to explore and shape the national self. Cultural reclamation of the historical past of a nation or territory was not an exclusively Norwegian trend in this period. Andrew Wawn and Patrick Geary, among others, have demonstrated how this was, and to some extent still is, part of the wider Western cultural tradition, and they have shown how this was a particularly popular trend in the nineteenth century. Part of this trend led the ecclesiastical and intellectual elite of Norway to interact with the pre-Reformation cults of saints, and especially those cults that had been popular in Norway in the Middle Ages.[1] Among the consequences of this trend was the 're-discovery' and promotion of native Norwegian saints as historical individual and symbols of local Christian virtue that linked local

---

[1] Wawn 2000; Geary 2002.

churches to the conversion and Christianisation of Norway at the end of the Viking Age. A further result of this linking was the identification of patron saints for episcopal sees in Norway. For the majority of the bishoprics, the saints selected were native saints, such as Hallvard in Oslo, Olav in Trondheim and Sunniva in Bergen. Like Oslo, Bergen and Trondheim (see Fig. 14.1 for locations), the Bishopric of Stavanger also returned to its medieval dedication, namely the ninth-century bishop of Winchester, St Swithun.

The medieval link between Stavanger and Swithun has received some excellent attention from Michael Lapidge in his 2003 book, *The Cult of St Swithun.*[2] In his extensive coverage and examination of the cult of St Swithun, Lapidge sheds light on the evidence for the cult of St Swithun in Norway, but recent scholarship in Norway has cast doubt on some of Lapidge's conclusions. Lapidge's book focuses on the surviving traces of the medieval cult and does not consider, perhaps justifiably, the post-medieval 'cult' and presence of Swithun. This is a general pattern in Lapidge's book, but in this instance it is a particularly important issue for this paper, as the discussions of Swithun in Norway cannot be complete on the basis of the surviving medieval materials, a point I will return to. Consequently, in this chapter I will attempt to illuminate both the ongoing state of scholarship regarding St Swithun in Norway in the medieval period alongside some evidence for the traces of the cult of St Swithun which are rarely considered when discussing his popularity and significance. I will also briefly consider why Swithun became popular in Norway and the problems surrounding seeking an answer for this question. The chapter will conclude by outlining the current cultural resonance of Swithun and Winchester in modern Norway.

This broad coverage stems from three overarching questions: when did the cult of Swithun arrive in Norway, what role has Swithun played in Norway and what role does he continue to play? The inspiration for these questions lies in the growing scholarship on the saints such as cult of St Olaf in Britain,[3] and an acknowledgement that we have yet to see a similar scholarly development in Norway. It should be acknowledged that some developments are under way, especially with regards to the studies of cults from a local history perspective, but broader scholarly surveys and detailed scholarship has yet to be produced. This does, in part stem, from the degree of survival in Norwegian sources, and the domination of political history in the Norwegian historical tradition, which is a theme to which I will return to in this chapter. The questions for this paper also stem from a wider consideration of the impact England had on religious life in Norway following its conversion and throughout its Christianisation.[4] It should be stressed that I am not arguing that Christianity only arrived in Norway from England, but it is important to acknowledge and consider Swithun in the light of this narrative and as an extension of the cultural impact of England, Wessex and Winchester at various times in Norwegian history and culture.

---

[2] Lapidge 2003.
[3] Alvestad 2020; Higham 2020.
[4] Abrams 1995.

As indicated above, the state of preservation of sources from or about medieval Norway, and especially about the religious life in Norway, is a crucial factor that impacts this study and all other studies of religious life in medieval Norway. The truth of the matter is that the document survival in Norway is very poor, fragmented and insufficient to gain a comparatively good overview of religious life in medieval Norway. Scholars are therefore reliant on fragmentary documents, as well as those few complete texts that do survive, such as letters, diplomas and documents collected in the *Diplomatarium Norvegicum* and *Regesta Norvegica*, as well as *Heimskringla* and other saga texts, the Gulathing and Frostating Laws, the national laws of Magnus Lagabøte, the *Old Norwegian Homily Book*, *Breviarium Nidrosiense* and *Missale Nidrosiense*, just to name a few. Of these, only the last three texts are explicitly religious in nature and cast direct light on the religious life in medieval Norway. Among the surviving materials, there is a trend in that more recent ones survive to a greater extent than older ones, and documents concerned with legal or political matters are more likely to be preserved than those concerning religious matters. This degree of survival imposes significant limitations on what can and cannot be concluded about the religious life in medieval Norway. Thus, this paper and other research into this subject have some significant methodological challenges when it comes to examining early Christian history in Norway, especially as an interdisciplinary approach offers limited conclusions about the immaterial traditions and culture in this period.

Swithun, Winchester and Stavanger: Setting the Background

In *The Cult of St Swithun*, Michael Lapidge presented the results of thirty years working on the Swithun's cult and hagiography, arguing that Swithun was 'one of the best-known and widely culted Anglo-Saxon saints, both in England and on the Continent.'[5] Following on from this, he acknowledges that little is known about Swithun's earthly life. Lapidge, Yorke and others have argued that Swithun was Bishop of Winchester between 852/3–863,[6] and that his cult began with the bishop's translation in 971.[7] Lapidge gives a detailed reconstruction of the spread of Swithun's cult in the centuries after the translation. Among the areas he catalogues is the cult in Scandinavia, its chronological and geographic origin and its spread on the basis of surviving sources. Yet in his review of the cult in Scandinavia, Lapidge contextualises

---

[5] Lapidge 2003, 3.
[6] *Ibid.*, 4; Attwater 1970, 316; Yorke 2004. Lapidge dates Swithun's tenure to 852–862/3 due to his interpretations of the sources. While Barbara Yorke, in her 2004 ODNB biography of Swithun, dates Swithun's tenure as bishop of Winchester to 852/3–63. This discrepancy between Lapidge and Yorke's interpretation is due to the surviving sources. Lapidge has used the earliest possible date for Swithun as his ordination to bishop of Winchester, while Yorke chooses to acknowledge in her text that there are some uncertainty surrounding the date of Swithun's ordination. At the same time, Yorke's date of Swithun's death in 863 is based on charter evidence, whereas Lapidge's date range points to the divergence of dates associated with the end of Swithun's tenure. I have therefore chosen to use the dates 852/3–63 as they seem most consistent with the surviving records.
[7] Lapidge 2003, 8.

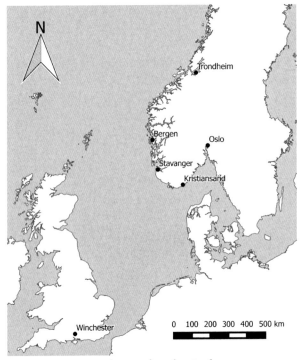

Fig. 14.1: Places referred to in the text.

the cult with the religious and cultural links between England and Scandinavia, especially Norway, and presents this as one of the plausible causes for the cult's spread to Norway. He does this through highlighting the number of Anglo-Saxon missionaries and bishops who, according to both Scandinavian and English sources, were active in Norway and Iceland during the late tenth and the eleventh century.

One of the many questions Lapidge raises in his assessment is whether any of these missionaries or bishops were from Winchester and if the cult could have arrived directly to Norway at this point.[8] This question reflects the number of Norwegian manuscript fragments that have been associated with Winchester. However, one of the challenges to the early introduction hypothesis is the uncertainties surrounding the identification of most of the Anglo-Saxon missionaries and bishops, and the lack of clear links to Winchester or other religious sites in England. For most of these men, the surviving sources are not detailed enough, nor do they correspond with information in other sources, thus it is at times difficult to identify these individuals and their networks. Lapidge highlights what he sees as a more plausible route of introduction, arguing that the cult of St Swithun most likely came to Norway directly from Winchester with the first bishop of Stavanger – Rainald (c. 1125/8–35).[9] Lapidge also argues that a subsequent bishop of Stavanger, Jon Birgisson, who was elected the first archbishop of Nidaros, brought the cult of Swithun into the liturgical calendars of the metropolitan see, facilitating the cult's spread in the north Atlantic.[10] Lapidge's conclusions and their implications for the understanding of the cult, and indirectly for the city of Stavanger and its religious institutions, have in recent years been somewhat challenged by Eldbjørg Haug, whose work on early Stavanger advocates the possibility that the cult and the relic of St Swithun in Stavanger might pre-date Bishop Rainald by

---

[8]   *Ibid.*, 56.
[9]   *Ibid.*, 56.
[10] *Ibid.*, 57.

up to a century.[11] Haug's argument has consequently been challenged by Knut Helle. As Haug and Helle's arguments forms the basis for the current state of scholarship on the cult of St Swithun in Norway, I will give what I hope is a balanced account of the two scholars' arguments in the subsequent paragraphs starting with Haug.

The Question of dating Stavanger's Link with Swithun

The discussion between Helle and Haug focuses on several questions, but for this paper, there are two key points of contention we need to consider: firstly, the dating of the St Swithun relic in Stavanger, and secondly, the evidence for the dating of the dedication of the cathedral in Stavanger to St Swithun. These two points of contention are related, so give the fairest possible analysis of this debate I will first examine Eldbjørg Haug's arguments and perspectives, before moving on to Knut Helle's response, with special attention to Haug's defence against Helle. Except for Haug's original texts, all the texts in the debate were published in the Norwegian journal *Historisk Tidsskrift* between 2008 and 2010.

Haug

Haug's 2008, 2009 and 2010 publications about Stavanger and its affiliated religious history came on the back of a series of earlier local history publications where she discussed the history of the area more broadly. Within these later publications Haug consolidates her arguments and interpretations, particularly concerning the religious history of Stavanger, and importantly for this paper, the cult of St Swithun in light of this.[12] Her core argument is that the cult of Swithun was introduced to Stavanger and Norway earlier than previously believed.[13] Haug bases her argument on several points, but three are important for this paper. Firstly, Haug acknowledges Hohler's 1964 argument that there are no documented openings of the reliquary of Swithun around the arrival of Reinald in Stavanger in the 1120s.[14] Based on Hohler's analysis Haug argues that it is likely that the Stavanger relic might have arrived either as part of the 1093 opening of the shrine, or a translation before 1066 or after 1150.[15] This leads us to the second important point for Haug, namely the statute in the *Canones Nidarosiensis* that dictates that every church should have a relic. Haug sees this in the light of the suggestion that Erling Skjalgsson had a church and priest at Stavanger in the 1020s.[16] Haug therefore argues that this earlier Stavanger church also must have had a relic at this point, and that it is plausible that this relic might have been of St Swithun.[17] There is sadly no evidence to enlighten us as to who this early church was

---

[11] Haug 2009, 462–5.
[12] Haug 2009; Haug 2010.
[13] Haug 2009, 462–5; 481.
[14] *Ibid.*, 463.
[15] *Ibid.*
[16] *Ibid.*, 463–4.
[17] *Ibid.*, 464–5.

dedicated to or who it held a relic of, but Haug proposes, based on Hohler's conclusions, that this might have been the Swithun relic said by the Lansdowne Redaction of the *Translatio et miracula S. Swithuni* to have been sent to 'Dacia' by Cnut, the king of Norway between 1028 and 1035.[18] Haug argues that there were no known Swithun liturgies in Denmark, or at the medieval Danish archbishopric of Lund, claiming that one could understand 'Dacia' as referring to all parts of Cnut's Scandinavian realm.[19] Haug thus argues that King Cnut's 'Dacia' relic might, in fact, have been the relic in Stavanger,[20] used to consecrate Erling Skjalgsson's church in Stavanger. If so, the act of sending this relic must have been part of Cnut's wider pattern of gift-giving targeted at Norwegian chieftains.[21]

Haug bases this interpretation of Dacia, as meaning all of Scandinavia, on both Russell's edited volume from 2005 and her own 2008 work on papal penitentiaries in thirteenth- through to fifteenth-century Scandinavia.[22] Haug's proposal that the Stavanger relic might have been part of Cnut's gifts in the attempt to undermine Olaf II Haraldsson's reign in Norway (1016–28) is something she problematises herself through her third point, namely the inclusion of Swithun among the saints whose mass was to be celebrated according to the oldest versions of the Gulathing Law code.[23] This law code claims to have been the product of Olaf II Haraldsson's 1024 legal revision of the Gulathing Law, suggesting that the veneration of Swithun in western Norway pre-dated Cnut's gift of a relic. Haug explains the inclusion of Swithun in the 1024 lawcode by pointing out that many of the missionary bishops active in Norway during the reign of Olaf I Tryggvason and Olaf II Haraldsson had roots in or links to the religious and political milieu in Winchester, making it possible that these bishops brought the veneration of Swithun with them to western Norway.[24] Because of this evidence and these interpretations, Haug draws a number of conclusions in her work about the religious history of Stavanger and its related institutions.[25] Crucially for this chapter, she concludes that it is plausible, maybe even likely, that the veneration and knowledge about St Swithun in Norway might have predated Bishop Reinald's arrival in the 1120s by about a century.[26] Moreover, this plausibility implies that the cult spread because of the efforts of several Anglo-Saxon missionary bishops active in the late tenth- and eleventh-century Norway. If this latter is true, this might help to explain the geographic spread of the late medieval and early modern references to St Swithun in Norway, which I will return to below.

---

[18] Lapidge 2003, 700–3.
[19] Haug 2009, 464.
[20] *Ibid.*
[21] Lawson 2011, 97; Lavelle 2017, 60.
[22] Russell 2005, 129; Haug 2008, 92; 2009, 465.
[23] Haug 2009, 464.
[24] *Ibid.*, 465.
[25] *Ibid.*, 480–3.
[26] *Ibid.*, 481.

Furthermore, in her 2009 article, Haug draws attention the dating of the Stavanger *Privilegium*, a document from the reign of Haakon Haakonson of Norway (r. 1217–1263), in which Haakon confirms a now lost grant by king Magnus Erlingson (r. 1161–84) to God and St Swithun as represented by the cathedral in Stavanger.[27] Haug claims the *Privilegium* is based on an even older grant, dated to the reign of Magnus Bærrføtt (1093–1103), on the basis of the shifting linguistic styles from *pluralis majestatis* in parts of the document to the first-person singular in other parts which she claims was likely the result of the later letter by Haakon Haakonsson quoting an earlier letter; to Haug's understanding it is unlikely that Magnus Erlingsson referred to himself as '... such a chieftain as king Magnus was, my kinsman...'.[28] Instead, she believes 'Magnus [...], my kinsman' is Magnus Erlingsson referring to his maternal great-grandfather Magnus Bærrføtt, thus dating the initial gift to St Swithun before 1103.[29]

The use of the lawcode evidence is one of the points of divergence that Haug addresses in her 2010 article directed at Helle. In this 2010 article she argues that the dating of the manuscript to the third quarter of the twelfth century as presented by Gjerløw in 1963, does not exclude the possibility that the cult might have been known earlier.[30] In doing so, Haug points to an earlier statement in the same article: 'we can rarely say that a phenomenon did not exist just because of the silence of the sources'.[31] In addition to re-opening the possibility of the cult pre-dating the third quarter of the twelfth century, Haug addresses Helle's argument that the Stavanger *Privilegium* does not refer to Magnus Bærrføtt (1093–1103) by highlighting the use of written documents in eleventh-century Norway, arguing that it is not implausible that Magnus Bærrføtt drew up such a document since other contemporary individuals actively used writing to further their economic, political and religious interests.[32]

Helle

Knut Helle (1930–2015) published an article in 2008 that he framed as a historiographical analysis of the research being conducted into the early religious and urban history of the Stavanger area, in reply to what he argued was 'radical reassessments' by Eldbjørg Haug.[33] Part of the 'radical reassessments' Helle argues Haug has produced relates to the understanding of the word *bæen* in the so-called Stavanger *Privilegium* from the reign of Haakon Haakonson of Norway (king 1217–1263), where Haakon confirms a now lost grant by king Magnus Erlingson (king 1161–84) to God and St Swithun as represented by the cathedral in Stavanger. Haug's radical act is according to Helle to translate *bæen* to mean farm or hamlet rather than the commonly accepted translation

---

[27] *Ibid.*, 469.
[28] Lange and Unger 1847, 38–9. Translated based on excerpt from Haug 2009, 474.
[29] *Ibid.*, 476.
[30] Haug 2010, 270–1.
[31] *Ibid.*, 266.
[32] Haug 2010, 271.
[33] Helle 2008, 577.

of town or city,[34] implying that the grant pre-dated the development of the urban settlement making a relatively early Swithun connection more plausible in Stavanger. Furthermore, Helle disagrees with Haug's interpretation of the *Privilegium*'s double reference to king Magnus, arguing it was Haakon Haakonsson referring to Magnus Erlingsson.[35] The consequences of Helle's argument are of interest for this paper, in that this suggestion would date the first contemporary attestation of the Swithun dedication in Stavanger to the third quarter of the twelfth century, rather than the end of the eleventh and beginning of the twelfth century. Helle's interpretation dovetails nicely with the long research tradition where the dedication is linked to the establishment of the episcopal seat in Stavanger to between 1123 and 1135, based on references to Bishop Reinald in *Heimskringla*, and on a description of Sigurd the Crusader's (king 1103–1130) last seven years as king in Orderic Vitalis.[36]

The dating offered by Helle in his article, based on the *Heimskringla* and Orderic, contrasts the materiality and dating of the church in Stavanger, which both Haug and Helle agree predates the episcopal see.[37] Helle argues that, although the building was begun before the establishment of the bishopric and the arrival of Reinald, the cathedral's dedication to St Swithun and its relic, attested in 1205 and 1507,[38] is unlikely to have arrived before Reinald's elevation to bishop in Stavanger. In his 2009 article, Helle draws on Lapidge's 2003 critique of Hohler and concludes that Haug's conclusions about an eleventh-century date on the arrival of the Swithun relic and the interpretation of Dacia as Norway are unlikely.[39] He instead endorses the 1150s as a more likely date for the arrival of the relic in Stavanger, as this corresponds to one of the times Swithun's Winchester shrine was opened, and argues that the veneration develops in Norway around this point.[40] Helle also leans on Gjerløw's dating of the Gulathing Law Code to the third quarter of the twelfth century in order to corroborate his own.[41] Helle's argument here is based on a reading of this aspect of the law code contemporary to the manuscript examined, and does not reflect a longer continuously evolving religious tradition. In doing so Helle relies on a more conservative, but still plausible, understanding of the text which infers less about the past than Haug does.

Extrapolating from this debate between Haug and Helle, it is evident that the preservation or lack thereof of documents from Norway in the eleventh and early twelfth century significantly affects what can be concluded about the dating of the cult of St Swithun in Norway. It is furthermore evident that some evidence, such as the liturgical fragments and the presence of Anglo-Saxon clergy in Norway in the eleventh century, point to a set of religious links that might have introduced Swithun

---

[34] *Ibid.*, 580.

[35] *Ibid.*, 587.

[36] *Ibid.*, 591.

[37] Haug 2009, 475–6; Helle 2008, 589.

[38] Helle 2008, 591.

[39] Helle 2009, 691.

[40] *Ibid.*, 690–2.

[41] Gjerløw 1963, 94–106, discussed in Helle, 2009, 691.

earlier than the accepted dating of the cult at the establishment of the episcopal seat in Stavanger. Other evidence such as the first datable references to Swithun in Stavanger in the *Privilegium*, the attestation of the relic in Stavanger and the manuscript date of the Gulathing Law manuscript points to a different verifiable date for the veneration of St Swithun. Yet, these verifiable dates raise the questions about the circumstantial evidence for a possible earlier introduction.

The Context of a Plausible Earlier Introduction

As Haug correctly points out, the earlier contact between Western Norway and England and through Winchester's religious and political milieu significantly influenced the early centuries of Christianity in Norway.[42] The role of Anglo-Saxon bishops in the conversion and Christianisation of Norway has been widely discussed by Lesley Abrams, among others. In her 1995 article on the topic, Abrams concludes that the English involvement in the conversion of Scandinavia is unarguable, but also that the details on especially the early process are unclear.[43] One of the many points that Abrams considers unclear is the identity of the individual involved, which as I have mentioned above then makes it difficult to pinpoint their relationships, networks and cultural contexts. Abrams also points out that among the exports English missionaries brought to Scandinavia were the cult of saints, and among the saints they might have introduced are St Birinus and St Swithun.[44] In this Abrams sees the introduction of these two West Saxon saints to Norway as part of the wider cultural transmission of the conversion period, opening up the possibility that familiarity with Swithun in Western Norway might pre-date bishop Reinald's arrival in Stavanger from Winchester.

Like other scholars,[45] Abrams and, more recently, Stefan Brink point to a number of possibly contacts between England and Norway: bishops, such as an unnamed bishop who came to Norway alongside Haakon I 'Athalsteinfostre' Haraldsson; a number of monks and Bishop John who accompanied Olaf I Tryggvason; and Bishop Grimkell, who attended Olaf II 'St Olaf' Haraldsson's court.[46] Abrams also highlights the possibility of continued and strengthened ecclesiastical interaction between these two regions during King Cnut's reign in Norway (1028–35).[47] Cnut's role in the Christianisation of Norway has so far been underappreciated, plausibly due to the unfavourable treatment Cnut and his regime in Norway gets in the *Heimskringla* and Norwegian historiography. Although *Heimskringla* and other sagas are silent on the Christianisation efforts under Ælfgifu and Svein beyond the continued activities of Olaf II's court Bishop Grimkel[48] and translation of Olaf II into a saint, the saga narratives do not suggest any deliberate

---

[42] Haug 2009, 465.
[43] Abrams 1995, 244.
[44] *Ibid.*, 248.
[45] Bagge and Nordeide 2007, 136–39; Winroth 2012, 119; Nordeide 2012, 7.
[46] Abrams 1995, 219, 221, 224; Brink 2008, 623, 626–7.
[47] Abrams 1995, 224.
[48] *Ibid.*, 223; Higham 2020, 491–5.

acts to slow these efforts either. In fact, Ælfgifu's attendance at the elevation of Olaf to sainthood actually points in the opposite direction: that the Danish regime supported the church, although Ælfgifu's involvement in the event is mostly remembered for her attempt to oppose the elevation. Looking beyond the sagas, the previously mentioned relic donation to Dacia, as well as a widely cited reference to 'an English source'[49] (most likely Matthew Paris) claiming Cnut founding a monastery on Nidarholm in 1028, also points to Cnut taking an active role in the integration of Norway and Denmark into a wider Christian world. The claims of 'the English source' about Cnut's foundation at Nidarholm have so far not been corroborated by archaeology, and are thus not widely acknowledged as the origins of Nidarholm or Munkholmen monastery near Trondheim. Without spending too much time considering the quality of this claim and its ramifications for the Christianisation of Norway, it can be agreed that Christianisation efforts did not stop in the seven years between 1028 and 1035.

The continuity of Christianisation efforts throughout the eleventh century, including the reign of Cnut in Norway, must be part of the explanation for the number of English liturgical manuscript fragments from this period found in Norway. Abrams noted that a closer examination of these fragments might demonstrate their point of origin,[50] as well as which monastic communities in England provided missionaries to Norway.[51] Lapidge drew on some of the same fragments when arguing for a Norwegian familiarity with a St Swithun liturgy in the eleventh century.[52] All this points to a cultural milieu where it is plausible that the veneration of Swithun might have been introduced prior to Reinald's arrival in Stavanger.

The cause of Swithun's introduction to and veneration in Stavanger and Norway is unclear. This is arguably due to the difficulty of precisely dating the arrival of the saint, and the state of survival of documentary evidence from the first centuries of Christianity in Norway. However, the scholarly hypotheses about the date of introduction of the cult and the relic presented by Haug and Helle can help us to see some possibilities, as the historical context of the introduction is likely to have influenced individuals involved in the introduction. If the introduction came with the first wave of organised Christianisation efforts in Norway at the beginning of the eleventh century as suggested by Haug,[53] the motivation is likely to have been different than if it came at the beginning of the twelfth century as Helle proposes.[54]

If the introduction happened in the eleventh century, it is possible that the cult and the relic was a statement of cultural affinity and/or socio-political ties between the region and England. A similar hypothesis has been presented by Bruce Dickins and, more recently, by Robert Higham as a contributing cause of the spread of the

---

[49] Bratberg and Arntzen 1996, 244, 368.
[50] Abrams 1995, 246.
[51] *Ibid.*
[52] Lapidge 2003, 56, 128–34.
[53] Haug 2009, 464.
[54] Helle 2009, 692.

cult of St Olaf in England in the eleventh century;[55] thus it is not impossible that this cultural exchange was two-ways. Yet, as there is no conclusive evidence for the dating of the cult and the relic in Norway, it could be just as likely that the cult and the relic arrived at different dates – and the first bishop of Stavanger, Reinald, who traditionally has been identified with a monk from Hyde Abbey in Winchester by the same name,[56] brought the relic to Stavanger as part of his and his new episcopal church's elevation. Yet why Reinald would bring this exact relic with him, or why this saint would be the one promoted in Stavanger in unclear, and it is likely that it will remain unclear forever.

Following the introduction of the veneration of Swithun to Norway, the cult seems to have been known in the metropolitan province of Nidaros, as attested by Swithun's inclusion in the Nidaros Breviary from 1519.[57] Lapidge argues that the veneration of Swithun was in retreat by the time of the printing of the Breviary as the 'feast of St Swithun's deposition ha[d] been omitted (having been replaced by the new feast of the Visitation of St Mary)'.[58] Beyond this, there is very little evidence for the veneration of Swithun in the Norwegian corpus of medieval materials. Yet, by broadening the scope of sources to also include other sources we might see a broader picture of the veneration.

Moving Beyond the Strictly Textual: The *Primstav* and their Evidence

In 2011 Audun Dybdahl published his study of the Norwegian perpetual calendars known as *primstav* from around Norway.[59] A *primstav* is a traditional wooden calendar marked on both sides with marks for each day, and symbols for each important date in the agricultural or religious calendar. Most of these calendars are ruler or sword-shaped and run from 14 April–13 October on one side, and 14 October–13 April on the other.[60] Such calendars seem to have been common in farming communities to help them keep track of time and agricultural tasks.[61] Although only 40 per cent of the 319 calendars which Dybdahl surveyed could be dated, the vast majority of these are dated to the seventeenth and eighteenth centuries, with the oldest example dated to 1457.[62] The geographic distribution of the sample Dybdahl examined covers the whole of late medieval and early modern Norway. When comparing the religious and agricultural dates marked on the whole corpus of 319 *primstav*, Dybdahl found a correlation between the religious feasts included and their religious classification in the early Norwegian law codes. According to Dybdahl, the religious feasts, which according to the Frostating Law were considered to be of the highest liturgical importance, could

---

[55] Dickins 1937, 45, 52–80; Higham 2020, 467–513.
[56] Lapidge 2003, 56–7.
[57] *Ibid.*, 57.
[58] *Ibid.*
[59] Dybdahl 2011.
[60] Dybdahl 2011, 279.
[61] *Ibid.*, 284.
[62] *Ibid.*, 261.

be found on all the *primstav*.[63] The feast of St Swithun (*Syftesok*) on 2 July is among these dates.[64] Moreover, Dybdahl demonstrates how Swithun is not included among the saints included in the prescribed list of feasts found in the laws of Eidsivating and Borgarting,[65] suggesting a regional difference in the saints venerated in Norway according to the lawcodes. Regardless of these regional differences, Dybdahl found Swithun's feast day marked on *primstav* throughout Norway. Even though the feast of St Swithun came under pressure following the introduction of the Visitation of Mary in the second half of the fifteenth century, Dybdahl found that the symbol for Swithun's feast, a crosier, was three times as popular as the symbol for Mary's feast.[66]

The only conclusion one might draw from Dybdahl's discoveries is that the feast of St Swithun was familiar and, to some extent, popular even outside the medieval dioceses of Stavanger. The question, however, is if this popularity was due to the extent of the saint's veneration or if it was due to the use of the day as an indicator for the summer weather until St Olaf's day (29 July).[67] In the post-reformation period, it is probably more likely that the weather was the prime cause of *Syftesok*'s popularity than it being remembered for its religious importance. There is no direct indication in the contemporary post-medieval sources that this meteorological importance was due to Swithun's weather miracle, yet this does not exclude the possibility of this importance having its roots in a folklore tradition based on this miracle. The cultural and religious changes in Norway following the Lutheran Reformation ended the cult of saints; thus, the religious importance of *Syftesok* is likely to have declined over the following centuries. The impact of the reformation might also explain the disconnection between *Syftesok* as a weather marker and *Syftesok* as a saint's day. In three Norwegian-Danish almanacs from 1644–1773 the date of the feast of St Swithun on 2 July is marked as the date of the Visitation of Mary, with a note that the 'old people' call the day *Syftesok* implying that Swithun had fallen out of fashion for the authors.[68] None of these almanacs attribute any particular meteorological importance to the date, but that does not mean that there were no traditional forecasting practices tied to the day, just that these did not manifest in these three texts. However, as noted in the opening of this paper, St Swithun was in time rediscovered. Therefore, the following section serves to briefly outline elements of the re-discovery of the Winchester saint in Norway.

Post-medieval 'Evidence' or Lingering Memory?

As was noted at the start of this chapter, Norwegian culture rediscovered its medieval past in the nineteenth and early twentieth century. This rediscovery of the medieval

---

[63] *Ibid.*, 281.
[64] Sandnes 1994, 27.
[65] Dybdahl 2011, 48.
[66] *Ibid.*, 171.
[67] *Ibid.*, 172.
[68] Nielszøn 1944, 350; Hammer 1773, 261; Brunsmand 1688, 120.

past, and in some cases its use in religious revivals, was part of a wider trend attested across the western world. Examples of such medievalisms can be found in Winchester, with its ties to Alfred the Great manifested in the 1901 anniversary and statue, and in New York with its Cloisters.[69] Among the ways this materialised was the promotion of the Viking Age kingdom of Norway as the origin of the Norwegian state, as well as the promotion of associated historical heroes and symbols who represented this past. I have discussed elsewhere how this medievalism can be seen through a national lens, as the broader patterns of inspiration for Norwegian medievalism has been connected to the national past.[70] However, this national emphasis does not apply to all medievalism and 're-discovery' of the medieval in Norway in the post-medieval period. For as I will demonstrate, the post-medieval life of St Swithun in Stavanger is not a matter of national but local concern based on the cathedral and city's medieval relationship with the saint.

As an indicative measure of printed communication in Norway, a search in the Norwegian National Library's catalogue indicates that the word 'Swithun' first appears in print in Norway in 1828, before reappearing in the 1850s. The Norwegian version of the saint's name, 'Svithun', demonstrates a similar pattern, with a few references to it in the 1830s before becoming more common in the 1850s and 60s. These search results are not wholly comprehensive, as they must be contextualised with a general but significant increase in publications in Norway in the second half of the nineteenth century as well as the selection of materials in the library. Yet what is noteworthy is that the majority of the references to Swithun or Svithun in the 1850s refer to a Stavanger-registered cargo ship named St Svithun.[71] By 1879 there were two ships named Svithun, both from areas in the medieval bishopric of Stavanger.[72] This naming pattern might point to increased familiarity with Swithun in this region. Further, in 1881, the Stavanger-based shipping company Holdt & Isachsen commissioned a new cargo ship from Flensburg, and publicly announced they intended to name her Svithun.[73]*Bergens Tidende* and *Morgenbladet* reporting on Holdt & Isachsen's familiarity with Swithun and his link to Stavanger, the modern relationship between the saint and the city starts to take shape.[74]

It is worth noting that the medieval bishopric centred on Stavanger was moved to the more strategic city of Kristiansand in 1682 (see Fig. 14.1 for location), so by the time Holdt & Isachsen named their ship Swithun, the medieval cathedral in Stavanger was no longer functioning as a cathedral, but rather as one of the city's many churches. Yet, by the time Holdt & Isachsen commissioned the Svithun, the Norwegian press had already run two anonymous articles reminding their readers about the church's

---

[69] Parker 2007, 1–32; Radnoti 2015, 307–15.
[70] Alvestad 2016; Alvestad 2019.
[71] *Christiania-Posten* 1851, 3.
[72] *Dagbladet* 1879, 3.
[73] *Bergens Tidende* 1881, 2; *Morgenbladet* 1881, 2.
[74] *Ibid.*

dedication to Swithun.[75] These two articles, from 1869 and 1877, both re-tell the history of the church and seems to follow the interpretations set out by P. A. Munch and Rudolf Keyser on the role of bishop Reinald in the cathedral's dedication to Swithun.[76] As such, these articles might be understood as part of the broader historical culture at the time. Although these articles and ships suggest an awareness of Swithun in Stavanger at the end of the nineteenth century, the revival of Stavanger as the city and cathedral of Swithun did not really happen until the twentieth century.

The crucial moments in the twentieth century that linked Stavanger and Swithun in the modern age, and promoted greater awareness of the saint, took place in 1918, 1925 and 1927. In 1918, St Swithun School in Stavanger opened;[77] this secondary school was the first Lutheran institution in the city that referenced the saint. Previously, in 1894, the Catholic community in the city had established St Swithun's Catholic Church in Stavanger.[78] There are no indicators in local newspapers of anti-Catholic sentiments around this use of Swithun in Stavanger at the time. In time for Stavanger City's 800th anniversary in 1925, the Lutheran bishopric of Stavanger was re-established. In the royal declaration that re-established the bishopric, the king and his government declared that 'Stavanger Cathedral, St Swithun's Church, shall be the bishopric's new Cathedral'.[79] With this, the Norwegian Lutheran Church reclaimed its historic link to and possession of Swithun in Stavanger. However, Stavanger's embracing of Swithun did not stop there, for, in 1927, the city council named two of the city's streets after the saint, creating *St Svithuns gate* (street) and *St Svithuns plass* (place).[80] Since the 1920s Stavanger has seen several other references to Swithun in form of a hotel, two statues and more, all adding up to a broader landscape of traces acknowledging Swithun and his role as the patron saint of Stavanger, much like Southwark in London remembers its historic parish of St Olaf and its relationship with the saint.[81] Stavanger's relationship with Swithun differs from that of Southwark's with Olaf. In Southwark, the community sought to preserve a continuous memory of the parish and saint, while Stavanger had to rediscover and revitalise its relationship with Swithun in the nineteenth and twentieth centuries. The process in Stavanger manifests itself chiefly in two ways: firstly, the revived and continuous ties between the cathedral in Stavanger and Winchester Cathedral (discussed below), and secondly in how Ernst Baasland in 2003 framed Swithun into his contemporary understanding of the religious life of Rogaland, the county in which Stavanger lies. Baasland claimed that Swithun's compassion and Christian charity was a great inspiration for local believers,[82] making Swithun not just a civic identity marker in the post-medieval world, but also a religious one.

---

[75] *Fædrelandsvennen* 1877, 1; *Morgenbladet* 1869, 2.
[76] Munch 1855, 610; Keyser 1866, 559.
[77] Olden 1949, 3–4.
[78] Baasland 2003, 255.
[79] *Ibid.*, 288.
[80] Berntsen 1939, 96.
[81] Alvestad 2020, 610–12.
[82] Baasland 2003, 107.

These observations only scratch the surface of St Swithun's role in modern Norway and have not considered if or how he is remembered or venerated outside Stavanger. What does appear to be clear on the basis of the modern evidence is that aspects of the contemporary religious movements in the area around Stavanger as represented by Baasland have found Swithun worthy of reverence due to his compassion and charity.[83] In stressing these qualities of Swithun, Baasland made the saint more 'Lutheran,' thus Swithun was suitable to be a Lutheran role model. A similar translation happened to St Olaf in the lead up to the 900-year-anniversary of his martyrdom in 1930.

Being a Christian role model does not seem to be the only reason Swithun remains relevant for Stavanger. A 2019 opinion piece in *Stavanger Aftenblad* by Tore Edland presents Swithun as both a civic and religious identity marker for the city, similar to Baasland in 2003.[84] Edland uses this to argue for the construction of a statue or depiction of Swithun within Stavanger Cathedral as part of the Cathedral's upcoming anniversary as a manifestation of Swithun's importance for the town's historic development.

Looking beyond just the direct references to Swithun in Stavanger, one can find some references to and depictions of the city of Winchester and its cathedral in contemporary newspapers and periodicals. When Norwegian periodicals and newspapers describe Winchester, most articles are unillustrated, but those that are illustrated depict Winchester Cathedral. The subject of the articles are rarely current events, but rather travel accounts by individuals or groups. There are among these a couple of trends. In the Stavanger region Winchester is first and foremost connected to Swithun, and through that the articles emphasises the historic ties between Stavanger and Winchester.[85] However, beyond Stavanger, Winchester is presented as the ancient capital of England,[86] a source of inspiration for the medieval cathedrals in Norway,[87] a lovely city with clean air and fair weather,[88] the home of the hospital of St Cross,[89] and above all the home of Winchester Cathedral, a site which all of the articles mention as worth visiting. What might appear surprising to someone who is familiar with Winchester and its heritage is that neither Jane Austen nor Alfred the Great are mentioned despite these historic figures being cornerstones of current tourism marketing of the city. I suspect this absence is not a reliable representation of all references to Winchester in Norwegian media after 1850. But it is notable that Winchester's religious history as represented by Swithun and the Cathedral dominates the image of the city in the modern Norwegian mind.

These modern depictions and references to Winchester, its cathedral and its religious history are not reflected in the surviving medieval sources from Norway.

---

[83] Baasland 2003, 107.
[84] Edland 2019.
[85] Aadnøy 1979, 28–30.
[86] Thun 1939, 1.
[87] Grieg 1968, 7–8.
[88] Svanøe 1969, 4.
[89] Offenberg 1910, 1–2.

What does exist within the medieval corpus is a short description of the miracles of St Swithun in the early sixteenth-century printed *Breviarium Nidrosiense*; among this we find a direct reference to Winchester.[90] This reference does not give us a description of the city or its structures, including the cathedral. Nevertheless, it does highlight Swithun's veneration as the text lists a number of his miracles, thus implicitly referencing the cathedral and shrine.[91]

Concluding Remarks

Although the origins of St Swithun's veneration in Norway is likely to remain unclear as scholars continue to discuss the surviving sources and circumstantial evidence from Stavanger and Norway in the Middle Ages, it remains apparent that his veneration in Norway was, by the end of the medieval period, focused on Stavanger and its relic. When this relic arrived in Stavanger is uncertain, but its longer historical impact goes beyond the religious. As I have shown, the cult of St Swithun in medieval Stavanger became a civic and religious identity marker for the local community in the post-medieval and modern period. More work needs to be undertaken to fully grasp the cultural significance of Swithun in modern Stavanger or Norway as a whole. However, I suspect that such work will return to the re-occurring theme of seeing Swithun in Norway as part of a broader cultural relationship and kinship between Norway and England in the past and present for it is within this narrative that Swithun's cult and the arrival of bishop Reinald, as well as the other plausible points of transmission, are framed. As such, the traces remaining of the veneration of St Swithun, and the modern re-claiming of the saint by the community, can represent the wider impact, real or imagined, of England, Wessex and Winchester on Norway and Norwegian culture through the centuries. The veneration of St Swithun in the north might thus help remind us that the impact of Winchester might be far greater than we first assume, and we should not forget to consider its echoes through the centuries.

Bibliography

Aadnøy, A. 3 November 1979. Dikterens Fødeby og Swithuns Kirke, *Stavanger Aftenblad*, 28–30. Available at: http://urn.nb.no/URN:NBN:no-nb_digavis_stavangeraftenblad_null_null_19791103_87_255_1. (Accessed 10 January 2021).

Abrams, L. 1995. The Anglo-Saxons and the Christianization of Scandinavia, *Anglo-Saxon England*, 24, 213–49.

Alvestad, K. C. 2016. Kings, Heroes and Ships: The Use of Historical Characters in Nineteenth- and Twentieth-Century Perceptions of the Early Medieval Scandinavian Past. Unpublished PhD thesis, University of Winchester.

Alvestad, K. C. 2019. Middelalders Helter Og Norsk Nasjonalisme Før Andre Verdenskrig, *Slagmark*, 79:1, 77–95.

---

[90] Valkendorf 1519, 723–4.
[91] These can be found, transcribed and translated in Lapidge 2003, 128–34.

Alvestad, K. C. 2020. Olavian Traces in Post-Medieval England, in A. Langlands and R. Lavelle (eds), *The Land of the English Kin: Studies in Wessex and Anglo-Saxon England Presented to Professor Barbara Yorke*, 602–20. Leiden: Brill.

Attwater, D. 1970. *The Penguin Dictionary of Saints*. Harmondsworth: Penguin Books.

Baasland, E. 2003. *Korsfylket*. Stavanger: Mosaikk Forlag.

Bagge, S. and Nordeide, S. W. 2007. The Kingdom of Norway, in N. Berend (ed.), *Christianization and the Rise of Christian Monarchy*, 121–66. Cambridge: Cambridge University Press.

Bergens tidende, 28 June 1881, 2.

Berntsen, M. 1939. *Stedsnavn i Stavanger by og nærmeste omegn*. Stavanger: Stabenfeldt.

Bratberg, T. T. V. and Arntzen, J. G. 1996. *Trondheim byleksikon*. Oslo: Kunnskapsforlaget.

Brink, S. 2008. Christianisation and the Emergence of the Early Church in Scandinavia, in S. Brink with N. Price (eds) *The Viking World*, 621–628. Abingdon: Routledge.

Brunsmand, J. 1688. *Almindeligt og Stedsevarende Kalender*. Christiania: Joachim Schmedigen.

Christiania-Posten, 12 April 1851. Ankomne og Afgaaende Skibe, 3.

Dagbladet, 16 Juli 1879. Ankomne og Afgaaende Skibe, 3.

Dickins, B. 1937–45. The Cult of St Olave in the British Isles, *Saga-Book of the Viking Society*, 12, 52–80.

Dybdahl, A. 2011. *Primstaven i lys av helgenkulten : opphav, form, funksjon og symbolikk*. Trondheim: Tapir Akademisk Forlag.

Edland, T. 17 February 2019. St. Svithun inn i Domkirken igjen?, *Stavanger Aftenblad*. Available at: https://www.aftenbladet.no/meninger/debatt/i/9m794r/st-svithun-inn-i-domkirken-igjen. (Accessed 10 January 2021).

Fædrelandsvennen, 10 September 1877. Stavanger Domkirke, 1.

Geary, P. 2002. *The Myth of Nations: The Medieval Origins of Europe*. Woodstock: Princeton University Press.

Gjerløw, L. 1963. Kalendrum II, in F. Hødnebø (ed.), *Kulturhistorisk leksikon for nordisk middelalder fra vikingtid til reformasjonstid*, Vol 8, 94–106. Oslo: Gyldendal Norsk Forlag.

Grieg, S. 5 January 1968. Winchester-Kathedralen – et forbilde for Stavanger Domkirke, *Nationen*, 7–8. 1968.01.05 Available at: http://urn.nb.no/URN:NBN:no-nb_digavis_nationen_null_null_19680105_51_4_1. (Accessed 10 January 2021).

Hammer, C. 1773. *Norsk Huusholdings Kalender*. Christiania: S.C. Schwach.

Haug, E. 2008. Minor Papal Penitentiaries of Dacia, their Lives and Careers in Context (1262–1408), *Collegium Medievale*, 21, 86–157.

Haug, E. 2009. Fra Stavanger-kirkens Tidligste Historie, *Historisk tidsskrift*, 88:3, 453–83.

Haug, E. 2010. Stavanger-privilegiet, Stavangers Romanske Domkirke og Klostersamfunnet på Utstein – Replikk til Knut Helle, *Historisk Tidsskrift*, 89:2, 263–71.

Helle, K. 2008. Stavanger By og Utstein Kloster, *Historisk Tidsskrift*, 87:4, 577–605.

Helle, K. 2009. Stavanger som By og Kirkelig Sentrum – svar til Eldbjørg Haug, *Historisk Tidsskrift*, 88:4, 685–97.

Higham, R. 2020. The Godwins, Towns and St Olaf Churches: Comital Investment in the Mid-11th Century, in A. Langlands and R. Lavelle (eds), *The Land of the English Kin: Studies in Wessex and Anglo-Saxon England Presented to Professor Barbara Yorke*, 467–513. Leiden: Brill.

Keyser, R. 1866. *Norges Historie*. Kristiania: Mallings Boktrykkeri.

Lange, Chr. C. A. and Unger, C. R. (eds). 1847. *Diplomatarium Norvegicum*. Vol. 1. 38–39. Oslo: P.T. Mallings Forlagshandel.

Lapidge, M. 2003. *The Cult of St Swithun*. Vol. 2. Winchester Studies, 4. Oxford: Clarendon Press.

Lavelle, R. 2017. *Cnut: the North Sea King*. London: Penguin Random House.

Lawson, M. K. 2011. *Cnut: England's Viking King 1016-35*. Stroud: The History Press.

Morgenbladet, 22 April 1869, Stavanger, 2.

Morgenbladet, 26 August 1881, 2.

Munch, P. A. 1855. *Det norske Folks Historie: Annen Deel*. Christiania: Tønsbergs Forlag.

Nielszøn, A. T. 1944. En Ny Allmanack paa det Aar Effter Jesu Christi Fødsel 1644 in W. P. Sommerfeldt (ed.), *Norske Almanakk Gjennom 300 År*, 334–350. Oslo: Universitetets Almanakkforlag.

Nordeide, S. W. 2012. *The Viking Age as a Period of Religious Transformation: The Christianization of Norway from AD 560 To 1150/1200*. Turnhout: Brepols Publishers.

Offenberg, R. 17 May 1910. Englandsbrev til Gudbr. Dølen: Fra Oxford til Winchester, *Gudbrandsdølen*, 1–2. Available at: http://urn.nb.no/URN:NBN:no-nb_digavis_gudbrandsdoelen_null_ null_19100517_17_58_1. (Accessed 10 January 2021).

Olden, O. F. 1949. *St. Svithuns skole*. Stavanger: Utgitt av Skolen.

Parker, J. 2007. *'England's Darling': The Victorian Cult of Alfred the Great*. Manchester: Manchester University Press.

Radnóti, S. 2015. The New York Cloisters: A Forgery?, in J. M. Bak, P. Geary and G. Klaniczay (eds), *Manufacturing a Past for the Present: Forgery and Authenticity in Medievalists Texts and Objects in Nineteenth-Century Europe*, 307–15. Leiden: Brill.

Russell, P. (ed.) 2005. *Vita Griffini Filii Conani: The Medieval Latin Life of Gruffudd ap Cynan*. Cardiff: University of Wales Press.

Sandnes, J. and Hagland, J. R. 1994. *Frostatingslova*. Oslo: Samlaget I Samarbeid med Frosta Historielag.

Svanøe, E. 31 January 1969. Fra det ene til det andre i 1968, *Aura Avis*, 4. Available at: http://urn. nb.no/URN:NBN:no-nb_digavis_auraavis_null_null_19690131_23_9_1. (Accessed 10 January 2021).

Thun, L. 18 February 1939. Brev fra England, *Dale-Gudbrand*, 1. Available at: http://urn.nb.no/ URN:NBN:no-nb_digavis_dalegudbrandtretten_null_null_19390218_5_7_1. (Accessed 10 January 2021).

Valkendorf, E. (ed.) 1519. *Breviarium Nidrosiense*. Paris: Jean Kerbriant & Jean Bienayse.

Wawn, A. 2000. *The Vikings and the Victorians: Inventing the Old North in 19th-Century Britain*. Cambridge: D. S. Brewer.

Winroth, A. 2012. *The Conversion of Scandinavia*. New Haven: Yale University Press.

Yorke, B. 2004. Swithun [St Swithun] (d. 863), bishop of Winchester. *Oxford Dictionary of National Biography*. Available at: https://doi.org/10.1093/ref:odnb/26854. (Accessed 20 May 2021).

Index

Numbers in *italic* denote pages with figures, numbers in **bold** denote pages with tables.

Kings are "of Wessex" or "the Anglo-Saxons" or "England", unless otherwise stated.